A Consumer's Guide to

MEDICINES IN FOOD

D0973280

Also by the Author

A Consumer's Dictionary of Medicines
A Consumer's Dictionary of Cosmetics Ingredients
A Consumer's Dictionary of Food Additives
A Consumer's Dictionary of Household, Yard, and Office Chemicals
Poisons in Your Food
Ageless Aging
Cancer-Causing Agents
How to Reduce Your Medical Bills

A Consumer's Guide to

MEDICINES IN FOOD

Nutraceuticals That Help Prevent and Treat Physical and Emotional Illnesses

Ruth Winter, M.S.

Crown Trade Paperbacks
New York

To my husband, Arthur,
my children, Robin, Craig, and Grant,
and especially to my grandchildren,
Samantha, Hunter, and Katelynd,
who will reap the benefits of nutraceuticals research.

Published by Crown Trade Paperbacks, 201 East 50th Street, New York, New York 10022. Member of the Crown Publishing Group.

Random House, Inc. New York, Toronto, London, Sydney, Auckland

CROWN TRADE PAPERBACKS and colophon are trademarks of Crown Publishers, Inc.

Manufactured in the United States of America

Design by Cindy Dunn

Library of Congress Cataloging-in-Publication Data
Winter, Ruth.
   A consumer's guide to medicines in food: nutraceuticals that help prevent and treat physical and emotional illnesses/by Ruth Winter.
       p.   cm.
   Includes index.
   1. Nutrition.   2. Diet therapy.   3. Dietary supplements.   4. Vitamins.
I. Title.
RA784.W675   1995   94-31427
615.8′54—dc20   CIP

ISBN 0-517-88349-X

10   9   8   7   6   5   4   3   2   1

First edition

Contents

WHAT IS A NUTRACEUTICAL AND WHY SHOULD YOU CARE?

Need a vaccination? Instead of a needle stick, a lettuce-and-tomato sandwich may give you immunity.

Trouble with your blood clotting? How about a drink of milk from a sow that is a living factory for anticoagulant drugs?

Arthritis bothering you? Why not sip milk from a "pharmaceutical" cow to soothe your aching joints?

If cancer is a worry in your family, order an anticancer pizza.

These are just a few of the nutraceuticals that exist or that are under development today.

A nutraceutical is any substance that may be considered a food, or part of a food, and provides medical or health benefits, including the prevention and treatment of disease. Such products may range from isolated nutrients, dietary supplements, and diets to genetically engineered "designer" foods, herbal products, and processed foods such as cereals, soups, and beverages.[1]

The term *nutraceutical* was coined by Stephen L. DeFelice, M.D., chairman of the Foundation for Innovation in Medicine, to give the wide-ranging field an identity because it extends from observing what chimpanzees eat when they don't feel well to creating superfoods through biotechnology.

At present, there is no legal term or definition in the United States for products emanating from this field of research. In addition to the term *nutraceuticals,* such foods are referred to as *designer foods, prescriptive foods, pharma foods, medicinal foods,* or *physiologically functional foods.*

The Japanese, however, who are far ahead of us in development and marketing plans, have officially named their nutraceuticals *foods for specified health use (FOSHU).* For more than a decade, Japanese government, academia, and industry have cooperated in the area. A license is issued for FOSHU goods, which allows the producers to claim that people who consume a particular product may expect a specific health benefit.[2]

At this writing, the United States Food and Drug Administration only permits health claims about the relationships between:

- Calcium and osteoporosis.
- Fat and cancer.
- Saturated fat and cholesterol and coronary heart disease.
- Fiber-containing products, fruits, and vegetables and cancer.
- Fruits, vegetables, and grain products containing fiber (particularly soluble fiber) and coronary heart disease.
- Sodium and high blood pressure.
- Folic acid and neural-tube defects (birth defects of the brain and spinal cord).

The minute an American food company makes a claim other than those above for a food product, it becomes a drug and must undergo rigorous, multimillion-dollar, premarket testing that could take years.

Changing the nutritive value of a food to combat a disease, of course, is not new. In 1928, pellagra, caused by a deficiency of niacin, was the leading cause of death in eight Southern states. After only two years of fortifying the traditional diet of cornmeal with niacin, pellagra was virtually eliminated. The fortification of milk in the United States with vitamin D in the 1930s has done away with rickets, the bone-bending disease due to a deficiency of that vitamin. The addition of iron to flour helps to prevent anemia in the population, and iodine added to salt has all but stopped the development of goiter, the enlargement of the thyroid gland, due to lack of that element.

The idea of certain whole foods for specific health purposes is also not new. In fact, it is as old as the first mother in biblical times who gave chicken soup to a family member suffering from a cold and the ancient Mexican woman who ate yams to help prevent pregnancy. (The most popular commercial birth-control pill in the world today is derived from yams.)

What is new is the ability of scientists through modern technology to:

- Break down and identify elements in plants that have medicinal potential.
- Rearrange and add to the genetic material in cells to create new and more beneficial plants and animals.
- Establish information networks that more accurately correlate the foods people eat with their health.

Nearly 35 percent of all new food products launched in 1992 were in a *no* or *low* category concerning calories, fat, salt, sugar, or cholesterol. There are some six thousand reduced-fat foods on grocery shelves today.[3] While our society now seems concerned primarily with *avoiding* those food elements mentioned above, such as cholesterol and sugar, to prevent disease, nutraceutical research emphasizes the *inclusion* of certain additional elements in food to avoid illness.

The road to proving the benefits of any nutraceutical, including vitamins, is fraught with the roadblocks of conflicting reports and bureaucracy. Take the case of folic acid, the B vitamin, and its use as a preventative against neural-tube defects (malformations of the nervous system including incomplete enclosure of the spinal cord or absence of a functioning brain).

In 1983, in an article published in the prestigious British medical journal *The Lancet,* British researchers reported multivitamin supplementation given to pregnant women could prevent the birth of offspring with neural-tube defect.[4] In August 1989, the equally prestigious medical publication *The New England Journal of Medicine* carried an article by multiple authors from the National Institute of Child Health and Human Development's Neural Tube Study Group, concluding that the use of multivitamins or folate-containing supplements by American women *does not* decrease the risk of having an infant with neural tube defect.[5] Less than three months later, in November 1989, in the respected *Journal of the American Medical Association*, Harvard and Boston University researchers authored an article: "Multivitamin/Folic Acid Supplementation in Early Pregnancy *Reduces* the Prevalence of Neural Tube Defects."[6] But wait, that's not the end of it. In March of 1993, four years later, the *Journal of the American Medical Association* carried an article by researchers at the Slone Epidemiology Unit, Boston University School of Medicine, concluding that pregnant women's intake of an over-the-counter multivitamin containing folic acid reduces the risk of neural-tube defects by 60 percent.[7] In the same *Journal of the American Medical Association* issue an editorial states: "One of the most exciting medical findings of the last part of the 20th century is that folic acid, a simple, widely available, water-soluble vitamin, *can prevent* spina bifida, [in which there is incomplete closure of the spine] and anencephaly (in which the brain fails to develop fully) [both are neural-tube defects]. Not since the rubella vaccine became available 30 years ago have we had a comparable opportunity for primary prevention of such common and serious birth defects."

It took ten years for United States government agencies to recommend that "all women of childbearing age in the United States who are capable of becoming pregnant should consume 0.4 mg of folic acid per day for the purpose of reducing their risk of having a pregnancy affected by spina bifida or other neural-tube defects."[8]

How many babies were born with spinal defects or the absence of a functioning brain for want of a simple over-the-counter vitamin pill in that decade?

And then there are the conflicting reports about diet that drive consumers crazy. In the 1960s, doctors told us to eat margarine instead of butter to lower our cholesterol levels and protect our hearts. The amount of butter consumed by Americans is now half of what it was in 1961.[9] In 1992, reports from United States Department of Agriculture researchers and other scientific institutions in Europe stated that margarines, which develop trans fatty acids during the processing to form "sticks," may be as bad or worse for our cholesterol levels and our hearts.[10] The sale of margarine immediately plummeted after publicity about the research.[11] Joseph T. Judd at the United States Department of Agriculture (which funded the $1-million margarine study) then said: "At this point, we really do not have all of the evidence to relate trans fatty acids to heart disease because in cardiovascular disease there are many factors. . . . And we don't know the effect of trans fatty acids in these other risk factors, all we're looking at is blood cholesterol."[12]

After much publicity about the benefits of the antioxidant vitamins beta-carotene and vitamin E in preventing cancer, a report about a well-controlled study from Finland in 1994 really shook things up. More than twenty-nine thousand men who smoked, ranging in age from fifty to sixty-nine years, were in the study. They were assigned to one of four regimens: vitamin E (50 mg per day) alone, beta-carotene (20 mg per day) alone, both vitamin E and beta-carotene, or a placebo. Follow-up was from five to eight years. The researchers found no reduction in the incidence of lung cancer among male smokers who received dietary supplementation with vitamin E or beta-carotene. In fact, the researchers said, the trial raised the possibility that these supplements may actually have harmful as well as beneficial effects.[13]

The antisupplement researchers said, "I told you so!" Those who were pro-supplementation were quick to point out that the men in the Finnish study were given low doses of supplements and had been smoking for more than twenty years, there was no information on their diets, and that it was a case of "too little too late."

As you will read in the following chapters, there is a tremendous amount of research concerning antioxidants in the prevention of cancer and heart disease, including one large study from China that showed dramatic benefits. Food companies are expected to promote antioxidant-fortified foods within two years.

An article in the *Journal of the American Medical Association*, commenting on the stir caused by the Finnish studies, concluded: "Vitamins and mineral supplements have entered the ranks of bona fide science. But it may be quite some time before those ranks determine how best to use them."[14]

"This issue is going to get hotter before it gets resolved," says Elizabeth Yetley, Ph.D., acting director of the Office of Special Nutritionals at the Food and Drug Administration.[15]

The fact that research reports can have an effect on what we eat is obvious. For years we were told a high-protein, meat-and-potatoes diet was the best for us. Now we are urged to ingest more carbohydrates and less protein, especially in the form of red meat.[16] Red-meat consumption has fallen by almost 50 percent and whole-milk consumption by 14 percent in the past twenty years.

It seems that reports about what we should eat are as solid as soup.

Intriguing Results From Population and Diet Studies

Still, epidemiologists and ethnobotanists—those who study medicinal plants used by populations—are persistently showing how diet affects the incidence of disease.[17] The worldwide network of researchers has made intriguing dietary observations. For example:

- Studies by Danish researchers showed a low incidence of heart disease among Eskimos. This prompted a University of Chicago study that isolated omega-3 fatty acids in fish, believed to be the heart-protecting ingredients in the Eskimos' diet.
- Onions have been used by Poles to cure a variety of ills, so Victor Gurewich, M.D., a cardiologist at Tufts University, fed onions to twenty patients and found that onions triggered a positive shift in cholesterol levels.
- Irwin Ziment, M.D., a professor at the University of California School of Medicine, was intrigued by the low incidence of respiratory trouble in Los Angeles among Mexicans

who smoke. For the past ten years, he has prescribed chilies to protect the lungs of his patients vulnerable to respiratory problems.

- James E. Enstrom, Ph.D., a University of California at Los Angeles epidemiologist, has studied the health habits of Mormons, who do not use tobacco, alcohol, or hot drinks but do use a lot of whole grains and fresh fruits. He has found that this group has very low cancer and heart-disease rates when compared to the population at large.

- James Duke, Ph.D., an ethnobotanist for the Department of Agriculture who is assisting the National Cancer Institute in its plant-drug research, began to study the link between garlic and cancer after noting the amounts of garlic eaten in certain provinces of China and the low incidence of cancer there.

"My favorite sport is finding the science behind the custom," says the sixty-year-old Dr. Duke, who likes to cite what he calls the "ginkgo-seed coincidence."

"In Japan ginkgoes are eaten with cocktails because they're believed to fight drunkenness," he said. "In completely unrelated research, we find that the ginkgo contains compounds that speed up the metabolism of alcohol."

A nutraceutical ginkgo to treat a hangover? Ginkgo is one of the most popular drugs in Europe today.

Chris Beecher, Ph.D., an assistant professor of medicinal chemistry at the University of Illinois at Chicago, has cataloged nine hundred plant substances (phytochemicals) that are common in nature that studies have found could prevent certain diseases.

Specific phytochemicals you will read about in this book include cancer-fighting ingredients such as indoles (found in the cabbage family) to deactivate estrogens; sterols (from cucumbers) to enhance cholesterol excretion from the body; polyacetylenes (from parsley) to buffer a potent cancer-causing agent, benzopyrene; quinones (from rosemary) to induce the body to produce detoxifying enzymes; and isoflavones (from legumes) to deactivate cancer-gene enzymes. Other plant chemicals have been found to stimulate the immune system; reduce inflammation; and help prevent blood clots, osteoporosis, and high blood pressure.

The potential applications of nutraceuticals have been encouraged by the National Cancer Institute. In 1989, this agency funded $20.5 million for a Designer Food Program to study phytochemicals. The first foods being studied under NCI grants include garlic, licorice root, flaxseed, citrus fruits, and umbelliferous vegetables (such as parsley, carrot, and celery).

The Food and Drug Administration (FDA) has expressed interest in cooperating with the program by assembling a multidisciplinary research group to assist with animal-growth and reproduction studies. The food industry and universities are cooperating.

The possibilities of prescribed health benefits from new food products made with phytochemicals or other techniques are mind-boggling. Herbert Pierson Jr., M.S., Ph.D., vice president, Research and Development, Preventive Nutrition Consultants, Woodinville, Washington, and former head of the Designer Foods Program at the National Cancer Institute, says:

"Imagine a frozen food that can be popped into the microwave. The product is devoid of cholesterol, fortified by huge concentrations of citrus or licorice that delivers natural molecules that fortify human tissue against chronic insults.[18]

"We could produce orange juice with the phytochemical content of twenty oranges or salt and fat-free beef Stroganoff with high concentration of allium [garlic and onion family, believed to have antibiotic and anticancer properties]."

Dr. Pierson believes we now have the technology to create superjuices. He says you can take the piths and peels of oranges and grapefruit, stir them into orange juice, and create high-octane super "life-cycle juice." You'd have to drink twenty glasses of orange juice to get the protective amount in one glass of life-cycle juice.

He says men and postmenopausal women might select a heart-protective superjuice rich in flavonoids. Flavonoid research shows that antioxidant flavonoids not only discourage oxidation of cholesterol that leads to clogged arteries, but also help prevent life-threatening clots by keeping blood cells from clumping.

Women with breast cancer might choose a different superdrink, spiked with d-limonene, a compound that has been shown to fight breast cancer in animals. And older folk with fading memories might opt for superjuices treated with another flavonoid that could discourage neurological diseases such as Alzheimer's. Some of these types of juices already exist. The technology is there but FDA approval is needed.

"It is more cost-effective than looking for new drugs," Dr. Pierson maintains.

The FDA agrees there is growing evidence that certain foods fight disease, but it wants to encourage the use of this information in labeling while at the same time discouraging producers from making false claims.

Food technologists say the production would be a breeze. "We could build certain properties into food products that are carcinogen scavengers," says Manfred Kroger, Ph.D., a professor of food technology at Penn State University. "For that matter, we could add birth control to cereal or feed students compounds that limit daydreaming and make them focus."

In the early 1990s, attendees at a National Institutes of Health Conference on Designer Foods joked about an anticancer pizza: "It would have a flaxseed crust and be topped with rosemary, licorice, and garlic. And served with orange juice."

That's not so far out, as you will understand as you read descriptions of the research now under way in the field of nutraceuticals. The technology to isolate and produce nutraceuticals, however, has outstripped the regulations for foods and drugs. Any product producer that makes a claim for a superjuice or an anticancer pizza, for example, would have to have the product rigorously tested—to show that it is indeed beneficial, that the compounds work together, and there are no side effects. All of this has to be worked out before FDA approval. It would require a tremendous amount of money to do this kind of testing. And if you are using standard, naturally occurring compounds, how do you keep others away from your idea long enough to pay off your investment? You can't patent it.

Although the development of such nutraceuticals may be promising, it is far from simple. Complexities of naturally occurring substances in plant foods are daunting. Effects of chemicals at one level may be benign, and at another level, hazardous. Vitamin D is a good example. We need it for strong bones, but it can become poisonous if body levels are too high. We need a certain amount of fat to live, but too much of it harms us.

Even manipulation of substances in foods by means of traditional plant-breeding techniques has provided some unforeseen problems. There was a near catastrophe in 1970 with the release of a new potato variety, named lenape. The potato had been bred especially for qualities that would make it suitable to produce potato chips. Shortly after its release, the lenape potato was promptly pulled from marketing channels. The variety was found to contain such a high amount of pharmacologically active substances, glucoalkaloids, that it might have poisoned many consumers.

So the development of nutraceuticals is fraught with problems, but it is hoped that once these substances derived from and/or added to plants and animals are well understood, they can be a beneficial, painless, and inexpensive way of preventing many human ills.

Despite the roadblocks to new nutraceuticals, there is much information about tried-and-true nutraceuticals that exist in vitamins and foods literally from soup to nuts. You can do a great deal right now to improve your health through educated use of existing elements. That casual carrot you munch and the rosemary you sprinkle on your chicken may help protect you against cancer, for example. The turmeric with which you spice your rice and the lettuce in your salad may aid in staving off heart disease. That piece of chocolate you feel guilty about swallowing may raise your spirits, while a cup of coffee may energize you while making your heart beat more rapidly.

Your body, however, is different from anyone else's, and what may be good for others may be bad for you. A lot of people, for example, cannot drink milk because they lack an enzyme to digest it (lactose intolerance) or cannot eat beans because of intestinal gas. Diabetics may die from ingesting sugar that would be harmless to the rest of us.

This book presents an overview of the reports of modern nutraceutical research as well as descriptions of the folk practices concerning therapeutic uses of food. As you will read, many of the highly schooled and skilled modern researchers are actually proving what the unschooled and folk-medicine practitioners discovered on their own—certain elements in foods can prevent and treat diseases.

As we progress through this book together, you will read about the controversies and barriers concerning nutraceuticals. It will raise questions. For example, when does a beneficial food additive, such as vitamin E or rosemary, become a drug? If a food is fortified with beta-carotene to help prevent heart attacks, can the public be made aware of it without moving the product from the supermarket to the pharmacy?

When conflicting reports are made by eminent scientists, which ones should we believe?

After educating yourself and, when necessary, seeking advice from professionals, what you put on your plate is your responsibility. You have no control over your heredity and limited control over your environment, but you do have control over what you eat. Those edibles that you ingest affect your mind, your body, and your longevity. If you choose wisely for yourself, you will feel and look better and live longer.

And someday, you may hear your doctor say to you, "Take two cookies and call me in the morning," and you will happily down your dose of nutraceuticals.

A Consumer's Guide to

MEDICINES
IN FOOD

Chapter 1

WHAT NOW PURPLE COW?

You may never have seen a purple cow and never hope to see one, but you will, if science continues along its path, see a cow that is literally a living medicine chest.

Cows have long given us proteins, calcium, and vitamins in their milk, but according to researchers, the bovines can produce human antibodies. These antibodies can be tailored to fight tooth decay, strep throat, stomach bugs, and other ailments. In June 1994, Enzon, Inc., a New Jersey–based company, asked the FDA for permission to market its bovine-derived blood substitute for humans. In the same barnyard, chickens are also being raised to lay eggs containing similar medicinal human antibodies.

Hyperimmune milk and eggs produced by cows and chickens have been developed by Stolle Research and Development, a subsidiary of Ralph J. Stolle Company, a diversified manufacturing concern in Cincinnati. Stolle Research is working with E.I. du Pont de Nemours & Co., and ConAgra, Inc., the big food processor, to develop nutraceutical eggs and milk.

Animals always produce antibodies in their milk, but only for their own species. In the Stolle products, however, a cow or chicken is repeatedly vaccinated with dead bacteria of the types that infect humans, causing the animals to produce large volumes of disease-fighting human antibodies. The antibodies are then secreted in a cow's milk or a chicken's eggs, and those products then become nutraceuticals.

One of the companies' earliest patents covers a form of hyperimmune milk loaded with antibodies to bacteria called *Strept mutans,* which causes tooth decay. Another early patent covers milk and eggs designed to ward off stomach infections. These dairy products contain antibodies to more than two dozen bacteria, including salmonella.

Lee R. Beck, Ph.D., executive vice president of Stolle Research, says the investigations, taken together, open broad new opportunities for "passive vaccines that would allow people to strengthen their defenses against infections simply by drinking milk every day."

Dr. Beck said the hyperimmune milk appears to lower cholesterol, provide relief from rheumatoid arthritis, and lower blood pressure.[1]

That's not all, Beck said. The company has also learned that milk contains a natural anti-inflammatory compound that can relieve pain as aspirin does but appears to be safer.

It also turns out that cows, pigs, and lambs have more protein and less fat when they are maintained in a hyperimmune condition. Stolle researchers believe farmers could use the hyperimmunity techniques instead of growth hormones. (United States beef producers have been using growth hormone, a powerful chemical from the pituitary gland at the base of the brain, to increase the cattle's weight from 10 to 20 percent for the same amount of feed.)

Pigs, which reportedly have body tissues and systems very similar to ours, are also being raised as nutraceutical factories. At the Gene Evaluation and Mapping Lab, Beltsville, Maryland, Robert J. Wall is working with a gene for whey acidic protein obtained from a researcher at the National Institutes of Health. This protein switches on only when the sows are lactating. Sows produce large amounts of it in their milk. The secret of this success is a "genetic switch" attached to the gene that turns on and off at lactation. To this "switch," researchers have attached the first medically important substance, Protein C (hPC), a scarce human anticlotting agent manufactured in small amounts in the liver. Its function is to prevent excessive clotting. Estimates are that about 1 million Americans each year could benefit from treatment with Protein C. One major area would be in patients undergoing hip, knee, and other joint-replacement surgery. Thousands of such operations are performed each year, often causing the body's system for regulating formation of blood clots to become overwhelmed. Protein C could prevent undesirable excessive clotting. Likewise, the toxins produced by some serious blood infections trigger the blood-clotting mechanism, and many patients actually die from extensive clotting. About 25 percent of heart-attack patients treated with clot-busting drugs develop secondary clots, which likewise might be prevented with Protein C.

Therapeutic proteins such as Protein C or antihemophiliac factor A, used to treat the blood-clotting disorder in hemophiliacs, can be very expensive. They exist in minute amounts and must be extracted from tissue or blood. It costs more than $30,000 per year to treat a hemophiliac with antihemophiliac factor A. Some simple therapeutic proteins such as tissue plasminogen activator (TPA), used to treat heart attacks, can be artificially produced by using genetically engineered cell cultures. But cell-culture production makes relatively small quantities at considerable costs. For instance, TPA is about $2,000 a dose. *A single pig or a goat or a cow genetically engineered for human protein production of antihemophiliac factor A, however, could produce enough to treat all the world's hemophiliacs.* Potential sales could exceed $1 billion per year.[2]

William Velander, Ph.D., is a biochemical engineering professor at Virginia Polytechnic Institute, whose research group, with funding from the National Science Foundation, the American Red Cross, and Virginia Tech, first developed the technique for pig production of Protein C. He and his coworkers began their efforts using cows but soon switched to pigs, which reproduce more rapidly and are better suited for research purposes.[3]

"We now have the ability to reproduce these needed proteins in very large amounts by using the same farm animals that have been bred for centuries to supply humans with food protein," Velander says.

Scientists are thus turning to transgenic animals as a potential source of therapeutic proteins in an effort to establish a new multibillion-dollar agribusiness sometimes called barnyard technology. The rationale is simple. Farm animals such as cows, goats, or pigs are given a foreign gene that orders their mammary glands to produce the desired protein and secrete it in their milk. The animals experience the production of the foreign protein as just another milk protein with no adverse ramifications upon health.

Instead of being sent to a dairy for processing into milk, cheese, and ice cream, transgenic milk goes to a pharmaceutical firm, where the therapeutic protein is extracted and processed into a drug.

Cow-derived, genetically engineered blood is, in fact, being tested in humans at this writing by Enzon, Inc., a New Jersey company, which has been developing the substitute, PEG-hemoglobin, since 1990.[4]

Biotech Nutraceuticals

Biotechnology is the use of living things—plants, animals, bacteria—to manufacture products. All cells contain DNA sequences that form genes; the genes in turn make up chromosomes. Think of the chromosomes as a strand of beads, with each bead representing a gene. These genes govern specific biological traits, everything from the way a cell uses food and fights off infection to how it reproduces. Thus every individual in every species would have a unique strand of beads.

In the 1970s, scientists discovered they could clip off a single gene (bead) from the chromosome and attach it to another. This technique is called gene splicing, which results in "recombinant DNA." With these manipulations, a characteristic of one living organism can be transplanted to another, even if the two are not of the same species.

The first farmer who bred the best bull with the best cow in the herd to improve the stock, rather than allowing the animals to breed randomly, was implementing biotechnology in a simple sense. The first baker who used yeast enzymes to make bread rise was likewise using a living thing to produce an improved product. Indeed, one anthropologist argues that a desire to raise grain for brewing beer—a classic biotechnology product—was the impetus for the first systematic farming ten thousand years ago.

The modification of crop plants began with ancient agriculturists, who selected for cultivation plants with desirable traits from domesticated relatives of wild species. In this century, plant breeders have pursued the transfer of genes from certain noncultivated plant species to a variety of different but closely related species. The new biotechnology springs from our ability to rearrange or recombine DNA, the basic genetic material of living things, a feat made possible in 1974, when American scientists first cloned (isolated and duplicated) a specific gene. From that beginning the new biotechnology has developed a wide range of applications. In food production it is revolutionizing old processes such as fermentation and crossbreeding.

The first food product of biotechnology was approved by the FDA in 1991. Rennin, a natural enzyme widely used in the dairy industry to make cheese, can be produced in pure form by growing it with bacteria. Before biotechnology, a not-so-pure rennin was extracted from the stomachs of newborn calves.

In the case of the MacGregor tomato, scientists at Calgene, Inc., a California biotech company, isolated the gene that produces the enzyme that makes a tomato rot. They cut it out of the tomato chromosome, altered it so that it would suppress the rotting function, and used the new genetic material to create a rot-resistant tomato. A new bead was added to the long string of the tomato's genetic material, and from then on, the tomato's offspring became rot resistant. DNA Plant Technology Corp. in New Jersey has made a tomato with an arctic flounder gene to keep it from being damaged by frost. The International Food Biotechnology Council has listed twenty-six companies that are working on some seventy new foods, such as celery sticks without strings, potatoes that absorb less oil when fried, presweetened melons, and cinnamon-flavored basil.[5]

Unlocking Nutrients

Many researchers believe there are beneficial substances in plants that may be ignored by the human digestive system because we lack certain enzymes to process them.

Biotechnology techniques are not only being used to create new versions of food products but to make existing but unavailable nutraceuticals in food obtainable. Even if foods do contain beneficial substances, they do no good if your body can't absorb them. Bioavailability of foods is a major consideration. That is achieved by breaking up the food into particles and increasing the surface area. Wayne M. Barnes, Ph.D., of the Washington University School of Medicine, for example, is trying to use plant genetic engineering to halt a form of childhood blindness caused by vitamin A deficiency. When plants rich in vitamin A are given to third-world children who are malnourished, they are unable to assimilate it. Their bodies don't have the enzymatic machinery they need to convert vitamin A to a usable form. The human body cannot assimilate carotene, the form of vitamin A found in plants, Barnes says, unless it is first broken down into retinoic acid by carotene cleavage enzyme (CCE).

Dr. Barnes theorizes that these children could be supplied with CCE by transferring the gene for the enzyme into plants like cassava, or rice, crops that are relatively abundant in the third-world countries.

"If you put this enzyme into something that these people commonly eat, the enzyme would make retinoic acid available and they would probably avoid blindness," Dr. Barnes says.[6]

Have Some Vaccine With Your Meal

Researchers in Texas are working to genetically engineer plants to provide vaccinations to humans. Hugh Mason, Ph.D., a professor at Texas A & M Institute of Biosciences and a consultant to Agristar, Inc., says that it is possible to insert genes into banana crops and into lettuce and tomatoes to provide immunity against cholera, strains of *E. coli*, and other intestinal diseases caused by bacteria or viruses.

Dr. Mason says, "Through recombinant technology, we would be able to insert genes into a banana crop that can be cultivated in third-world countries. This food could be consumed without cooking. A mother could mash it up and feed it to her infant and protect that child against *E. coli* or some other enteric disease."[7] He is also testing a lettuce and tomato vaccine to fight intestinal upsets.

The Texas researcher says that human albumin has been produced in plants and so has enkephalin, a human brain chemical that is linked to pain suppression. A company already has the patent on a streptococcal antigen in plants to combat that bacterial infection in humans.

Plants can become factories for pharmaceutical products through genetic engineering performed by plant molecular biologists. Such "factories" could easily produce nutraceuticals inexpensively and in large amounts.

David Russell, director of plant moleculor biology at Agracetus, a Middleton, Wisconsin firm, points out pharmaceuticals that are too expensive to produce with conventional technology may make it to market if a technique to "grow" them in genetically engineered plant seeds is successful. Agracetus is collaborating with a number of pharmaceutical companies that have developed some "hot" drugs that are too costly to produce.[8]

Russell says that Agracetus researchers use a "gene gun" to shoot foreign genes into a plant such as corn or soybean. To make the neutraceutical, for example, the borrowed gene typically would be cloned from a human tissue sample and injected into corn or soybean cells. The transplanted gene then would cause the plant to produce the desired product—generally a valuable protein—and the accumulate this material in its seeds. The ability to produce the chemical is passed on to successive generations of the plant, which can be cultivated in a field to increase commercial production. The desired chemical can then be recovered from the seeds or the seeds can become a nutraceutical to be eaten or perhaps processed into an injectable or pill medication.[9]

Russell told an American Chemical Society audience in 1994 his firm has been working with seven companies, including Bristol-Meyer's Squibb, to include in plants therapeutic proteins for autoimmune and genetic disorders, and monoclonal antibodies for tumors and infectious diseases.

In the meanwhile, in addition to putting anti-cholera medication in bananas, scientists at Texas A & M University are working on producing hepatitis B antigens in the fruit.[10] The viral illness kills more than a million people a year in third-world countries. The vaccine now in use is about three dollars a shot, too expensive for the poor nations. Dr. Charles Arntzen, head of the hepatitis-fighting banana project, hopes the altered bananas will deliver the vaccine at a cost of about two cents a dose, and save on such costs as refrigeration, needles, and sterilization equipment. Bananas don't have to be cooked, can be eaten by very young children, and are easy to grow. And, he says, they have a type of protein that potentially lets them deliver very high levels of antigens, making them promising as a nutraceutical.

"The food business has become a technology business," maintains John M. McMillin, a food analyst with Prudential Securities. "It is getting to the point where people are starting to call it 'software for the microwave.'"[11]

Flaxseed oil, for example, is rich in omega-3 fatty acids. A study by Dr. Lillian Thompson of the University of Toronto found that in addition to its cholesterol-lowering ability, flaxseed oil caused a 50 percent reduction in precancer cells in lab animals. Instead of selling food for what it doesn't do, big food companies are increasingly developing and marketing products with what advertisers call "proactive" health claims, extolling specific health enhancements.

Prospects include meats with lower sodium and cholesterol content and longer shelf life, as well as weather-resistant crops with more abundant yield and nutritional content. There will be low-fat, low-cholesterol steaks, long-lasting, nutritionally superior vegetables, and pesticide-free fruits.

The position of the American Dietetic Association concerning biotechnology and the future of food is that "techniques of biotechnology are useful in enhancing the quality, nutritional value, and variety of food available for human consumption and increasing the efficiency of food production, processing, and waste management."[12]

The techniques for the genetic manipulation of plants—recombinant DNA methodology—should pose risks no different from the techniques of classical genetic methods for similar traits. The molecular methods are more specific, and thus users of genetic engineering will be more certain about the traits they introduce into the plants.[13]

The FDA's labeling policy for foods from new plant varieties has stirred controversy. A common objection is, "Why shouldn't consumers be informed that their food is genetically engineered, especially when new tomatoes might contain animal genes?" The FDA's general position is that the information on labels must be accurate but also material, a criterion that in the agency's view does not apply to plant-breeding techniques. As a longtime advocate of consumer information, I personally believe the label can state whether or not genetic engineering has been used. Why shouldn't we have a choice?

As for allergies, many foods elicit an allergic response, including milk, eggs, fish, shellfish, nuts, and wheat. Since all known food allergens are proteins, the transfer of proteins from one food source to another could confer allergenic properties from the donor plant. This is possible, and scientists must study whether a suspected allergen has been transferred or is allergenic in the new variety.[14]

Worried about "Frankenfood," Jeremy Rifkin, president of the Foundation on Economic Trends, maintains biofoods are not necessarily safe and insists the public deserves the right to know what they are buying.

"DNA is a chemical. When you mix genes across species in ways that cannot be done through evolution or classical breeding, there is no way of knowing in advance how that gene will line up,"[15] Rifkin maintains.

Natural Nutraceuticals From Plants

While genetic engineers are interested in creating new plants and animals, other researchers are seeking to unlock old health secrets that have always been in flora and fauna but may have been unrecognized by our technologically advanced society.

Botanicals are currently the source of 25 percent of our pharmaceuticals and researchers are tramping through jungles and accompanying witch doctors to find new medicines from plants. They are also watching animals that instinctively eat certain plants when ailing.

For example, a sick chimp with intestinal upset, lethargy, and loss of appetite was observed in East Africa. A few hours after her illness began, the chimp began gathering shoots of *Vernonia amygdalina*, a shrub native to Tanzania's Mahle Mountains National Park but rarely eaten by any of the chimpanzees there. She sucked and swallowed the bitter juice from the macerated pith, spitting out the fibrous remains. She was in much better health the next day. Researchers at the Tanzania's Wildlife Research Center say that African tribes use extracts from the plant's bark, stems, roots, seeds, and leaves to treat a variety of human ailments—including intestinal upset and appetite loss. Other researchers have found that chimps in Uganda eat *Rubia cordifolia* when they are not feeling well. Monkeys in the province of Santiago of the Dominican Republic, near Puerto Rico, eat dirt for its mineral content. Certain clay soils contain high concentrations of kaolin, the active ingredient in the popular antidiarrheal medication Kaopectate.[16]

At the National Cancer Institute (NCI) natural products branch, created in 1975, contractors all over the world are collecting plants, marine organisms, and microorganisms that might contain some anticancer chemical. Matthew Suffness, Ph.D., head of the NCI Natural Products Branch, says that those herbal medications that work generally work only on minor diseases. Dr. Suffness is not surprised that some do work; after all, he says, "You're looking at thousands of years of clinical experience."[17]

Humans have used plants as medicines since the beginning of

time. Quinine, a soluble salt extracted from the bark of a tree, was the first drug found effective to treat malaria. Treating fevers with a beverage made from tree bark is a long-used folk remedy, and that knowledge led to the development of one of our most popular medications, aspirin. Other folk remedies, since they may involve as many as sixty ingredients, some secret, are more difficult to find.

In recent years, there has been increasing scientific interest in natural or folk sources of medicines. U.S. Department of Agriculture researchers have been testing seeds chemically for biologically active compounds, and the National Cancer Institute has a program to test more than five thousand extracts a year from some two thousand plants collected from around the world.

A seed from a native evergreen bush of China and Japan, the plum yew, has been tested against a variety of cancers in mice. It was found to extend the lives of leukemic mice by at least 300 percent over the length of time they would live without treatment. The NCI is planning to test this treatment on humans. While drugs that are promising in animals can prove disappointing in human trials, if results from the plum yew tests are promising, it may be a significant new treatment. Before the current budget cuts, about a hundred extracts entered testing at the NCI every week— even though only one out of every couple of thousand became a candidate for clinical evaluation. The NCI has six compounds from plants under development for clinical trials, at this writing.

What researchers are aiming for now, however, is to identify those substances within human food plants that contain health benefits and to increase their potency and availability.

Phytochemicals

Phytochemicals are natural compounds found in plants, fruits, vegetables, grains, and legumes. Phytochemicals give therapeutic properties to herbs that have been used in folk medicine for centuries.

Hundreds of different phytochemicals affect our health. Some are essential to our hormone regulation. Others trigger the release of various chemical messengers between nerves, neurotransmitters, critical to emotional and mental well-being. Some protect our DNA from being damaged. Many are anticancer, antimutagenic, antioxidative, and anti-inflammatory. Clues to the benefits of these phytochemicals come from the diets of certain populations. The high plant-based diets in certain regions of China have been associated with low blood cholesterol, cancer, and heart disease.

You will read in the next chapters about research concerning phytochemicals as well as vitamins, minerals, and other substances ingested with our meals that may prevent and in some cases treat common illness. It is important to remember that this is research in progress, that none of the findings are conclusive, and that any substance can be toxic when taken in excess.

Honey is ordinarily a perfectly safe food, but under certain circumstances it may be hazardous. This depends upon what kind of plant the honeybees have used as their source of nectar. If nectar is gathered from species of rhododendron, azalea, and in particular, mountain laurel, it may cause poisoning. People who eat large amounts of rhubarb may become acutely ill from oxalate toxicity. Potatoes contain solanine, which inhibits the enzyme cholinesterase, and in turn can interfere with the transmission of nerve impulses. Shrimp contain arsenic; lima beans contain hydrogen cyanide. Milk contains about two hundred known chemical substances. Many natural foods contain both toxins and carcinogens. To complicate matters more, different species of the same plant, such as licorice root, can have widely different phytochemical profiles. And where the plant is grown can greatly affect its content of phytochemicals. Then the solvents and methods of extraction can influence the phytochemicals.

Scientific literature and studies have identified more than eight hundred foods that researchers say warrant further investigation for use in preventive medicine.

The phytochemicals in cruciferous vegetables called indoles have the potential, for example, to prevent breast and uterine cancer.

Legumes such as soybean, peas, lentils, seeds, and licorice are rich in isoflavones.

Whole grains such as oats, wheat, flax, rice, and barley are good sources of dietary fiber and phenolic acids. Food fibers are thought to benefit human health by binding to artery-clogging cholesterol and dangerous steroid hormones. This causes their elimination from the body more quickly. These same fibers raise the acidity in the large intestine, which prevents the recycling of potentially harmful bile acids. Whole grains, particularly flax, are high in lignins and phenolic compounds (*see* glossary). Both are believed, from animal studies, to be important factors in resisting breast and colon cancer.

Phytochemicals in garlic are under intensive study for their cholesterol-lowering, immune-enhancing, and cancer-preventive activity, as you will read in the following chapters.

Most of the pharmacology research of the past thirty years has sought chemical agents among microbes. But other natural sources of medicine and plants have through the ages provided these for humans.

Nutrition research today holds the key to a promising future where food—and products formulated from food components—may actually help us treat disease and promote optimal health.

Because foods are complex mixtures of various phytochemicals, studying them is a complex task. In nature phytochemicals can be both beneficial and toxic. At present the specific role of each phytochemical and the potential synergistic effects of different phytochemicals in cancer prevention are mostly unknown. There is much, however, we have already learned. Our new understanding of the relationship between diet and chronic diseases like cancer and osteoporosis has led to legitimate health claims for foods. Food components offer a veritable smorgasbord of possibilities for nutraceutical researchers. And today, special dietary products—including hypoallergenic foods, infant formulas, and nutritional supplements—are commonly used to nourish patients and mitigate existing disease. As you read on, you will learn about the observations and research concerning the human diet and prevention of disease through the use of foods, nutrients, and phytochemicals.

DIET AND CLUES TO
CANCER PREVENTION

When I was a young reporter on the staff of the *Star-Ledger* in Newark, New Jersey, I was assigned to write a series of articles on medical quacks. One of the targets of the exposé was a doctor who plied cancer patients with carrot juice. The medical and legal authorities came down hard on him because he allegedly exploited desperate people with a phony "cure."

Today, researchers are enthusiastic about the cancer-fighting properties of beta-carotene, a precursor of vitamin A contained in large amounts in carrot juice. While no one claims that carrot juice will cure cancer, few would deny that substances such as beta-carotene in food play a part in protecting us from out-of-control malignant cells.

In fact, researchers funded by the National Cancer Institute and the American Cancer Society and others worldwide are seeking nutraceuticals that will interfere with the process that turns a normal cell into a cancerous one.

Since the 1960s, scientists have believed that cancer develops in two steps:[1]

- Step one: *Initiation.* Some substances, such as tobacco smoke, serve as initiators, which start but cannot finish the cancer-causing process without the help of promoters.

- Step two: *Promotion.* Most promoters cannot work in cells that have not been initiated. Interfering with promoters offers the best approach in our lifetime of reducing cancer incidence.[2] This was demonstrated, for example, when the "promoter" estrogen supplementation given to postmenopausal women was found to cause cancer of the uterine lining. When the estrogen medication was curtailed, the cases of endometrial cancer in postmenopausal women dropped dramatically. Saccharin is another cancer promoter (although a weak one), hence the warning on the artificial sweetener's packaging.

It is feasible, scientists believe, that we all may be victims of step one, but that if step two does not occur, we don't get cancer. *The greatest effort today in the field of nutraceuticals is to identify those components in the diet that can be used to inhibit step two from taking place.* This quest is difficult because

- In most instances exposure to cancer-causing agents (carcinogens) takes place twenty to thirty years before a statistically significant increase in cancer can be detected. Only then can it be adduced that the increase in cancer may have been caused by exposure to specific cancer-causing agents.[3]
- Animal studies may give clues, but laboratory conditions and the bodies of other creatures may not result in valid conclusions for us.
- Each of us is unique in the way our bodies process chemicals based on our age, sex, heredity, medical history, diet, and behavior.
- Since it is unethical to deliberately feed humans cancer-causing agents, researchers must rely on epidemiological studies, which can be confounded by many factors including the environment.

Nevertheless, scientists are making great progress in understanding what in the diet may cause cancer and what may protect against it. You have to understand it yourself in order to grasp the realities of current nutraceutical research. Most of the information has come from *epidemiologic studies* that relate number of cancers in certain groups to their diet. For example, vegetarians and Seventh-Day Adventists have far less cancer than the general population.

Why?

Vegetarians have strikingly lower rates of colon and prostatic cancers. Two major factors appear to contribute to these surprising differences, according to Walter Troll, Ph.D., professor of environmental medicine, New York University Medical School, a pioneer in the study of the diet-cancer connection.[4]

1. Vegetarians don't eat meat, which has a high fat content, and fat has been associated with an increase in prostate and colon cancer.
2. Vegetables contain a variety of substances that suppress the progression of cancer by interfering with tumor promotion (as you will read in this chapter and the next).

The same factors may contribute to the low number of cancer deaths in Seventh-Day Adventists—50 to 70 percent below that of the general population for most cancers unrelated to smoking and drinking.[5]

Seventh-Day Adventists abstain from smoking and drinking; about 50 percent follow a lacto-ovo-vegetarian diet (dairy, eggs, vegetables, but no meat); and most avoid the use of coffee, tea, hot condiments, and spices.

The typical lacto-ovo-vegetarian diet has about 25 percent less fat and 50 percent more fiber than the average nonvegetarian diet.

Researchers at Loma Linda University in California believe several aspects of the typical Adventist diet might affect their risk of cancer. Again, the relatively low content of fat (especially saturated fat) and cholesterol and the relatively high content of fiber could influence other body functions that may relate to cancer risk. Increased speed of food through the intestines, for example, and/or changes in intestinal bacteria as well as a lesser output of bile acids may reduce exposure to cancer-causing agents in the diet.

The fact that Seventh-Day Adventist vegetarians have a relatively low intake of protein and are usually not obese suggests that eating fewer calories may delay the onset of the beginning of menstruation (menarche) and also influence hormone status at other periods of life. If such effects were documented, the Loma Linda researchers say, this could explain all or part of the reduced risk of Adventists for breast, ovary, and endometrial cancer. The lack of coffee consumption by most Seventh-Day Adventists could account for a good share of their reduced bladder-cancer risk.

Tying the observations of the Adventists to those noted in animal studies, the Loma Linda investigators speculate that:

- The relatively low intake of protein and fat by members of this religious group may favorably alter the body's response to chemical carcinogens.
- Exposure to potentially cancer-causing food additives or contaminants among Adventists may be quite different from that of the general public.
- Response to potential carcinogens such as nitrosamines (powerful carcinogens caused by the ingestion of nitrites that combine with chemicals in the body, amines), aflatoxin (a cancer-causing mold), or hydrocarbons (organic compounds such as chlorine) might be less detrimental because of a relatively high intake of vitamin C and vitamin A, both of which are potentially protective against a number of chemical carcinogens.
- The lower use of meats also reduces the use of backyard charcoal broilers, which are capable of producing considerable benzopyrene (a component of soot recognized as a cancer-causing agent for more than two hundred years) content in broiled meat.
- Although relatively little is known regarding environmental influences on the human enzyme system, several fruits and vegetables are abundantly used by Adventists. These fruits and vegetables contain compounds (such as flavones, *see* page 46) that are potent inducers of enzymes intimately involved

in the detoxification of absorbed carcinogens. Thus they help to prevent step two, cancer promotion, from taking place.

Roland Phillips, Ph.D., of Loma Linda University's Department of Biostatistics and Epidemiology, notes, "Although the evidence is quite scanty, it seems reasonable to assume that the Adventists' diet might influence the functioning of the immunological system. It is quite conceivable that a very low intake of foreign animal protein could influence the ability of the immunological surveillance system to recognize and destroy small, early clones of tumor cells. This possibility is particularly attractive because of the rather general decrease in cancer mortality from almost all cancer sites in Adventists, which is more suggestive of a stronger defense system against cancer than lack of exposure to a few of the known multiple environmental carcinogens."[6]

In addition to the studies of Seventh-Day Adventists and vegetarians, there have been thousands of investigations concerning the links between diet and cancer. The relationships noted in human epidemiologic studies are, in many cases, supported by evidence from laboratory-animal studies. The following are just a few of the research efforts that relate specific cancers to diet in certain populations and point to the future development of nutraceuticals to prevent and to treat cancers. They provide clues based on the diets of people who do and do not get malignancies.

Migrating Populations

Among the most intriguing studies are those deduced from migrating populations. Peter Greenwald, M.D., director, Division of Cancer Prevention and Control, National Cancer Institute in Bethesda, Maryland, points out, for example, that the Japanese who migrated to Hawaii have developed a cancer pattern closer to other Hawaiian residents than to the Japanese in Japan as their diet gradually became similar to the Hawaiian diet.[7] Other studies of migrating populations—eastern Europeans who migrated to the United States and Canada, Icelanders who migrated to

Canada, and southern Europeans who migrated to Australia—have shown similar types of changes in cancer incidence.[8]

Breast cancer and cancer of the colon and rectum annually account for approximately 30 percent—or 337,000—of all newly diagnosed cancers and for approximately 20 percent—or more than 100,000—of all cancer deaths in the United States.[9]

"These numbers contrast sharply with cancer mortality rates for other Westernized countries, such as Japan and Finland," Dr. Greenwald says. *"For example, if the United States had the same breast-cancer mortality rate as Japan, approximately eleven thousand—rather than the current forty-six thousand—American women would die each year from breast cancer. Similarly, if colon-cancer death rates in the United States were at the level of Finland, the number of Americans dying each year from colon cancer would drop from sixty thousand to below twenty thousand."*

The Japanese have historically followed a low-fat diet that is high in vegetables and sources of complex carbohydrates such as rice. However, as the Japanese diet has become "Westernized" to include larger amounts of animal fats and higher caloric intake, incidence and mortality rates for breast and colorectal cancers have shown a marked increase, says Greenwald.

In contrast, the Finnish diet, like the American diet, is relatively high in fat, accounting for nearly 40 percent of all calories consumed. However, Finns, who have a relatively low incidence of colorectal cancer, consume more dietary fiber, particularly wheat and rye fiber, than Americans.[10]

Migrant studies show similar results for endometrial (lining of the uterus) and ovarian cancers in women, suggesting environmental factors are more important than genetic differences between populations and that diet can explain much of the international variation. Most suspicion has fallen on dietary fat.[11]

The Fat Connection

The link between dietary fat and the development of tumors was first proposed in 1942.[12] Since that time, studies using animal models have confirmed an effect of fat—both saturated and unsaturated—on the development of breast tumors that is independent of total caloric intake. Experiments involving the administration of cancer-causing agents have demonstrated that dietary fat exerts its effect during the *promotional* stage of cancer development.[13]

There are at least as many epidemiologic studies showing an association between fat intake and breast-cancer risk as there are to the contrary.[14] The results of these studies in conjunction with those of animal studies, however, have convinced many researchers that there is sufficient evidence that some relationship does exist between high fat intake and cancer risk in humans.[15, 16]

Again, it is epidemiological studies that provide clues. And one of the best places to do such investigations is Israel, where citizens have come from many lands. When immigrants abandon their native diets for Israeli menus, the changes in their incidence of cancer development are telltale.

Cancer–Israeli Study

Prof. Baruch Modan, head of the Department of Epidemiology at the Chaim Sheba Medical Center in Israel, and his colleagues completed a four-year study on nearly one thousand women with cancer and found that they consumed more fat and less fiber in their diet than did a group of women matched for age, residence, and length of stay in Israel who did not have cancer. In fact, Professor Modan's group found that women with a high-fat, high-animal-protein, low-fiber diet are twice as likely to develop cancer in the postmenopausal period.[17]

Professor Modan wants to utilize the findings on diet and cancer to prevent the disease. Of the various factors contributing to cancer, he says, diet is the most easily manipulated. "I'm for women consuming less fat and more fiber, more fruits and vegetables including the peels. As a matter of fact, this advice is valid for men as well."

Other studies have concluded high-fat diets are linked to cancer recurrence after treatment. In an investigation reported in the

Journal of the National Cancer Institute, researchers took dietary histories from 240 patients undergoing treatment for stage I or II cancer, then followed their progress for four years. The results? Women with estrogen-responsive tumors who experienced a recurrence reported higher intakes of total fat than did the successfully treated women.

When the researchers looked at the women's percentage of daily calories derived from fat, they found that for every 1 percent increase in fat, the risk of recurrence increased 10 percent.[18]

In a review of twelve studies of dietary factors and the risk of cancer reported in the *Journal of the National Cancer Institute*, an international group of researchers concluded there was not only a statistically significant, positive association between cancer risk and saturated fat intake in postmenopausal women, but there was a consistent protective effect from fruit and vegetables, and particularly for vitamin C intake, against cancer. The researchers concluded that if these dietary associations are correct, 24 percent of the cancers in postmenopausal North American women and 16 percent of the premenopausal could be prevented.[19]

The Finnish Women's Study and Vitamin E

Vitamin E may also be a factor in preventing female cancers. The Finnish Social Insurance Institution's Mobile Clinic Health Survey enrolled 15,093 Finnish women, aged fifteen to ninety-nine, who were initially free from cancer between 1966 and 1971.[20] Eight years later, cancer had stricken 313 women. Vitamin E levels were measured from previously stored samples of the cancer patients' blood and that of 578 controls matched for municipality and age. Those who had high levels of vitamin E in their blood when they first entered the study had a lower risk of cancer.[21]

Cancer of the Cervix and Uterus

Can vitamins prevent cancer of the cervix, the opening to the uterus? Cervical cancer affects about thirteen thousand women a year in the United States and results in about five thousand deaths annually. But the cancer is rampant in poor nations. It has been described as the most common cancer among women in the developing world. Dysplasia—the development of abnormal cell growth—in the uterine cervix is the earliest detectable stage of cervical cancer in women. It can be diagnosed with a Pap smear test.

In a study of oral contraceptive users studied for as long as seven years, there is an increased risk of progression of abnormal cells of the cervix to carcinoma in situ—a local and curable malignant growth. The risk of developing cervical cancer increases with the duration of oral contraceptive use. While this doesn't mean, according to researchers, that carcinoma of the cervix is caused by oral contraceptive hormones, it at least suggests enhanced susceptibility to spread or progression of lesions and perhaps some impairment of natural protective mechanisms.

B Vitamins Protect the Cervix

The B vitamin, folic acid, is often deficient when oral contraceptives are used, and the deficiency tends to become more pronounced with prolonged exposure. In addition, it has been widely recognized that age at first intercourse, smoking, and sexual promiscuity also contribute to cancer of the cervix. Much evidence indicates that dysplasia is caused by sexually transmitted infection, particularly the papillomavirus (HPV), which can cause genital warts. The latest research found that none of these factors were as powerfully linked to dysplasia, the precancerous lesions, as the combination of the HPV virus and folic acid deficiency.

Researchers from several universities led by Charles Butterworth Jr., M.D., professor of nutrition at the University of Alabama at Birmingham, found a link between the virus and the vitamin deficiency by testing blood levels of 294 women with precancerous cell changes in their cervixes.[22]

Dr. Butterworth notes that "even mild folic acid deficiency, a condition that has no detectable symptoms, appears to promote abnormal cells in the cervix." For this reason, he says, adequate dietary folic acid prior to HPV infection can possibly prevent cervical dysplasia. Prevention using better nutrition is a very desirable alternative to today's expensive detection and treatment programs."[23]

The concept of *localized nutrient deficiency* is emerging along with recognition of a regulatory role for certain folic acid derivatives. It has been known for many years that folic acid plays an important role in the effect of hormones on target tissue.

Dr. Butterworth said the vitamin deficiency is most often caused by poor diet, one lacking sufficient amounts of vegetables, fruits, and especially orange juice. The conclusion of the researchers in this study and others is that folic acid deficiency is not carcinogenic by itself, but it makes cells more susceptible to cancer-causing agents. It looks as if many cases of dysplasia could be prevented with a healthy diet.[24]

In fact, giving folic acid as a nutraceutical seems to prove this. Forty-seven young women with mild or moderate dysplasia of the uterine cervix, diagnosed by Pap smears, received oral supplements of 10 mg of folic acid or a placebo daily for three months. All had used a combination type of oral contraceptive for at least six months and continued "the pill" while returning monthly for follow-up examinations. Biopsies showed that the condition of the cervix improved considerably after three months in those receiving the folic acid compared to those receiving placebos.[25]

Vitamin E Against Cervical Cancer

Folic acid is not the only protector of the cervix, according to other researchers. The blood levels of beta-carotene, the substance found in vegetables that turns into vitamin A in the body, and vitamin E were measured in 116 women. The less there was of these two nutrients in the blood, the greater the risk for the women of advanced cervical cancer.[26]

In an Italian study, beta-carotene was also found helpful in discouraging the development of cervical cancer.[27]

Vitamin C Against Cervical Cancer

Vitamin C (ascorbic acid) in the precancerous condition of cervical dysplasia has been reported to be even more effective than beta-carotene. Women who took less than 88 mg of vitamin C per day had more than four times the risk for severely abnormal cells of the cervix or carcinoma in situ (localized cancer). Vitamin C intake remained a significant factor even after control for age and sexual activity.[28] Researchers in Sydney, Australia, also found vitamin C, fruit juices, and beta-carotene showed protective effects against cervical cancer, reducing the risks by as much as 80 percent with beta-carotene and 60 percent with vitamin C, and 50 percent with fruit juices.[29]

The answer as to whether vitamins—folic acid, vitamin E, vitamin C, and beta-carotene—can protect the cervix against cancer seems to be clearly "Yes!" The usefulness of vitamins in other female cancers is not as certain.

Cancer of the Uterus

Cancer of the uterus usually starts in the endometrium, or lining. After growing in the lining, the cancer invades the wall of the uterus and, if not treated, spreads to the fallopian tubes, ovaries, and other organs. Cancer of the uterus is the second most common form of cancer of the genitals in women and may be first ahead of cancer of the cervix, the most common, in some developed nations. The highest recorded incidence rates are from La Plata in Argentina with a rate of 31.1 per 100,000. Incidence rates elsewhere are highest in U.S. whites, in Canada, in Hawaiians and Maoris, and in western Europe. More than thirty-three thousand American women each year develop uterine cancer, and four thousand of them die of it. Low rates of incidence (2–4 per 100,000) are seen in the Far East and Near East populations, except for Jews in Israel and Chinese in Singapore and Hong Kong.[30]

Dietary studies are not as numerous as with other types of female cancers, but in an Italian study of endometrial cancer of 206 patients and age-matched hospital control subjects in Italy, the cancer patients reported significantly lower intake of green vegetables than control subjects, and lower intake of fruit.[31.]

Beta-Carotene and Ovarian Cancer

Cancer of the ovary includes several distinct types with probably different causes. The highest rates are reported among white females in northern and western Europe and in North America— 8–15 per 100,000. In the three Nordic countries the incidence rates exceed 14 per 100,000; however, in Finland the rate is less than 10. Incidence is also high in Israeli Jews. Ovarian cancer is less common in Indian, Chinese, and Japanese populations, with rates of 2–5 per 100,000.

A study of eighty-three Buffalo, New York, women with ovarian cancer compared to 113 matched who did not have the disease again found that those with cancer had low levels of beta-carotene in their blood. They had diets low in carotene-containing vegetables.[32]

Vitamins Against Breast Cancer

What about vitamins and breast cancer? Researchers at Harvard Medical School entered 89,494 cancer-free women thirty-four to fifty-nine years old into a study in 1980. Their intakes of vitamins C, E, and A were noted at the time. Breast cancer was diagnosed in 1,439 of the women during the next eight years. After adjusting for other risk factors, it was discovered that women who were in the highest group for intake of vitamin A had the lowest risk. Large intakes of vitamin C or E did not protect women in this study from breast cancer. The Harvard researchers stopped short of recommending vitamin A supplementation and said that pills may help only with those women whose diets were low in vitamin A. They suggested women increase their intake of the vitamin through vitamin A rich vegetables. They also said a typical multivitamin supplies an adequate amount of vitamin A if women wish to supplement their dietary intake.[33, 34]

Colorectal Cancer

Colon cancer, the second leading cause of cancer deaths in the United States, will be diagnosed in 111,000 people here this year and will cause about 51,000 deaths. Epidemiological studies in humans and laboratory studies of animals indicate that an increased dietary intake of fat and a decreased intake of dietary fiber add to the risk of colon cancer development.[35]

Vitamins and Fruits Against Colon Cancer

A large study of colon cancer and diet by the American Cancer Society was analyzed in 1992 by Michael Thun, M.D., director of analytical epidemiology for the American Cancer Society.[36] The prospective study used data from the Society's Cancer Prevention Study II (CPS II) to assess the relation of diet and other factors to risk of fatal colon cancer. CPS II is an ongoing mortality study started in 1982 that analyzes the diet, behavior, and lifestyles of 1,185,124 American men and women through the use of questionnaires. It is one of the largest research studies ever carried out in the United States.

Dr. Thun and his colleagues found that men and women who consumed fewer servings of vegetables and high-fiber grains had an increased risk of fatal colon cancer. Men who consumed the least vegetables and grains and no aspirin had 2.5 times higher risk, and women had a 2.9 times higher risk compared to those who consumed the most vegetables and used low-dose aspirin sixteen or more times a month.[37] "The study is one of several promising new developments with respect to colon cancer," Dr. Thun says.

The results support recommendations by the American Cancer Society and the U.S. Department of Health and Human Services encouraging consumption of a variety of vegetables, fruits, and high-fiber grains.

Fiber Against Colon Cancer

Geoffrey Howe Jr., M.D., of the University of Toronto found that in twelve of thirteen studies, eating lots of fiber in foods can indeed slash the risk of colon cancer about in half.[38]

A high-fiber, lower-fat diet may be especially important for persons at high risk of developing colorectal cancer, such as middle-age and older adults and persons with a family history of the disease.

Dr. Howe and colleagues figure that if everyone ate about 70 percent more fiber than usual, the rates of colon and rectal cancers would drop 31 percent, preventing an annual fifty thousand new cases in both men and women of all ages.

This would mean adding at least thirteen grams of food fiber daily for most people, about the amount in a serving of high-fiber bran cereal. However, the scientists stress you should get fiber from fruits, vegetables, and legumes, as well as cereals. Such foods all contain numerous anticancer substances in addition to fiber, as you will read in the next chapter.

Vitamins and Colon Cancer

A few studies have found a statistically significant protective effect of vitamin C. People with the lowest intake of vitamin C had three times the risk of colon cancer. Both dietary and supplemental vitamin C were significantly protective.

The possible role of vitamin C may be in prevention or reduction of fecal mutagens (substances that adversely affect the programming of a cell) in stool. In a study of diet and the mutagen fecapentaene levels conducted by the National Cancer Institute, a strong protective effect was observed for both dietary and supplemental vitamin C intake. Consumption of citrus fruit and of supplemental vitamin E was also significantly protective against fecapentaene. Thus, if fecal mutagens are associated with colon cancer development, vitamin C may play an independent role or may act together with vitamin E in blocking their cancer-causing potential.[39]

Can vitamins stop rectal polyps—growths—from occurring, reoccurring, and/or turning malignant? A Canadian study showed patients receiving supplemental vitamins C and E following surgical removal of precancerous colon polyps were much less likely to have a recurrence of their polyps than were those who received a placebo. Preliminary data from a similar U.S. study suggests that a combination of vitamins C, E, and beta-carotene is effective at preventing recurrence of polyps.[40]

Pursuing this research lead, the NCI has implemented the Polyp Prevention Trial, a four-year study to determine whether a low-fat, high-fiber, and vegetable- and fruit-enriched eating plan will reduce the likelihood of recurrence of colon polyps in persons over the age of thirty-five. Half of the one thousand men and one thousand women who are participating will consume a low-fat diet including five to eight servings of vegetables and fruits each day. Persons on this diet will be individually counseled on how to meet these goals, with a strong emphasis on behavior modification. The other participants will receive only information on basic nutrition. The difference in polyp formation between the two participant groups will be measured at one and four years.

A study of people at high risk for colon cancer in the Polyp Prevention Study Group reported negative results when vitamin supplements were given to protect against the development of precancerous growths in colon. People who took vitamin C or vitamin E or beta-carotene or all three over four years were no freer of the disease than those who took dummy pills.[41] The 864 people involved in the study previously had colorectal tumors or polyps that precede cancer.

The findings came as a surprise to some researchers because epidemiological studies have shown that people who eat a lot of fruit and vegetables have lower rates of colon cancer than those who eat less of these foods. Commenting on the study performed at Dartmouth-Hitchcock Medical Center in Hanover, New Hampshire, other researchers said the final answer to the question of whether vitamin supplements can protect against cancer is not known. They said it may be necessary to conduct longer studies or studies with different designs to see an effect. Or, it may be something else about fruits and vegetables that protects against colon cancer.

Vitamins and Protein Against Bladder Cancer

Eating vegetables and fruits containing carotenoids, the plant form of vitamin A, appears to decrease the chances of developing bladder cancer, a study by State University of New York at Buffalo researchers has found.[42]

The study compared the dietary histories of 351 men with confirmed bladder cancer with the diets of 855 men with no bladder cancer. It was conducted by a team of investigators from the University at Buffalo Department of Social and Preventive Medicine, headed by John Vena, Ph.D., associate professor.

Participants were selected from similar neighborhoods in western New York between 1979 and 1985. Nutrients considered in the study were total vitamin A, vitamin A from animal sources (retinol), vitamin A from plant sources (carotenoids), vitamin C, vitamin E, vitamin D, fiber, calcium, thiamine, riboflavin, and niacin. Total caloric intake; calories from fat, carbohydrates, and protein; sodium; total daily fluid intake; and level of cigarette smoking were also analyzed. In general, the study showed a positive link between bladder cancer and diet. Researchers found a "strong dose-response relationship" between eating large amounts of fruits and vegetables containing carotenoids and lower risk of bladder cancer.

Participants with bladder cancer consumed significantly more coffee, soda, white bread, crackers, sugar, presweetened cereals, macaroni, gravy, eggs, canned ham, liverwurst and cold cuts, smoked dried meat, and smoked fish than participants without cancer. They ate significantly less celery, lettuce, carrots, green peppers, squash, peas, bananas, oranges, and hard cheese than participants without the disease.

"Our study reinforces the importance of diet in the development of bladder cancer," Dr. Vena says. "It suggests that, for this disease, diet intervention has strong public health potential."

In other studies, vitamin C seems to be especially protective against bladder cancer because it can fight nitrites and nitrates. These chemicals, used in fertilizers and in food additives, combine with natural body chemicals to form powerful cancer-causing agents, nitrosamines. Several investigators have demonstrated that vitamin C (ascorbic acid) inhibits nitrosation in humans and animals. In the laboratory it has been definitely shown to inhibit carcinogen-induced bladder tumors in animals. Following up on this lead, other researchers examined 123 male and 41 female patients with bladder cancer and population control subjects in Hawaii.[43] Vitamin C intake from supplements was lower in bladder-cancer patients than in control subjects.

Vitamins Against Lung Cancer

By now, it is well-accepted that tobacco is the major cause of lung cancer, but why do some heavy smokers not develop lung cancer? Is it because of some inherited defense or some behavior pattern not linked to smoking that protects smokers against the development of the disease?

Could it be high levels of vitamin A or its relatives, the retinoids, in the diet?

Researchers at Roswell Park Memorial Institute in Buffalo had a theory. Vitamin A is essential for controlling the normal changes in cells lining organs (epithelial tissues). Therefore, ingestion of vitamin A would be higher in heavy smokers without lung cancer than in those who had the disease.[44] Indeed, in their study of 292 lung cancer patients and 801 controls, they found smokers who had higher levels of vitamin A had a lower risk of lung cancer than smokers who did not.

The vitamin A lung-cancer risk finding was a side benefit of the Multiple Risk Factor Intervention Trial (MRFIT), originally aimed at studying risks for heart disease.[45] The MRFIT project included a study of 12,866 men at high risk of coronary heart disease who were between thirty-five and fifty-seven years at baseline. The participants were selected on the basis of a risk score derived from a combination of their cigarette smoking, high blood pressure, and high levels of blood cholesterol at an initial screening examination. Men were excluded if they had a history of or evidence of any life-shortening cancer, clinical coronary artery disease, or any other chronic disease likely to result in substantial life-shortening or to make it difficult for them to participate in the intervention trial. Approximately 63 percent of them were cigarette smokers.

John E. Connett, M.D., Ph.D., and his colleagues at the University of Minnesota evaluated the average blood levels of beta-carotene, total carotenoids, and vitamins A and E among 156 initially healthy men who participated in MRFIT and who subsequently died of cancer, and 311 controls individually matched for age and smoking status. Both total carotenoids and beta-carotene levels were lower in the 66 lung cancer cases than in their matched controls. The relationship between lower blood-serum carotenoid level and lung cancer persisted after adjusting for the number of cigarettes and alcohol intake. The results of this study provide further evidence for a possible protective effect of beta-carotene against lung cancer among cigarette smokers.

The authors conducted a case control study among the multiethnic population of Hawaii to test the theory that lung cancer risk is inversely associated with dietary intake of total vitamin A, carotene, and vitamin C. Detailed dietary interviews were done for 364 primary lung cancer patients and 627 similar persons without lung cancer. After adjusting for the number of confounding variables, including ethnicity, smoking history, and occupation, evidence was found that total vitamin A intake (food sources plus supplements), vitamin A intake from food sources alone, and carotene intake were each linked to a decrease in lung cancer risks in males. Men who reported no regular use of vitamin A preparations were at approximately 1.8 times the overall cancer risk of regular users. Compared with the controls, those who developed cancer had lower levels of vitamin A in their blood at least twelve months before cancer diagnosis.[46]

This MRFIT ancillary study was the first to include measurements of blood levels of both beta-carotene and total carotenoids (*see* both in glossary).

Dr. Connett concludes it is possible that beta-carotene dietary supplements are effective only in individuals at high risk of lung cancer who have low blood levels or low intake of carotenoids. He says it also is possible that the lung cancer–protective effects of beta-carotene are due to other micronutrients in green or yellow vegetables that are highly correlated with beta-carotene. From the current study and similar recent studies, he notes the possible link between lung cancer and beta-carotene, other carotenoids, and other nutrients in green or yellow vegetables certainly deserves further evaluation and research.

Most of the thirty epidemiologic studies that have examined the relationship between dietary factors and lung cancer have focused on vitamin A or carotenoids. Four studies, however, have found stronger protective effects for vitamin C than for carotenoids. In fact, one researcher maintains that *a 55-year-old, male, one-pack-a-day smoker with low dietary and supplemental vitamin C had a 25 percent chance of dying from lung cancer within 25 years, while a fifty-five-year-old, male smoker with high dietary and supplemental vitamin C had only a 7 percent chance of dying from lung cancer.* Fruit intake was also significantly and inversely related to subsequent lung cancer mortality.[47]

Women and Lung Cancer

What about lung cancer and women? Until recently, studies have concerned men and the malignancy, but women are catching up to men in becoming victims of the disease. In 1986, Iowa researchers began assessing the diets of 41,837 Iowa women, ages fifty-five to sixty-nine. After four years of follow-up, 179 cases of lung cancer were identified. Intakes of eleven vegetable and fruit groups as well as the nutrients beta-carotene and vitamin C were evaluated in 138 of the lung cancer victims and more than two thousand women who did not have the disease. High intakes of all vegetables and fruit were linked to cutting the risk in about half. A lower lung cancer risk was also seen for high vitamin C intake and beta-carotene intake.[48]

Vitamins Against Mouth and Throat Cancers

New evidence suggests people who regularly consume vitamin E supplements have half the risk of oral and throat (pharyngeal) cancer after adjusting for the effects of tobacco, alcohol, and other risk factors for these cancers. The conclusions are drawn from the largest population-based investigation of oral cancer to date, and the first study to show an association between vitamin E intake and reduction of oral cancer in humans.[49]

Statistician Gloria Gridley and colleagues from the National Cancer Institute gathered data from interviews with more than 1,100 people with oral cancer and 1,300 healthy controls from four regions of the country. They compared use of vitamins—including A, C, E, minerals, and multivitamins—with incidence of cancer.

When the analysis was complete, they found that those who took vitamin E had a 50 percent lower risk of oral cancer compared with non–vitamin users.[50]

Most of the study population (95 percent) who took vitamin E took other vitamin supplements as well, Gridley notes. "Thus, we cannot rule out that it is a combination of the vitamins that is producing the protective effect, particularly since vitamins A, C, and E are all antioxidants [which are known to help neutralize carcinogenic effects]. However, we must also consider that the reduced risk could be attributable to some hidden factor common to users of vitamins, and not to the vitamins per se," she adds.

The researchers also found that multivitamins containing vitamins A, B, C, and E had no visible effect on lowering cancer risk. "We speculate that the vitamin E dosage in multivitamins [usually 30 IU] was not sufficient for a protective effect," Gridley says.

Tablets sold over-the-counter contain at least 100 IU, which is ten times the recommended daily allowance.

In an earlier analysis, the researchers reported that they did not find an effect of vitamin E from dietary sources alone. Vitamin E is found primarily in vegetable oils, nuts, seeds, whole grains, and wheat germ, but in low concentrations.

Vitamin C and Cancers of the Oral Cavity, Larynx, or Esophagus

Intake of Vitamin C seems to protect against cancer of the oral cavity, larynx, or esophagus. Of eight studies that have reported on vitamin C and these cancers, every one found a statistically significant elevation in risk associated with low intake. A study in Iran discovered oranges were the most protective of the fruits. In an investigation of esophageal and oral cancer in regions of India, where incidence of these diseases is among the highest in the world, vegetable consumption was found to significantly lower risk.[51]

Vitamin C Against Pancreatic Cancer

Pancreatic cancer is the fifth most common cause of cancer mortality in the United States and is a disease with extremely poor prognosis. Therefore, prevention is of prime importance. All five pancreatic cancer studies have found statistically significant protective effects for fruit, and in some instances for vegetables as well. The one study that calculated a vitamin C index found a significant twofold reduction in risk associated with high intake. Frequent consumption of dried fruit was significantly protective: use of tomatoes, fresh citrus fruit, and fresh winter fruit showed a "suggestive," though not very significant, protective relationship.[52]

Antioxidant Vitamins and Fiber Against Stomach Cancer

The stomach is the first organ that comes in prolonged contact with food. Since the human diet contains a variety of both carcinogens and anticarcinogens, it seems reasonable that diet affects risk of gastric cancer, and that a suitable modification of diet can reduce such risk.

There are studies correlating food-item consumption rates with stomach-cancer incidence in countries and in various ethnic groups.[53]

Perhaps most well known is the hypothesis that dietary nitrate and nitrite are converted in the stomach to nitrosamines, powerful cancer-causing agents, as pointed out earlier. In addition, vitamins C and E have been shown to inhibit nitrosamine formation. Nitrate is also ingested from water supplies, especially in rural areas, and is converted by bacteria to nitrite in foods stored without refrigeration. Some nitrosamines may be directly ingested from foods as well. However, the extent of conversion of nitrate to nitrite in the stomach is dependent upon stomach acid and other factors, which may also be related to risk.[54]

A second theory about the cause of stomach cancer concerns tissue stress or damage resulting from intake of polyunsaturated fats. Unsaturated fatty acids appear to participate in free-radicals (*see* glossary) production and may affect the risk of stomach cancer. Antioxidants such as vitamin E are thought to inhibit this process, probably by scavenging the oxygen-tainted fat deposits in cell membranes.[55]

Fiber and Stomach Cancer

A three-year case control study of diet and stomach cancer was conducted in Toronto, Winnipeg, and St. John's, Canada.[56] Two hundred forty-six verified cancer cases were individually matched by age, sex, and area of residence to 246 randomly selected population controls.

The Canadians said their data strongly suggest, in consonance with several previous studies, that nitrite intake is associated with risk of stomach cancer occurrence. They concluded that some protection appears to be afforded by consumption of citrus fruit.

Vitamin C and Stomach Cancer

Citrus fruits contain both fiber and high levels of vitamin C. In seven investigations of vitamin C dietary intake and stomach cancer risk, all found statistically significant protective effects approximately twofold. One prospective study found lower blood vitamin C levels in those who subsequently developed stomach cancer.[57]

Vitamin C has been found to be three times as high in the gastric juice of persons with normal stomach cells than in those with chronic stomach irritation (gastritis). Moreover, in normal persons it is predominantly in the form of vitamin C, which is required for the combat of those cancer-linked nitrosamines. In gastritis patients, by contrast, it is predominantly in the oxidized form of dehydroascorbic acid, which is not as effective against nitrosamines. Most studies have not differentiated between the forms of vitamin C—ascorbic or dehydroascorbic acid—nor considered the conversion of the first to the latter during cooking.[58]

The big question now is, how much cooking destroys the anti-cancer properties of vitamin C?

As for the protection against stomach cancer offered by fruit, in Poland researchers found a statistically significant relative risk of 3.2 for those who ate fruit less often than twice a week compared with those who ate it daily. In Greece, scientists observed a statistically significant protective effect of frequent consumption of citrus fruits and of raw salad-type vegetables. In England, investigators determined a statistically significant reduction in risk, twofold or greater, for fruit and for salad vegetables. For fruit intake, the high-consumption category consisted of those consuming it six or more times per week. In studies of Japanese Americans, both native born and immigrant, only tomatoes, a source of vitamin C, showed protective effects.

The Chinese Studies

Because studies such as the ones described above and many others throughout the world have shown that people who eat more fresh fruits and vegetables have a lower risk of cancer, the National Cancer Institute decided to determine how vitamins work to prevent cancer.[59] The site chosen was Linxian, a rural county in north-central China with one of the highest rates of cancer of the esophagus and stomach in the world. Death rates from these cancers are ten times higher than elsewhere in China, and one hundred times higher than in the United States. The possible factors in the area include nitrosamines (cancer-causing agents found in some preserved foods), mycotoxins (substances produced by fungi in stored foods), silica (microscopic bits of hard minerals) in grain, and a tendency to gulp down scalding hot tea—but no clear culprit emerged.

The Linxian diet, however, is low in fruits, meats, and other animal products, and blood levels of micronutrients such as vitamins A, B, C, and E are low by Western standards.

"If vitamins work to help prevent cancer, then they were going to work in this population where the people have had a consistently poor intake of several vitamins and minerals, and the cancers we're trying to prevent are known to be diet-related," said William J. Blot, Ph.D., of the National Cancer Institute's (NCI) biostatistics branch, and one of the principal investigators for the study.

Working with Chinese health officials, the researchers combined compounds for the greater effect at levels one to two times the U.S. recommended daily allowances.

The compounds, called factors, were

- **Factor A.** Retinol, a form of vitamin A (5,000 IU) plus zinc (as 22.5 mg of zinc oxide), which enhances delivery of retinol to tissues.
- **Factor B.** Riboflavin (3.2 mg) and niacin (40 mg), two B vitamins that are lacking in the diet in the county.
- **Factor C.** Vitamin C (as 120 mg of ascorbic acid) and molybdenum (as 30 mcg of molybdenum, yeast complex), which may inhibit the formation and activity of nitrosamines.

- **Factor D.** The antioxidants beta-carotene (15 mg) and vitamin E (as 30 mg of alpha tocopherol) with selenium (as 50 mcg of selenium yeast). Antioxidants are compounds that pair with carcinogens to prevent them from damaging DNA.

Beginning in March 1986, the participants in the trial were randomly assigned to take one or more factors or a placebo, so that about half of the people would be taking each factor. This design permitted analysis of the benefits of each group of nutrients. The participants took the supplements for five and a quarter years.

After five years of supplementation, the group receiving beta-carotene, vitamin E, and selenium showed significant benefits, with the effects beginning to appear less than two years into the trial. The biggest benefit was the reduction in the cancer death rate, the principal cause of death in Linxian.

For the participants taking the antioxidants (factor D) the number of deaths from esophageal cancer was reduced about 4 percent while the number of deaths from stomach cancer was reduced 21 percent. The overall risk of dying from cancer was reduced by 13 percent.

The number of cases of cancer diagnosed during the time also decreased due to factor D. Overall, 7 percent fewer cancers were diagnosed, 6 percent fewer esophageal and gastric cancers, and 12 percent fewer other cancers.

The National Cancer Institute has a number of dietary intervention or chemoprevention studies under way. Several large trials include the agents found to reduce cancer deaths in the Linxian trial. Among them are

- **The Physicians' Health Trial:** Twenty-two thousand men have been taking beta-carotene or placebo since 1980 and were also taking aspirin or placebo until 1987, when this study showed that aspirin can reduce the risk of heart attack by half in healthy men. The researchers showed in the 1990s that beta-carotene reduces the risk of a fatal heart attack in men with preexisting heart disease. The group is being monitored to see if a reduction in overall cancers and/or specific cancers comes from the beta-carotene. The trial is scheduled for completion next year (1996).

- **The Women's Health Study:** Forty thousand healthy women age fifty and older are being recruited to take combinations of beta-carotene, vitamin E, and low-dose aspirin in this study. The women will be monitored for cancer and heart-disease benefits, similar to the Physicians' Health Trial. The trial began in 1992.

- **The Alpha Tocopherol, Beta-Carotene Cancer Prevention Study:** Twenty-nine thousand male smokers and former smokers aged fifty to sixty-nine are taking beta-carotene, vitamin E, or both, in Finland. Stomach cancers—which were reduced by a mix of the same nutrients in the Linxian trial—are also prevalent in this population. The study began in 1985, and the results are now being evaluated.

- **CARET—The Carotene and Retinoid Efficacy Trial:** Eighteen thousand men and women who are either smokers or have been exposed to asbestos are taking beta-carotene plus retinyl palmitate (a chemical cousin of vitamin A) as part of this study. Researchers in Seattle, Washington; Portland, Oregon; San Francisco, California; Baltimore, Maryland; Irvine, California; and the state of Connecticut will assess whether taking the supplements results in a reduction in lung cancer incidence. Accrual of 3,881 males exposed to asbestos and 13,600 male and female smokers and former smokers was completed in the 1990s, and the studies are now in progress.

While the above research is exciting, as you will read in the next chapter, a number of naturally occurring dietary constituents besides vitamins also appear to act as inhibitors of cancer development.

Chapter 3

NUTRACEUTICALS THAT FIGHT CANCER

What substances in foods fight cancer? Once identified, can they be added to a product just as vitamin D fortifies milk or iodine improves salt?

The National Cancer Institute's Designer Food Program is testing the most promising of the chemicals isolated from plants. For people at high risk of developing certain cancers—those who have premalignancies, a risky family history, or a previous cancer, for example—the NCI researchers hope to formulate the purified substances into nutraceuticals to be taken as medicine or to be added to foods.

Taking anticancer supplements from foods seems like a great idea. The problem is that, as with most medication that works, there are side effects. Some substances identified as anticarcinogens in animals such as protease inhibitors, for example, are natural pesticides made by plants to ward off predators. Under some circumstances protease inhibitors may have beneficial effects, including the inhibition of cancer. But under other conditions, they may be toxic or even cause cancer.

An important challenge is how to use anticancer nutraceuticals in a rational way to greatly reduce the incidence of human cancer without inadvertently exposing us to increased health risks.

Phytochemicals—Natural Cancer Fighters

Phyto is from the Greek meaning "to bring forth," and it is used as a prefix to designate "from a plant." Hence *phytochemical* means a chemical from a plant. Epidemiological studies, as you have read in the previous chapter, have shown that diets containing large quantities of vegetables and, to a lesser extent fruits, are associated with lowering risks of certain cancers. There is a growing scientific acknowledgment that phytochemicals as well as vitamins and minerals may possess cancer-fighting properties. The following describe some of the phytochemicals and other food substances being studied for their anticancer potential.[1, 2, 3]

The Antioxidants

We oxygen-breathing humans face a curious paradox: we cannot live without oxygen, yet our cells are constantly traumatized by its toxic side effects. The culprits are *free radicals*, highly reactive molecules generated when a cell "burns" its foods with oxygen to fuel life processes. Free radicals act like "loose cannons" rolling around and damaging cells. This damage is thought to be a first step in cancer development. Antioxidants such as vitamin C, vitamin E, and a number of phytochemicals found in food can suppress free-radical cell damage.

Among the most interesting antioxidant anticancer phytochemicals are the *protease inhibitors*.

The Seeds of Protection—Protease Inhibitors

Found in plants' reproductive parts including soybeans and other beans, rice, and potatoes, protease inhibitors are believed to provide these edibles with natural protection against insect predation. In order to assure the survival of the species, plants use protease inhibitors to prevent seed digestion by insects.

Protease inhibitors, because they block the activity of an enzyme that aids the digestion of proteins, were thought to be antinutritious. Walter Troll, M.D., of New York University Medical Center, who is conducting protease-inhibitor cancer studies, notes that the U.S. Department of Agriculture spent a lot of time removing them from soybeans because it was believed the removal would make young children grow better.[4] Now, however, protease inhibitors have been shown to have great potential as anticancer nutraceuticals.

Ann Kennedy, Ph.D., of the Harvard School of Public Health's department of cancer biology in Boston, and her colleagues have found that protease inhibitors may be capable of neutralizing the effect of a wide range of cancer-causing agents, from radiation and steroid hormones to potent components of diesel exhaust.

Remember in the previous chapter it was noted cancer is believed to be a two stage process with *initiation*, exposure to a cancer-causing substance, and *promotion*, stimulation by another substance that makes the first become active and causes cancer to develop. It had been assumed once cells have been both *initiated* and *promoted* they may go haywire and become cancerous. What Dr. Kennedy and her coworkers have found is that even brief exposure of initiated and/or promoted cells to minute quantities of certain protease inhibitors—such as the Bowman-Birk inhibitor derived from soybeans—not only prevents the transformation of those cells into cancers, but also "reprograms" their precancerous changes back to the pre-initiation, normal state.[5] Dr. Kennedy and her group reported treatment with the protease inhibitor from soybeans could start 45–135 days after the beginning of exposure to a cancer-causing agent and still suppress the malignant process. The only real limit to the achievement seems to be the dose of the cancer-causing initiator. If the amount of cancer-causing agent is too high, the protease inhibitor may reduce but not stop tumor development.

Dr. Kennedy says some cancer researchers have labeled her findings "heresy," on the assumption that changes during cancer initiation were irreversible. Her research now suggests that both initiating and promoting changes are indeed reversible with protease inhibitors.

To understand how these compounds work, both Drs. Kennedy and Troll are focusing on protease inhibitors' recently identified ability to restrain the action of cancer-causing genes (oncogenes) carried by retroviruses. It is generally assumed that specific cancer-causing genes must be "turned on" for cancer to develop, and the hope is that protease inhibitors will keep those bad genes from becoming active.

CLA—Heads or Tails

As mentioned above, some potential anticancer nutraceuticals are like two sides of a coin. On one side, they cause cancer, and on the other they suppress it. A substance in vegetable oil and in fat manufactured by the body—linoleic acid—is apparently just such a compound.

The weight of evidence in epidemiological studies in humans links high-fat diets involving both saturated (solid at room temperature) and unsaturated (liquid at room temperature) fats to the development of certain cancers, particularly those of the colon and prostate.[6] The AMA's Council on Scientific Affairs (CSA) report states: "It is now clear from numerous animal experiments that the cancer-enhancing property of dietary fat is the result of two effects:

- A general effect due to excessive calories.
- A specific effect due to the essential fatty acid linoleic acid.[7]

Linoleic acid, an essential (for nutrition) unsaturated fatty acid found in vegetable oils and produced in the human body, is required for growth. It has been shown in animal studies to induce breast, pancreatic, and probably colon cancer. Enhancement of cancer was observed when linoleic acid was about 5 percent of the diet. Linoleic acid makes up 40 percent of the fatty acids in corn oil. Corn oil enhanced rat breast cancer more than beef tallow. So far, linoleic acid seems to be the only fatty acid to exhibit such an unequivocal cancer-enhancing effect.

Linoleic acid may explain why those who eat fish oil may have lower cancer rates. Researchers from Cornell University in Ithaca, New York, and Dartmouth Medical School in Hanover, New Hampshire, induced the development of precancerous tumor nodules by injecting two-week-old rats with azaserine—a potent pancreatic-cancer-causing agent. After four months on diets containing 20 percent corn oil, the rats showed a proliferation of growing precancerous lesions. Other rats on diets containing 20 percent menhaden (fish) oil developed only about one-third as many lesions.[8] Though the fat level in the two diets of the rats was high—about 45 percent of the calories—it was only 18 percent higher than the level consumed by the average American adult. By lowering the fat in the rats' diets after tumors had begun to develop, the researchers slowed the growth of tumors. Rats started on corn oil but switched to fish oil two months later received virtually the same benefits in reduced precancer development as those dining on fish oil only.

To demonstrate what a tough task researchers have in identifying anticancer nutraceuticals, it has been discovered a derivative of culprit linoleic acid—CLA (conjugated dienoic derivatives of linoleic acid)—seems to be a powerful anticancer agent. As little as 0.5 percent CLA in the diet significantly reduced carcinogen-induced breast cancer in rats. The discovery of CLA is confounding because:

- It represents the first clear example of a fatty acid that inhibits cancer in animals.
- CLA, which inhibits cancer, is derived from cancer-enhancing linoleic acid.
- The principal dietary sources of CLA appear to be animal products, specifically dairy products, meat from cud-chewing animals, and turkey.

Several laboratories are conducting research into the potential of CLA as a nutraceutical to reduce cancer risk at the promotion stage in humans, particularly those at high risk of developing malignancies.

Flavonoids—The Color of Anticancer Agents

There is a lot of scientific interest in flavonoids, the pigments that constitute most of the yellow, red, and blue colors in flowers and fruits. Since the mid-1900s when Nobel Prize winner Albert Szent-Györgyi indicated that citrus bioflavonoids had vitaminlike activity, there have been literally hundreds of individual plant flavonoids isolated, characterized, and subdivided into some fifteen classes. The flavonoids include *catechins*, *leucoanthocyanidines*, *flavins*, *flavones*, *anthocyanins*, and *flavonols*. Bioflavonoids, which have vitaminlike activity, are in citrus fruits. Other flavonoids that are potential nutraceuticals are in green tea, soybeans, cereal grains, cruciferous vegetables such as broccoli (*see* page 57), umbelliferous vegetables such as celery (*see* page 59), solanaceous vegetables such as eggplant (*see* page 59), curcuma herbs such as turmeric, licorice root, and flaxseed—all of which are being studied for their anticancer properties. It is believed the flavonoids act to inhibit enzymes that may activate cancerous cells at the initiation stage.[9]

Polyphenols—The Smell of Anticancer Agents

Polyphenols are compounds found in many plants including garlic, green tea, soybeans, cereal grains, cruciferous vegetables such as broccoli, umbelliferous vegetables such as celery, citrus, solanaceous vegetables such as potatoes, curcuma such as ginger, licorice root, and flaxseed. Polyphenols are believed to act at both the initiation and the promotion stages of cancer development. They have been reported to interfere with tumor promotion by dampening steroid hormones. Polyphenols are also antioxidants and act as "garbage collectors," disposing of mutagens and cancer-causing agents.[10] One plant phenol, *ellagic acid* (EA), is of great scientific interest today as a potential anticancer nutraceutical. It is in various plants, fruits, and nuts and has been found to inhibit the induction of tumors of the esophagus in rats caused by a powerful cancer-causing agent, NBMA (N-nitrosobenzylmethylamine). Ellagic Acid inhibited the tumors at both the initiation and promotion stage of cancer development.[11] Ellagic acid also acts against cancers caused by the mold aflatoxin, hydrocarbons such as cigarette smoke, and aromatic amines such as benzene.[12]

Another plant polyphenol, *anethole trithione*, which occurs in cruciferous vegetables such as broccoli, has been found by researchers to reduce colon cancer in laboratory animals exposed to a powerful colon-cancer-inducing agent.[13]

Terpenes—Antioxidants

Terpenes are in a class of unsaturated, liquid hydrocarbons occurring in most essential oils and plant resins. They are found in garlic, soybeans, cereal grains, cruciferous vegetables, umbelliferous vegetables, citrus fruits, solanaceous vegetables, cucurbitaceous vegetables, licorice root. Among terpene derivatives are camphor and menthol. Terpenes act as antioxidants and are believed to interrupt both initiation by cancer-causing agents and promotion by steroid hormones.

Sulfides—Repair Mechanics

Compounds containing sulfur are in garlic and cruciferous vegetables. They are believed to stop initiation of a cell by cancer-causing agents from becoming malignant and to prevent steroid hormones from promoting tumors. They also are believed to stimulate DNA repair (DNA is the genetic programming of the cell that breaks down during cancer development).[14] Investigators at the American Health Foundation, Division of Nutritional Carcinogenesis in New York City, investigated dietary *diallyl disulfide* (occurs in garlic) and found it significantly inhibited cancer of the colon in laboratory animals exposed to cancer-causing agents.[15]

Plant Sugars—Sweet Protection

Plant sugars (glucosinolates) have breakdown products that include *isothiocyanates*, *indoles*, and *dithiothiols* found in plants. Plant sugars are high in Chinese cabbage, followed in descending order by American cabbage, radish, kale, and mustard. The highest levels are in fresh vegetables followed by sun-dried, oven-dried, and cooked.[16] The plant-sugar breakdown products stimulate the production of protective enzymes to fight cancer initiation.[17] Rats fed diets containing isothiocyanate, for example, a naturally occurring constituent of cruciferous vegetables, before and during treatment with the powerful cancer-causing agent N-nitrosobenzylmethylamine (NBMA), developed 99–100 percent fewer esophageal (gullet) tumors than NBMA-treated control rats.[18]

Isothiocyanate in the diet inhibited the development of cancer caused by tobacco extracts in the lung tissue of animals.[19]

Some sugars that occur naturally in certain food plants such as tomatoes, onions, and bananas have the tongue-challenging name, *fructooligosaccharides* (FOS).

These sugars are unusual because:

- They are not digestible in the stomach and travel intact to the intestine.
- They promote the growth of friendly bacteria, *Bifidobacteria* and *Lactobacilli* (both are used to culture yogurt), as well as other beneficial microorganisms in the intestines.

A number of scientific investigations conclude that these bacteria may play a role in increasing resistance to intestinal infection by pathogens such as salmonella.[20] The friendly bacteria may reduce the production of known cancer-causing chemicals in the intestine and in addition, may reduce the levels of serum triglycerides and cholesterol in the blood. FOS, while not yet fully approved for human consumption, are being added to poultry feed to enhance growth properties and to reduce pathogens.

Phytoestrogens—The Female Hormone in Plants

Dr. Leon Bradlow of the Strang-Cornell Cancer Research Lab, New York, has explored how plant chemicals influence estrogen metabolism and thus how a diet high in fruits and vegetables might inhibit breast cancer. Scientists know that estradiol, the precursor to estrogen, can take one of two metabolic pathways in the body, turning into either a 16-hydroxylated form or a 2-hydroxylated form of estrogen. The 16-form is stimulatory and more dangerously reactive. Women with a high risk of breast cancer have elevated levels of the 16-form in their blood. Tissue from breast tumors contain more of the 16-form of estrogen than does surrounding noncancerous breast tissue. The 2-form of estrogen is relatively inert and has been found to be elevated in women who are vigorous athletes and in those who eat many cruciferous vegetables (*see* glossary). Phytoestrogens—isoflavones, genistein, and diadzeins—are contained in soy products and may be one reason Orientals, who eat a lot of soy sauce, have a much lower rate of breast and prostate cancer.[21]

Some Other Potential Anticancer Nutraceuticals

Among other potential anticancer nutraceuticals now being studied by researchers are the amino acids *acetylcysteine* (occurs in salmon and oatmeal) and *taurine* (occurs in oysters and milk). They significantly inhibited colon tumors in laboratory animals exposed to a colon-cancer-inducing chemical.[22]

What Should You Eat?

A diet that will prevent cancer is not yet defined. In this chapter and the previous one you have learned about research with nutraceuticals that seem to offer protection against specific cancers. Certainly, if you know you are susceptible to a type of cancer either because of family history or environmental exposure, it would be wise to talk things over with your physician and a nutritionist to make sure that you have in your diet an ample supply of the substance particularly effective against the cancer to which you may be vulnerable. You may wish to take supplements. Until more research is done to develop powerful cancer-fighting nutraceuticals derived from food, moderation in the diet and the taking of supplements is sensible. No one will guarantee that any diet or nutraceutical will prevent any specific human cancer. Scientists now believe there is sufficient inferential information to make a series of interim recommendations about nutrition that, in the judgment of experts, are likely to provide some measure of reduced cancer risk.[23] The following is based on a consensus of experts from the National Cancer Institute, the American Cancer Society, the National Research Council of the National Academy of Sciences, and researchers interviewed for this book.

Facts About Fiber

Dietary fiber is not a single substance. It is a complex mixture of materials. Some dietary fiber is crunchy like shredded wheat or carrots and others are gummy or sticky like oatmeal.

Fiber is contained in plants, but unlike foods that are broken down and absorbed during the normal digestive process, the fiber content of plant foods is not affected by our digestive enzymes. It passes virtually unchanged through the stomach and small intestine into the colon.

In the colon, some forms of dietary fiber are fermented by bacteria. Other forms resist this fermentation and pass unchanged from the body in the stool.

Just as fiber differs in form, it differs in biologic effect. Fiber might help clear the colon of substances that are perhaps changed by bacteria into cancer-promoting chemicals.[24] Fiber absorbs water and thus increases the water content and size of the stool. Perhaps this reduces the concentration of chemicals that might cause cancer. Fiber also speeds elimination of these chemicals in the stool. Still, some cancer specialists are skeptical that fiber itself protects against colon cancer. They note diets rich in animal fat may promote colon cancer and high-fiber diets may discourage colon cancer not because of the fiber but because such diets generally are low-fat.

A combined analysis of thirteen international studies by

Canadian researchers provided strong evidence that high intakes of fiber-rich foods decrease cancer risk for both the colon and the rectum.[25]

Fiber, however, can remove from your body essential minerals, such as calcium, iron, and zinc. Wheat fiber, for example, can have this effect, and as you will read in this chapter, calcium and other minerals may protect against cancer, so eat fiber in moderation and make sure you obtain sufficient minerals in other foods and supplements.

The National Cancer Institute does not currently promote the use of fiber supplements or fiber-fortified foods for the general public because the specific food components in fiber-rich foods that may protect against cancer have not yet been identified, and although dietary fiber supplements are not harmful when properly used, too often they are misunderstood or misused, according to NCI experts. They say the mistaken impression persists that a supplement such as wheat bran will suffice; although wheat bran (the most widely available supplement) may improve bowel function, it may not offer the possible health benefits available in other forms of fiber.

Keep processed foods to a minimum. Refining, for example, removes the outer coat (bran) from grain; thus, this highly desirable form of fiber is lost. This is why whole-grain products are higher in fiber content than those made with refined flour. Similarly paring fruits and vegetables reduces their fiber content. And an orange contains considerably more fiber than the juice squeezed from it.

Although fiber can help you feel comfortably full after a low-calorie meal, too much fiber can lead to bloating, intestinal gas, and diarrhea. Therefore, although most of us need to increase the amount of fiber we consume, don't overdo it. Instead, increase the fiber content in your diet gradually. Your body may need several weeks to adjust.

Based on current scientific evidence, the NCI is encouraging Americans to eat at least five servings of fiber-rich foods each day to help reduce the risk of cancer and other diseases. Eating more high-fiber foods may not only reduce your risk of colon cancer, but they are good, low-calorie substitutes for fatty or high-carbohydrate foods. Dietary fiber (sometimes referred to as bulk or roughage) comes in many forms, and natural sources such as whole-grain products, fruits, vegetables, and legumes are good and widely available.[26]

Pick These Foods to Increase Fiber Content of Your Diet

- Grain products—look for whole-grain cereal, bran cereals, whole-wheat flakes, shredded wheat, whole- and cracked-wheat bread, pumpernickel, and bran muffins. Also look for brown or wild rice, barley, whole-wheat pasta, and bulgur (cracked wheat).
- Fruits—good fruit choices include apples, pears, berries, and all kinds of dried fruits.
- Vegetables, especially broccoli, brussels sprouts, carrots, corn, parsnips, peas, potatoes, squash, and yams.
- Legumes such as lentils, dried peas, and dried beans such as navy, kidney, pinto, and lima beans.
- Snack foods—select nuts, seeds, popcorn, fresh and dried fruit, raw vegetables, whole-grain crackers, and bran muffins.

Soybeans Believed to Be a Super Anticancer Food

Japanese-style soy sauce (shoyu) is produced through a complex microbial fermentation of soybeans and wheat. During its manufacture characteristic flavors and aromas develop due to the action of microbes and reactions between various chemical substances. Shoyu has been reported to promote anticancer activity and significantly reduced stomach cancer in mice exposed to a powerful cancer-causing agent, benzopyrene.[27]

Epidemiological studies provide further evidence that soybeans are beneficial because of the low rates of certain cancers in the Orient where soy foods are consumed in large quantities—twenty to fifty times more than in the United States. In the United States, women consuming soy foods had 50 percent less incidence of cancer than those who did not eat soy-based products. Soy foods appear to reduce the risk of breast, colon, lung, and stomach cancers.[28]

What potential anticancer nutraceuticals are in soy products besides the protease inhibitors described earlier in this chapter? Soybeans contain *plant estrogens* (phytoestrogens, *see* page 48), *HEMF, genistein, isoflavonoids,* and perhaps a number of other as yet unidentified anticancer agents.

Michael W. Pariza, Ph.D., and his associates at the University of Wisconsin's Department of Food Microbiology and Toxicology wanted to know why Japanese-style soy sauce inhibited cancer of the stomach in animals induced by the potent carcinogenic substance benzopyrene.[29]

The Wisconsin researchers extracted a major flavor/aroma compound from soy sauce, HEMF (4-hydroxy-2(or 5)-ethyl-5(or 2)-methyl-3(2H)furanone) and found it to be an antioxidant and a powerful anticancer agent.

The Wisconsin researchers discovered that in animals, HEMF inhibited tumor promotion.

Another recently identified potential anticancer agent in soybeans is genistein.[30] Scientists from several countries have found it in the urine of people who ate a traditional Japanese diet. Genistein, an isoflavonoid (*see* glossary), is found in high concentrations in soybeans and to a somewhat lesser degree in cruciferous vegetables.

In the laboratory, Dr. Lothar Schweigerer and his colleagues at Heidelberg University discovered that genistein blocks an event called angiogenesis, the growth of new blood vessels. That could have implications for the treatment of solid tumors, including malignancies of the breast, prostate, and brain. Once a tumor grows beyond a millimeter, it must foster the growth of new blood vessels around it. When it is fully vascularized, the malignancy then receives the oxygen and nourishment it needs to grow and eventually to send fatal metastatic colonies elsewhere. By inhibiting blood-vessel growth, genistein may keep new tumors from growing beyond harmless dimensions.[31]

In those on a Japanese diet, the scientists found the urine level of genistein is much higher than that of Westerners. This could be an explanation of why, when Japanese men leave their country for several years to work in the United States or Europe, their rate of invasive prostate cancer rises sharply. Dr. Schweigerer postulates that tiny prostate tumors that had been kept in check by the daily intake of, say, miso soup would finally be free to grow once the Japanese men ate a more Western diet.

And in other laboratory studies, researchers at the University of Alabama at Birmingham, found phytoestrogens in soybeans prevented breast cancer in rats. The researchers believe that the plant estrogens inhibit estrogens in the body of the animals, or that they have some beneficial effect on liver metabolism.[32]

Other researchers have reported genistein suppresses the growth of human leukemia cells, prostate cancer cells, and melanoma (potentially lethal skin cancer) cells.[33] Genistein in soybeans is now also being tested against Kaposi's sarcoma, a cancer frequently linked to AIDS.

Food researchers and producers, however, were alerted that not all soy products are created equal, as far as nutraceutical potential at the 208th American Chemical Society meeting in Washington, D.C., in 1994. Dr. Stephen Barnes, professor of Pharmacology at the University of Alabama in Birmingham, reported that recently it has been found that genistein takes on different chemical forms depending on its soy source, and it is not certain whether all these forms are absorbed equally well in the body.[34]

Tofu, an increasingly popular soybean-based food in the United States, contains high levels of the phytoestrogen, daidzein. Until recently, scientists did not believe that soybeans contained enough phytoestrogens to fight cancer. Johanna Dwyer, director of the nutrition center at the New England Medical Center in Boston, and her colleagues discovered that different brands of tofu contain anywhere from 73 to 97 mcg of daidzein in each gram. As tofu intake increases in the American diet, diadzein may help prevent breast cancer.[35]

Have a Cup of Tea

Again the Japanese diet, which includes not only soybeans but green tea, seems to diminish the risk of cancer. There is tremendous interest among researchers worldwide to identify those nutraceuticals in tea that may help prevent malignancies. Cultivated principally in China, Japan, Ceylon, and other Asian countries, tea leaves come from an evergreen of the camellia family, *Camellia sinensis*, and are processed in different ways to produce green, black, and oolong tea. Each emerges with different chemical properties. To produce black tea, which most Americans drink, leaves are subjected to warmth for a few hours and heated to 200° F to finish the drying process. Green tea is popular in Asia and is not heated but simply steamed, rolled, and crushed. Oolong tea is less heated than black, but just enough to give it a different character from green.

Green tea, which has been used in Japan for more than a thousand years, is now believed to have the most beneficial effects and may explain the low incidence of certain cancers in eastern Asia. A recent epidemiological study showed a lower risk of gastric cancer among those with a high consumption of green tea (ten or more cups per day).[36]

Black tea, on the other hand, may prevent skin cancer. A team headed by Zhi Y. Wang of the Department of Chemical Biology and Pharmacognosy of Rutgers University gave one group of mice water and another group black tea for thirty-three weeks while the animals were exposed to ultraviolet irradiation. The group that drank the tea had far fewer skin tumors and when the growths did appear, they were smaller than those just drinking water.[37]

Since ancient times tea has been known to help keep the body and soul in good condition. Until recently, most of the physiological functions of tea have been attributed to just one of its constituents—caffeine. Meanwhile tea tannin, that is, tea polyphenols, which constitute the major part of soluble solids in tea, have been rather overlooked. Green tea contains more polyphenols (*see* page 46) than the other teas. Scientists at the Cancer Prevention Division of the National Cancer Center

Research Institute in Japan are studying the main polyphenol of Japanese green tea—epigallocatechin gallate (EGCG)—on tumor development. They report that EGCG was effective in preventing development of tumors in the skin, duodenum, and liver in animals.[38]

Summing it up, tea reportedly has the following benefits:

- *Antioxidative action:* The polyphenols—catechins—found in tea are strong antioxidants, twenty times as potent as vitamin E. In addition, the antioxidant activity of vitamin E or vitamin A is enhanced when trace amounts of EGCG and other tea polyphenols are mixed with the vitamins.

- *Antiradiation action:* Radiation causes various damage in the animal and human body. A certain strain of rat is prone to developing lymphomas by irradiation. Three hundred female rats of this strain were fed a green-tea polyphenol, catechin, diet for two years following repeated radiation. As a result, the life span of the catechin-fed group was comparatively longer than the group that was not fed catechins. Accordingly, the incidence of malignant lymphomas in the thymus and spleen were lower in the catechin-fed group.

- *Anticancer action:* By feeding catechins to rats or mice, considerable suppression of tumor development was observed in cases such as the growth of implanted tumors, the development of tumors by the injection of a cancer-causing agent, or the spontaneous growth of breast cancers in mice. In Shizuoka prefecture in Japan, where green tea is a staple product, the mortality rate of stomach cancer for those who drink a great deal of tea is as low as 20 percent of the national average. It is widely accepted that changes in intestinal microflora may be related to colon cancer. Fecal profiles of intestinal bacteria in patients with colon cancer and patients with nonhereditary large-bowel polyps are different. Recent research has suggested tumor growth or malignant transformation of the polyps into cancer may be related to an increase of the intestinal bacteria *Clostridium.*[39]

Since green-tea polyphenols have selective inhibitory activity against the growth of intestinal *Clostridium*, scientists are theorizing that green tea may inhibit the development of colon cancer, at least partially, through its inhibitory effect on the intestinal bacteria.

Eat Lots of Anticancer Vegetables

The American Medical Association's Council on Scientific Affairs report on diet and cancer states: "In general the epidemiologic reports of the past decade reinforce the conclusion that vegetable and fruit consumption is linked to reduced cancer risk."[40]

There is strong epidemiological and laboratory evidence that green leafy vegetables, in particular, contain nutraceuticals that protect against cancer. The greatest research emphasis is on cruciferous vegetables belonging to the mustard family whose plants have flowers with four leaves in the pattern of a cross. They include cabbage, bok choy, collards, broccoli, brussels sprouts, kohlrabi, kale, mustard greens, turnip greens, and cauliflower.

Broccoli—Filled With Anticancer Agents

Broccoli, especially, has been the object of a great deal of scientific interest because it is apparently full of nutraceuticals against cancer. Like most other vegetables and fruits, broccoli contains antioxidants—vitamins C and E and beta-carotene. These nutrients mop up dangerous free radicals (*see* page 42 and 77), which can lead to cancer. In animal studies, vitamin E and beta-carotene slow tumor growth. Broccoli is rich in fiber (*see* page 50), which may protect against colon cancer.

As if that weren't enough, broccoli also contains *sulphoraphanes* and other *isocyothionates*, which seem to guard against cancer by stimulating the production of protective enzymes in the body. Such enzymes detoxify cancer-causing agents and swiftly flush them from the body.[41]

And there are still more potential nutraceuticals in broccoli and its relatives. They contain *indoles*, the products of fermentation that give cabbage and broccoli their characteristic odors and that may help prevent hormone-dependent cancers by inactivating estrogens.

Jon Michnovicz, Ph.D., and Leon Bradlow, Ph.D., tested different chemicals found in cabbage to see which caused female rats to break down most of their bodies' estrogen to an inactive form. Earlier studies had suggested that the breakdown of estrogen into an active form can promote tumors.[42]

Then Drs. Michnovicz and Bradlow fed 500 mg per day of indole-3-carbinol to seven healthy men. That's as much as in four to seven cups of raw cabbage-family vegetables.

After a week, the men produced 56 percent more inactive estrogen breakdown product. In later studies, women showed a similar response.

Since those first experiments, the two researchers found indole-3-carbinol effective against spontaneous tumors in female mice.[43]

The next step was to find out how much indole to use, how long the effect lasts, and whether there are any toxicities.

A study is now under way in which sixty women are taking daily capsules of 400 mg of indole carbinol, equivalent to the amount in half a head of cabbage. Within several weeks, their levels of the harmless estrogen breakdown product had already risen to concentrations seen in marathon runners, and the levels have stayed elevated throughout the months of the ongoing trial. Dr. Bradlow and his colleagues are now testing lower doses of the compound on larger groups of women.[44]

Indoles also may protect against cancers of the colon, stomach, lung, esophagus, and prostate as well as breast cancer.

In addition to the indoles, fiber, vitamins, and sulphoranes, broccoli and other cruciferous vegetables also contain *quercetin*, a bioflavonoid (*see* glossary) that has been found to inactivate aflatoxin, the cancer-causing mold that may contaminate, nuts, and to inhibit the development of aflatoxin-caused cancer in laboratory animals.[45]

A Salad of Anticancer Nutraceuticals

Another family of vegetables, the Umbelliferae, which includes carrots, celery, parsnips, winter squash, and parsley, also contains cancer-fighting ingredients, including beta-carotene and chlorophyll. Extensive epidemiological evidence suggests that these vegetables may be effective against some forms of cancer.

Carrots, which contain high levels of beta-carotene, are being tested by National Cancer Institute researchers against smoking-related cancers.

Still another family of vegetables, the Solanaceae, which includes tomato, eggplant, and peppers, may contain cancer-fighting chemicals. The Solanaceae contain bioflavonoids and perhaps many other ingredients that may be anticarcinogenic.

Eat Lots of Fruit

Citrus fruits have long been touted as "good for you," but the Florida Department of Citrus has been supporting research for years to determine just how good oranges, tangerines, lemons, limes, and grapefruit are for you.

Epidemiological evidence indicates these fruits help in the treatment of several forms of cancer, particularly pancreatic cancer. They contain particularly high concentrations of vitamin C, and preliminary evidence indicates vitamin C may help fight certain viruses and protect against some cancers.[46]

Three types of flavonoids (see page 46) also occur in citrus: flavanones such as *hesperidin* in orange juice and *naringin* in grapefruit juice; *anthocyanins*, important only in blood oranges; and *flavones*. The flavones, such as *nobiletin*, *tangeretin*, and *sinesetin*, are almost unique to citrus and they exhibit high levels of biological activity including anticancer capability.[47, 48, 49]

Current cancer treatments, such as chemotherapy and irradiation, attempt to slow its rate of growth and spread, but have serious side effects and limited anti-invasive activity.

Early research found that tangeretin—from tangerines—was

the most potent of all flavonoids tested for the ability to inhibit invasiveness of cancer in laboratory animals. Studies are now being conducted to determine whether oral administration of tangeretin can reduce liver metastasis of one or more types of human tumors.[50]

The effects of tangeretin and nobiletin on the growth of small, scalelike malignant tumors of the skin (squamous-cell carcinoma) have also been investigated in the laboratory. It was found that these citrus flavonoids markedly inhibited growth at all concentrations tested.

Research into how tangeretin may work against the spread of breast and other cancers was described at the 208th Annual Meeting of the American Chemical Society, in 1994, in Washington, D.C.[51] Normal breast epithelial cells, from which nearly all breast cancers originate, are held together by a coating on the cell surface called E-cadherin. In cancer, adhesion between the cells is lost because E-cadherin is no longer produced or has become inactive. Because of this, researchers believe that E-cadherin may be an "invasion suppressor." Tangeretin in laboratory dishes is able to restore the E-cadherin function and thus protects the breast cells against invasion by cancer cells. At this writing, researchers at University Hospital, Gent, Belgium, were testing tangeretin in mice with liver cancer.

Fruits Against Cancer-Causing Nitrites

Pineapple and strawberries (as well as green peppers, tomatoes, and carrot juice) can block the formation of nitrosamines, powerful cancer-causing agents formed when nitrites and nitrates are ingested and form the compound with amines in the body, according to a study by Michael A. Helser and Joe Hotchkiss, Ph.D., Cornell University.[52] Nor is it just because the vegetables contain vitamin C, a well-known nitrosamine inhibitor. There's something else in the vegetables, something that may explain why fruits and vegetables are linked to lower rates of cancer, especially stomach cancer.

Anticancer Boost in Berries

Berries, grapes, and nuts contain another potential nutraceutical, ellagic acid. Ellagic acid has been shown to scavenge cancer-causing agents and prevent cancer in laboratory animals. Gary D. Stoner, Ph.D., and his colleagues at the Medical College of Ohio, Toledo, found that in human and animal cell cultures exposed to cancer-causing agents such as auto exhaust and tobacco smoke, and afla-toxins (cancer-causing molds), ellagic acid in berries inhibited the development of cancer. Dr. Stoner emphasizes that ellagic acid can be used only as a preventive, because it must be added to the system just before or during exposure to a cancer-causing agent. Although the researchers have yet to define the exact mechanism of cancer inhibition, they suspect that the ellagic acid competes for DNA receptors that are also used by the cancer-causing agents. Because purified ellagic acid has difficulty crossing intestinal walls, the group is tinkering with its structure to improve its absorption into the body. The substance, which apparently is bound to sugar in nature, may be more easily absorbed in its natural state.[53]

Fighting Cancer With the Spices of Life

Herbs and spices that have reportedly been found to have potential anticancer activity include mints, oregano, rosemary, sage, thyme, ginger, chives, basil, tarragon, turmeric, peppers, and garlic.

Dr. Alan Conney, director of the Laboratory for Cancer Research at Rutgers University, has also found in animal experiments that many of the herbs and spices suppress cancer growth by acting as antioxidants, neutralizing free radicals.[54]

The following herbs and spices are being intensively studied for their cancer-fighting potential.

Garlic and Onions

Garlic is a member of the onion family and was cultivated in

Egypt from earliest times and known in China more than two thousand years ago. Garlic contains lots of potassium, fluorine, sulfur, phosphorous, and vitamins A and C as well as seventy-five different sulfur compounds. In addition it contains *quercetin* and *cyanidin* and *bioflavonoids* (*see* glossary). Garlic also contains *selenium*, which has been found to have anticancer potential. Garlic has been used since ancient times to treat all sorts of ailments including the Great Plague in Europe and dysentery during World War I. The herb has recently been found to contain antibiotic, antiviral, and antifungal ingredients. It has also been reported in the scientific literature that garlic may decrease nitrosamines, modulate cancer-cell multiplication, increase immunity, and protect the body against ionizing radiation. Three Rutgers University researchers in 1992 reported at the American Chemical Society meeting in Washington, D.C., that chemicals in garlic may protect the liver from damage caused by large doses of the popular nonaspirin painkiller acetaminophen (it's in Tylenol and dozens of other painkillers and cold medications) and may prevent growth of lung tumors associated with tobacco smoke. Garlic also reportedly inhibits the production of prostaglandins, which may explain why allium oils have antitumor activity.

A study by the National Cancer Institute showed that those with diets high in allium vegetables, such as onion (*Allium cepa*) and garlic (*Allium sativum*), suffer from fewer incidences of stomach cancer. Both contain sulfides, which probably explains their actions as strong disinfectants. Michael Wargovich, Ph.D., and his team at the University of Texas MD Anderson Cancer Center in Houston have shown that sulfides, the substances that give garlic and onions their strong odor, inhibit cancers of the colon and esophagus in animals. Other researchers have found that the substances also inhibit stomach cancer. Sulfides work in two ways: they block the action of cancer-causing substances, and they slow tumor development.

Dr. Sydney Belman of New York University has reported experiments in which onion and/or garlic oil was applied thirty minutes before or thirty minutes after mice were exposed to a cancer-causing agent. The results were that tumor development was significantly inhibited at both the initiation stage (the oil was applied before the cancer inducer) and the promotion stage (the oil was applied after the carcinogen) when compared to mice exposed to the cancer-causing agent without the application of the oils.[55]

Research reports about the effects of garlic and onions in human cancer, however, have been criticized by scientists, who say that it is difficult to do double-blind studies in which neither the subjects nor the scientists know which compound contains the placebo and which the garlic. The odors that emmanate from garlic and onions give their presence away.

Epidemiological studies, nevertheless, point to the cancer-fighting benefits of the onion family. In China, where the intake of garlic and related allium vegetables is high, stomach cancer is low. Those Chinese who ate less than 11.5 kilograms per year had more than twice the number of stomach cancers than those who ate more than 24 kilograms per year. And in Georgia where Vidalia onions are grown, the stomach-cancer mortality rate among whites is one-third the average in the United States and one-half of the average level of stomach cancer in Georgia as a whole.[56]

The National Cancer Institute plans to study garlic as a potential cancer-fighting substance. Excessive amounts of raw garlic can be toxic, but when dried, extracted, and aged to form a powder, its sulfur compounds can enter the body's cells and stimulate immune response, according to Dr. Herbert Pierson, formerly a toxicologist in the division of cancer prevention and control at the National Cancer Institute.[57]

Rosemary—For Remembrance

Rosemary *(Rosmarinus officinalis)* contains *rosmaricine*, the derivatives of which possess smooth-muscle stimulant activity and some analgesic properties. Rosemary is also high in minerals such as calcium, magnesium, phosphorus, sodium, and potassium. Rosemary contains phenolic diterpenes and *quinones*, which are antioxidants and have been found to suppress tumors in laboratory studies. University of Illinois researchers, for example, found that adding rosemary to the diet of mice exposed to a breast-cancer-inducing chemical decreased the breast tumor incidence by 47 percent.[58] Other researchers have found rosemary contains two other powerful antioxidants, *carnosol* and *carnosic acid*, which inhibit oxygen damage to cells.[59]

In fact, Rutgers researcher M. T. Huang, Ph.D., reports that rosemary is a better antioxidant than BHT or BHA, widely used as antioxidant food additives. He said that rosemary is chemoprevention for tumors of the skin, stomach, colon, lung, and mammary gland in animals. It was 92 percent effective in inhibiting skin cancer in mice after a powerful cancer inducer had been applied.[60]

Turmeric—Yellow Cancer Fighter

Turmeric *(Curcuma longa)* is a perennial plant that is being widely studied for its anticancer properties. Native to East Indian and most of the Pacific islands, it belongs to the ginger family and is widely used in Indian foods. The active principal of turmeric, *curcumin*, the chemical responsible for turmeric's and curry's yellow pigment, is a potent antimutagenic agent and is being studied for its activity against cancer and inflammation.[61] A related substance, cumin, is a natural flavoring obtained from the seeds of *Cuminum cyminum*, a fragile plant cultivated in Asia and the Middle East and used in spice and sausage flavorings. Cumin contains *cuminic aldehyde*, which may have some antiviral properties, and cumene, which is narcotic in high doses and potentially toxic by ingestion. The seed was used in medicine in ancient times as a stimulant and remedy for stomach ailments. Although nontoxic, curcumin does have the potential to cause a reaction to light, but it also can kill salmonella and *E. coli*, two types of bacteria that can cause intestinal ills.[62] *E. coli* is suspected of playing a part in colon cancer.

Licorice—The Black Knight

A perennial shrub, it is native to Europe and Asia, China and Mongolia. *Glycyrrhiza glabra*, also called sweetwood, was introduced into Britain in the sixteenth century by black friars. Among the contents of the dried root are sugars with cortisonelike activity, flavonoids (*see* glossary), coumarins (blood thinners), and estrogen. It stimulates the production of two steroids, *cortisone* and *aldosterone*. It has also been found to produce sodium and water retention with subsequent loss of potassium in some instances. Scientists in the United States and Japan are studying extracts of licorice as a nutraceutical to fight cancer, protect the liver, and slow cell mutation. Licorice can elevate the blood pressure and may cause allergic reactions and be toxic if taken in large amounts.

What About Vitamins and Minerals?

Most researchers and certainly the majority of physicians believe supplemental vitamins may be less promising than increased fruit and vegetable intake, because supplements may not contain all the protective factors and will not modify overall dietary patterns. What happens to the vitamin and mineral content of foods when they are stored or cooked is a big question. It may be that it is not possible to get all the necessary nutrients in our diet as constantly proclaimed by many in the medical field. As for supplements, at pharmacologic dosages, studies are sparse, but those that exist are promising, according to Regina Ziegler, Ph.D., MPH, nutritional epidemiologist at the National Cancer Institute in Bethesda, Maryland.[63] She says more analytic epidemiology and clinical trials are under way. You read about the antioxidant vitamins—A, beta-carotene, E, and C—in the previous chapter. What other nutrients and phytochemicals may protect us against cancer?

Calcium—The Protector

Calcium, a mineral found in dark green, leafy vegetables and dairy products, is now known to be highly effective at preventing colon cancer. Calcium helps prevent abnormal growth of colon cells in people who have polyps, small growths that increase the risk of colon cancer. Half of all Americans are deficient in their daily intake of calcium.[64] Researchers at Memorial Sloan-Kettering in New York, and at Cornell University Medical Center, found that dietary supplementation with calcium significantly reduced the proliferation of epithelial cells lining the colon within two to three months after supplementation. The overproduction of epithelial cells is often a forerunner of cancer, and thus people at high risk for colon cancer can take calcium to help protect their colons against the development of malignancy.

Approximately 1 percent of calcium is distributed in body fluids, where it is essential for normal cell activity. If the body does not get enough calcium from food, it steals the mineral from bones. Abnormal loss of calcium from bones weakens them and makes them porous or brittle and susceptible to fractures.

Selenium—A Trace of Help

Discovered in 1807 in the earth's crust, it is the most toxic of the dietary minerals. Selenium, which is included in the Chinese studies described in the previous chapter, works in association with vitamin E to preserve elasticity in the tissues. It is necessary for the formation of prostaglandins, very active substances found in tissues involved in many bodily activities such as blood pressure, temperature, and the stimulation of involuntary muscles.

A connection between cancer of the colon and selenium deficiencies has become apparent in recent years. Epidemiologists have determined that rates for colorectal cancer are high in geographical areas where selenium is in short supply.

Further, earlier studies demonstrated a link between selenium and the prevention of colon cancer when the inorganic form (sodium selenite) was added to the drinking water or diets of rats. Although inorganic forms of selenium have been shown to deter colon cancer, their toxicity is of concern.

If either not enough selenium was in the diet of animals or too much, the cancer-inducing effects of the mold aflatoxin were enhanced.[65]

Researchers believe that selenium works to prevent oxygen damage to the cells, but it may have other ways of protecting against cancer. It has been reported that it inhibited virus-caused tumors in animals.[66]

Dr. Bandaru S. Reddy and his associates from the American Health Foundation in Valhalla, New York, synthesized a less toxic, organic form of selenium. They added small or large amounts of it to a high-fat diet two weeks before exposing young rodents to a cancer-causing agent, during, and up to three days after cancer was induced. Control animals ate a standard high-fat diet free of additional selenium. The researchers found that supplemental selenium had significant tumor-inhibiting effects.[67]

Although there is evidence that selenium, a trace element, may offer protection against some cancers, this evidence is much too limited to justify a recommendation that selenium intake be increased.[68] Potential adverse reactions include nausea, vomiting, baldness, loss of nails and teeth, fatigue, and bad breath. A massive overdose can be fatal. Because of the potential hazard of selenium poisoning, the *medically unsupervised* use of selenium as a food is hazardous.

Choline—The Egg and You

Choline is normally ingested as part of the human diet in eggs, meat, and some cereals. It is required to make fats and fatlike substances that are essential components of all membranes.[69] The demand for choline in normal adults is likely to be smaller than the demand for choline in the infant, as large amounts of choline must be used to make fat in growing organs. In animal studies, deficiency of choline alone is sufficient to trigger spontaneous liver cancer in rats without exposure to any known carcinogen. Healthy humans fed diets deficient in choline develop liver dysfunction similar to that seen in choline-deficient animals.

Some Other Potential Nutraceuticals

In addition to the potential nutraceuticals mentioned in this chapter and the prior one, many others have been used in folk medicine for years and are now being studied by modern scientists for their anticancer potential. Among them:

Burdock (*Arctium lappa*) is also called lapp, bardane, and beggar's-buttons. The root, seed, and leaves of this common roadside plant contain nearly 45 percent inulin (*see* glossary) and many minerals. Burdock-root extract has been shown to have antitumor effects.

Celandine (*Chelidonium majus*), also called swallowwort, is a tall herb that contains alkaloids, choline, histamine, tyramine, saponins, chelidoniol, chelidonic acid, carotene, and vitamin C. Herbalists use it for the treatment of hepatitis and cancer. It also reputedly detoxifies the liver and relieves muscle spasms and bronchospasms.

Clivers (*Galium aparine*) is also called burweed, catchweed, loveman, and scratchweed. A weed used by herbalists as a solvent for bladder stones and to treat colds, it reputedly has anticancer activity.

Coumarin is a fragrant ingredient of tonka beans, sweet woodruff, cramp bark, and many other plants. It is made synthetically as well. It has anti-blood-clotting effects and anticlotting agents are derived from it. Coumarin is prohibited in foods because it is toxic by ingestion and carcinogenic. Natural coumarins, however, are believed to contain anticarcinogenic factors that interfere with initiation by cancer-causing agents. In animal experiments, pretreatment with coumarin inhibited development of malignancies in male—but not female—mice from the cancer-inducing chemical benzopyrene. The sex difference is, as yet, unexplained.[70]

Cranesbill Root (*Geranium maculatum*) is also called wild geranium, storksbill, and alumroot. The root contains tannic and gallic acids, starch, pectin, and gum. It was used by early

American Indians to treat dysentery, vaginal discharges, and hemorrhoids, among other conditions. These people passed on knowledge of the herb to early settlers. It is used by herbalists today to treat diarrhea and dysentery, colitis, bleeding, and vaginal discharge. It is being studied by researchers at the National Cancer Institute and universities as a potential cancer remedy.

Kelp—From the Sea. Recovered from the giant Pacific marine plant *Macrocystis pyrifera*, kelp is used by herbalists to supply the thyroid gland with iodine, to help regulate the texture of the skin, and to help the body burn off excess fat. In Japan, where kelp is a large part of the diet, thyroid disease is almost unknown. Kelp was banned from over-the-counter diet pills by the FDA, February 10, 1992. Kelp does contain many minerals, and herbalists claim that it has anticancer, antirheumatic, anti-inflammatory, and blood-pressure-lowering properties.

Other Anticancer Chemicals in Fruits and Vegetables

Animal studies have shown that the following nutraceuticals from fruits, vegetables, and herbs protect against cancers:

Nutraceutical—Site Protected

Black tea—skin
B-sitosterol (wheat germ, corn oil)—colon, prostate
Cafestol (green tea)—mouth
D-limonene (citrus fruits, particularly red grapefruit)—breast, lung
Fiber—colon
Folic acid—cervix, mouth
Garlic oil—skin
Green tea extract—skin, esophagus
Kahweol **(green tea)**—mouth
Lemon oil—lung, stomach
Mace—skin
Menthol (herbal teas)—breast

Nomilin (citrus fruits)—forestomach
Oltipraz (cruciferous vegetables)—colon, small intestine, liver
Onion oil—skin
Orange oil—breast, lung, forestomach
Phenethyliosthiocyanate (cruciferous vegetables)—lung, esophagus
Rosemary extract—breast
Selenite (grain cereals)—breast
Sulphoraphane (broccoli)—breast
Tangeretin (tangerines)—breast

As you have read in this chapter, animal and test-tube experiments and epidemiological studies make it clear that many foods contain potent anticancer components, often several working in concert. Whether eating more foods containing these components will fend off cancer in humans remains to be proven. But dozens of studies that correlate eating habits and cancer rates in different parts of the world indicate that certain foods are protective in people. Simply eating these foods on a regular basis may strengthen the body's defense against cancer, a disease that kills half a million Americans each year.

The report of the American Medical Association's Council on Scientific Affairs "Diet and Cancer: Where Do Matters Stand?" states: "Simply identifying substances that inhibit cancer in animals is not enough. For each prospective anticarcinogen it is necessary to determine the precise mechanism of action." The CSA report cites examples in which a substance can be both an animal anticarcinogen and carcinogen, depending upon the amount of the dose administered.

The potential adverse side effects of anticancer nutraceuticals must be identified. Just as with any powerful anticancer pharmaceutical now on the market, if a substance is biologically active, it can have side effects.

While it might be best to get all your anticancer nutraceuticals in foods, other big questions remain—what happens to the vitamins, phytochemicals, and other anticancer compounds in foods during processing, storage, and packaging? Are they removed or weakened?

The key to the diet/cancer puzzle may lie in nutrient interactions and in individual response to dietary factors, determined in turn by genetic, physiologic, and lifestyle factors, according to the American Medical Association's CSA report, which concludes: "Given the rapid strides being made in furthering our understanding of the biochemistry and molecular biology of cancer, we may look forward to the day when optimal dietary and lifestyle guidelines can be tailored on a specific individualized basis. An important challenge is learning how to use these compounds in a rational way to substantively reduce the incidence of human cancer without inadvertently exposing the public to increased health risks."

Despite all the problems in identifying and understanding the anticancer chemicals in our diets, scientists hard at work to develop anticancer nutraceuticals envision consumer products, such as pizza, being fortified with anticancer sulfides from cruciferous vegetables, and green tea being enriched with anticancer citrus terpenes and flavonoids.

Chapter 4

DIET AND THE HEART AT RISK

Your heart beats sixty to eighty times a minute, hour after hour, day after day, year after year. Where does it get its energy? How can it be protected from all the physical and psychological problems that may affect it?

To understand how nutraceuticals in particular and diet in general can prevent or ameliorate cardiovascular disease, you have to recognize how heart and blood-vessel disease develops.

Heart disease, like cancer, is not a one-step process. Blood starts out like a river flowing freely, carrying nutrients to tissues along the way. Arteries are the tunnels that carry blood from the heart to the rest of the body. Healthy arteries have walls that are muscular, smooth inside, and elastic enough to accommodate extreme variations in blood pressure. As a result of high cholesterol, high blood pressure, cigarette smoking, or other factors, injuries occur to the smooth lining. Once the area has been damaged, there is a buildup at the spot of a thick, fatty patch called plaque. Two types of blood cells contribute to the accumulation of plaque:

- Platelets, small blood cells that assist in the coagulation of blood.
- Macrophages, "cleanup" cells that become engorged with cholesterol and debris.

Plaque is made up of a hard jumble of fatty tissue, macrophage cells, and platelets, which erodes the wall, diminishes the elasticity of the artery, and narrows the passageway, interfering with blood flow. A clot may detach itself from the site and move toward the heart or into a small artery, blocking it. An obstruction inside the coronary artery causes angina—chest pain—or a heart attack.[1]

Coronary artery disease and cancerous tumors apparently involve some of the same biological processes.[2] Both diseases result in the growth of a rich network of blood vessels around the site of the disease. In heart disease, it's a buildup of fatty plaque in the coronary arteries, similar to rust collection in an iron pipe, that creates a need for additional blood vessels in the artery wall. In cancer, it is the tumor that requires additional blood vessels for more nourishment. While the production of abnormal blood vessels is not fully understood, it is believed to involve hormonelike substances—prostaglandins—and growth factors secreted by the cells themselves.[3]

Heart disease is responsible for more than 550,000 deaths in the United States each year—more deaths than all forms of cancer combined. Some 5.4 million Americans have symptomatic coronary heart disease, and a large number of others have undiagnosed coronary diseases, many of them young and highly productive. It has been estimated that coronary heart disease costs the United States more than $60 billion a year in direct and indirect costs. Therefore, it would pay everyone—victim and society at large—to prevent it.[4]

How can nutraceuticals—either naturally in our foods or as supplements—protect us against heart and blood-vessel disasters?

Risk Factors

A number of risk factors have been identified as strongly associated with heart disease. Cigarette smoking, high blood pressure, and high blood cholesterol levels are the most clearly established of these factors. Risk is greater in men, increases with age, and has a strong genetic component. Obesity, diabetes mellitus, physical inactivity, and behavior patterns are also risk factors.[5]

Let's begin with the first and one of the most talked about risk factors—high cholesterol.

Cholesterol

A fatlike, waxy substance, cholesterol is found in animal tissue. It is present in foods from animal sources such as whole-milk dairy products, meat, fish, poultry, and egg yolks. An estimated 400 to 500 mg or more of cholesterol is ingested each day in the average American diet. Cholesterol is also produced in your body—primarily your liver—in varying amounts, usually about 1,000 mg a day.

Cholesterol is essential for producing new cells and manufacturing certain hormones. It is delivered throughout your body by tiny packages made of fat and protein called *lipoproteins*. Lipoproteins are flat, disklike particles produced in the liver and intestines and released into the bloodstream. There are basically two major types, *high-density lipoproteins* (HDLs) and *low-density lipoproteins* (LDLs). It is believed HDLs pick up cholesterol and bring it back to the liver for reprocessing. Some researchers believe HDLs may also remove excess cholesterol from fat-engorged cells, possibly even those in artery walls. Because HDLs clear cholesterol out of the system and high levels of it are associated with decreased risk of heart disease, HDL is often called "good" cholesterol. An LDL package, on the other hand, is considered "bad" because it drops its contents along artery walls as it travels from the liver to body cells.

The National Institutes of Health's National Cholesterol Education Program Guidelines say our total cholesterol should be below 200 mg/dl, LDL below 100, and HDL cholesterol should be above 35 mg/dl. So it is not only the total amount of cholesterol in your blood that is important, but which lipoprotein package is carting it around.

Triglycerides are fatty substances that ride around with cholesterol and other fats in the bloodstream. When present in excessive amounts in the blood, they are also related to the occurrence of coronary heart disease.

A great deal of evidence links elevated blood cholesterol levels to coronary heart disease. The National Heart, Lung and Blood Institute and the National Institutes of Health Office of Medical Applications convened a Consensus Development Conference on lowering blood cholesterol to prevent heart disease in 1984.[6] The expert panel recommends we:

- Reduce fat in the diet to 30 percent of total calories.
- Reduce saturated-fat intake to less than 10 percent of total calories.
- Increase polyunsaturated fat intake but to no more than 10 percent of total calories.
- Reduce daily cholesterol intake to 300 mg or less.

Food labeling now includes cholesterol, sources of fat, and saturated- or unsaturated-fat information.

Beyond Cholesterol

Just as cancer researchers now believe that a cell must first be initiated by a cancer-causing agent and then promoted by another agent to cause malignancy, heart researchers believe there are several steps to the development of cardiovascular disease. Low-density lipoprotein (LDL) cholesterol, the "bad" cholesterol, may not be harmful to our arteries until it is oxidized.

The idea that LDL has to be exposed to oxygen developed because of victims of an inherited disease, type II hypercholesterolemia. A baby we'll call Timmy contributed greatly to medical knowledge about cholesterol. Timmy's arteries became choked with cholesterol when he was an infant, and he had his first heart attack at the age of two. He died at five years, and when doctors performed the autopsy, they found his arteries were indeed streaked with fat, and inside the fatty streaks were foam cells, scavenger white blood cells stuffed with droplets of cholesterol. The researchers then mixed the scavenger cells and LDL cholesterol in a laboratory dish and expected plaque to result. Nothing happened. They discovered that LDL had to be exposed to oxygen before the scavenger cells would engulf it.

Evidence of the LDL-oxygen connection was added when Dr. Daniel Steinberg and his colleagues at the University of San Diego gave rabbits prone to clogged arteries one of two routines. In one, they received probucol, a medication that not only lowers but deters oxidation of cholesterol. They gave the other set of rabbits lovastatin, a medication that just lowers cholesterol. The cholesterol was reduced by the same amount in both sets, but those receiving the antioxidant probucol had their fatty lesions in the arteries reduced by half.[7]

Similar results were later found in human studies at Southwestern University, Texas, as you will read under descriptions of the research with the antioxidant vitamin E. Oxidized LDL cholesterol, therefore, is a dangerous substance. How does LDL get oxidized? The culprits are believed to be free radicals, highly reactive molecules generated when a cell "burns" its foods with oxygen to fuel life processes.

We oxygen-breathing humans face a curious paradox, as pointed out in the previous chapter: we cannot live without oxygen, yet our cells are constantly traumatized by its toxic side effects.

Dangerous Radicals

A free radical is any molecule that is "single" and looking for a partner. It's not unlike the singles ads placed in publications. Sometimes a person who answers an ad is dangerous. The most common and potentially hazardous free radicals are oxygen "singles" that look for a mate by stealing someone else's partner or by attaching themselves to a couple. Just like the "other" woman or man, they cause a lot of disturbances and destroy relationships. They can deform and corrode any partner they touch. There is a large body of evidence that free radicals can directly and indirectly cause substantial damage to cells lining blood vessels and arteries.[8] Platelets tend to aggregate at the site of injury.

This leads to deposits of *fibrin*, a protein in the blood that enmeshes blood cells to form clots. Cholesterol also gets stopped at the site—all of which contributes to the formation of an atherosclerotic plaque.

Free radicals have their good side. They play a big part in our ability to kill microbes, and without them we would be helpless to break down food, twitch a muscle, think a thought, or reach for vitamins. Free radicals are controlled with extraordinary precision by our bodies, and they are usually kept in line. It is only when we age or under conditions of abnormal stress that reactive radicals escape the bounds of disciplined performance and begin nicking our cells to pieces.

Many investigators believe that excessive free-radical damage can be fought by eating the right nutraceuticals. Antioxidants such as vitamin C, vitamin E, and a number of phytochemicals found in plants can suppress *free radical* cell damage. They get rid of free radicals' extra electron, rendering the compound inactive.

Stroke and Free Radicals

Free radicals are suspects in the development of strokes. More than half a million Americans a year, most of them over the age of sixty-five, suffer strokes. A stroke occurs when a blood vessel bringing oxygen and nutrients to the brain bursts or is clogged by a blood clot or some other particle. Because of this rupture or blockage, part of the brain doesn't get the flow of blood it needs. Deprived of oxygen, nerve cells in the affected area of the brain can't function and they die within minutes. And when nerve cells can't function, the part of the body controlled by these cells can't perform either. Some 2,980,000 Americans now alive are victims of the cardiovascular disease that affects the arteries of the central nervous system. Many are left with language and mobility problems and become dependent on other family members for their daily needs.[9]

Strokes, like heart disease, are associated with atherosclerosis, high blood pressure, and oxygen damage. Although serum cholesterol is a strong risk factor for coronary heart disease, its importance in stroke remains controversial. Lowering cholesterol with diet or drugs, however, does not reduce stroke mortality, according to researchers from the University of Washington, Seattle. To assess the impact of cholesterol reduction on the risk of stroke, they conducted a meta-analysis (an evaluation of many studies) of cholesterol-lowering trials that used either dietary or therapeutic intervention.[10]

In thirteen studies evaluated, lowering cholesterol did not reduce the risk of fatal strokes and the effect on nonfatal strokes was minimal.

High Blood Pressure and the Heart and Blood Vessels

High blood pressure is a risk factor for both heart disease and stroke. It is estimated that more than 60 million Americans have hypertension.[11] Blood pressure is the force created by the heart as it pushes blood into the arteries and through the circulatory system. When the heart pumps, it causes the blood to flow through the arteries into the arterioles (small arteries). The walls of the arterioles can contract or expand, altering both the amount of blood flow and the resistance to blood flow. Expansion of the arterioles allows increased blood flow and reduces the resistance to the flow. Contraction of the arterioles has the opposite effect. Hence, regulation of the size of the arterioles plays an important role in regulating blood flow and determining blood pressure. If the arterioles remain constricted, they can create a condition we know as high blood pressure. Physicians generally diagnose high blood pressure when an otherwise healthy adult has consistent readings above 140/90. The upper number in a blood pressure reading is a measurement made when the heart contracts, the *systolic* pressure. The lower number in a blood pressure reading is recorded when the heart is at rest, called the *diastolic* pressure.

Elevated blood pressure indicates the heart is working harder than normal, putting both the heart and the arteries under a greater strain. This may contribute to heart attacks, strokes, kidney failure, and atherosclerosis. When the heart is forced to work harder than normal for an extended time, it tends to enlarge. A slightly enlarged heart may function well, but one that's significantly enlarged has a hard time adequately meeting the demands put upon it.

Arteries and arterioles also suffer the effects of high blood pressure. Over time, they become scarred and hardened and less elastic. This may occur as we age, but elevated blood pressure speeds the process and is believed to accelerate atherosclerosis.

In almost all cases, as of this writing, the cause of high blood pressure is unknown. In a few instances, the high blood pressure is due to an underlying problem such as kidney disease, a tumor of the adrenal gland, or a defect of the aorta, the largest artery emanating from the heart.

Diabetes—A Major Culprit

Diabetes is a disease in which the body doesn't produce or properly use insulin. Insulin is needed to convert sugar and starch into the energy needed in daily life. Diabetics often suffer from high blood pressure and are more prone to suffering a heart attack or a stroke than persons without the condition. The frequency of heart disease in diabetics is two to three times that of the population.[12]

Diabetes and diabetes complications are the third major cause of death in the United States. An estimated fourteen million people in the United States have diabetes. Approximately 25 percent of people with diabetes have type I, that is, are insulin dependent, whose bodies produce little or no insulin. Approximately 75 percent of the people with diabetes have type II, that is, are noninsulin dependent, whose bodies produce insulin but do not use it properly.[13]

Overweight—A Heavy Burden

Based on National Health and Nutrition Examination Survey (NHANES II) data, an estimated 46.3 million American adults are 20 percent or more over their desirable weight. This overweight condition exists in 24.4 percent of white males, 25.7 percent of black males, 25.1 percent of white females, and 43.8 percent of black females. Think of yourself carrying a heavy package up a flight of stairs, and you get some idea of the strain excess weight puts upon your cardiovascular system.[14]

No Buts About Butts

Cigarette smoking is another risk factor. The major connection that it has with diet is that many people continue to smoke so they won't gain weight. Happily, smoking has declined 32 percent in the last twenty-two years.[15]

What Can Be Done to Lower the Risks of Cardiovascular Disease?

We can't change our heredity that makes us prone to cardiovascular disease, but we can help reduce our risks. If we smoke, we can give it up. If we are overweight, we can lose weight. If we drink too much alcohol—more than two ounces a day is said to raise blood pressure—we can forgo it. We can reduce the sodium and cholesterol in our diets, and we can ingest nutraceuticals that lower blood pressure and cholesterol and/or protect our arteries against free radicals.

Many medications are available to lower high blood pressure. They include:

- Diuretics, which remove excess fluids and salt from the body by increasing the flow of urine.
- Beta-blockers, which reduce the heart rate and the heart's output of blood.
- Sympathetic-nerve inhibitors, which suppress the self-made nerve chemicals that constrict the arteries.
- Vasodilators, which relax the muscles in the walls of the blood vessels allowing the artery to widen.
- Angiotensin-converting enzyme (ACE) inhibitors, which interfere with the body's production of angiotensin, a chemical that causes arteries to constrict.

- Calcium antagonists (calcium channel blockers), which can reduce the heart rate and relax blood vessels.

In the next chapter, you will read about how nutraceuticals can aid or substitute for many pharmaceuticals.

Chapter 5

NUTRACEUTICALS THAT COMBAT CARDIOVASCULAR DISEASE

Nutraceuticals—natural medications in diet or derived from food—have been used since ancient times to achieve what the prescription drugs mentioned in the previous chapter do. In fact, some of the prescription medications now in use, such as digitalis and reserpine, are based on plants. Modern researchers are now investigating many other natural compounds in the laboratory and by studying the rate of cardiovascular diseases in specific populations.

The greatest emphasis in the field of nutraceuticals, however, is prevention of heart disease. This includes elements in or from the diet that lower blood pressure and cholesterol and protect the cells against the ravages of oxygen and diabetes.

The Vitamin and Mineral Nutraceuticals

A great deal of research is in progress to determine how medicinal doses of vitamins and minerals may be used to prevent and to treat cardiovascular diseases. At the same time, the U.S. government has lowered most of the recommended dietary allowances (RDAs) for these nutrients and changed the name of the advisory to "daily value" intake (*see* appendix I). The following describes some of the studies concerning the use of nutrients to protect the cardiovascular system and to help it heal once something goes wrong.

The Power of Vitamin E

In 1922, two American researchers, Dr. Herbert M. Evans and Dr. Katherine S. Bishop, tried to find out whether reproduction was dependent on "some nutritive substance different from those which produced growth and adulthood." The two scientists noticed that female rats given a diet of rancid lard conceived young in a normal manner but failed to carry to term. When they were given lettuce, the fertility problem was corrected.

At first, Evans and Bishop thought that the vitamin C in lettuce cured the rat mothers' problem, but it was then found that only the oil of the vegetable worked. To their amazement, they discovered that wheat also cured infertility.

Intrigued, Dr. Evans tested the oil content of wheat—the germ. He found that "single daily drops of the gold-yellow wheat germ oil proved remedial." The substance in the lettuce oil and wheat germ was vitamin E.

Because the substance allowed animals to bear offspring, it was named *tocos*, the Greek word for "childbirth," combined with the Greek verb *phero*, meaning "to bring forth," and the suffix *ol* for *alcohol*; thus vitamin E was named *tocopherol*.

Tocopherols are widespread in nature. They are in almost all plants and animals. The most active form is alpha tocopherol. For years, it was taught in medical schools that the only known biologic function of vitamin E was the prevention of miscarriage in rats. However, advocates of alternative medicine have for years extolled vitamin E as a way to forestall aging, improve sexual function, and prevent atherosclerosis. Evidence is emerging that the last may certainly be true. Vitamin E is a major target of mainstream medical researchers seeking chemoprevention of heart and blood-vessel disease.

Vitamin E and the Heart

Two epidemiologic studies reported on in the 1990s demonstrated that vitamin E consumption is associated with a reduced risk of coronary artery disease.[1] The Nurses' Health Study enrolled more than 87,000 women in 1980 who were free of diagnosed cardiovascular disease and cancer. After eight years of follow-up, the researchers identified 437 cases of nonfatal myocardial infarction (heart attack due to a blood clot) and 115 coronary-disease deaths. For women who were in the top fifth of vitamin E intake, the relative risk of major coronary disease was 0.66 compared with those in the bottom fifth—even after adjustment for age and smoking. Only women who took vitamin E for longer than two years had this benefit.[2]

The United States Health Professions Follow-up Study, which enrolled almost 40,000 male health professionals in 1986, identified 667 cases of coronary disease during four years of follow-up. A lower risk of coronary disease was found among men with higher intakes of vitamin E. Men who took one hundred units or more of vitamin E a day for at least two years had a risk of coronary disease of 0.63. Neither study found that a high intake of vitamin E in the diet—with no supplements—significantly reduced the risk of coronary disease.

Reaction to the above two studies was mixed. The doubters said that the two studies could have been skewed by the fact that healthy persons who self-treat with large doses of vitamin supplements might very well have other lifestyle habits that lower their risk of coronary heart disease.[3] Others said that the addition of vitamin E to other means of controlling blood fats couldn't be harmful and might help.[4] And still other researchers started swallowing vitamin E themselves.

How Does Vitamin E Work?

Remember in the previous chapter, steps in the development of cardiovascular disease include clumping of platelets, those blood cells involved in clotting? Vitamin E has been shown to reduce platelet aggregation in blood samples from volunteers taking high levels of vitamin E supplements and to inhibit the platelet prostaglandin-release reaction. The concentration of vitamin E in platelets has been found to decline with age.

Women using oral contraceptives, who were found to have reduced vitamin E levels and increased platelet clotting, were given a vitamin E supplement of 200 mg per day for two months. Following this, blood samples showed markedly reduced platelet activity. Healthy volunteers not taking oral contraceptives showed no such changes after taking vitamin E.

Taking 400 IU per day of vitamin E strongly inhibited platelet adhesions to collagen, fibrinogen, and fibronectin, all substances believed to be involved in the creation of plaques sticking to the inside of the arteries. This affect of vitamin E would complement the action of potent agents, such as aspirin, that inhibit blood platelet clumping but have no effect on adhesion.[5]

In a large clinical study, researchers showed megadoses of vitamin E added to the diet can slow the development of atherosclerosis. When nutrition researchers at the University of Texas Southwestern Medical Center at Dallas gave volunteers daily doses of 800 IU of vitamin E, they discovered that the oxidation rate of the subjects' LDL was reduced by half. As pointed out earlier in this chapter, scientists are now beginning to believe it is the oxidation of LDL—the bad form of cholesterol—that triggers the buildup of cholesterol in the artery wall, leading to atherosclerosis.

Dr. Ishwarlal Jialal, associate professor of internal medicine and clinical nutrition, and Dr. Scott Grundy, director of the University of Texas Southwestern's center for human nutrition, published their findings in the June 1992 issue of the *Journal of Lipid Research*.

Two groups of twelve normal men were given either a placebo or vitamin E for twelve weeks. None had side effects.

When the researchers tried to oxidize the LDL in the blood samples, they found that in the vitamin group, the ability to oxidize was 55.7 percent less than in the placebo group.

Remember cholesterol-engorged scavenger cells contribute to artery blockage? In France, J. C. Fruchart of the Pasteur Institute, Lille, gave twenty men with high blood cholesterol either a placebo, a cholesterol-lowering drug, one gram of vitamin E (1,000 IU), or vitamin E plus the drug. After two months, the rate of LDL ingestion by those scavenger cells, the macrophages, was slower in the vitamin E group than either the drug-treated or the placebo group. Those who took the drug plus vitamin E had the greatest decrease in blood cholesterol levels.

Bypass Surgery and Vitamin E

A loss of blood supply and oxygen to an area of the body (ischemia) can cause tissue damage. Bypass surgery, an operation to improve blood flow, involves a temporary cessation of blood flow to the heart, followed by a restoration of blood flow to the heart, and thus the heart may be subject to ischemia-reperfusion injury. Those villainous free radicals form as surgeons briefly flood the heart with richly oxygenated blood. Vitamin E has been found to serve as a bodyguard during bypass surgery.

In one study, thirty patients undergoing the bypass procedure participated in a study of the effects of vitamin E supplementation on reducing free-radical damage to membranes. Ten of the subjects received an oral supplement of 2,000 IU of vitamin E twelve hours before surgery. The supplemented group showed no significant increase in hydrogen peroxide, an indicator of oxygen-caused stress, during the procedure. The supplement also prevented the significant reduction in blood levels of vitamin E observed in the control subjects twenty-four hours after surgery.[6]

In a small study, Terrence Yau, M.D., of the University of Toronto reported presurgical supplementation with vitamin E improves the heart's ability to pump during the especially risky five-hour postoperative period after bypass surgery. While the results seem promising, Dr. Yau stressed the preliminary nature of the small-scale study calls for further research.[7]

In countries with relatively high ischemic heart-disease deaths (Scotland and Finland), the blood level of vitamin E has been found to be about 25 percent lower than in countries with low or moderat.e coronary mortality—Italy, Switzerland, and Northern Ireland.[8]

In one of the most important studies, researchers at Brigham and Women's Medical Center in Massachusetts, found that women who took vitamin E supplements totaling at least 100 IU daily for two years had half the risk of cardiovascular disease as did women who hadn't taken supplements. Higher doses did not appear to cut the risk further.[9]

Intermittent Claudication and Vitamin E

Intermittent claudication is the result of various blood-vessel disorders, such as atherosclerosis, that result in insufficient blood flow. This lack of blood to exercised muscles can cause cramping, pain, numbness, and fatigue.

The treatment of intermittent claudication with vitamin E supplements has been investigated for many years with mixed results. In one early double-blind placebo study of high-dose vitamin E, intermittent claudication showed improvement in 67 percent of only those subjects who had poor circulation in the lower leg.[10] In later studies in Northern Ireland, physicians wanted to know if oxygenation of blood fats played a part in lower-limb swelling after vein-grafting surgery to increase circulation in the legs. The doctors tested vitamin E in the blood before, during, and after the operation. They found that those who had the least swelling after surgery had the higher levels of vitamin E.[11]

Angina—Chest Pain and Vitamin E

Angina is another condition in which the heart muscle doesn't receive enough blood, resulting in pain in the chest. Vitamin E has been found to be effective in angina.

Rudolph A. Riemersma, M.D., and his colleagues at the University of Edinburgh in Scotland, working with K. Fred Gey, M.D., at the University of Berne, Switzerland, studied 110 men with previously undiagnosed chest pain and 394 healthy men who reported no heart-disease symptoms. The researchers took blood samples and analyzed the clear plasma portion for carotenes and vitamins E and C. Their statistical analysis revealed men with higher than average plasma levels of these nutrients, particularly vitamin E, were less likely to experience chest pain than were men with lower than average plasma concentrations of the nutrients. Those with the lowest levels were 2.7 times as likely to have angina as those with the highest levels.[12]

Swiss research compared blood levels of antioxidants in groups of about one hundred men from each of sixteen different European communities. The rates of coronary heart disease in those communities ranged from about 65 to nearly 500 deaths per 100,000 males. Men in communities with the highest coronary-disease death rates had the lowest blood levels of vitamin E. Low levels of vitamins A and C were weakly associated with such increased risk.

Preliminary, unpublished findings from the ongoing Nurses' Health Study in the United States suggest that low intake of vitamin A, including carotenoids, and of vitamin E increase the risk of cardiovascular disease.

How Much Vitamin E Is Protective?

As you have read, current research indicates that vitamin E may lower risk of cardiovascular diseases (hardening of the arteries, angina, heart attack, and stroke) by reducing oxidation of harmful LDL cholesterol, inhibiting platelet (*see* glossary) activity, and preventing blood clots.

The recommended daily allowance for newborns to six months is 4 IU. Infants from six months to one year, 6 IU. Children over one year to three years, 9 IU. Children four to ten years, 10 IU. Males eleven years and over, 12 IU. Females eleven years and over 12 IU. Pregnant women 15 IU. Lactating women 16 to 18 IU. Used to treat vitamin E deficiency in premature infants and in patients with impaired fat absorption.

In the newer set of dietary references based on and replacing the recommended dietary allowances (RDAs) for essential vitamins and minerals, the RDI for vitamin E is 30 IU (*see* appendix I).

The United States recommended daily allowance of vitamin E was set years before studies emerged suggesting that vitamin E can help prevent a wide array of diseases. While the newer RDIs have upped the recommended daily intake, several recent research reports have indicated doses far higher than the new RDIs may be needed to yield such benefits. Studies show that it takes a daily vitamin E supplement of at least 100 IU to raise blood levels.

Researchers with the National Cancer Institute and the U.S. Agricultural Research Service looked at the relationship between vitamin E intake and blood levels in sixty-five men. Vitamin E intake from the diet did not differ significantly among the men. Their diets provided less than 15 IU per day. But they fell into three groups based on their use of vitamin supplements: those who did not take the supplements on any regular basis; those who got an extra 15 to 60 IU daily from multivitamin supplements; and those who got an extra 100 IU or more from a vitamin E capsule. Compared with those who did not take any supplements, the blood levels of vitamin E were 14 percent higher in the group that took multivitamin supplements. But levels were more than twice as high in the group that took vitamin E capsules on a daily basis. It is virtually impossible to get 100 IU of vitamin E from diet alone. The normal adult intake is 10 to 15 IU.[13]

In some cases, such as those where people consume mineral oil or a fat-and-cholesterol-lowering medication, cholestyramine resin (Cholybar or Questran), intestinal absorption of oral vitamin E is inhibited and higher levels of vitamin E may be needed.

The main dietary sources of vitamin E are vegetable oils, nuts, and other fatty foods, says Jeffrey Blumberg, Ph.D., associate director of the Human Nutrition Research Center on Aging, a federal laboratory in Boston. "We're telling people to cut back on fats, which makes it hard to get much vitamin E," Dr. Blumberg says. "So there is some rationale to get vitamin E supplementation."

A person would have to drink two quarts of corn oil or eat more than five pounds of wheat germ to get 400 IU of vitamin E, the amount in a typical supplement capsule, according to the Vitamin E Research & Information Service, a La Grange, Illinois, concern funded by Henkel KGaA, a German company that sells vitamin E supplements.

Harmful effects are rare from vitamin E intake, but prolonged use of more than 250 IUs daily may lead to nausea, abdominal pain, vomiting, and diarrhea. Large doses may also reduce the amounts of vitamins A, D, and K absorbed from the intestines.

Vitamin C and the Heart

Vitamin C, ascorbic acid, is like vitamin E, an antioxidant vitamin and is the object of numerous studies for its possible role in ameliorating atherosclerosis. As pointed out earlier in the chapter, oxidation of low-density lipoprotein (LDL) speeds the formation of atherosclerotic lesions. Researchers have shown vitamin C may also protect against the process in humans. Cooperating investigators at Harvard, the University of California at Berkeley, and the University of Texas Southwestern Medical Center exposed human blood to oxidative substances and found that vitamin C protects LDL cholesterol from oxygen damage.[14]

The beneficial effects of vitamin C may be through an increase in HDL, the so-called good cholesterol, rather than through a lowering of total cholesterol. It has been suggested that vitamin C significantly alters cholesterol levels only in people with high cholesterol. Others have theorized that vitamin C mobilizes the cholesterol in arterial walls, thereby improving the condition of the arteries without significantly lowering and sometimes even raising serum lipid levels.[15]

Paul F. Jacques, ScD, a researcher at the USDA Human Nutrition Research Center on Aging at Tufts University in Boston, found that low vitamin C intake had an adverse effect on three major heart-disease risk factors—LDL cholesterol, the cholesterol-laden fat carrier in the bloodstream that may contribute to heart disease; high-density lipoprotein, a fat carrier with protective qualities; and blood pressure.

Dr. Jacques conducted separate studies on three groups of adults: 491 individuals aged twenty to sixty years, 696 aged sixty to one hundred years, and 259 Chinese Americans between the ages of sixty and ninety-six. "The persons who had the highest blood levels of vitamin C [the top 25 percent of each group] had more HDL ["good"] cholesterol and less LDL ["bad"] cholesterol. They also were far less likely to have high blood pressure," said Dr. Jacques.

The average HDL was 7 percent higher in the group with the highest blood levels, and the LDL was 11 percent lower. Persons in the top 25 percent also had lower blood pressure over all. The highest intakes of the persons in the high vitamin C group was over 180 mg per day, or three times the RDA.[16]

Similar observations were made in persons who consumed higher amounts of vitamin C—over 180 mg/day or the equivalent of more than three times the RDA. Dr. Jacques noted, "Those persons with high vitamin C intakes had higher HDL cholesterol levels and lower blood pressure than did persons who consumed less vitamin C."

Studies in animals have also shown that atherosclerosis induced by a high-cholesterol diet can also be prevented or reversed by a high vitamin C intake. A single dose of vitamin C—two grams—injected intravenously, caused inhibition of platelet aggregation when the blood was later examined in the laboratory and reduced the concentration of debris caused by oxidation.[17]

In another study, individuals with existing coronary-artery disease were given either a fake pill or one or two grams of vitamin C in two daily doses for six months. At the higher vitamin C dose there was a significant increase in fibrin-dissolving activity (which is thought to be a factor in clearing arteries) and a 27 percent decrease in blood platelet adhesiveness, which, as you have read, is involved in the development of blocked arteries. The subjects who had mild high cholesterol also had a drop in that. Furthermore, the addition of one gram of vitamin C to food prevented an increase in platelet stickiness and aggregation that occurs in coronary-artery-disease patients who eat a high-cholesterol meal. The studies indicate that perhaps a high threshold level of vitamin C is required to influence blood platelet activity. It has been suggested that a daily dose of one gram of vitamin C is the minimum necessary to help protect against blood-clotting disease.[18]

Strokes and Vitamin C

A rise in blood levels of vitamin C in elderly patients was associated with a lower number of pinpoint hemorrhages caused by a blood-pressure cuff in comparison with subjects who received a fake pill. It has been suggested that low vitamin C levels increase the fragility of arteries and capillaries and, when coupled with hypertension, may lead to hemorrhages and stroke.

British researchers noting an association between declining strokes and an increase in fruit and vegetable consumption in Britain and the United States have proposed that these foods may be protective against stroke. The authors suggest that the reduced risk of cardiovascular disease associated with eating fresh fruit and vegetables may be due to their vitamin C content. They also point out that fresh produce is a good source of potassium, also a factor in lowering the risk of high blood pressure.[19] Vitamin C also works together with vitamin E, another antioxidant vitamin, to help maintain vitamin E's antioxidant capability.[20]

Vitamin C and Diabetes

Levels of vitamin C (ascorbic acid) are decreased in various tissues of diabetic patients. Glucose and vitamin C have similar structures and are thought to share a cellular-transport mechanism. Because diabetics typically have high blood sugar, the competition between glucose and vitamin C for transport into cells is likely to cause vitamin C inadequacy in tissues and organs, and diabetics may require more vitamin C than normal subjects.[21] Increased intake of vitamin C may help to protect diabetics against the cell damage associated with chronic high blood sugar, and the inflammation, susceptibility to bacterial infections, and delayed wound healing.[22]

In one study, twelve diabetics, six of whom had damage to the retina of the eye, and twenty-four controls participated. Half the diabetics and a quarter of the controls were found to have an intake of less than the recommended 316 mg/wk of vitamin C.

The diabetics randomly received either a placebo for one month followed by one gram of vitamin C daily for two months, or one gram of vitamin C for one month followed by a placebo for another month. In all subjects negative pressure was applied to the forearm causing blood spots (petechiae), to test blood-vessel fragility. The diabetics showed blood spots at much lower negative pressure than the controls, and all diabetics with damage to the retina had fragile capillaries. Blood-vessel fragility failed to change during the placebo treatment. Capillary strength in all diabetics improved during vitamin C treatment. No further retinal changes were observed during vitamin C treatment.[23]

High Blood Pressure and Vitamin C

High blood pressure is considered a major risk factor for cardiovascular disease. Calcium, magnesium, and particularly vitamin C help keep blood pressure in check. In fact, both systolic and diastolic readings are generally 5 to 10 percent lower in persons with high bloodstream levels of vitamin C than in persons with low levels. An evaluation of the United States National Health and Nutrition Examination Survey (NHANES I) data show that people with lower vitamin C consumption had higher blood pressure.[24]

Researchers at the Medical College of Georgia, Augusta, and their colleagues looked at 678 healthy men and women, twenty to sixty-nine years of age with normal blood pressure. They discovered that people in the group with the highest blood levels of vitamin C had significantly lower blood-pressure values than people with low levels. Scientists found a mean blood-pressure reading of 104/65 mm of mercury for high vitamin C participants compared with 111/73 for low vitamin C participants. The people in the study obtained their vitamin C through diet alone.

Other investigators at Tufts University, Boston, studied 241 elderly Chinese Americans, some of whom had high blood pressure. The researchers found that participants with the highest blood levels of vitamin C tended to have the lowest blood-pressure values in the group.

The new results raise the possibility that vitamin C may lower blood pressure. The USDA said that people with borderline hypertension may benefit from one gram daily of vitamin C supplement.[25]

How Much Vitamin C?

Recommended daily allowance for newborns to six months was 30 mg. Infants six months to one year, 35 mg. Children one to three years, 40 mg. Children four to ten years, 45 mg. Children eleven to fourteen years, 50 mg. Children fifteen years and over and adults, 60 mg. *The newer reference daily intake is 60 mg.*

Potential adverse reactions to very high levels of vitamin C may be diarrhea, heartburn, acid urine, and kidney stones or failure, and with fast IV administration, faintness or dizziness.

Best food sources of vitamin C are green peppers, honeydew melon, brussels sprouts, broccoli, cantaloupe, strawberries, and oranges. Four ounces of broccoli contains twice the amount of vitamin C in an equivalent amount of reconstituted frozen orange juice—about 100 mg. If the broccoli is especially fresh, evidenced by a blushing green hue, it can contain up to 40 percent more of this vitamin. Freezing, boiling, blanching, steaming, or otherwise cooking broccoli roughly halves its vitamin C.[26]

Beta-Carotene and Cardiovascular Disease

The body stores beta-carotene in fatty tissues and converts it to vitamin A in a regulated way, so toxicity appears to be virtually nonexistent.

Charles Hennekens, M.D., and his team of Harvard researchers offered a peek from the Physicians Health Study, originally an intervention trial of aspirin for the heart and beta-carotene for cancer prevention. In the ongoing beta-carotene part of the study, some twenty-two thousand men were randomly assigned to take either a 50-mg supplement or a placebo every other day.

After six years, the researchers analyzed data on 330 men who had signs of coronary disease when they entered the study. The researchers found that those who took beta-carotene had half as many major cardiovascular events such as heart attack or stroke as those on the placebo.[27]

Julie Buring, D.Sc., associate professor of preventive medicine at Harvard Medical School, is now studying forty thousand post-menopausal women, healthy nurses with no history of cardiovascular disease or cancer. The nurses are being tested to see if low-dose aspirin as well as beta-carotene and vitamin E may reduce their risk of cardiovascular disease. The research is being funded by the National Cancer Institute and the National Heart, Lung and Blood Institute.

Evidence that antioxidant vitamins protect against cardiovascular disease is intriguing although not yet conclusive. In one nested case-control study, there was an inverse association between serum beta-carotene levels and myocardial infarction, but two other such studies did not demonstrate a significant association between serum levels of vitamins A or E and subsequent cardiovascular mortality. The Nurses' Health Study, which examined the effect of beta-carotene and vitamin E intake on cardiovascular disease in 87,245 women, found that those in the highest fifth of beta-carotene intake had a 22 percent reduction in risk as compared to those in the lowest fifth; for vitamin E, risk was reduced 34 percent in the highest quintile of intake. Additionally, a study following 1,299 elderly people for almost five years found a 43 percent reduction in fatal coronary heart disease and a 68 percent decrease in risk of fatal myocardial infarction among those in the highest fourth of beta-carotene intake. Finally, among 333 doctors in the Physicians Health Study with chronic stable angina or a prior coronary revascularization procedure, those given 50 mg of beta-carotene every other day had a 51 percent reduction in risk for coronary events and a 54 percent reduction in risk for vascular events.

In a major study examining the incidence of cardiovascular problems over thirteen years, researchers at the University of

North Carolina at Chapel Hill confirmed that beta-carotene and other carotenoids may significantly reduce the risk of heart attack.[28] Dr. Tony Morris, who was a member of the study team, said, "Our research shows that particularly in individuals who didn't smoke, the higher the serum carotenoid levels, the lower the risk of getting a heart attack."

Orange, yellow, and green fruits and vegetables such as carrots, sweet potatoes, spinach, apricots, and cantaloupe contain beta-carotene, which can easily be depleted by overcooking.

B_6, B_{12}, and Folic Acid Against Heart Disease

VITAMIN B_6 (pyridoxine) metabolizes protein, helps produce red blood cells, and maintains proper functioning of nervous-system tissue. Vitamin B_6 is believed to act as a partner for more than one hundred different enzymes. Vitamin B_6 also reportedly helps rid body tissues of excess fluid.

The suggestion that vitamin B_6 plays a role in cardiovascular health is consistent with epidemiological observations. Atherosclerosis is prevalent in developed countries where meat intake is high and diets are typically high in sulfur-containing amino acids and relatively low in vitamin B_6.

In laboratory animals, vitamin B_6 deficiency causes atherosclerotic lesions similar to those seen in spontaneous human atherosclerosis.[29] Advanced atherosclerosis is also seen in children with homocystinuria, a genetic disorder. The metabolism of amino acids, which requires vitamin B_6, is impaired in individuals with this disease, which causes an accumulation of homocysteine. Homocysteine is a component of protein. Individuals with congenital defects of B_{12} metabolism, or a deficiency of folic acid or vitamin B_6, also have high levels of this substance, which is associated with clots in the veins and an increased risk of heart and blood-vessel disease in humans.[30] Homocysteine has been found to plug arteries with fatty plaques in animals and may contribute to atherosclerosis in humans.[31]

High circulating levels of homocysteine were found in a group of postmenopausal women. Folic-acid supplementation (5 mg per day for four weeks) lowered homocysteine levels in this group.[32]

Patients are likely to have a deficiency of vitamin B_6 if they are alcoholics or have burns, diarrhea, heart disease, intestinal problems, liver disease, overactive thyroid, or are suffering the stress of long-term illness or serious injury. Patients on dialysis or who have their stomachs removed are also probably deficient in the vitamin.

Overdosing on B_6 is unwise. A study reported in the *The New England Journal of Medicine* in 1983 described the loss of balance and numbness suffered by seven young adults who took from two to six grams of pyridoxine daily for several months to a year. Other potential adverse reactions include drowsiness and a feeling of pins and needles in limbs.

Recommended daily allowance of B_6 for newborns and infants to six months was 0.3 mg. Children six months to three years, 0.9 mg. Children four to six years, 1.1 mg. Children seven to ten years, 1.4 mg. Males eleven to fourteen years, 1.7 mg. Males fifteen years and over, 2 mg. Females eleven to fourteen years, 1.4 mg. Females fifteen to eighteen years, 1.5 mg. Females nineteen years and over, 1.6 mg. Pregnant women, 2.2 mg. Lactating women, 2.1 mg. The newer reference daily intake for B_6 is 2 mg.

Best food sources of B_6 are wheat germ, bananas, brewer's yeast, buckwheat flour, sunflower seeds, peanuts, and tomatoes.

FOLIC ACID aids cell growth and regeneration, red blood cell formation, and protein metabolism. It is used to treat deficiency caused by alcoholism, anemia, diarrhea, fever, hemodialysis, prolonged illness, intestinal diseases, liver disease, prolonged stress, and surgical removal of the stomach. Recommended daily allowance: newborns and infants to six months, 25 mcg; infants six months to one year, 35 mcg. Children over one year to three years, 50 mcg. Children four to six years, 75 mcg. Children seven to eleven years, 100 mcg. Children eleven to fourteen years, 150 mcg. Males fifteen years and over, 200 mcg. Females fifteen years and over, 180 mcg. Pregnant women, 400 mcg. Lactating women, from 260 to 280 mcg. The newer reference daily intake for folic acid is 0.4 mg. Potential adverse reactions include rash, itching, redness, allergic bronchospasms, and general malaise.

VITAMIN B$_{12}$ helps form red blood cells; maintains healthy nervous system. Deficiency symptoms include anemia, brain damage, and nervousness. Recommended daily allowances were neonates and infants to six months, 0.3 mcg. Infants six months to one year, 0.5 mcg. Children over one to three years, 0.7 mcg. Children four to six years, 1 mcg. Children seven to ten years, 3 mcg. Adults and children eleven years and over, 2 mcg. Pregnant women, 2.2 mcg. Lactating women, 2.6 mcg. The newer reference daily intake is 6 mcg. Potential adverse reactions include allergic reactions and, rarely, blood clots.

NIACIN. (Nictonic Acid) Introduced as a nutritional supplement in 1937, it is an essential nutrient that releases energy from foods, and aids in the maintenance of a normal nervous system. A component of the vitamin B complex, niacin is a water-soluble vitamin involved in carbohydrate, protein, and fat metabolism.

Niacin stimulates histamine release and causes a temporary dilation of the blood vessels resulting in unpleasant symptoms of flushing associated with doses of about 75 mg or more. If levels are increased gradually, people can often increase their tolerance to it.

Highly successful treatment for high blood fats has been reported for niacin in combination with other drugs. Significant improvement and in some cases a normalization of blood cholesterol and LDL was reported in patients with inherited high cholesterol after treatment with niacin plus a cholesterol-lowering drug. Niacin reduces so-called bad cholesterol and increases good cholesterol. In a study comparing it with other coronary drugs in men who had had a heart attack, fifteen-year follow-up (nine years after treatment ended) showed an 11 percent lower mortality rate in the group receiving niacin compared with the placebo group.[33]

Unlike other agents used in the treatment of high blood lipids, niacin appears to block the initial manufacture and secretion of LDL rather than removing LDL after it is already present. This is consistent with the earlier discovery that niacin has anti-blood-fat properties and therefore reduces the release of lipids in the bloodstream. However, the exact mechanism by which niacin improves blood-fat profiles and cardiovascular health is not definitely known.[34]

Most adverse reactions are dose dependent and include nausea, vomiting, diarrhea, dizziness, headache, possible activation of peptic ulcer, stomach pain, liver dysfunction, high blood sugar, high uric acid, flushing, itching, and dryness. Blood-pressure-lowering drugs may have an additive blood-vessel-dilating effect and cause a drop in blood pressure when standing. Niacin is contraindicated in liver dysfunction, active peptic ulcer, severe low blood pressure, or bleeding of the arteries. Should be used with caution if you have gallbladder disease, diabetes, or gout. It is most effective when taken on an empty stomach, but may be taken with food to avoid stomach upset.

Best food sources of niacin include tuna, halibut, chicken, turkey, sunflower seeds, enriched cereal grain products, cheese, eggs, milk, ham, peanuts, mushrooms, and potatoes. Niacin in many foods such as grains is bound to other substances and therefore nutritionally unavailable.

Vitamin K Against Heart and Blood-Vessel Diseases

Vitamin K, the last of the commonly accepted vitamins to be discovered, wasn't fully identified until the 1930s. The important role of many of the clotting factors was not even suspected until the 1940s. It wasn't until the 1960s that scientists started to look at vitamin K action in clotting.

Vitamin K is required for the manufacture of proteins essential in blood clotting—the cascade of reactions that forms a fibrin clot to prevent excessive loss of blood from injuries. Vitamin K is also required for the manufacture of two plasma protein anticoagulants—substances that interfere with clotting—and two bone proteins. And there are other vitamin-K-dependent proteins in the body whose functions are as yet unknown.

Vitamin K deficiency is infrequent, and the bleeding disorders associated with vitamin K deficiency are rare except when people are exposed to certain types of antibiotics, including some of the new cephalosporins. Newborns are also at risk for vitamin K deficiencies because it does not efficiently cross the placenta and the fetal gut is sterile. This helps to explain why bleeding disorders are more common in newborns than in adults. Pharmaceutical researchers are seeking a vitamin K nutraceutical that may eventually be used as an alternative, safer anticoagulant than those now in use.[35]

There is no recommended dietary intake or reference daily intake for vitamin K.

Good sources of the plant form of vitamin K, *phylloquinone*, are green, leafy vegetables, particularly kale, brussels sprouts, and broccoli. A closely related form of the vitamin, *menaquinones*, are synthesized by bacteria. A large amount of them are found in the gut. The synthetic form of the vitamin, *menadione*, is commonly used in animal feed.

Alpha-Linolenic Acid and the Mediterranean Diet

It has been noted among researchers for many years that the Italians and the French, who eat a high-fat diet, have less heart attacks than Americans. Some say it is the wine they drink with their meals and others say it is the presence of alpha-linolenic acid found in olive oil, and canola oil. The typical Mediterranean diet has more bread, root vegetables, green vegetables, fish, and less meat than the typical American diet. The Mediterraneans also eat a great deal of fruit. In a French study of post-heart attack patients, one group of 302 patients was prescribed a diet of less saturated fats but more alpha-linolenic acids. A control group of

302 patients ate their normal diets. After five years, the group that had the increased alpha-linolenic acid suffered only three deaths while the control group had sixteen deaths.[36]

Purslane, walnuts, and soybean oil are all high in alpha-linolenic acid.

Coenzyme Q$_{10}$ (Ubiquinone)—The Strengthener?

Coenzyme Q$_{10}$ is a vitaminlike substance made by the human body and also found in food. Coenzyme Q$_{10}$ has been found to be lower in patients with heart disease. Administration of coenzyme Q$_{10}$ for twelve weeks to heart patients significantly increased their hearts' ability to pump, reduced shortness of breath, and increased muscle strength. The improvements lasted as long as three years in patients treated continuously, but cardiac function deteriorated when CoQ$_{10}$ was discontinued.[37]

Coenzyme Q$_{10}$ has been successfully used in combating irregular heartbeat in both heart and diabetic patients.[38]

Most coenzyme Q$_{10}$ comes from eating fish. Sardines, for example, have the most—64 mcg. Mackerel is also high with 43 mcg. It may be the reason why fatty fish reportedly helps prevent artery clogging.

Taurine—An Amino Acid Against Heart Disease

Taurine is an amino acid found in almost every tissue of the body and high in human milk. Most infant soy-protein formulas are now supplemented with taurine. Taurine is almost absent from vegetarian diets. It is believed necessary for healthy eyes, and it is an antioxidant.

Irregular heartbeat is characteristic of lack of blood to the heart and may be partly due to loss of intracellular taurine, some researchers theorize. Much like magnesium, taurine affects membrane excitability by normalizing potassium flux in and out of the heart muscle cells. Supplementation may prevent digitalis-induced arrhythmias.[39]

Taurine may also lower blood pressure. In a group of nineteen young patients with borderline high blood pressure, some received six grams daily of taurine and others a placebo. After seven days, systolic and diastolic blood pressure fell significantly in patients receiving taurine. Epinephrine, which stimulates heartbeat, was blunted by taurine, suggesting that its anti-high-blood-pressure effect may be mediated by reduction in signals from the nervous system.[40]

Calcium—An Important Player in Heart Function

Antioxidant vitamins are not the only nutraceutical weapons against heart disease. The same pill you swallow for heartburn may help your heart in some instances by lowering your blood pressure and cholesterol.

Epidemiological studies have shown an inverse relationship between blood pressure and calcium in the body.[41] Calcium metabolism is regulated by several factors, including the hormones parathyroid and calcitonin, and by vitamin D. There are several ways calcium may lower blood pressure: a reduction in parathyroid hormone production, reduction of calcium concentration within the cell, and an alteration in smooth-muscle contraction.

Your body contains about three pounds of calcium, 99 percent of which provides hardness for bones and teeth. Approximately 1 percent of calcium is distributed in body fluids, where it is essential for normal cell activity. If your body does not get enough calcium from your food, it steals the mineral from your bones.

Calcium carbonate, a commonly used antacid and osteoporosis therapy, appears to have yet another benefit: it helps lower cholesterol among people with mild to moderately elevated levels.

In a study reported in the *Archives of Internal Medicine*, researchers placed fifty-six patients on a low-fat, low-cholesterol diet. The patients were assigned to receive calcium carbonate or a placebo for six weeks, then were switched to the alternate treatment for another six weeks.[42]

The results: compared with the placebo, calcium carbonate

lowered LDL cholesterol (the bad cholesterol) 4.4 percent and raised HDL cholesterol (the good cholesterol) 4.1 percent. Though modest, these improvements still have the potential to reduce heart-disease risk—and without the side effects of some cholesterol-lowering drugs.

Calcium is essential to life, but too much can lead to illness. Thus, a class of drugs called *calcium entry blockers* has dramatically improved medical practice. These drugs are highly effective in treating abnormal heart rhythms and chest pain due to coronary heart disease. When calcium enters a muscle cell, it triggers a contraction. So calcium channels are vital in heart muscle cells for the generation of heartbeats. They also are essential for contraction of smooth-muscle cells in blood-vessel walls. The force of contraction determines blood pressure. If calcium channels admit too much calcium, abnormally fast heart rates and high blood pressures may result. Many diseases seem to be related to calcium overload of the cells.

Calcium chloride, an oral medication, may cause gastrointestinal hemorrhage, nausea, vomiting, thirst, or abdominal pain. Other reactions to calcium medications include frequent urination and kidney stones. Before taking any calcium supplements, it is wise to check with your physician. Calcium must be used cautiously in patients with kidney or heart disease.

What about too little calcium? The percentage of calcium absorption declines progressively with age. Oxalic acid found in rhubarb and spinach, phytic acid in bran and whole cereals, and phosphorus in milk and dairy products may interfere with absorption of calcium. Caffeine and alcoholic beverages may also make calcium channel blockers (medications for cardiovascular problems) less effective.

Calcium can also lower blood pressure, as well as raise it. Monitoring the diets of eighty three- to five-year-olds, researchers at Boston University found that those who took the most calcium had the lowest blood pressure. Specifically, for each 100 mg of the mineral consumed per 1,000 calories, there was an average drop of two millimeters in systolic pressure. Systolic pressure is the top number in a blood pressure reading of, say, 140 over 80 and is a measure of the pressure exerted by the artery walls each time the heart contracts to pump blood out to them.

Calcium may also keep down the blood pressure of pregnant women. A report published in the *The New England Journal of Medicine* suggests that expectant mothers who take calcium supplements have a reduced risk of high blood pressure during the nine-month stretch.

Babies born to mothers who take in plenty of calcium might benefit too. Scientists working in Providence, Rhode Island, discovered that mothers who ate relatively large amounts of food rich in calcium, as well as magnesium and potassium, bore babies whose blood pressure readings were lower than those of other babies throughout the first year of life.[43]

The RDA for calcium is 1,000 mg for adults. The newer reference daily intake is the same. High-calcium foods include dairy products, sardines, and salmon with bones.

Magnesium—The Enzyme Helper

Magnesium is a trace element that exists in tiny amounts in the body. It participates in more than three hundred enzymatic reactions that maintain cell structure. Lower than normal dietary intake of magnesium can be a strong risk factor for high blood pressure, irregular heartbeat, ischemic heart disease, fat-clogged arteries, and sudden cardiac death.

The heart, with its dense membranes and high enzyme activity, is particularly vulnerable to magnesium loss. The epidemiological evidence that populations consuming more magnesium from hard water or diet are less prone to cardiovascular disease and sudden death than those with lower magnesium intakes substantiates the relevance of the animal findings to human atherosclerosis, high blood pressure and its treatment, heart attack, and sudden death.

In one large study, 419 males from ages twenty-five to sixty-five at risk of or with coronary heart disease were assigned to a group receiving a heart and blood-vessel protective diet (group A) or to a group receiving a normal diet (group B). Those in group A received a significantly higher percentage of calories in complex carbohydrates, vegetable proteins, and polyunsaturated fatty acids and had a higher polyunsaturated to saturated fatty-acid ratio compared to group B, which received more saturated fat and cholesterol in their meals. Group A also received more soluble dietary fiber and magnesium, and participants were more physically active than those in group B. Exercise and dietary adherence were tested by a questionnaire. After twelve weeks, results indicated those in group A had a significant decrease in total cholesterol in the blood, LDL cholesterol, and triglycerides and an increase in blood magnesium. No significant changes were noted in group B.[44]

It has long been known that the heart drug digitalis can be toxic and that when that occurs, there is a drop in magnesium and the heart beats irregularly. Scientists have more recently reported that magnesium may prevent arrhythmia, irregular heartbeats, even when digitalis doesn't play a part.[45]

Evidence is accumulating that magnesium is protective for the heart and blood vessels, especially in controlling blood fats and fat uptake by those scavenger cells, the macrophages. Magnesium-deficient diets cause lesions in the arteries and the heart in all animals studied, and diets that are high in saturated fats and deficient in magnesium intensify the heart and blood-vessel lesions, whereas magnesium supplementation helps to prevent them.[46]

Magnesium injections at the time of heart attack reduced deaths by a fourth in a study of more than 2,300 patients British researchers reported in *The Lancet*, June 27, 1992. The magnesium injections also reduced by 25 percent the incidence of heart failure among patients during their stay in a coronary care unit after a heart attack. Magnesium effectiveness in the study was about equal to the highly beneficial results found from aspirin and drugs that dissolve the blood clots that produce heart attacks.

Intravenous magnesium is an effective treatment for irregular heartbeat. In patients with congestive heart failure, low serum magnesium concentrations are associated with frequent arrhythmias and high mortality. This suggests that magnesium administration may decrease the frequency of ventricular arrhythmias in patients with heart failure.[47]

In a second British study involving 2,000 patients, there was a 20 percent reduction in deaths over four years in myocardial infarction (heart attacks due to blood clots) patients treated with magnesium compared with those who did not receive the therapy.[48]

In still another British study undertaken by Dr. Peter Elwood of the Medical Research Council Epidemiology Unit in South Wales, 2,182 men ages forty-five to fifty-nine were followed for ten years. During that time, 152 died of heart attacks. Those who succumbed had an intake of 235 mg/day of magnesium versus 266 mg/day in the survivors. Dietary magnesium can be found in bread, eggs and dairy products, potatoes, and beer.[49]

Researchers suspect that magnesium benefits heart attack victims by helping to widen coronary arteries and improve blood flow. Or it may somehow protect heart muscles from damage. Alternatively, the mineral may help by reducing the incidence of irregular heartbeats or lowering the risk of blood clots.[50]

Another theory is that magnesium competes with calcium, the body's most abundant mineral, which may be involved with irregular heartbeat, as pointed out before.

And again, those old devils, free radicals, enter the scene. Some researchers believe that oxygenation of fat may cause heart problems. It has been found that cholesterol was more vulnerable to damage by oxygen when magnesium in the body was deficient.

Whatever the reason, in a follow-up study of British patients who had received magnesium in heart attacks caused by blood clots, the death rate was reduced by 21 percent and the all-cause mortality rate by 16 percent. The heart attacks had occurred two to seven years before. The researchers who conducted the study concluded that magnesium protects the heart.[51]

Are you deficient in magnesium? It is widely assumed, especially in the United States where food intake is generally ample, that magnesium inadequacy is unlikely. However, the foods that are highest in magnesium—vegetables, especially legumes and dark green, leafy vegetables, fish including shellfish, and whole grains and nuts—are not major constituents of the average American diet. Nutrients that are high in the American diet—such as fat, sugar, salt, vitamin D, inorganic phosphates, proteins, and the more recently supplemental calcium and fiber—all increase dietary intake requirements for magnesium.

Dietary magnesium deficiency is more prevalent than generally suspected and can cause heart and blood vessel lesions leading to disease at all stages of life. The average American diet is deficient in magnesium, especially in the young, in alcoholics, and in those under stress or with diseases or receiving certain drug therapies. Diuretics and digitalis can intensify an underlying magnesium deficiency leading to irregular heartbeats that are refractory unless magnesium is added to the regimen.[52]

If you eat a lot of sweets, you may be low in magnesium. Diabetes mellitus, which causes magnesium wasting, is marked by high blood fats and lesions of small blood vessels that resemble those seen in experiments or with magnesium deficiency. Deficiency may also occur in pregnancy, aging, or stress, both physical and psychological. Diets with enough magnesium to prevent death in rats but not enough for optimal growth caused heart and artery lesions similar to those found in humans.

Vegetarians have a much higher magnesium intake than meat eaters, which could be a factor in their lower incidence of cardiac and vascular disease. High-fat diets increase the need for magnesium.

You may need more magnesium than the 400 mg per day of the recommended daily allowance and the new reference daily intake.

Manganese—The Activator

A mineral first isolated in 1774, it occurs in the earth and in minute quantities in animals, plants, and in water. Manganese salts are activators of enzymes and are necessary to the development of strong bones. They are used as nutrients and as dairy substitutes.

Manganese helps the human body manufacture cholesterol. Diets deficient in manganese have been associated with the development of clogged arteries. Manganese may help to stabilize LDL and HDL cholesterol and blood sugar.[53] Vegetables are high in manganese and so are nuts and whole grains. There are no U.S. government recommended daily allowances for manganese.

Potassium—The Protector

Today's health foods are the staples that mimic those of our prehistoric past: potatoes, bananas, and other fruits and vegetables that are high in potassium and low in sodium. Louis Tobian Jr., M.D., professor of medicine and chief of the hypertension section at the University of Minnesota Hospital and School of Medicine, studied rats prone to develop high blood pressure and strokes. Death rates were reduced by more than 90 percent in rats given extra potassium—even though blood-pressure levels were equal in the groups compared. It appears a high-potassium diet allows brain arteries to carry a usually damaging level of blood pressure without sustaining damage to the arterial walls. There are some suggestive bits of evidence that the same is true in humans. Blacks in the southeastern United States have less potassium in their diets than any other ethnic group in the country, and because the rocky Scottish soil is poor for vegetable growing, the people of Scotland take in less potassium than most Europeans. It may be a coincidence, but both these low-potassium groups have a very high incidence of strokes and heart attacks. However, the Minnesota scientist does not recommend taking potassium supplements. For the general population, he recommends eating foods high in potassium.[54]

If you are healthy, your body contains about nine grams of potassium. Most of it is found inside your cells. Potassium plays an important role in maintaining water balance and acid-base balance. It participates in the transmission of nerve impulses and in the transfer of messages from nerves to muscles. It also acts as a catalyst in carbohydrate and protein metabolism. Potassium is important for the maintenance of normal kidney function. It has a major effect on the heart and all the muscles of the body.

Some diuretics (water pills) commonly used to treat high blood pressure cause potassium to be lost from the body. To compensate, physicians may advise the addition of potassium-rich foods such as bananas, oranges, and dried peas. Other potassium foods include apples, apricots, avocados, beef, blackstrap molasses, brewer's yeast, broccoli, chicken, halibut, peanut butter, potatoes, raisins, sesame seeds, sunflower seeds, tomatoes, tuna, and wheat germ. Avoid peeling foods. Avoid cooking them in large amounts of water.

Potassium supplements should not be taken unless a physician monitors them. If potassium supplements are prescribed, caution is necessary about the amount of potassium in the diet. Potential adverse reactions due to potassium tablets include ulcers, compression of the esophagus, nausea, vomiting, diarrhea, and abdominal discomfort. Also tingling of the hands and feet, listlessness, confusion, weakness, increased blood pressure, and irregular heartbeat.

Chromium vs. Sugar

Chromium occurs in the earth's crust and plays a vital role in the activities of some human enzymes. It helps break down sugar for conversion into energy and in the manufacture of certain fats. It works together with insulin and is essential to the body's ability to use sugar. Traces of chromium are widely available in food. However, chromium deficiency may frequently occur because the soil in the United States contains low levels. Those who are deficient may show symptoms similar to diabetes such as tiredness, mental confusion, and numbness or tingling of the hands and feet. Deficiency may worsen preexisting diabetes, depress growth in children, or contribute to the development of narrowing of the arteries.

A chromium-rich diet may prevent type II diabetes, the non-insulin-dependent form of the disease that starts in adulthood. Richard A. Anderson, a biochemist at the USDA Human Nutrition Research Center in Beltsville, Maryland, has shown that diets high in simple sugars such as glucose and fructose rob the body of chromium, while those high in complex carbohydrates such as pasta preserve it.

The new research builds on data from Anderson's lab showing that chromium supplementation in rats improves glucose tolerance—the ability to transport blood glucose into cells.

Mexican Americans appear to have a strong genetic predisposition to insulin resistance, obesity, and type II diabetes. Chromium picolinate, brewer's yeast and a very low-fat diet are being studied to see if the risk factors for diabetes and heart disease can be lowered in this group.[55]

Chromium is poisonous in large amounts. Ingestion can result in violent gastrointestinal irritation.

Foods that contain chromium include fruits, beer, oysters, liver, egg yolk, potatoes with skin, mushrooms, brewer's yeast, and wines. It is not always absorbed; for example, much of the chromium in potatoes never gets incorporated into the body cells. Furthermore, simple sugars cause the body to excrete large amounts of the mineral.

When fats such as lard, shortening, and oils are refined, then chromium necessary for their proper utilization in the body is largely lost. Butter, however, has plenty of chromium manganese, as well as cobalt, copper, and molybdenum.

Even a balanced diet doesn't provide enough chromium, according to the Carbohydrate Nutrition Laboratory, Human Nutrition Research Center, Beltsville, Maryland. Analysis of the trace element that helps regulate blood sugar shows that the average content of twenty-two balanced diets prepared at the Center was 13.4 micrograms (mcg) per 1,000 calories; it was 15 mcg per 1,000 calories for diets study volunteers prepared at home. At these levels, a person would have to eat between 3,500 and 4,000 calories per day to get the minimum suggested intake of chromium—50 mcg. But the eleven women in one study actually consumed an average of 2,273 calories per day, the eight men, 2,950. These levels are typical for Beltsville Center studies. Breakfast cereals made with whole bran and those fortified with extra vitamins and minerals, including instant oatmeal, provide 10 to 30 mcg of chromium per serving. To get the maximum suggested intake of 200 mcg, people would need a chromium supplement.[56]

Copper and Cholesterol

Diets high in fructose (fruit sugar) significantly increased cholesterol levels, specifically the bad LDL. A small group of men were studied to see if excess dietary fructose would aggravate the signs of copper deficiency. Copper is an integral part of several enzymes that act to defuse free radicals in the body. Fructose metabolism is known to generate free radicals. So the men alternated for seven weeks each between diets low and adequate in copper containing either 20 percent fructose or an equivalent amount of starch. The combination of low copper and excess fructose decreased some of the body's defenses against oxygen-free radicals. Excess fructose alone increased serum cholesterol, regardless of the copper content of the diets. If the findings are repeated in larger studies, it will raise questions about the growing consumption of sugar, which is half fructose, and high-fructose corn syrups regularly added to processed foods and soft drinks. This may increase oxidative stress in the body.[57]

Copper deficiency interferes with the ability of rats' arteries to relax. This may explain why rats develop high blood pressure when fed diets devoid of copper, and it could have implications for people who consistently eat diets with low copper levels. In the last decade, scientists have learned that cells lining the arteries are not passive. When stimulated by certain blood-borne chemicals, these cells release substances that cause the adjacent smooth-muscle cells to either relax or contract. When the muscle cells are signaled to relax, blood pressure goes down. U.S. Department of Agricultural Research Services (ARS) investigators found that copper deficiency decreased the effectiveness of the relaxing factor in the aorta—the largest artery in humans and animals. In a second study, ARS and University of Louisville researchers saw the same response in smaller vessels known as arterioles.[58]

In several studies, copper deficiency had produced adverse cholesterol changes in people and animals. And it's well known that excess zinc interferes with copper metabolism and vice versa because the two metals are similar in their chemical properties. So researchers wanted to test whether the drop in HDL cholesterol that was attributed to high zinc was actually due to copper deficiency induced by high zinc. They used pigs because their circulatory and digestive systems are similar to those of humans. The result: animals exposed to excessive zinc—about thirty-three times normal—had lower HDL.[59]

The daily reference intake for copper is 2 mg. Prior to that, the government had established the safe and adequate daily dietary intake of copper as 20 to 30 mg for an adult.

Foods high in copper are dried yeast, lobster, oysters, almonds, avocado, beans, beef liver, peas, pecans, and walnuts.

Iron—The Good and Bad of It

A certain amount of iron is essential for your health. Hemoglobin, the protein in the red blood cells that ferries oxygen around the bloodstream, can't function without it. Some enzymes use it to speed up crucial reactions inside the cell. New research on the biology of heart disease suggests how iron switches from helper to villain. Free iron floating through the bloodstream unbound to any protein may force oxygen to react with freely circulating LDL cholesterol. These oxidized LDLs settle into artery walls, so the thinking goes, narrowing and sometimes completely clogging them.

Relatively low levels of dietary iron may also contribute to the risk of fat-clogged arteries.[60] Many studies have shown that drinking tea can inhibit absorption of important dietary minerals such as iron. A mineral is more bioavailable the more soluble it is. University of Wisconsin researchers found that iron was totally soluble in instant tea, but only 85 percent soluble in green and oolong teas, and just 69 percent soluble in regular black tea. Tea's effects on calcium were even more pronounced. Calcium was 88 percent soluble in oolong, 66 percent in black, 46 percent in green, and only 35 percent soluble in instant teas.[61]

Foods high in iron are apricots, beans, blackstrap molasses, brewer's yeast, eggs, green, leafy vegetables, nuts, organ meats, sunflower seeds, wheat germ, and whole grains. Steam vegetables instead of boiling. Cook for a short time and avoid excessive water in cooking.

Zinc

This mineral is, like iron, apparently both good and bad for the blood vessels. Saul Powell, Ph.D., Chief of Basic Science Research in North Shore-Cornell's Department of Surgery, has been examining the role of free radicals following injury to the heart caused by insufficient blood flow. Recent work under a grant from The National Heart Institute, indicates that under certain circumstances, Dr. Powell reports, zinc may help decrease heart injury from free radicals and lessen heart rhythm disturbances after cardiac surgery. Zinc appears to work by interfering with the most active oxygen-free radicals.[62]

Chapter 6

PLANTS THAT HELP THE HEART

When you were told as a child to "eat your vegetables—they're good for you," you were given advice that could help protect you against not only cancer but heart and blood-vessel disease.

Nutraceuticals and Diabetes

Diabetes, as pointed out, is one of the major risk factors for cardiovascular disease. Those who have it find it difficult to process sugar. When the substance rises too high in the blood, serious problems may occur, including coma and death.

Absorption of sugar (glucose) is slowed by legumes such as peas and beans and by pectins and gums commonly found in fruit. Pectins are in roots, stems, and fruits of plants and form integral parts of such structures. Gums are the dried exudates from various plants obtained when the bark is cut or other injury is suffered.

Plant pectins and gums are also used as food additives. Pectin-containing foods may reduce the need for insulin or other antidiabetic drugs, according to the Agricultural Research Services of the U.S. Department of Agriculture. Pectins are the main structural substances binding adjacent cell walls in plants. Especially prevalent in the rinds and fleshy parts of citrus and other fruits, they are often used as binders in jams and jellies.

In laboratory tests on various folk medicines reputed to have antidiabetic effects, nine of the twenty-four plants boosted insulin activity from 2 to 4.5 times. The common weed loosestrife *(Lythrum salicaria)* produced the biggest increase. Others were bearberry *(Arctostaphylos uva-ursi)*; hops *(Humulus lupulus)*; lavender *(Lavandula stoechas)*; oregano *(Origanum vulgare)*; sage *(Salvia officinalis)*; dandelion *(Taraxacum officinale)*; sweet bay *(Laurus nobilis)*; and birch *(Betula lenta)*. These substances are generally prepared as teas or tinctures. Sage and oregano are common herbs used in cooking. Hops and lavender are food additives generally recognized as safe. Earlier assays found several spices such as cinnamon and turmeric to be effective.[1]

Other Plants That Lower Blood Sugar

GINSENG. *Panax ginseng* (Asia). *Panax quinquefolius* (North America). *Eleutherococcus senticosus* (Siberian ginseng). Chinese esteem ginseng as an herb of many uses and have been using it in medicine for more than five thousand years. The Chinese and Koreans also use it in combination with chicken soup. The word *panax* comes from the Greek *panakos*, a panacea. Among ginseng's active ingredients are amino acids, essential oils, carbohydrates, peptides, vitamins, minerals, enzymes, and sterols. In the Orient, it is esteemed for its abilities to preserve health, invigorate the system, and prolong life. It is taken in an herbal tea as a daily tonic. North American Indians used ginseng as a love potion. It has been found to normalize high or low blood sugar.

FENUGREEK *(Trigonella foenum graecum)* is one of the oldest known medicinal plants. Use of fenugreek dates back to the ancient Egyptians and Hippocrates. A folk remedy for sore throats and colds, this herb is also reputed to be an aphrodisiac. Fenugreek may also be used against diabetes. In a study done in India involving insulin-dependent diabetics on low doses of insulin, pulverized seeds of fenugreek were shown to reduce blood sugar and other harmful fats. The saponin-containing plant fibers of fenugreek may inhibit the intestinal absorption of cholesterol.

Plant Substances That Lower Cholesterol

High cholesterol is another major risk factor for heart and blood-vessel problems. Certain forms of dietary fiber and other phyto-chemicals may lower blood cholesterol.

OAT FIBER *(Avena sativa)* is an extract used by herbalists to treat anxiety and to aid digestion. It is also used by herbalists to treat general debility and exhaustion. It has been found by modern scientists to lower cholesterol by helping to prevent reabsorption of bile acids from the small intestine. Oat fiber is rich in calcium (*see* page 103) and contains soluble beta-glucan (*see* glossary) for lowering blood cholesterol. Food companies have produced food additives and low-viscosity beverages fortified with soluble beta-glucans from barley or oats, but they are not allowed, as yet, to make a health claim for the products.

PSYLLIUM *(Plantago psyllium)* is a cultivated weed and has been used as a laxative since the early 1930s. It absorbs water and expands to increase bulk and moisture content of the stool to encourage bowel movement. Psyllium contains a soluble fiber that studies have shown can lower cholesterol levels.

General Mills introduced the first psyllium cereal, Benefit, in April 1989. Heartwise was introduced in August of that year. Procter and Gamble Company, which makes the psyllium laxative Metamucil, had asked the FDA to prohibit General Mills from making claims that its cereal could reduce cholesterol. Procter and Gamble contended psyllium was a drug, not a food, and thus the cereal could only be marketed after extensive tests to prove to regulators that it is safe and effective in performing as claimed. Procter and Gamble is barred from making claims about Metamucil's ability to reduce cholesterol.

General Mills withdrew Benefit from the market in December 1989 citing poor sales. Heartwise is the only major brand of cereal containing a significant amount of psyllium, three grams in a one-ounce serving. Bran Buds is made by Kellogg but has less psyllium. Allergic reactions occurred in some people who ate the cereal Heartwise, made by the Kellogg company. Reported reactions ranged from itchy eyes and runny noses to severe difficulty in breathing. In September 1989 the FDA sent a letter to Kellogg raising new questions about its use of psyllium, which has been employed for decades in bulk laxatives such as Metamucil and Fiberall. On October 30, 1990, the FDA published proposed regulations in the Federal Register that would require a warning label on over-the-counter drugs containing water-soluble fibers, including psyllium, which is not absorbed systemically.

Bearing Citrus Fruits Against Heart Disease

We have long been told to drink our orange juice, it's good for us, but citrus fruit may be even better than its reputation. Oranges, lemons, limes, and grapefruit contain particularly high concentrations of vitamin C, and preliminary evidence indicates vitamin C may help lower blood cholesterol and reduce arterial plaque.[2]

At the University of Florida, Gainesville, researchers reported that about three tablespoons of grapefruit pectin a day either in capsule form or as a nontoxic dietary additive can lower blood cholesterol levels an average of almost 8 percent. For sixteen weeks, volunteers with high serum cholesterol levels consumed unidentified capsules with each of their three major meals daily. Roughly half the twenty-seven subjects got capsules containing a placebo; the others got capsules with pure grapefruit pectins. Eight weeks into the experiment, each group was switched to the opposite capsule.

Although the average blood cholesterol reduction for those on pectin was 7.6 percent, levels in some dropped by as much as 19 percent. Moreover, thirteen participants experienced a drop of more than 10 percent in LDL. Agriculture Department scientists reported that vegetable pectins, like those in carrots, appear capable of comparable cholesterol lowering and that fruit is more protective than cereal fiber.

The University of Florida scientists have now introduced into the marketplace a powdered form of grapefruit pectin, ProFibe, to help reduce cholesterol levels. It is designed to be blended into beverages, mixed into baked goods or sprinkled onto fruit salad or cereal as a daily supplement to a low-fat diet.[3]

Prunes Really Do Work

Researchers at the University of California studied the effect of prunes as a source of fiber on blood cholesterol and on fecal output and bile acids. They had forty-one men with mild high cholesterol in the community add twelve prunes a day to their regular diet for four weeks. The men substituted grape juice for the prunes during a four-week control period. Their low-density lipoprotein (LDL), the "bad" cholesterol, was measured after both the prune and the grape-juice periods. They found that prunes lowered cholesterol significantly more effectively than grape juice.[4] Three years later, researchers decided to test prunes in rats with high cholesterol to add evidence to the human findings. The results indicated that prunes lowered cholesterol in the animals 6 percent more than did cellulose fiber.[5]

LECITHIN. From the Greek meaning "egg yolk," lecithin is a natural antioxidant and contains choline, phosphoric acid, fatty acids, and glycerin. Commercially isolated from eggs, soybeans, corn, and egg yolk, it is employed as an antioxidant. Herbalists and some physicians are using it to lower cholesterol.

WHEAT GERM. The golden germ of the wheat is high in vitamin E. About 2.5 percent of the whole wheat kernel, the germ contains about 64 percent of the thiamine, 26 percent of the riboflavin, and 21 percent of the pyridoxine. The germ is used to lower cholesterol and may work because of its high vitamin E content.

Nuts About Walnuts

A six-year study funded by the California Walnut Commission found frequent consumption of nuts was associated with a reduced risk of ischemic (insufficient blood supply) heart disease. Dr. Joan Sabate of Loma Linda University observed that out of 31,208 Seventh-Day Adventists, those who ate nuts at least five times a week had half the risk of fatal heart attacks as those who ate nuts less than once a week. To explore the possible explanations for this finding, researchers at Loma Linda University placed eighteen healthy men on two carefully controlled diets for two months. One was a nut-free version of a standard low-cholesterol diet. The other was nutritionally similar, except that 20 percent of the calories came from walnuts. The walnuts, therefore, were fitted into the recommended cholesterol-lowering diet while maintaining the intake of total dietary fat and calories. The fat in walnuts was offset by lesser amounts of fatty foods, meats, and visible fats, oils, margarine, and butter. Half of the volunteers ate the diet with nuts for a month while the others ate the nonnuts version. Then the two groups switched diets. On the nonnut diets, the volunteers' cholesterol fell 6 percent. On the walnut diet, the volunteers' cholesterol declined an additional 12 percent. The conclusion of the Loma Linda University researchers was the blood-fat profile was favorably modified in normal men who ate the walnuts as part of their regimen.[6] While the study was criticized by many scientists because it was sponsored by those interested in promoting walnuts, the nuts do contain omega-3 oils, the same oils in fish that are said to protect the heart (*see* fish oils, page 135).

Nature's Diuretics

Diuretics are substances used to remove excess fluids from the body by increasing the flow of urine, and reducing blood volume. The heart, therefore, doesn't have to work as hard. Among herbs that are considered diuretics are:

BARLEY (*Hordeum vulgare*) contains seeds that are used by Chinese herbalists as an anti-inflammatory diuretic.

CELERY SEED *(Apium graveolens)*, also called smallage, was one of the first condiments to reach the country of the Gauls and Franks. It was introduced into northern Europe by military men upon returning home from Roman conquests. Celery seed is used by herbalists as a diuretic and blood cleanser. Modern scientists reported in 1992 what herbalists had known for a long time: celery lowers blood pressure. In Europe, celery seed is a common treatment for gout and rheumatism. Some persons are allergic to celery.

CLEAVERS *(Galium aparine)*, also called catchweed, goosegrass, or clivers, is a native of Europe, Asia, and North America. The Greeks called it *philanthropon* because they considered its clinging showed a love of mankind. The whole herb is used by herbalists to treat kidney and bladder problems. It has diuretic properties.

CUCUMBER *(Cucumis sativus)* is used by herbalists as an effective diuretic, and modern scientists are now studying its effect on cholesterol.

DANDELION *(Taraxacum officinale)*, also called blowball, clock, gowan's milk, priest's-crown, and wiggers, is native to Britain and is believed to have derived its name from the Norman *dent de lion*, referring to its sharply toothed leaves. It was reputedly so effective as a diuretic, it was nicknamed piss-a-bed in the United States and Britain. It is rich in beta-carotene (*see* glossary) and lecithin. Among the substances in dandelions are tannin and inulin (*see* both in glossary) and sugars. In 1992, the FDA proposed a ban on *Taraxacum officinale* in oral menstrual drug products because it has not been shown to be safe and effective for its stated claims.

FLAX *(Linum usitatissimum)*, also called linseed or lint bells, is a native of the Mediterranean countries. It was cultivated in Mesopotamia in prehistoric times and was widely grown in ancient Egypt and has been reported to have been used in medicine as far back as the beginning of recorded history. Flaxseed contains important demulcent and emollient qualities that soothe mucous membranes and skin. Flax is combined with other herbs today by herbalists for the treatment of kidney stones and as a diuretic, and as a laxative.

GERMANDER *(Teucrium chamaedrys)* is a member of the mint family and has been used by herbalists as far back as Hippocrates and Pliny. It is a diuretic and stimulant and has been used in the treatment of excess fluid due to heart failure. Cases of liver toxicity have been reported to the Centers for Disease Control due to its use in tea or in capsules.

HOLLY *(Ilex aquifolium, Ilex opaca)* is a small evergreen, the berries of which were used as a diuretic.

HOLY THISTLE *(Cnicus benedictus)*, also called blessed thistle or cardin, is an annual herb. The plant is a native of the south of Europe and is cultivated in gardens all over the world. Its use in medicine has been recorded since A.D. 100. Once believed to be a panacea, it has been credited with reducing excess fluid.

HORSE CHESTNUT *(Aesculus hippocastanum)* is traditionally used by herbalists to reduce fever. It contains *escin*, widely used in Europe as an anti-inflammatory agent for a variety of conditions including varicose veins. Escin has also been found to be a powerful diuretic.

JUNIPER *(Juniperus communis)*, also called viscum and mistletoe, has berries used by herbalists to treat urinary problems. It acts directly on the kidneys, according to herbalists, stimulating the flow of urine. Juniper berries and extracts are in several over-the-counter drugstore diuretic and laxative preparations. In fact, gin was created in the 1500s by a Dutch pharmacist using juniper berries to sell as an inexpensive diuretic. The berries have long been used by herbalists to treat gout caused by high uric acid in the blood. The berries are high in vitamin C. Juniper is also used to lower cholesterol and to treat arthritis. Large amounts may irritate the kidneys. The FDA issued a notice in 1992 that juniper has not been shown to be safe and effective as claimed in OTC digestive-aid products and oral menstrual drugs.

PUMPKIN SEED *(Cucurbita pepo)* has a reputation among herbalists as being a nonirritating diuretic. Among its ingredients are fatty oil, albumin, lecithin, phytosterol, and alcohol.

TARRAGON *(Artemisia dracunculus)* is a perennial herb native to southern Europe and parts of Asia and cultivated in the United States. The name is derived from *dracunculus,* meaning "little dragon," and it is a member of the wormwood family. In medicine it is employed as a diuretic.

XANTHINE is a chemical that occurs in animal organs, blood, urine, yeast, potatoes, coffee beans, and tea. First isolated from gallstones. Xanthines are in chocolate and many drugs, such as aminophylline and caffeine *(see* both in glossary). They stimulate the brain, heart, and muscles. They act as a diuretic and dilate the heart's blood vessels.

YARROW *(Achillea millefolium),* also called milfoil or soldier's woundwort. A strong-scented, spicy, wild herb, it is used in commercial food and beverage flavorings and in herbal medicine as a diuretic. It is also used to cause sweating and is reputedly anti-inflammatory. Yarrow may cause a sensitivity to sunlight and artificial light, in which the skin breaks out and swells.

Plants That Reputedly Lower Blood Pressure

High blood pressure is another major risk factor for cardiovascular disease. Folk doctors have used plants to lower it, and in fact, some of our most popular antihypertensive drugs are derived from plants. The following are plants used in traditional and, some of them, in modern medicine:

CALENDULA *(Calendula officinalis)*, also called pot marigold, has flower heads with essential oil containing carotenoids, saponin, resin, and bitter principle *(see* all in glossary). Marigold flowers have been reported to lower blood pressure. It may be harmful if taken internally by pregnant women.

CAYENNE *(Capsicum annuum)*, also called red or green pepper, is derived from the pungent fruit of a plant. It originated in Central and South America where it was used by the natives for many diseases, including diarrhea and cramps. It contains capsaicin *(see* glossary), carotenoids, flavonoids, essential oil, and vitamin C. Cayenne is a stimulant, astringent, laxative, and antispasmodic. Cayenne is not irritating when uncooked. It is reported by herbalists to lower blood pressure and serum cholesterol. Modern scientists report that cayenne prevents the absorption of cholesterol.

CHERVIL *(Anthriscus cerefolium)* is an herb of the carrot family native to Europe. Used as a restorative for the elderly, it was called cerefolium because it was said to be a powerful brain stimulant. The juice is used for edema. An herbal infusion is made to lower blood pressure. In herbal medicine, *infusion* means the steeping in boiled water of the softer parts of plants such as leaves, flowers, and twigs and the juice from leaves.

CHRYSANTHEMUM *(Chrysanthemum sinense)*, also called *ye ju* or corn marigold. It belongs to a large family of perennial herbs thought to have originated in Asia. A tea made from this flower is used to lower blood pressure.

EPIMEDIUM *(Epimedium grandiflorum)*, also called lusty goatherb, is an herb widely used in Chinese medicine. It contains benzene, sterols, tannin, palmitic acid, linolenic acid, oleic acid, and vitamin E *(see* all in glossary). It is used to treat kidney dysfunction and high blood pressure.

EVENING PRIMROSE *(Oenothera biennis)* is also called sundrops. The leaves and oil from the seed are used by herbalists to treat liver and kidney dysfunctions. The oil has a high content of linoleic acid (GLA), an essential polyunsaturated fatty acid that is converted into prostaglandins (*see* glossary) and hormones. It is used as a tonic for inflammatory conditions. It is said to relieve high blood pressure, and anxiety associated with inflammatory conditions. It also reputedly lowers cholesterol.

RAUWOLFIA is a small shrub native to the Orient, where it has been used for medicinal purposes for hundreds of years. The active ingredients are usually in the root. Rauwolfia contains the basics for many widely used modern drugs including *reserpine, serpasil,* and *yohimbine.* Rauwolfia extracts work by blocking nerve signals that trigger constriction of blood vessels. Rauwolfia is used in pharmaceuticals to treat mild to moderate high blood pressure. It has many potential adverse reactions including mental confusion, depression, drowsiness, nervousness, nightmares, headache, a drop in blood pressure upon rising from a sitting or prone position, faintness, dry mouth, stuffy nose, glaucoma, hypersecretion of gastric acid, nausea, vomiting, GI bleeding, skin rash, impotence, and weight gain. Rauwolfia may predispose patients taking digitalis to irregular heartbeats. When given with MAO inhibitors (*see* glossary), it may cause excitability and high blood pressure. Alcohol and other central-nervous-system depressants including antihistamines will add to the depressant effects of rauwolfia.

RUE *(Ruta graveolens)* is also called garden or German rue. It is an evergreen shrub. The oil is a spice agent obtained from the fresh aromatic blossoming plants grown in southern Europe and the Orient. Rue is mentioned in the Talmud as a valuable medicine. In the sixth century A.D., it was used to treat gout. The plant is mentioned in more than thirty-five prescriptions in a fourteenth-century manuscript for almost every known disease, including tuberculosis, and for itches, boils, and ulcers. It was used to ward off pestilence during the Great Plague and to combat witches. It was considered good for toadstool poisoning, the stings of hornets, bees, and wasps, and the bites of serpents. It is still used in folk medicine in an herbal tea for high blood pressure, to reduce swelling, and to increase local circulation. May be toxic and causes sensitivity to light.

VERATRUM *(Veratrum viride)* is also called American hellebore or Indian poke. Herbalists used the dried rhizome and roots of the plant, which grows in North America, to lower blood pressure. *See* hellebore (page 128).

Plants That Act Upon the Heart

The folk doctors were way ahead of Western medicine when it came to using plants to help the heart. Among those in use in both folk potions and modern pharmaceuticals:

BORAGE OIL is from the seed of the borage plant, a wildflower that has been used as food for thousands of years. The oil is one of three major sources of GLA, the acronym for *gamma-linolenic acid*—a prostaglandin/eicosanoid precursor. Prostaglandins work much like hormones. GLA is similar in chemical structure to a better-known prostaglandin precursor, EPA, the active ingredient in fish oil. The body creates GLA, a type of prostaglandin that may be deficient. The prostaglandins created from GLA are identified as a factor in widening blood vessels and helping to keep blood platelets from sticking together, in the inhibition of cholesterol production, in circulation improvement, and in strengthening the immune system. GLA is a part of the metabolic process that begins with linoleic acid, the most common dietary essential fatty acid, found in corn, soybean, sunflower, and many other common vegetable oils. To be converted to a prostaglandin, linoleic acid must be converted to GLA by enzymes. Many aspects of our lifestyles may reduce the efficiency of this conversion to GLA. These include saturated and trans fatty acids, aging, stress, illness, alcohol abuse, diabetes, and premenstrual syndrome. GLA supplementation may bypass the negative effects of these enzyme blockers and may enhance prostaglandin formation.

CALAMUS *(Acorus calamus)*, also called sweet flag or sweet sedge, has a rhizome that contains essential oil, mucilage, glycosides, amino acid, and tannins *(see* all in glossary). Calamus root is an ancient Indian and Chinese herbal medicine used to treat irregular heart rhythm, low blood pressure, and lack of mental focus. Native Americans would chew the root to enable them to run long distances with increased stamina.

FO-TI *(Polygonum multiforum)*, also called *ho shou wu,* is one of the most popular herbs in China. It is believed to increase fertility and maintain strength and vigor. Modern studies in humans have shown *fo-ti* can reduce high blood pressure, high blood cholesterol, and the incidence of heart disease among people prone to these conditions.

FOXGLOVE *(Digitalis purpurea)* is found wild in the English countryside and along the west coast of the United States. It is the plant from which the heart drug digitalis *(see* glossary) is derived. It is often cited as an example of an herbal medicine that became a widely used prescription medication. A Welsh woman used it to treat dropsy, fluid retention caused by congestive heart failure. An English botanist, Dr. William Withering, observed this use in 1775 and isolated digitalis from the leaves. Digitalis, the active principal of foxglove, is widely used today as a stimulant for heart failure, as a diuretic, and as a heart tonic in chronic heart disorders. Prior to the discovery of its effect on the heart, foxglove was used in folk medicine as an expectorant, in epilepsy, and to reduce swollen glands. The plant was used externally to heal wounds and reduce swellings. The herb also contains a deadly poison and should be used only under proper medical supervision.

GINGER *(Zingiber officinale)* is native to Asia but cultivated in many parts of the tropics. Hippocrates used it as a medicine. It is an important herb for low blood sugar. Some studies have shown that gingerroot is a mild stimulant for the heart and brain and may even help ease learning. Modern studies have shown that ginger inhibits prostaglandins (*see* glossary), as do NSAIDs (non-steroidal anti-inflammatory drugs such as ibuprofen), and thus reduces inflammation. They concluded that the use of ginger in folk medicine was effective because of a constituent, zingiberene. Scientists have also found that ginger slows the formation of platelet clumping and thus may help to prevent blood clots. Such functional characteristics of ginger have important meanings for human health because ginger is a daily foodstuff.

HELLEBORE *(Veratrum viride, Helleborus niger)*, also called green hellebore, Indian poke, itchweed, veratrum, and Christmas rose, was employed by ancient physicians to treat insanity. The doctors believed that patients brought to near death by the medication would be shocked into sanity. Hellebore is used by homeopathic physicians as a means to slow heartbeats. Black hellebore is used to treat fluid retention associated with heart failure. Hellebore is toxic and can cause severe nausea and extreme depression of the nervous system.

LILY OF THE VALLEY *(Convallaria majalis)*, also called May lily, May blossom, or convallaria, grows wild in woodlands. The powdered root is used to slow the heartbeat. It is used by herbalists to reduce fluid retention. It contains cardiac glycosides (*see* glossary) similar to digitalis, a drug that strengthens contractions of the heart muscle and promotes the elimination of fluid from the body.

MOTHERWORT *(Leonurus cardiaca)*, also called heart wort, mother weed, mother herb, heart gold, heart heal, and lion's-tail, is used worldwide in folk medicine for the heart due to its glycoside (*see* glossary) content. Motherwort has been used to treat high blood pressure, and as a sedative and antispasmodic. It reputedly calms palpitations and generally improves heart function.

PURSLANE has been identified by Norman Salem Jr., a lipid bio-chemist with the National Institute of Alcohol Abuse, Bethesda, Maryland, as the richest known omega-3 source in the world of leafy greens. Purslane is a weedy herb sometimes thrown into salads.[7] Salem and his collaborator, Artemis P. Simopoulos of the American Association for World Health, Washington, D.C., found range-fed chickens at one Greek farm voluntarily feast on purslane. Just one yolk from a large-sized egg produced by these chickens contains roughly 300 mg of omega-3 fatty acids, the same amount contained in a standard fish-oil capsule and ten times more than what's found in a typical U.S. supermarket egg. The eggs from purslane hens lack the fish taste and smell of eggs from hens feeding on fish oil. The Mediterranean diet that seems so effective in preventing heart attacks contains high amounts of alpha-linolenic acid, which is also found in purslane.

ROSEMARY (*Rosmarinus officinalis*) contains *rosmaricine*, the derivatives of which possess smooth-muscle stimulant activity and some analgesic properties. The herb possesses essential oils that reputedly calm and soothe irritated nerves and upset stomach. Rosemary is also high in minerals such as calcium, magnesium, phosphorous, sodium, and potassium. Rosemary contains more than a dozen antioxidants. In fact, Greek fishermen often cover their fish with rosemary to retard spoilage.

RUTIN, found in many plants, especially buckwheat and eucalyptus, is believed to protect blood vessels.

STROPHANTHUS (*Strophanthus chlorzoxazone* or *Strophanthus hispidus*) is a shrub native to Africa and Asia. It was originally used by natives in Tanganyika and Nyassa for arrow poison. Strophanthus is a heart stimulant. Its action is similar to digitalis's, but its effect is quicker. Its action is less predictable than that of digitalis. Because its effect is more rapid than digitalis's, it is being studied for use during emergency heart failure, given intravenously.

Relax and Eat Well—The Three Newly Recognized Old Heart Nutraceuticals

The common dietary substances green tea, wine, and garlic have been found by modern scientists to have an overall beneficial effect on the heart.

Green Tea

Take a green-tea break instead of a coffee break and you'll not only relax, you may help your heart. Green tea has been cultivated in Japan for about a thousand years. It has been found to have the following benefits for the cardiovascular system:

- **Blood-Pressure Controlling Action:** An enzyme in the blood, *angiotensin 2 (ACE)*, induces sodium retention and constriction of peripheral blood vessels, raising blood pressure. Substances in tea, *polyphenols*—particularly *catechins*—have been proven to inhibit at fairly low concentrations the activity of the ACE enzyme. In experiments, spontaneously hypertensive rats (SHR) show elevated blood pressure similar to that of humans. When SHR rats were fed catechins, their blood pressure was significantly lower when compared with those SHR rats not fed catechins. The high-pressure rats almost all succumb to strokes. Those on the catechins, however, had an extended life span of more than fifteen months, indicating the apparent delay of strokes. In human trials, similar suppression of blood pressure was observed. Large-scale epidemiological data in northern Japan showed that the more daily cups of green tea consumed, the less the occurrence of strokes.
- **Cholesterol-Controlling Action:** A high-fat diet increases the blood cholesterol level of rats. In particular bad LDL cholesterol increases excessively while good HDL cholesterol decreases. However the addition of tea catechins in a high-fat diet suppresses the increase of LDL cholesterol considerably and prevents the lowering of HDL cholesterol.

In human trials where tea catechins were administered to volunteers with marginally high cholesterol, a similar tendency was observed.[8]

Have Some Wine With Your Tea?

The catechins in tea are phenols, and if you want to add some wine to your tea break, you'll be increasing your intake of potentially cholesterol-lowering substances.

"The French paradox" alludes to the low incidence of heart disease in France despite a cuisine rich in butter, cream, and cheese. A study reported in *The Lancet* offers an explanation—the chemicals that give wine its color.

The compounds—*phenols*—are antioxidants like vitamins C and E and beta-carotene. As pointed out many times so far in this book, antioxidants reportedly clean up free radicals, toxic particles formed as cells that use oxygen.

A comparison of wine, fruits, and other sources of phenolic compounds shows that wine is a particularly rich source of these substances. When the researchers added phenols from red wine to human low-density lipoprotein (LDL) in laboratory experiments, they found the phenolic compounds in the wine significantly inhibited the oxidation of the so-called bad LDL cholesterol by 98 percent in one experiment and 60 percent in another.[9] Oxidation of LDL cholesterol is believed to promote coronary artery disease. In fact, the phenol compounds were much more effective at blocking this process than was vitamin E. That's not only how red wine acts to protect the heart, however. Research from France, Wales, and the United States has shown that wine helps to prevent blood platelets from becoming sticky.[10]

Garlic—From Vampires to Blood Vessels

GARLIC *(Allium sativum)* is a member of the onion family. It was cultivated in Egypt from earliest times and has been known in China more than two thousand years ago. Garlic contains lots of potassium, fluorine, sulfur, phosphorous, and vitamins A and C.

Many modern studies have reported that garlic can lower blood serum cholesterol and triglyceride levels, decrease the ability of platelets to clot, and possibly to lower high blood pressure. It is theorized that garlic expands blood vessels. It has also been reported in the scientific literature that garlic may decrease nitrosamine formation (a powerful cancer-causing agent created when nitrates combine with natural amines in the stomach), modulate cancer-cell multiplication, increase immunity, and protect the body against ionizing radiation. Such research reports have been criticized by some scientists, who say that it is difficult to do double-blind studies (in which neither the subjects nor the scientists know which compound contains the placebo and which contains the garlic) when the odor is a dead giveaway.

Dr. James Duke, an economic botanist at the U.S. Department of Agriculture, is studying epidemiological evidence that garlic may help reduce the incidence of blood clots.

Dr. David Kritchevsky, of the Wistar Institute, reported that ingestion of a diet containing 2 percent garlic led to a slight lowering of cholesterol in rats. A significant research finding in recent years was that garlic may enhance the regression of fatty lesions in rabbits. Kritchevsky cited a study on coronary heart disease patients in which garlic led to reduction in serum cholesterol, low-density lipoprotein, and very low-density lipoprotein (VLDL) levels and to an increase in serum high-density lipoprotein levels. However, he cautioned that other studies have shown no effect of garlic on serum parameters.

Nilofer Qureshi of Advanced Medical Research in Madison, Wisconsin, fed aged garlic extract and s-allyl cysteine (a sulfur compound derived from garlic) to sixty chickens. After four weeks of daily garlic supplements at doses as high as 8 percent of body weight, the garlic-supplemented chickens showed cholesterol decreases of much as 30 percent when compared to six chickens receiving no garlic.[11] Qureshi said the cholesterol-lowering effect of dietary commercial garlic powder, garlic extract, garlic oil, or allyl cysteine from garlic in chickens was due to a decrease in the manufacture of cholesterol caused by inhibition of a liver enzyme (HMG-CO-A). The most potent inhibitor was reported to be the aged garlic extract. However, it is not clear which component of the aged garlic is responsible for the inhibition. One component of aged garlic extract, ajoene, was reported by Rafael Apitz-Castro (Instituto Venezolano de Investigaciónes Científicas, Venezuela) to prevent blood-platelet clumping during the dialysis of dog blood.[12]

Arun Bordia, Tagore Medical College, India, presented the results of a study of 432 heart-disease patients in India. Subjects received in milk each morning the juice squeezed from six to ten grams of garlic. The most significant effect was a 50 percent reduction in mortality in the second year and a 60 percent reduction in the rate of heart attacks by the third year. He also reported decreases in blood pressure, lower blood cholesterol, increased energy, increased appetite, and a decreased incidence of joint pain in the group fed garlic. However, some of the participants dropped out of the study for a variety of reasons including odor, burning in the urine, and gastrointestinal irritation.[13]

Dr. Benjamin Lau at Loma Linda University is currently investigating garlic in treating high blood pressure.

Anti-blood-clot factors have been found in garlic and onion.[14] Thrombosis—artery- and vein-clogging blood clots—is a common cause of heart attacks and strokes as well as fatal blood clots to the lung. The clot forms in a blood vessel because the blood platelets clump, which is mediated with the hormonelike substances prostaglandins. As we age, certain prostaglandin formation is depressed, and a wayward blood clot is easily formed in a blood vessel.

In a meta-analysis (overview of several studies) of garlic and its effect on blood fats, researchers at the Radcliffe Infirmary in Oxford, England, found that one-half to one clove of garlic a day can reduce total cholesterol by 8 percent and triglycerides by 13 percent, and the effect persists for at least six months.[15]

Chapter 7

Fish, Fat, and the Healthy Heart

Your mother may have told you fish is brain food, but it is also good for your heart. Fatty fish and marine mammals are excellent sources of omega-3 fatty acids, proven to inhibit production of prostaglandins, hormones that, among other things, modulate cell metabolism.

A twenty-year study of the effects of fish consumption on the health of 852 middle-aged men in Zutphen, the Netherlands, found that death from coronary heart disease was more than 50 percent lower for those men who ate thirty grams (one ounce of fish per day) than among those who did not eat fish.[1]

The Zutphen study supports the findings of a previous study in which the low death rate from coronary heart disease among Greenland Eskimos was attributed to an average per capita fish consumption of four hundred grams per day.

Since the publication in 1985 of the Zutphen study in *The New England Journal of Medicine*, omega-3 fatty acids have been used to help reduce cholesterol and are now being studied as a possible treatment for other prostaglandin-related disorders such as rheumatoid arthritis and multiple sclerosis.[2]

Additional information on the effectiveness of omega-3 fatty acids in reducing cardiovascular disease comes from the 1973 to 1982 Multiple Risk Factor Intervention Trial (MR/FIT) of coronary heart disease prevention in American men. Therese A. Dolecek, Ph.D., of the Bowman Gray School of Medicine, Wake Forest

University, Winston-Salem, North Carolina, reported there were nearly one-third (31 percent) fewer deaths from cardiovascular disease among 1,250 men in the study whose diet included omega-3 fatty acids, amounting to the equivalent of two to three meals of fish per week, compared with 1,300 men who ate no fish at all.

In still another study, Michael Burr, M.D., Medical Research Council, Epidemiology Unit, Cardiff, Wales, reported data from the first prospective intervention trial to look at the effects of dietary fat, fish, and fiber. He and his colleagues found that in subjects with a history of heart attacks, there was a 29 percent reduction in mortality from all causes during a two-year period among those advised to eat fish compared with those who were not given this advice. The fish-eating group ate about three hundred grams of fish per week. Burr says, "Compliance was reasonably good and there was little tendency to eat fish among those not advised to do so."

Why are fish oils nutraceuticals for the heart?

A tremendous amount of research is in progress to find out. Some explanations have already surfaced. Forty percent of patients dying of heart attacks do so because of arrhythmia, irregular heartbeat. In animal studies, fish oil reduces the vulnerability of the heart to develop arrhythmias. Omega-3 fatty acids reduce cardiac-muscle sensitivity to catecholamines, body chemicals that are involved in starting the heart beating irregularly.[3]

Fish oil also seems to reduce the stickiness of blood platelets and to reduce fibrinogen, both of which play a part in the formation of blood clots.[4]

Fish oil, in addition, reduces triglycerides, fatty substances that some researchers consider to be a precursor of low-density lipoproteins (the bad cholesterol). The addition of omega-3 fatty acids to a high saturated-fat diet reduced after-meal blood fats.[5] Triglyceride is the fat present in blood plasma, which, in association with cholesterol, forms the plasma lipids (fats). When present in excessive amounts in the plasma, it is related to the occurrence of coronary heart disease.

In a four-week study of twenty patients with high blood levels of triglycerides, a diet containing fish oil caused total plasma cholesterol and triglyceride levels to fall in every patient. By contrast, a diet containing vegetable oil was much less effective. Indications are that polyunsaturated fatty acids found in fish oil have a special potentially therapeutic effect on triglyceride metabolism.[6]

The effect of fish oil on triglycerides and cholesterol may be the answer to why fish oil has been found to help keep newly opened coronary arteries clear. From 30 to 45 percent of coronary arteries opened by balloon angioplasty will narrow again within six months. Various drugs have been tested for their ability to prevent artery reclosure (restenosis). An analysis of studies on fish-oil supplements published in the *Archives of Internal Medicine* in 1993 indicates that these omega-3 fatty acids can reduce reclosure rates by 14 percent. Patients took a daily dose of six to eighteen fish-oil pills.[7] If omega-3 oils can keep the arteries open after procedures, it is a big advantage not only to the patient but to society. The average coronary bypass costs $25,000 and the average angioplasty, $10,000. Eating the equivalent of half a pound of salmon a day or taking omega-3 fish-oil capsules would cost less than $1,000 a year.[8] In a large Canadian study in 1994, however, fish oil proved ineffective in keeping the opened blood passage from reclosing.

Fish oil can lower blood pressure. It operates much like a low-sodium diet, according to Constance Kies of the University of Nebraska at Lincoln, by increasing urine output. It reduces the volume of fluids pressing against the inside of blood-vessel walls. People on fish oil in her study increased their urine output by roughly 10 percent, and unlike most diuretics, fish oil did not increase the excretion of potassium, important in regulating blood pressure. Kies suspects the changes may be traced to the regulation of kidney function by eicosanoids—a class of "biological activators" that can speed or slow many bodily activities.[9]

In addition, fish are a source of B vitamins, calcium, magnesium, chloride, potassium, phosphorus, sulfur, fluoride, selenium, copper, zinc, and other trace elements in amounts similar to meats. Only iron content is lower than in meats. Saltwater fish are the richest source of iodine in food, and some studies suggest iodine may reduce the risk of breast cancer.[10] Iodine is essential for proper thyroid function, which plays a part in the body's processing of cholesterol as well as the rhythm of the heart.

A number of studies have now shown that fish contain nutraceuticals that:

- Decrease blood pressure in persons with normal and moderately high blood pressure.
- Decrease blood viscosity.
- Decrease blood-vessel leakage in insulin-dependent diabetics.
- Decrease blood triglycerides.
- Decrease vascular response to norepinephrine, a hormone that stimulates.
- Decrease irregular heartbeats.
- Decrease cardiac toxicity of cardiac glycosides (sugars).
- Decrease platelet stickiness.
- Increase platelet survival.[11, 12]

The consumption of as little as one or two fish dishes per week may be of preventive importance in relation to coronary heart disease.[13] Fish-oil supplements, on the other hand, do carry a small but potentially serious risk of bleeding complications and can cause gastrointestinal side effects, such as nausea and diarrhea, so they should not be taken in large amounts or over a long period of time without medical supervision.

Fat in the Fire

What about other fats? Which ones are helpful to the heart and which ones are harmful? Fat is a component of most foods of plant or animal origin and is an essential part of the diet. It is not only a major source of energy, but fat also plays a key role as a carrier of the fat-soluble vitamins A, D, E, and K. Dietary fat also supplies the body with essential fatty acids.

Fatty acids are the basic chemical units of fat. They can be either saturated, monounsaturated, or polyunsaturated, depending on how many hydrogen atoms they hold. All dietary fats are mixtures of these three types of fatty acids, but they vary in the amount of each they contain. These three types of fatty acids influence cholesterol levels in our blood as follows:

SATURATED FATTY ACIDS tend to raise blood cholesterol levels. They are found in the largest amounts in meat and dairy products, but also in some vegetable oils, including coconut and palm-kernel oil.

MONOUNSATURATED FATTY ACIDS are found in varying amounts in both plant and animal fat. Olive oil, peanut oil, some margarines, and vegetable shortening tend to be high in monounsaturated fatty acids. Research has shown that substituting monounsaturated fat for saturated fat reduces blood cholesterol.

POLYUNSATURATED FATTY ACIDS tend to lower blood cholesterol levels. They are found mainly in fat of foods from plants. Safflower, sunflower, corn, soybean, and cottonseed oils contain large amounts of polyunsaturated fatty acids.

Cholesterol is a fatlike substance found in all foods of animal origin (meat and dairy products), but not in foods from plants. Some cholesterol is needed by the body, but too much can build up in arteries leading to heart disease, heart attack, or stroke.

Fake Fat—Negative Nutraceuticals

Fat substitutes have been called *negative nutraceuticals*. Since fat is so bad for us, especially those of us who want to lose weight and/or lower our blood cholesterol, fat substitutes can serve as nutraceuticals. The fat replacers developed to date generally fall into one of three categories:

* carbohydrate based
* protein based
* fat based

Most of the low-fat products on the market at this writing use carbohydrates such as cellulose, maltodextrin, or gums. Carbohydrates have been used as food additives for many years as thickeners and stabilizers. These ingredients are effective fat replacers in many formulated foods, but they are not suitable for frying foods.

Protein-based fat replacers received a boost in 1990 when the FDA gave a *generally recognized as safe* (GRAS) approval to microparticulated protein for use in frozen desserts. Employed primarily in frozen and refrigerated products, protein-based fats are also not suitable for frying foods.

Vinegar and Rice-Bran Oil

Vinegar and rice-bran oil could become the salad dressing of choice for people who want to lower their cholesterol, substituting for saturated fat in the diet. University of Massachusetts studies found the oil is unique in that it contains all three substances—tocotrienol, oryzanol, and ample amounts of plant sterols—known to either reduce circulating cholesterol or to protect it from being oxidized to a more damaging form. Researchers fed monkeys about two tablespoons of rice-bran oil alone and in blends with other oils, accounting for 35 percent of their total daily calories as fat. Rice-bran oil alone produced the greatest reductions in cholesterol—up to 40 percent when the animals' levels were highest after eating a typical U.S. diet. Only the damaging LDL cholesterol dropped, while the beneficial HDL cholesterol stayed constant or rose. A second study confirmed the findings, showing that LDL cholesterol drops 1 percent for every 1 percent rice-bran oil substituted in the diet. Many grocery and health food stores carry rice-bran oil.

The Heart-Healthy Diet

GET YOUR SHARE OF ANTIOXIDANTS. Antioxidants such as the vitamins and some of the plants mentioned in the chapters dealing with the heart are excellent nutraceuticals, but as with any medication that works, they do have side effects. If you include fruits and vegetables in your diet, you will provide yourself with chemopreventive agents that will help to protect your heart and blood vessels. In a study reported in the *American Journal of Cardiology*, researchers placed more than six hundred men at risk of heart disease on the American Heart Association's Prudent Diet. One group, however, was instructed to eat more fruits, vegetables, and complex carbohydrates—a strategy that resulted in a high intake of soluble fiber and antioxidants and a lower intake of saturated fat and cholesterol. Both groups were advised to exercise regularly and to do some stress-reduction activity such as yoga or meditation. At the end of six months, the men on the enhanced diet had greater reductions in heart-disease risk factors: total cholesterol dropped 13 percent; low-density lipoprotein, 17 percent; triglycerides, 19 percent; blood sugar levels, 19 percent; and blood pressure, 11.5/6.2 mm Hg.[14] The use of the substances in larger doses as medication should be done only under a knowledgeable physician's guidance.[15]

EAT FISH AT LEAST TWICE A WEEK. It's a wise choice if you want to lower fat in your diet and ingest the omega-3 fatty acids that have been found in recent studies to be potential nutraceuticals for the heart.

TRY A MEATLESS ALTERNATIVE FOR A FEW MEALS PER WEEK. Vegetables with beans and legumes give you needed protein as well as the other nutraceutical benefits described in this chapter. Of course, include fruit.

CHANGE YOUR OIL. Choose liquid vegetable oils that are highest in unsaturated fat, such as canola, safflower, sunflower, olive, sesame, and soybean, in cooking and in salads.

GO FOR FIBER. Fruits and vegetables and grains will give you the fiber that can help lower cholesterol and provide other benefits.

SUBSTITUTES CAN HELP. If you are vulnerable to heart problems, substitute low-fat or nonfat yogurt for sour cream in recipes or as toppings, and substitute low-fat sour creams, mayonnaises, and margarines for the regular versions.

Chapter 8

NUTRACEUTICALS THAT
BOOST IMMUNITY

Fighting Infections From the Common Cold to AIDS

It wasn't so long ago that scientists first realized that we have an immune system just as we have nervous, gastrointestinal, and cardiovascular systems. In the 1960s, they found the immune system is a widely distributed whole-body network that includes the lymph nodes, spleen, tonsils, thymus gland, bone marrow, and white blood cells. These organs are in total communication with each other, and they are, in ways as yet not fully understood, orchestrated.

When the system is operating at its optimal level, our defenses are in harmony and we are protected against all sorts of potential enemies from the common cold to cancer. If our immune instruments don't play in concert, we become ill. If one or more elements overreacts or plays an off note, we develop allergies or arthritis or some other malady in which our cells attack our own bodies.

The "music" for our immune system is very much influenced by what we eat.

It has been known for many years that if we have a large deficiency of certain vitamins and nutrients, we will become ill and die. The association between malnutrition and lowered disease resistance is taken for granted. It is also well accepted that children and older adults do not have immune systems as strong as young adults'. But what about subclinical deficiencies that may affect our health in subtle ways? Is it possible that genetic facts make some of us less able to use certain elements in our food necessary to our well-being?

Are there nutraceuticals that can be used as medication to shore up a weakened immune system? Some people think so. They are sucking on zinc tablets at the first sign of a sore throat, taking the herb echinacea to ward off the flu, and downing vitamin C as a weapon against the common cold and other ailments.

Are they swallowing false hope?

Top scientists are trying to determine if such alternative medicine practices have a real basis in restoring immunity. Nutritional immunology is a newly recognized subdiscipline, but its history goes back to 1810 with the recognition that lymph tissue atrophies when there is malnutrition. The discovery of vitamins in the early 1900s was followed by reports on their contribution to immunity and other host defenses. Progress in immunonutrition faltered during World War II with the advent of antibiotics. Interest began again in the 1960s and early 1970s, triggered by epidemiological reports linking nutrition and health and by new diagnostic technology.[1]

Researchers and the organizations for which they work are now aiming at identifying nutraceuticals that may promote *optimal immunity*. This means the enhancement of the body's natural defense systems in apparently healthy people making them less susceptible to illnesses and more responsive to immunizations. In addition, scientists are attempting nutraceutical strategies against more than forty diseases that result when the body's defense system mistakenly turns against the body. Such autoimmune diseases include arthritis, lupus, and allergies.

What may nutraceutical research efforts mean to you?

Your body's immune system reflects your life history: the genes you inherited, the vaccinations you received, the infections you have fought, and the allergies you may have developed. Your cells form an exclusive "fraternity" recognizing only their own members by means of chemical signals that serve as "passwords."

Your immune "fraternity of cells" is a powerful fighting force. It searches out and destroys all kinds of foreign invaders including bacteria, viruses, and chemical toxins.

Your body has basically two types of "fraternities" to which your immune cells belong—the *humoral* and the *cellular.*

HUMORAL IMMUNITY comprises *immunoglobulins* in the blood and the *complement system*—protein components that aid and abet other portions of your immune system. The immunoglobulins are:

- *IgM*, the earliest immunoglobulin produced in most first responses and thought to be useful in eliminating parts of "invaders" in the blood.
- *IgG*, the major protective immunoglobulin. It is important for the neutralization of "enemies" such as bacterial toxins. Its concentration increases with repeated battles, and it tends to be present in large amounts in the hyperimmune state.
- *IgA*, the defender in saliva, colostrum, tears, and in nasal, bronchial, and intestinal secretions. IgA is not well understood but is believed to signal the manufacture of antibodies.
- *IgE*, the immunoglobulin that plays a major part in immediate hypersensitive reactions such as an allergic reaction to a bee sting or sulfites in food.

CELLULAR IMMUNITY is produced by *B* and *T white blood cells* that bind to invaders such as germs or cancer cells.

- *B cells* are produced in bone marrow and make *antibodies*. Each B cell antibody is specifically tailored to latch onto just one kind of invader.
- *T cells*, which mature in the thymus, are "fraternity brothers" that stand guard on the surface of other cells and identify specific enemies by shape. Cancer cells and some other foes are attacked directly by *"killer" T cells*. Other T cells

attract "the cleanup squad"—*phagocytic cells*—which then
engulf and destroy the enemy. There are also *helper T cells*
and *suppressor T cells*, which aid or inhibit the production of
B cell antibodies.

* *Lymph nodes*—those "glands" that may feel swollen when you
have an infection—are the "closets" where defensive T and
B white blood cells hang out until challenged.[2, 3] The spleen,
in the upper left of the abdomen, also provides a meeting
ground for immune defenses.

*The immune system, therefore, is a massive fraternity of defensive
cells that need an adequate supply of nutrients for peak operation. The
nutrients support rapid manufacture of antibodies, complement factors,
T cells, and B cells. If the sustenance is inadequate, the speed and power
of immune response will falter.*

Immunity and Aging

Jeffrey B. Blumberg, Ph.D., professor of nutrition and associate
director of the USDA Human Nutrition Research Center on
Aging at Tufts University, Boston, says of the research on vitamin
E and other nutraceutical research and immunity:

"Implications of this research are especially important to
older adults. It now appears that the 'age-related' decline in
immunity among the elderly is more attributable to their
changed nutritional requirements than simply the passage of
years. Therefore, it is critical that future research determine the
specific relationship between these nutrients and the aging
immune system—with the ultimate goal of achieving optimal
physiologic function and decreasing the risk or delaying the
onset of chronic disease.

"In the final analysis, this effort will not only allow us to
develop foods and nutraceuticals that promote wellness, but also
help us reduce the ever-growing costs of health care amidst an
aging population."[4]

Vitamins, Minerals, and Immunity

Billions are spent each year on over-the-counter vitamin and mineral supplements by consumers hoping to treat illness and/or maintain health.

Deficiencies of macronutrients such as protein and fatty acids and micronutrients such as vitamins do, indeed, impair the immune system, which in turn decreases resistance to disease.

Scientific evidence is growing that antioxidant nutrients such as vitamin E, beta-carotene, and selenium may be important in preventing cancer, heart disease, and other degenerative diseases associated with aging, as pointed out in previous chapters. Certain oxygen molecules called free radicals have been found to be underlying factors in aging and degenerative diseases because they damage DNA, the blueprint for life, within the cells. They also adversely affect enzymes, the workhorses of the cells, and damage cell membranes. Free radicals are formed during the course of normal metabolism, as well as from exposure to cigarette smoke and other environmental influences.

The cells of the immune system are rich in polyunsaturated fatty acids, which are prone to oxygen damage and thus are sensitive to changes in the level of antioxidants in the body. The body's built-in "fraternity of defensive cells," however, are not powerful enough to ward off all harmful attacks on DNA. Over time, damage caused by free radicals accumulates in cells. For instance, in a young rat, there are a million oxidative lesions per cell, with one hundred thousand new ones occurring every day; the number of lesions per cell doubles as the animal ages.[5]

Impairment of immunity is the underlying factor for increased incidence of infectious disease and tumors as we age. The relationship between our nutrient intake and immunity is under intensive study. One reason is because the elderly are increasing by leaps and bounds and many are not consuming enough vitamins and minerals. At the same time, they are suffering from chronic diseases that affect their nutrient status. And if that weren't enough, they are taking drugs that interfere with the absorption of nutrients from their food.

Vitamin E and Immunity

Many scientists have reported vitamin E wields a wide-ranging and profound influence over cellular and humoral immunity in farm and laboratory animals. Indeed, the concentration of vitamin E is significantly higher in defensive white blood cells than in red blood cells and has been shown to stimulate the activity of T cells. The vitamin has also been found to increase antibody production in laboratory experiments with mice.

It is believed that the antioxidant function of vitamin E may be aiding the manufacture of antibodies as well as helping those scavenger phagocyte cells to gobble up invaders.[6] In one experimental study, volunteers injected with histamine—a substance released into the body when an allergic reaction occurs—showed far less swelling around the injection site when pretreated with vitamin E for five to seven days.[7]

In another experiment, twenty healthy premature human infants with decreased levels of vitamin E and decreased B cell (antibody) function were divided into two groups. One group received a total dose of 120 mg/kg vitamin E, and the other served as controls. At five days of age, the index and frequency of the action of the phagocytes—those cells that gobble up enemies—in the treated group increased significantly but remained unchanged in the control infants. At fourteen and thirty days, however, the action of the phagocytes was normal in both groups. Restoration of normal white-blood-cell function was also reported in an infant with glutathione synthetase (an intrinsic antioxidant deficiency) when treated with 400 IU of vitamin E daily for three months.[8]

A group of diabetics with defective immunity also significantly improved after vitamin E supplementation of approximately 28 IU/kg/day over two to three weeks.[9]

Antioxidant Vitamins and the Elderly

For certain age groups, higher than U.S. government recommended daily intakes of nutrients may be needed for optimal immune-system function. Department of Agriculture nutritionist Simin N. Meydani, DVM, Ph.D., and her colleagues recruited thirty-four healthy volunteers over the age of sixty years who moved into a dormitory at the USDA Human Nutrition Research Center on Aging at Tufts University for thirty days.

Half the volunteers received a normal diet containing about fifteen international units of vitamin E. The other half received the same diet but in addition took two 800 IU vitamin-E capsules daily. Neither the patients nor the researchers knew which volunteers received the vitamin E.[10]

After one month on the diet, those receiving the vitamin showed a marked increase in immune responsiveness.

The U.S. Department of Agriculture researchers concluded one or two capsules of vitamin E daily can at least partially reverse the decline in immunity that normally occurs during aging and might thereby make it easier for the elderly to fight off disease.

Investigators at Memorial University of Newfoundland reported in *The Lancet*, the prestigious British medical journal, that a modest multivitamin and mineral supplement may strengthen the immune response in people over age sixty-five and reduce the incidence of infections. Dr. R. K. Chandra and colleagues assigned ninety-six healthy elderly volunteers to one of two groups. One group received placebos and the other a multivitamin and mineral supplement for twelve months. Vitamin and mineral amounts in the supplement were similar to the U.S. recommended dietary allowances (RDAs), except for vitamin E and beta-carotene. These nutrients were given in doses about four times the usual. Volunteers who received the supplement improved in several measures of immune function. Moreover, the supplement group had a significant reduction in infection-related illnesses . . . twenty-three sick days versus forty-eight days for the placebo group.[11]

Vitamin E also showed immune-boosting effects in a European study that examined serum vitamin levels in relation to the incidence of infections in a retrospective study of one hundred healthy persons over the age of sixty. A statistically significant correlation was found between blood levels of vitamin E and number of infections during the previous three years. The higher the levels of vitamin E, the lower the number of infections.[12]

Researchers in America, Canada, and Europe are gathering more and more evidence that vitamins, particularly the antioxidants such as vitamin E, may boost immunity. Indeed, since the concentration of vitamin E is significantly higher in defensive white cells, it is understandable that vitamin E supplements may make it easier for the elderly to fight off disease.

The B Vitamins

The B vitamins are known to help the body use sugars, fats, and proteins. They have been shown to work with other vitamins to shore up the immune response and may even act as controllers of the rapidly dividing cells of the immune system.

When vitamin B_6 (pyridoxine) is deficient, both cellular and humoral immunity in animals is depressed. Their lymph glands shrink, their skin-hypersensitivity reactions fail to develop, and their normal rejection of a skin transplant is inhibited. Their antibody production is also impaired.[13]

In a study at Tufts, Dr. Meydani evaluated the number and function of white blood cells in eight subjects who had their B_6 intake lowered and then raised in three stages. Dr. Meydani found that when B_6 intake was lowered, the number of white blood cells and their ability to proliferate and produce interleukin-2—the message carrier between them—dropped significantly. When B_6 was replenished, the white-blood-cell count climbed to its original level.[14]

Dr. Meydani and her colleagues at the Department of Agriculture are studying the combination of vitamin B_6 and vitamin E and immunity in the elderly because she says research has shown deficiencies of the two vitamins in humans compromises the immune response.[15]

Inadequate levels of another B vitamin, B₅ (pantothenic acid), is one of the most common of all vitamin insufficiencies, especially in the elderly. When vitamin B₅ is deficient in humans, as in animals, antibody and new immunoglobulin (IgE, IgA, etc.) production is impaired and response to vaccines is inadequate.[16]

Vitamin C and Immunity

The *C* in *vitamin C* could stand for "controversy" or "conflicting reports." Ever since Nobelist Linus Pauling caused a run on vitamin C in 1970 by endorsing it as a cold medicine and immunity builder, the nutrient has been popular with the population at large. Many scientists disputed the nutrient's immune benefits in the past, but today vitamin C is being intensively studied at some of the most prestigious medical institutions supported by government grants.

It is well accepted that vitamin C (ascorbic acid) helps to form connective-tissue collagen; promotes wound healing; keeps blood vessels strong; and enhances iron absorption. Deficiencies are known to cause bleeding gums, easy bruising, slow-healing wounds, painfully swollen joints, and impaired digestion. Supplementary vitamin C is used to prevent scurvy, a debilitating condition, in persons with extensive burns, severe fever, poor diet, or chronic-disease states. The recommended daily allowance for newborns to six months is 30 mg. Infants six months to one year, 35 mg. Children one to three years, 40 mg. Children four to ten years, 45 mg. Children eleven to fourteen years, 50 mg. Children fifteen years and over and adults, 60 mg.

How does vitamin C work in the immune system?

It has been theorized vitamin C stimulates the immune system through enhancement of white-blood-cell function. The concentration of vitamin C is quite high in phagocytes, those white blood cells that gobble up foreign invaders. Mounting evidence supports the vitamin's role in helping with the duties of phagocytes—especially their "safety patrolling" and their bacteria killing. Some researchers report that vitamin C may help the immune system by neutralizing the harmful byproducts of phagocyte activity. When the scavenger cells "digest" bacteria, they produce potentially harmful residues that can inhibit the actions of other white blood cell defenders.[17]

It is also believed that vitamin C may improve resistance to infection by stimulating collagen formation in the skin and the linings of openings in the body, thus helping to maintain a physical barrier against germs.[18]

Researchers at the University of California at Berkeley wanted to determine what happens when vitamin C intake is low in healthy individuals. They recruited eight male volunteers and had the men consume less than one-third of the recommended daily allowance of 60 mg of vitamin C. When the investigators tested the volunteers' blood, it was discovered that the glutathione levels had fallen by 50 percent. Glutathione, a building block of protein, helps guard against heart disease, cancer, and inflammatory disease such as arthritis. When the volunteers raised their vitamin C intake, glutathione increased. It has been reported many times that a low intake of vitamin C weakens the body's disease defenses, but this study showed that lowering glutathione is another path by which a low vitamin C intake impairs defenses.[19]

In another research project at the Human Nutrition Research Center on Aging at Tufts, Simin N. Meydani and her colleagues wanted to see if extra glutathione could improve the function of white blood cells, especially T cells, where most of the age-related loss of immune response occurs. So they tested the peptide first in aging mice with successful results, then on white blood cells from both young and older people. Glutathione improved the cells' ability to divide and produce substances that mobilize other players in the immune response. It also dampened the cells' production of inflammatory substances. And it had a greater effect on the more sluggish cells from the older people, boosting their function close to that of young people's cells. Researchers were planning to test glutathione supplements in a human study.[20] (*See* also Glutathoine S-transferase in glossary.)

Current research indicates that vitamin C may reduce the risk of cancer of the mouth, esophagus, and stomach; may reduce risk of cataracts; may protect lungs against pollutants; and may ease common colds. Higher intakes are associated with higher beneficial HDL cholesterol levels and lower blood pressure. Potential adverse reactions include faintness or dizziness with fast IV administration, diarrhea, heartburn, acid urine, and kidney stones or failure.

Because of epidemiological evidence that citrus fruits help in the treatment of several forms of cancer, particularly pancreatic cancer, the National Cancer Institute is studying them. Citrus fruits contain particularly high concentrations of vitamin C, and preliminary evidence does indicate vitamin C may help fight certain viruses.

Vitamin A and Beta-carotene

Poor vitamin A status is also associated with compromised immune-system function. Animal experiments have shown that a deficiency of vitamin A leads to depletion of those defender T cells from the thymus and an increase of severe bacterial and virus infections. The incidence of spontaneous infections is also said to increase in vitamin A–deficient humans. Immunoglobulin (IgA) production may be impaired. Supplemental vitamin A given to premature infants reduces the incidence of lung problems.[21] These effects may be related to the action of vitamin A in keeping cell membranes healthy.[22]

In addition, vitamin A is required for normal production of *lysozyme*, an antibacterial enzyme found in tears, sweat, and saliva.[23] Thus, vitamin A is important as a first-line defense against bacterial infections.

Evidence is growing regarding vitamin A and childhood resistance to infection in nonindustrialized societies. The morbidity and mortality associated with measles infection in marginally nourished children can be reduced by high-dose supplementation with vitamin A. Supplementation appears to benefit children with even mild deficiency.[24] Sickness and death have reportedly been more closely correlated with vitamin A status than with overall nutritional status.[25, 26]

Children at risk for diarrhea and acute respiratory infections can be helped by periodic vitamin A supplementation, according to a study conducted in Brazil. More than 1,200 children aged six to forty-eight months were assigned to vitamin A or a placebo every four months for a year. The incidence of diarrhea during a year's follow-up was about 20 percent lower in the vitamin A group. The reduction in respiratory infections was not significant. The results were important because diarrhea is a major killer of children in third-world countries.[27]

Beta-carotene and Immunity

Beta-carotene is converted to vitamin A by enzymes in the body on an as-needed basis, mainly in the intestinal lining. Apart from its vitamin A activity after conversion, intact beta-carotene appears to influence various components of the immune system on its own. The following are some of the effects noted by researchers concerning beta-carotene and immunity:

- Beta-carotene increased helper T lymphocytes (human).
- Beta-carotene enhanced T- and B-cell proliferation.
- Beta-carotene increased the ability of phagocytes to kill invading cells.
- Beta-carotene increased natural killer T cells that battled tumors.

Minerals and Immunity

Minerals, inorganic materials found in the earth's crust, are vital to health. They interact with enzymes, the workhorses of the cells. Magnesium, for example, is part of ninety enzymes. People with marginal or insufficient minerals are much more susceptible to infectious diseases than those in an optimal state. Some estimate that 90 percent of the fatal diseases in this country involve minerals in one way or another.[28]

IRON helps hemoglobin, the substance in red blood cells that captures oxygen and carries it to all parts of your body. When iron and oxygen are low, you are pale, fatigued, depressed, headachy, and most of all weak. Why?

Iron deficiency, in general, causes immune dysfunction in large numbers of people. It is accompanied by shrinkage of lymphoid tissue and impaired white-blood-cell responsiveness to a challenge. Antibody and phagocyte function is impaired. Too much iron, of course, can be harmful. Studies suggest, however, that the immune system of man is exquisitely sensitive to iron availability and responds adversely to deficiencies of iron that are too small to lower red-blood-cell oxygen values.[29]

MAGNESIUM. Researchers in Nottingham, England and at Brigham and Women's Hospital have linked magnesium and lung function.[30] Magnesium is involved in a wide range of biological activities, including some that may protect against the development of asthma and chronic airflow obstruction. Dr. John Britton and his colleagues at Nottingham University measured the magnesium in the diets of 2,633 adults aged eighteen to seventy years. They found that low magnesium was associated with reduced lung function and wheezing. Magnesium has been identified as a broncodilator. Magnesium is easily leached out of foods such as nuts, greens, and cereals during cooking so that low magnesium may be a hidden factor in many cases of lung disorders.

ZINC is a mineral needed for wound healing, healthy skin, enzyme power, and normal levels of vitamin A in the blood. It is added as a nutrient to food. Results of both animal and human studies with zinc have been puzzling. When there is a slight deficiency, it seems to make the scavenger cells, the phagocytes, work harder. When there is more of a deficiency, there is atrophy of lymphoid tissue and abnormalities in both cellular and humoral immunity. In the laboratory dish, white blood cells from zinc-deficient animals show a depressed ability to fight infections. In fact, in zinc-deficient animals, skin grafts are not rejected, as they normally are. Humans who are zinc deficient show a restoration of immune functions when body zinc is replenished.[31]

Incidentally, taking zinc with bran may make zinc less effective. As with any other chemical, zinc can have side effects. Ingestion of zinc salts can cause nausea and vomiting.

A doctor's daughter reluctantly took a zinc tablet for a condition, and her sucking on the zinc made her sore throat disappear. From a letter in a journal, the idea that zinc could stop sore throats grew. Sublingual forms of the white, brittle metal are now on the market. Zinc is also widely used as an astringent for mouthwashes.

Does it help ease sore throats and colds? In a study by the Dartmouth College Health Service, a zinc lozenge resulted in a 42 percent reduction in the duration of common colds as well as reduced symptoms when taken within forty-eight hours of the start of a cold.

In other observational studies, children between three and seven years with frequent upper-respiratory-tract infections had significantly lower zinc concentrations in their hair.[32] In double-blind experimental studies, volunteers received lozenges of either zinc gluconate (23 mg) or a placebo every two hours while awake, for four and a half days. The volunteers were challenged with human cold viruses on the second day. Zinc reduced the total mean clinical score from 8.2 in the placebo group to 5.7; the reduction of the mean clinical score was significant on the second day after virus challenge. Sixty-nine volunteers were inoculated with human rhinovirus 2, and those who developed cold symptoms were randomly allocated to receive either zinc gluconate lozenges or a placebo every two hours while awake, for six days. Zinc reduced the mean daily clinical score; this was significant on the fourth and fifth days. Similarly, zinc reduced the mean daily nasal-secretion weight and total tissue count. The cold symptoms were less severe in the volunteers taking the zinc.[33]

In another study, 146 volunteers were given a seven-day supply of zinc gluconate tablets (23 mg of elemental zinc) or placebo tablets. Adults and youngsters were to suck on two tablets for at least ten minutes at the onset of cold symptoms, followed by one tablet every two waking hours up to a maximum of twelve daily for adults and nine daily for youngsters. Treatment was stopped six hours after symptoms ceased and no other treatments were permitted. While cold sufferers receiving zinc completely recovered in an average of 3.9 days, those who received placebos took 10.8 days to become symptom free. Many zinc-treated subjects became asymptomatic within hours and one-fifth of the zinc-treated group fully recuperated within one day.[34] This later study was criticized because of the higher rate of side effects in the zinc group and the lack of any confirmation that it was the zinc that was beneficial. Furthermore, it was noted that unflavored zinc-gluconate tablets can easily be distinguished from unflavored calcium-lactate tablets, the placebos. Furthermore, high zinc levels have been reported to decrease immunity, not increase it.[35] Therefore, the use of zinc as a nutraceutical for the common cold has to await further study.

SELENIUM, discovered in 1807 in the earth's crust, is used as a nutrient. Selenium is necessary for the formation of prostaglandins, a group of extremely potent hormonelike substances present in many tissues. More than sixteen effects of prostaglandins are known, such as dilating or constricting blood vessels, stimulating intestinal or bronchial smooth muscle, uterine stimulation, antagonism to hormones, and influencing metabolism of fat. A modest increase in dietary selenium, alone or in combination with vitamin E, appears to enhance the immune responsiveness to vaccine antigens in animals. Selenium has also been reported to work with vitamin E to preserve elasticity in the tissues and to increase endurance by improving the supply of oxygen to the heart muscle.

Amino Acids and Immunity

AMINO ACIDS. Amino acids are the building blocks of proteins and neurotransmitters, the chemical signals between nerve cells. About twenty amino acids are called *essential* because the body cannot make them and they must be obtained from food. Dietary deficiencies of many single essential amino acids (phenylalanine, tyrosine, valine, threonine, methionine, cystine, or tryptophan) impair humoral antibody responses in mice but have little apparent effect on cellular immunity. An excessive dietary intake of the essential amino acid leucine, however, if sufficient to cause an amino acid imbalance, reduces the antibody response to immunization in animals. Whether it does so in humans is not, as yet, known.

GLUTATHIONE (GSH). A precursor of amino acids such as glycine and cystine, and glutamic acid. Found in plants and animals and usually isolated commercially from yeast, glutathione and other natural antioxidants may help restore some of the capabilities of the immune system in elderly individuals. Dr. Simin Meydani and her colleague Dr. Dayong Wu at the USDA Human Nutrition Research Center on Aging at Tufts University found that the addition of GSH to cultured immune cells from young and old human volunteers increased their responsive capabilities, suggesting that GSH supplementation may help reduce the incidence of infectious disease, especially in the elderly.[36]

Nutraceuticals From the Sea

In addition to vitamins, minerals, and amino acids, immunity-bolstering nutraceuticals may be found in the oceans. Sea creatures are another unusual but logical source for pharmaceuticals. Sea dwellers must protect themselves against disease and the environment as much as land creatures do. It is likely they are full of biologically active agents. Researchers recently obtained a powerful antiviral and anticancer substance from sea squirts, gelatinous creatures that attach themselves to rocks and piers. The substance, didemnin, has killed a variety of viruses in tests including herpes viruses, influenza viruses, and some rhinoviruses, which cause the common cold. Other sea creatures have been the source of antibiotics and psychoactive agents.

Chapter 9

Plants, Minerals, and Vitamins That Fight Infections From Colds to AIDS

Plants growing on land were used by humans to improve immunity and treat ailments long before vitamins and antibiotics were discovered. Scientists are now rediscovering the power of botanicals and attempting to isolate the beneficial elements within them in order to create new and more powerful nutraceuticals.

Fighting Infections

Infections, of course, are caused by germs. But the term *germ* can mean a whole host of things from a virus that causes a cold or AIDS to bacteria that cause food poisoning or pneumonia.

Antimicrobials are medications that can help the body destroy or resist germs. Some plants contain ingredients that kill or inhibit the growth and reproduction of bacteria and are considered antimicrobial. Until recently, the use of plants in folk medicine has been based on trial and error. Twenty-five percent of prescription drugs on the market today are based on botanicals and have been studied extensively for their active properties. Much is still unknown, however, about why and how certain plant substances do their jobs. In 1993, researchers at Rutgers University, New

Brunswick, New Jersey, discovered that plants use a material that is a basic component of aspirin to fight off their infections.[1] Using tobacco and cucumber plants, the investigators discovered that salicylic acid inhibits the action of catalase, an enzyme that normally converts hydrogen peroxide to water and oxygen. This in turn leads to a buildup of hydrogen peroxide within the plant cells. The elevated levels of hydrogen peroxide then activate genes to mobilize the plant's fight against infection.

The Rutgers researchers Klessig Zhixiang Chen and Herman Silva said the compound may hold important clues for the use of aspirin. Although much research has been conducted on the physical effects of aspirin, scientists still know relatively little about how it and related chemicals achieve so many effects in both plants and animals. Unlike animals, plants produce salicylic acid naturally.

Following are examples of plant nutraceuticals that are reputed to be general immune boosters.

GARLIC—THE TASTE OF IMMUNITY. Garlic *(Allium sativum)* is a member of the onion family. It was cultivated in Egypt from earliest times and known in China more than two thousand years ago. Ancient herbalists made a syrup of garlic and honey to treat colds, coughs, asthma, and bronchitis. Hippocrates used garlic to treat pneumonia and infected wounds. Garlic was used during the Great Plague in Europe and in World War I to treat typhus and dysentery. Albert Schweitzer, the saintly physician who practiced in Africa, used garlic effectively against typhus, cholera, and typhoid. Garlic contains lots of potassium, fluorine, sulfur, phosphorous, and vitamins A and C. Modern scientists have found it also contains antibiotic, antiviral, and antifungal nutraceuticals. Garlic, according to current scientific literature, may decrease formation of nitrosamine (a powerful cancer-causing agent created when nitrates combine with natural amines in the stomach), modulate cancer-cell multiplication, and protect the body against ionizing radiation.

ECHINACEA—THE OLD/NEW WONDER HERB. Also called snake-root, stoneflower, and coneflower, *Echinacea angustifolia* is increasingly popular today among people who wish to enhance their immunity by "natural" means. The roots and leaves of this herb served as a medicine for the American Plains Indians. It is said by herbalists to be a natural antibiotic and immune enhancer. It contains a volatile oil that is antiseptic and glycosides (*see* in glossary), as well as phenol, which is also an antiseptic. It was widely used by Dr. Wooster Beach, who in the mid-1800s founded Eclectic Medicine, a blending of homeopathic and North American herbalism. It has been found that echinacea increases the ability of white blood cells to fight, destroy, and digest toxic organisms that invade the body. Echinacea, which can be bought over the counter in supermarkets, health-food stores, and pharmacies, is taken to combat colds, infections, and inflammations. The herb produces a numbing sensation when held in the mouth for a few minutes.

SUMA—THE LAUDABLE. Also known as *para todo* and Brazilian ginseng, *Pfaffia paniculata* is the South American version of ginseng (*see* glossary). The name *para todo*, meaning "for all things," was given to the plant by Brazilian Indian tribes who first discovered its medicinal uses. In North America it has been used to treat exhaustion resulting from viruses such as Epstein-Barr and chronic fatigue syndrome. Among its constituents are saponins and germanium (*see* both in glossary). Herbalists use it as a tonic to increase energy.

TEA AND IMMUNITY. One of the hottest areas of nutraceutical research involves tea. Long the favorite drink of many from the English in the afternoon to the Japanese at mealtimes, tea has been found to have antibacterial and antiviral actions. For a long time tea has been thought to be effective in mitigating diarrhea caused by bacterial infection. Specifically, this antibacterial property is contained in the polyphenolic fraction of tea. Research has revealed that various kinds of food-borne pathogenic bacteria are susceptible to tea polyphenols, even in a concentration far lower than that from everyday consumption of tea. The daily intake of tea catechin tablets influenced the intestinal microflora of human subjects and made bowel movements more regular. One of the features of tea polyphenols is that they are prone to bind with protein. This leads to the inactivation of such viruses as tobacco mosaic, influenza, or others even when in contact with tea polyphenols at a remarkably low concentration.[2]

Some other general immunity boosters:

MYRRH GUM. *Commiphora molmol.* Guggul. One of the gifts of the Magi, it is a yellowish to reddish brown, aromatic, bitter gum resin that is obtained from various trees, especially from East Africa and Arabia. In Asia and Africa, it was used as an antiseptic for mucous membranes. In modern studies, myrrh was shown to inhibit gram-positive bacteria such as *Staphylococcus aureus.* The herb contains volatile oils, including limonene, eugenol, and pinene. These oils help to ease breathing during colds and to increase circulation. Myrrh also contains tannin, which is thought to be the reason it allays the pain and speeds the healing of mouth ulcers and sore gums. It is also used as a stimulant tonic.

HONEY OF AN INFECTION FIGHTER. Manufactured by bees from flowering plants, honey speeds healing and combats infections. In a study reported in the journal *Infection,* unprocessed honey effectively eliminated several common bacteria and significantly reduced the growth of a host of other organisms. The researchers tested unprocessed honey, commercially prepared honey, and syrup against laboratory cultures of various bacteria and fungi that commonly infect surgical wounds. Only unprocessed honey possessed consistent germ-killing activity.

The investigators note that honey also speeds healing by promoting cell growth at the edges of the wound and by helping absorb fluid buildup.[3]

On the other hand, under certain circumstances, honey may be hazardous. This depends entirely on what kind of plant the honeybees have used as their source of nectar. Nectar gathered from species of rhododendron, azalea, and in particular mountain laurel may cause poisoning.

YOGURT—CULTURED MILK. Folklore has long given cultured milk health-preserving powers. Yogurt has been said to cure insomnia and hold the fountain of youth. Modern science has found that yogurt can fight bacteria. An eight-ounce serving provides between 30 and 45 percent of the 1,000 mg of calcium we are advised to consume daily.

Dr. Sherwood Gorbach, professor of community health at Tufts University School of Medicine, and Dr. Barry Goldin, associate professor of community health, have added a new fermenting ingredient to yogurt, *Lactobacillus GG.*

GG—short for Gorbach and Goldin—is a bacterial strain found in people. What separates GG from other bacteria is its ability to colonize in the intestine and fend off other bacteria. When GG enters the body, it stays in the intestine for several days and produces a substance that prevents many harmful bacteria from growing. Several studies completed by Goldin, Gorbach, and researchers in Finland have shown that GG rids the body of persistent forms of diarrhea, including traveler's diarrhea and diarrhea found in hospitalized infants. It's also being tested in animals as a combatant against colon cancer.

Traditionally, yogurt is made with two fermenting bugs, *Lactobacillus bulgaricus* and *Streptococcus thermophilus.* These strains give yogurt its creamy consistency, and technically, without them, a fermented-milk product can't be called yogurt. But according to Goldin, *Lactobacillus bulgaricus* and *Streptococcus thermophilus* can't survive in the human intestine and have little or no therapeutic value.

In Lima, Peru, where half of all children die by age five, usually due to diarrhea, a study sponsored by the International Child Health Foundation is testing the effectiveness of GG in treating diarrhea.

GG yogurt is available at this writing only in Finland. GG makes for a sweeter yogurt, and the product made in Finland, Gefilus, contains just 1.5 percent fat.

Other Plant Anti-infective Candidates

BEARBERRY (*Arctostaphylos uva-ursi*), also called uva-ursi, is used by herbalists to treat colds and bladder problems. It contains the antiseptic arbutin, which in the system yields hydroquinone, a urinary disinfectant. Bearberry leaves have also been found to contain anesthetic and an antibiotic activity.

GOLDENSEAL (*Hydrastis canadensis*), also called puccoon root or yellowroot, was used by American Indians to treat sore eyes. Early pioneers, along with many Indian tribes, used goldenseal as a general tonic. Herbalists claim it dries and cleanses the mucous membranes. It reputedly has potent antibiotic and antiseptic properties. It contains berberine, a mild antiseptic and decongestant used in eye lotions on the market today.

Fighting the Common Cold

A tremendous amount of research is under way to find nutraceuticals for specific ailments ranging from the common cold to AIDS. Starting with the first, there are many folk remedies, the benefits of which are now being determined in scientific laboratories. Your grandmother, however, probably knew their worth all along.

The common cold is an inflammation of the upper respiratory tract caused by infection with any one of a large number of viruses. There are at least one hundred subtypes of rhinoviruses. Adults eventually develop antibodies to about 55 percent of the subtypes. You would have to get two colds a year for fifty years to develop immunity to every strain.[4] Most people have two or three colds per year, but some people never have colds. Other people can resist colds after exposure to a virus if they are in good general health, but succumb to the virus if they are fatigued, chilled, poorly nourished, or under some other stress.

Many natural remedies for colds have been given throughout history to ease the cough and the inflammation that may accompany that common malady. In Russia, for example, a scratchy throat was sometimes wrapped in a cloth containing a salty herring. In France, heated glass cups were placed on a victim's back and chest to clear up congestion. Colonial Americans applied kerosene or mustard plasters to the chest to combat a cold, or they inhaled vapors of steaming-fresh dung. Another remedy was to wrap a dirty stocking filled with salted pork and onions about the neck in order to keep a cold from entering the chest. It also probably kept other people away. In China, herbal teas have been used for centuries. Mixtures include licorice, ginger, cinnamon, mint, and apricot seeds, among others. "Natural" remedies have one or more of the following properties:

Expectorants to help thin and loosen the thick mucus of the respiratory tract, making it easier to expel.
Anticatarrhals to soothe the mucous membranes.
Febrifuges to lower fever.

The following are some of the common "natural" nutraceuticals used to ward off or treat colds and flu.

Chicken Soup—The Great Cold Cure

In 1978, the Mount Sinai Medical Center in Miami Beach published a study that concluded chicken soup, "Jewish penicillin," worked better than hot or cold water in fighting the congestion that accompanies a cold. More than ten years later, Dr. Irwin Ziment of the University of California at Los Angeles found that chicken, a protein, contains an amino acid, cysteine, which is chemically similar to the drug acetylcysteine. Acetylcysteine is prescribed for people with respiratory infections because it thins the mucus in the lungs.[5]

And if you still don't believe chicken soup is good for a cold, Dr. Stephen Rennard, chief of pulmonary and critical-care medicine at the University of Nebraska Medical Center in Omaha, and his wife, Barbara, tested the old "nutraceutical." She made chicken soup from her grandmother's recipe and he tested it.

Dr. Rennard reported at the 1993 International Conference of the American Lung Association and the American Thoracic Society that the chicken soup had an effect on neutrophils, white blood cells that are part of the immune system.[6] White blood cells are chiefly responsible for the problems caused by inflammation, when they attack the body's own cells. Chemotaxis is the process by which white blood cells are attracted to the site of inflammation.

"We postulated that an anti-inflammatory action of chicken soup might explain its general salutary effects," the Rennards reported. "As an initial test of this hypothesis, we tested the ability of the chicken soup to inhibit neutrophil chemotaxis."

As Barbara Rennard made the soup, Stephen Rennard took nineteen samples at various stages of preparation. The eighteenth sample, with matzo balls carefully screened out, was added to a standard laboratory system for assessing neutrophil chemotaxis.

The results: chemotaxis was significantly reduced. The response was seen even when the chicken soup was diluted two hundred times, the researcher reported.

The Rennards said that perhaps it wasn't the soup alone since the first inhibitory activity was seen after the onions, sweet potatoes, carrots, turnips, and parsnips were added.

The University of Nebraska researchers said the good news was that the chicken soup did not appear to be toxic. The white blood cells weren't killed by any dose of the liquid, no matter how concentrated.

They noted, "There's a large worldwide therapeutic tradition of recipes, local plants, and animals. Modern medicine tends to ignore traditional medicine even though it includes potent remedies. There is something to be learned by studying traditional remedies in a scientific way."

Baker's Yeast

The yeast you buy at the supermarket to make cakes and breads just may contain an element that can prevent the common cold. When a University of California professor isolated a molecule of yeast in a dish with the cold virus, the yeast stopped the virus dead, preventing the virus from spreading to other cells. Dr. Asim Dasgupta, professor of microbiology and immunology at UCLA, says that at the first sign of a cold, you should spray the yeast molecule into your nose and throat to prevent the virus from doing its dirty work.[7]

Vitamin C and Colds

There has been a great deal of controversy over whether vitamin C offers any protection from or palliation of the common cold. Nobel laureate Linus Pauling, as pointed out earlier, caused a run on vitamin C in 1970 by endorsing it as a cold medicine. He recommended hundreds of milligrams a day to ward off and treat colds.

Actually, vitamin C, as an immunity builder, was touted by its discoverer, Albert Szent-Györgyi, who won the Nobel Prize in 1937. Dr. Szent-Györgyi pointed out that although 10 mg was enough to protect most people against scurvy, a much larger amount might be needed for the best of health. He himself began taking 1,000 mg per day, together with other vitamins.[8]

For several decades, medical scientists did not credit increased doses of vitamin C with the power to enhance immunity. Physicians told patients it was useless in fighting colds.

A great deal of study is now in progress, however, on vitamin C and colds, and the results have thus far been inconclusive.

A double-blind study to evaluate vitamin C supplements for the treatment of respiratory disease was conducted among 641 children at a Navajo boarding school over a fourteen-week period. Half the children received vitamin C supplements, the other half an identical-appearing placebo, with the tablets distributed to teachers in containers labeled only by code number.

Children aged six to ten receiving vitamin C were given 1 g daily, and children aged ten to fifteen received 2 g daily. Children in the placebo group received the same number of tablets as in the vitamin C group. The same number of tablets were given whether a child had symptoms of illness or not. Although there was no difference between the two groups in the number of respiratory illnesses, the children receiving vitamin C had fewer days of illness than those receiving the placebo. Among the younger children, there were 26 percent fewer days of illness in the vitamin C group and 33 percent fewer in the older girls. No such difference was seen in the older boys. The two symptoms that appeared to benefited by vitamin C were nasal discharge and cough.[9]

In a study with "smoking" rodents, the animals did not get emphysema if they were given vitamin C.[10] University of Munich pathologists, Hans Anton Lehr and colleagues reported in 1994 that vitamin C halts more than 90 percent of the damage from cigarette smoke to white blood cells known as leukocytes—the main trigger for emphysema and atherosclerosis. Again, the researchers believe the vitamin protects the lungs against those bad old free radicals.

Protocols for nearly all of the studies of vitamin C and colds have been criticized. In many cases, subjects were living in the community and exposed to many infectious organisms of varying strength. The subjects were also evaluating their own symptoms and compliance with the regimen prescribed.[11]

A well-controlled study in which neither the investigators nor the subjects knew which pills were the vitamin C and which were the fake ones was conducted in 1988. Subjects were isolated and exposed to a single type of cold virus through contact with an infected person. The group receiving vitamin C—500 mg four times a day—had symptoms that were half as severe as those determined in the placebo group. Vitamin-supplemented subjects had significant increases in vitamin C blood levels, whereas those receiving the fake pills had a substantial decline in vitamin C levels.[12]

Could it be that vitamin C works as an antihistamine? Histamine is a substance released in the body when an allergic reaction occurs. Taking antihistamines for an allergy or a cold is common. In both animal and human experiments, vitamin C depressed hist-amine and improved breathing. Moreover, in a double-blind crossover study, vitamin C supplementation prevented inhaled his-tamine from impairing lung function in patients with stuffy noses due to allergy.[13] (When the study includes a crossover, subjects serve as their own controls. For half the regimen they are given the targeted medication and for half they are given the placebo. If it is a double-blind study, neither patients nor participating researchers know which subjects are receiving the medication and which the fake pill until after completion of the study.)

Increases were also shown in the proportions of total T cells and helper T cells in the vitamin C treated group. Much work has been done with prophylactic vitamin C for upper-respiratory viral illness, and current evidence supports a lessening of severity and/or duration of symptoms. The shorter duration of cold symp-toms that has been associated with vitamin C prophylaxis may be related more to the role of the vitamin in influencing phagocyte (scavenger) cell interactions with secondary bacterial invaders than to any direct antiviral effects of vitamin C on the causal res-piratory viruses.

The use of rose petals (*Rosa gallica*) dates from early history. Ancient pharmacists used them as a tonic, and in the treatment of chronic lung diseases. The medicinal properties of the petals are generally considered mild. The buds and petals are astringent, and high in vitamin C, tannins, and phenolic compounds (*see* the latter two in the glossary).

Taking too much vitamin C, whether through pill, food, or herb, has it dangers. Potential adverse reactions include diarrhea, heartburn, acid urine, and kidney stones or failure.

Other "Natural" Cold and Flu Nutraceuticals

AMALAKI (*Phyllanthus emblica*) is an herb used for thousands of years in India to treat coughs.

ANEMONE *(Anemone ranunculaceae)* is also known as windflower, pulsatilla, and lily of the field. Common throughout Europe. References to the small herb can be found in Greek and Chinese ancient medicinal literature. Anemone is still used today as a homeopathic remedy for the common cold as well as various emotional ills.

ANGELICA *(Angelica officinalis)* is also called masterwort and archangel. The benefits of this northern-European wild herb were said to have been revealed by an angel to a monk during a time of plague. In medicine, herbalists use it as a tonic and for coughs, colds, and arthritis pain. A beverage of dried leaves with lemon and honey is used as a cold cure. It is also used to improve the circulation and warm the body and as an astringent.

BALM *(Melissa officinalis)* is also known as lemon balm and sweet balm. A sweet-tasting herb introduced into Britain by the Romans, it has been used from early times in England for nervousness, menstrual irregularity, and for surgical dressings. The Greeks used it for fevers and to treat scorpion stings and the bites of mad dogs. A hot tea made from it causes perspiration and is said to stop the early symptoms of a cold.

BAYBERRY *(Myrica cerifera)* is also called candleberry, waxberry, and wax myrtle. The bark contains volatile oil, starch, lignin, albumin, gum, tannic and gallic acids, astringent resins (*see* all in the glossary), and an acid resembling saponin. It is used by herbalists as a stimulant, astringent, expectorant, and to induce sweating. A famous patent medicine, *Dr. Thompson's Composition Powder*, was used by many physicians to treat colds, coughs, and flu. Several modern versions are used by herbalists.

BONESET *(Eupatorium perfoliatum)* is also called feverwort and thoroughwort. Native Americans introduced the settlers to this herb. Its name reflects its use for a severe strain of flu called breakbone fever. The herb contains flavonoids, quercetin, vitamin C, volatile oil, and sterol (*see* all in the glossary). Herbalists use it to treat fevers, colds, and flu today. It reportedly loosens phlegm, clears nasal passages, relieves constipation, and reduces fever. It is also used in over-the-counter cold medicines.

BORAGE *(Borago officinalis)*, also called herb of gladness, is a beautiful plant with blue flowers. The folk saying "borage for courage" has a basis in fact. The chemicals present in the herb act upon the adrenal gland, which releases hormones needed to fight or flee during threat. Borage also contains potassium and calcium. It is used for bronchial, lung, and chest disorders. Borage tea is used by herbalists to reduce fevers. It is used in a gargle for sore throats. Borage may cause liver damage.

BUGLE *(Ajuga reptans)* is a mint used in rock gardens. Bugle was used by herbalists to treat tuberculosis, coughs, and as a mild narcotic.

CARAWAY *(Carum carvi)* is a plant native to southeastern Europe and western Asia. The use of this herb dates back to ancient Egypt. The seeds are used to ease intestinal gas and colic and to stimulate the appetite. It is also used by herbalists to treat bronchitis and laryngitis.

CHAMOMILE *(Matricaria recutita)* of the English, Roman, and Hungarian variety has a daisylike white or yellow flower. The heads of these flowers contain sesquiterpene lactones, essential oil, calcium, coumarin, and tannic acid (*see* all in the glossary). Herbalists use it for the common cold and the flu.

CHAPARRAL *(Larrea indentata)* is a dwarf evergreen. Its leaves contain antioxidants and what is believed by herbalists to be an antibiotic. The leaves are ground and may be used in a tea or in capsules. It is used for blood purification, cancer and tumors, arthritis, colds and flu, diarrhea, and urinary tract infections. The American Indians used it to treat arthritis. A modern Argentine study showed that the primary constituent of chaparral, NDGA (nordihydrogua-iaretic acid), an antioxidant, possesses pain-relieving and blood-pressure-lowering properties. Two cases of chaparral-induced toxic hepatitis were reported in 1992 by the FDA.

CHESTNUT *(Castanea vulgaris)*, also called Spanish chestnut, sweet chestnut, and horse chestnut. Nuts from the European tree are used as a remedy for piles, backaches, and for coughs. An astringent, the bark and leaves were used to make a tonic that was also reportedly useful in the treatment of upper-respiratory ailments such as coughs and particularly whooping cough.

CUDWEED *(Gnaphalium ulginosum)* is grown widely in North America. The plant is used by herbalists to treat upper-respiratory inflammation including laryngitis, tonsillitis, and bronchitis.

CYPERUS *(Cyperus rotundus)*, also called sedge root, is a common wayside weed. The root contains essential oils including pinene and sesquiterpenes. Related to Egyptian papyrus, it is used by herbalists to treat stomach cramps, colds, and flu.

ELDERFLOWER *(Sambucus nigra, S. canadensis)* is also called sambucus, black elder, bourtree, or Judas tree. In China, the herb is added to tea. It contains essential oil, terpenes, glycosides, rutin, quercitrin, mucilage, and tannin (*see* all in glossary). The fruits are high in vitamin C. Elderflower is used to treat colds and flu. It reputedly reduces fever. Hippocrates mentioned its use as a purgative. The inner bark and the young leaf buds, as well as the juice root, are all considered cathartics. The berries induce sweating and act as a diuretic. Only the black elder is safe to use internally. Red elder is toxic.

EUCALYPTUS *(Eucalyptus globulus)* is also called blue gum and dinkum oil. It is used in many cold and cough products on the market today such as Halls Mentho-Lyptus cough-suppressant tablets, Listerine antiseptic, and Vicks VapoRub. The colorless to pale yellow volatile liquid from the fresh leaves of the tree has a camphorlike odor. The chief constituent of eucalyptus, eucalyptol, is used as an antiseptic, antispasmodic, and expectorant. Herbalists maintain that, as a disinfectant, it destroys bacteria, fungi, and viruses. Most commonly, the oil is rubbed directly on the chest or back for respiratory ills. Herbalists claim it lowers fever. The FDA proposed a ban in 1992 for the use of eucalyptus oil to treat fever blisters and cold sores because it has not been shown to be safe and effective for stated claims in over-the-counter medications for these sores.

EYEBRIGHT *(Euphrasia officinalis)*, also known as euphrasy, is an annual herb native to Europe and western Asia, and grown in the United States. It belongs to the foxglove family. It contains tannins, iridoid glycosides, phenolic acids, and volatile oil *(see* all in the glossary). It has been mentioned in medical literature since the early 1300s. It had the reputation of being able to restore eyesight in very old people and is still used today as an eyewash for inflamed and tired eyes and to treat sinus congestion. Astringent infusions are made by herbalists for coughs, colds, and sore throats.

GARLIC *(Allium sativum)* is another old folk remedy for warding off and treating colds. One folk method involves hanging a bunch of garlic around the neck. Some skeptics said that the garlic kept people away from you and therefore you were not exposed to other people's germs and that's how garlic prevented colds. Garlic is high in vitamins A and C, and ancient herbalists made a syrup of garlic and honey to treat colds, coughs, asthma, and bronchitis. And in one study at Brigham Young University in Utah, James North, chief of microbiology, found that garlic extract killed nearly 100 percent of both a human rhinovirus, which causes colds, and parainfluenza 3, a flu and respiratory virus. As pointed out previously, the herb has recently been found to contain antibiotic, antiviral, and antifungal ingredients. Herbalists have long used it to treat respiratory infections and the flu.

GROUND IVY (*Glechoma hederacea*) is a plant with many names including alehoof, benth, cat's-foot, devil's candlesticks, hale house, hay house, May house, hay maids, hedge maids, thunder vine, and tun-hoof. Common on wastelands, it is used by herbalists for coughs and bronchitis. It contains tannin, volatile oil, bitter principle, and saponin, all of which have some physiological activity (*see* all in glossary).

HEMP (*Cannabis sativa*) is an herb of the nettle family native to northern India, southern Siberia, and Asia. It was widely cultivated for its narcotic properties. It was used in folk medicine to treat the flu and colds.

ICELAND MOSS (*Cetraria islandica*), also called Iceland lichen, was named because Icelanders reputedly were the first to discover its benefits. It is high in mucilage with some iodine, traces of vitamin A, and usnic acid (*see* all in glossary). Herbalists use the lichen to treat upper-respiratory problems associated with degenerative wasting, as a gentle laxative, and to treat dysentery and anemia. It is also used to treat bronchitis.

IPECAC (*Cephaelis ipecacuanha*), also called ipecacuanha, is from the dried rhizome and roots of a creeping South American plant with drooping flowers. Used by herbalists and sold in conventional pharmacies, ipecac is primarily used to induce vomiting when ingestion of noncaustic poisons has occurred, but it may also be used in medicine to induce expulsion of mucus in lung congestion.

LOBELIA (*Lobelia inflata*) is also called Indian tobacco, pukeweed, and asthma weed. The leaf and seeds of this bitter, common weed contain lobeline, which has an effect similar to nicotine and is used to help break the nicotine habit. It is also used by herbalists as an expectorant, stimulant, and as an antispasmodic. It is primarily used to treat asthma, bronchitis, and coughs. Externally, it can be applied to wounds. Potential adverse reactions include nausea, vomiting, breathing problems, convulsions, and even coma and death when used in large amounts.

LOQUAT *(Eriobotrya japonica)* is a plant whose leaves and fruit are used by herbalists to treat coughs and lung inflammations. Loquat contains amygdalin *(see* glossary), which is also found in cherry bark and apricot kernel, both of which are used to treat coughs.

LOVAGE *(Ligusticum scoticum)* is also called shunis. An ingredient in perfumery from an aromatic herb native to southern Europe and grown in monastery gardens centuries ago for medicine and food flavoring. It has a hot, sharp, biting taste. The yellow-brown oil is extracted from the root or other parts of the herb. It has been used by herbalists as an eyewash and as a cold cure.

LUNGWORT is also called wall hawkweed and Virginia cowslip. It refers to any of several plants, including mullein, thought to be helpful in combating lung diseases and coughs and hoarseness. Lungworts are also used by herbalists to treat diarrhea. The leaves contain mucins, silicic acid, tannin, saponin, allantoin, quercetin, and vitamin C *(see* all in glossary). Externally, this plant is used to heal wounds.

LYCII *(Lycium chinensis)* is also known as gay gee. The berries are used by herbalists to make a cooling tonic used to reduce fevers and thirst, and to treat bronchial inflammations.

MALLOW *(Malvaceae sylvestris)* is also known as malva. An erect European perennial herb with rosy purple flowers. It contains mucilage, essential oil, and a trace of tannin *(see* all in the glossary). The herb is used to soothe inflammation in the mouth and throat and to treat earaches.

MULBERRY *(Morus alba* or *Morus nigra)* is a plant of which the fruits, leaves, twigs, and root bark are used by herbalists as a tonic, to treat coughs and inflammation of the lungs, to reduce fever. The mulberry contains citric acid, vitamin C, carotene, succinic acid, choline, coumarin, and tannin *(see* all in the glossary), among other constituents.

MULLEIN *(Verbascum thapsus)* is a perennial of the figwort family native to Europe, Asia, Africa, and the United States. It grows wild. Its dried leaves were smoked to treat asthma. Indians use it for upper-respiratory problems. A high content of mucilage and saponins *(see* both in the glossary) reportedly makes this herb useful to treat coughs. It has also been found to have antibiotic properties. During the Civil War, the Confederates relied on mullein for treatment of respiratory problems whenever their medical supplies ran out.

OSHA *(Ligusticum porteri)* was used by western Indians to treat colds, flu, and upper-respiratory infections. Osha is reputed to build immunity.

PLEURISY ROOT *(Asclepias tuberosa)* is also called butterfly weed and Canada root. Native Americans used this root to treat bronchitis, pneumonia, and diarrhea. Herbalists use it to induce sweating, as an expectorant, to induce vomiting, and as a laxative. It contains glycosides and essential oil *(see* both in the glossary).

PRIMROSE *(Primula vulgaris)*, also called Easter rose, is a perennial native to Britain and Europe. It flourishes in meadows, hedges, and ditches. The name comes from the Latin word for first, *primu*, because it was the first rose of spring. A decoction of the root is given for catarrh, coughs, and bronchitis. It is also used to cure insomnia.

PUERARIA *(Pueraria lobata)*, also called ko ken and kudzu root, grows wild in the Southern states, where it is considered the scourge of the South. Its fast-growing, hardy vines creep over everything and are difficult to eradicate. The root or vine is used by Chinese herbalists as a treatment for cold and flu. It is high in starch.

QUILLAJA EXTRACT. The extract of the bark of *Quillaja saponaria* is also called soapbark, quillay bark, Panama bark, and China bark. The inner dried bark of a tree grown in South America, it is used in flavorings and in folk medicine to treat bronchitis.

QUINCE SEED (*Cydonia oblonga*) is a plant grown in southern Asia and Europe for its fatty oil. Thick jelly is produced by soaking its seeds in water. It is used in fruit flavorings for beverages and foods and by herbalists as an expectorant to treat dry coughs.

SAFFLOWER (*Carthamus tinctorius*) is also known as bastard saffron and American saffron. It is an annual plant that is a native of Egypt, but is cultivated in various parts of Europe and America. Safflower in large doses is reputed to have laxative value and, when given as a warm infusion, is said to have a fever-reducing effect. It is used in an herbal tea for colds.

SAINT-JOHN'S-WORT (*Hypericum perforatum*) is also called amber, blessed, devil's scourge, God's wonder herb, grace of God, goatweed, hypericum, and Klamath weed. A perennial native to Britain, Europe, and Asia, it is now found throughout North America. The plant contains glycosides, volatile oil, tannin, resin, and pectin (*see* all in glossary). It was believed to have infinite healing powers derived from the saint, the red juice representing his blood. A spray has been used for colds. It is now being studied by researchers from the National Cancer Institute and universities as a potential treatment for cancer and AIDS. The FDA listed Saint-John's-wort as an "unsafe herb" in 1977. The FDA issued a notice in 1992 that Saint-John's-wort has not been shown to be safe and effective as claimed in OTC digestive-aid products. That does not mean, however, that it cannot be used for other purposes.

SQUILL *(Urginea maritima)* is a plant, the bulb of which contains glycosides, mucilage, and tannin *(see* all in glossary). It is used by herbalists as a powerful expectorant to treat chronic bronchitis. The mucilage content eases and relaxes the bronchioles.

SUNDEW *(Drosera rotundifolia)* is an herb that contains quinones, flavonoids, tannins, and citric acid *(see* all in glossary). It is used by herbalists to treat bronchitis and infections caused by streptococcus, staphylococcus, and pneumococcus bacteria. It is also used to treat asthma.

SUNFLOWER *(Helianthus annuus)* is also called lady eleven o'clock, and marigold of Peru. It was introduced into this country from South America, and the seeds are used in medicine as a soothing tonic for coughs. It is high in vitamin E.

VIOLET *(Viola odorata)* is also called sweet violet. The violet is used as a syrup for sore throat, dryness of the upper-respiratory tract, chronic coughs, and asthma. It contains saponins, salicylate, alkaloids, flavonoids, and essential oil *(see* all in glossary). It is also used by herbalists against tumors, to lower blood pressure, and to treat urinary-tract infections.

WHITE POPLAR *(Populus tremuloides)* is a tree bark that contains glycosides, flavonoids, essential oil, and tannin *(see* all in glossary). It is used by herbalists to treat colds and fever, cystitis and diarrhea.

WILD CHERRY *(Prunus serotina, Prunus virginiana)* is the dried stem bark of the wild cherry. It is collected in autumn in North America. Used in cherry flavorings for medicines, it is also used as a sedative and expectorant medicinally. It is soothing to the mucous membranes and is widely used in over-the-counter cough medicines. The American Indians and early settlers were aware that the bark is effective in calming coughs, and the wild cherry is still included in the U.S. Pharmacopoeia (USP), a compilation of standards for the strength and purity of drug ingredients and directions for making medicinal preparations.

WILD GINGER *(Asarum heterotropoides)* is also called *xi xin.* The root is used by Chinese herbalists to treat congestion in the lungs and nose. Its warm, pungent action relieves spasms. The American wild ginger is not as strong as the Chinese, but the Chinese can be mildly toxic.

AIDS and Nutraceuticals

Human immunodeficiency virus (HIV) is a causative agent of acquired immune deficiency syndrome (AIDS). AIDS leads to a weakening of the immune system, which in turn results in opportunistic infections, malignancies, and neurological lesions. Nutritional deficiencies can, of course, impair immunity and so influence susceptibility to AIDS. A variety of nutrients affect several of the immune functions that are defective in HIV-infected individuals. Since there are many conflicting reports concerning nutrients and AIDS, great caution must be exercised. It was reported in 1994 that men infected with HIV who take a multivitamin supplement are about one-third less likely to develop full-blown AIDS than those who don't take these vitamins.[14] The survey of 296 HIV-infected men also showed that those who had a higher than average intake of vitamins A, B_1, B_2, or niacin tended to have a higher CD4 count, indicating higher immunity. In addition, those who consumed vitamin E and iron from food supplements seemed less likely to develop AIDS than those who did not take these supplements.

Beta-carotene and AIDS

Several indicators of immune response improved in patients infected with the AIDS virus who received beta-carotene in a double-blind, placebo-controlled clinical trial conducted at Oregon Health Sciences University in Portland.[15] Beta-carotene is in natural pigments in fruits and vegetables and is a precursor of vitamin A.

Twenty-one HIV seropositive patients under treatment with antiviral drugs were randomized to receive either 180 mg of beta-carotene or a placebo daily for four weeks. They were then switched over to the alternate treatment for the following four weeks. Two important markers of immune function in HIV-infected people improved when the subjects were treated with beta-carotene and declined when they were given the placebo.

"We initiated this trial based on earlier research showing that CD4 counts rose in healthy people after they were given beta-carotene and on the results of a pilot study we did with three HIV-positive patients," said Gregg O. Coodley, M.D., the principal investigator for this study. CD4 cells, also known as T helper lymphocytes, are a type of white blood cell that orchestrates the functioning of other immune cells. CD4 cells are the primary target of the AIDS virus. In fact, one of the parameters of the Center for Disease Control's newly revised definition of AIDS is a CD4 count of two hundred or less per deciliter of blood on two occasions (the normal level is one thousand). The body's ability to fight infections is compromised as CD4 levels drop. For this reason, the CD4 count is used to track the progression of AIDS.

In this latest study, both total white-blood-cell and CD4 counts increased with beta-carotene supplementation. "Beta-carotene supplementation may prove to be a useful complement to treatment with antiviral drugs. Perhaps patients given beta-carotene will not succumb to opportunistic diseases as readily or the progression from HIV infection to full-blown AIDS may be delayed," Coodley said.

Dr. Coodley's findings differ from those in a study reported a year before. In that study, conducted at the Tucson VA Medical Center and University of Arizona Health Sciences Center, there was no change in CD4 count, but natural killer cells (a type of lymphocyte that seeks out and destroys infected cells) increased in eleven HIV patients supplemented with 60 mg of beta-carotene daily for four months.

"It is possible that the effect on CD4 levels is dose-related. More research needs to be done to establish an optimal dose," Dr. Coodley says.

Scientists do not yet know why beta-carotene stimulates immune response in HIV-infected people. "It is possible that beta-carotene may prompt increased production of specific white blood cells or may block their destruction," Coodley speculated. "In future trials that follow a large number of patients over a longer period, if there is a sustained increase in immune response with beta-carotene, then it could be useful as an adjunct therapy in the treatment of HIV-infected patients. Beta-carotene has the benefit of being quite safe and inexpensive."

Studies reported in 1994 have been shown that pregnant, HIV-infected women transmit the virus to their babies 10 to 40 percent of the time, raising the question about why some babies become infected and others don't. Richard Sembra and colleagues at Johns Hopkins School of Hygiene and Public Health, in collaboration with John Chiphangwi from Malawi Medical College, tested whether vitamin A levels may be a factor. They tested the blood of 338 pregnant, HIV-infected women, and tested their children for the virus once they were born.[16]

The researchers found that mothers who transmitted HIV had serum vitamin A levels averaging 0.86 micromoles per liter. Infected mothers who did not transmit the virus had levels averaging 1.07 (1.05 or less is considered vitamin A deficiency).

AIDS and Selenium Depletion

University of Georgia researchers published a hypothesis in the *The Journal of Medicinal Chemistry*, in August 1994, stating that AIDS depletes the body of the trace mineral, selenium. According to the hypothesis, the AIDS virus needs selenium, which preserves the elasticity of body tissues to trigger growth. Once the virus exhausts the selenium in an infected cell, it breaks out in search of more, spreading infection to new cells. Many AIDS patients have been found to lack selenium and have had it prescribed by their physicians or taken it on their own. Some researchers believe the latency period may be due to the time it takes the virus to deplete the body's stores of selenium.

AIDS and Tea

Researchers at the Aichi Cancer Center Research Institute in Nagoya, Japan, are studying substances in tea to combat HIV. Since HIV is a kind of retrovirus, various chemotherapeutic approaches have been conducted for the treatment of AIDS. One of the appropriate approaches is the inhibition of reverse transcriptase because this enzyme is unique to retroviruses and is crucial for retrovirus infection. A number of reverse-transcriptase inhibitors including azidothymidine (zidovudine, AZT) have been shown to inhibit HIV replication in both the laboratory dish and in humans. Although AZT is helpful in the treatment of AIDS, serious side effects (i.e., bone-marrow dysfunction and muscle problems) and AZT resistance occur in the long-term use of AZT. The development of novel anti-HIV drugs is, therefore, an urgent task.

To find novel anti-HIV compounds, Japanese researchers have been looking for natural products inhibitory to the reverse transcriptase. They found that a Chinese traditional drug inhibited HIV reverse transcriptase. They identified 5,6,7-trihydroxyflavone (baicalein) from *Scutellaria baicalensis* as an effective substance. Then they extended the survey to other flavonoids and their related compounds and found that (-)-epicatechin gallate (ECg) and (-)-epigallocatechin gallate (EGCg), the two major components of Japanese green tea, were strong inhibitors of HIV reverse transcriptase. The method of inhibition was different from that of AZT, and it did not inhibit beneficial enzymes. The inhibition of such enzymes is believed a major cause of severe side effects in drugs used to combat HIV.[17]

The activity of tea polyphenols might explain, at least in part, the epidemiological finding in Japan that the mortality rate of digestive-tract cancer is significantly lower in the area where green-tea ingestion is high.

Black tea contains some novel polyphenols called theaflavins as the oxidation products of green-tea polyphenols. Japanese investigators have shown that these theaflavins are also strong inhibitors of HIV reverse transcriptase. The mechanism of inhibition of the reverse transcriptase by theaflavins was similar to that by ECg and EGCg.

The anti-HIV substances from both green tea and black tea are toxic to cells. One possible explanation for the cell toxicity, the Japanese believe, is that tea polyphenols bind to and cannot pass through the cell membrane because of their strong affinity to cell-membrane proteins. To reduce cytotoxicity and to enhance anti-HIV effect, they are, at this writing, trying some structural modifications of these tea polyphenols to develop effective and safer anti-HIV nutraceuticals.

Herbs Against AIDS

Many persons with AIDS or HIV, frustrated by the toxicity and ineffectiveness of the few prescription medications available, have turned to herbal medications. Whether or not they are any more effective than other compounds is yet to be proven. There is always the possibility that hidden within some botanical somewhere is an effective substance to combat this devastating disease. The following are some of the plants being studied for their potential.

CHINESE CUCUMBER. TAP 29 is an agent from the root of *Trichomatoses kirilowii*, a Chinese herb. It was reported by researchers at New York University in 1991 to have potential against the AIDS virus. It is reportedly nontoxic to normal cells and may eventually be used in condoms, vaginal jellies, and toothpastes to minimize the risk of HIV transmission.

PRUNELLA. An extract, obtained from *Prunella vulgaris*, a Chinese herb, was able to significantly inhibit HIV-1 replication with relatively low toxicity to cells.[18]

SAINT-JOHN'S-WORT *(Hypericum perforatum)*, also called amber, blessed, devil's scourge, God's wonder herb, grace of God, goatweed, hypericum, and Klamath weed. A perennial native to Britain, Europe, and Asia, it is now found throughout North America. The plant contains glycosides, volatile oil, tannin, resin, and pectin *(see* all in glossary). It was believed to have infinite healing powers derived from the saint, the red juice representing his blood. It is now being studied by researchers from the National Cancer Institute and universities as a potential treatment for cancer and AIDS.

Can Sharks Take the Bite out of AIDS?

In addition to the plants above, a fish is being intensively studied, shark. The sharks' immune systems are different from humans', and shark derivatives are now under intensive study. The killer of the deep is being studied as a source of squalamine, a unique compound that kills a variety of bacteria, fungi, and parasites. Shark cartilage has been used in alternative medicine as an anticancer and anti-AIDS compound because sharks apparently do not suffer from cancer. Mainstream medical researchers are now investigating shark derivatives for their potential in the treatment of both AIDS and cancer.

Chapter 10

NUTRACEUTICALS TO EASE
ARTHRITIS AND ALLERGIES

Since the early 1900s, scientists have been denying that there is any real connection between food and rheumatic diseases with the exception of gout. In that case, "overindulgence in rich food or alcohol" can raise the uric-acid level and bring on painful swellings of the joints, often in the big toe, elbow, knee, or hand.

The idea that food can play a part in either causing or ameliorating arthritis remains controversial. Some scientists believe that the relationship between nutrition and rheumatic diseases could occur through two possible mechanisms that are not mutually exclusive:

1. Nutrition factors might alter immune and inflammatory responses and thus modify manifestations of rheumatic diseases.
2. Food-related antigens might provide hypersensitivity responses—food allergies—leading to rheumatologic symptoms.[1]

While skeptical professionals denigrate the idea that diet has an effect on arthritis, the fact is that arthritis is an autoimmune disease involving inflammation and that reactions to certain elements in food can cause an allergic reaction, so it stands to reason that diet has an influence on arthritis. Folk medicine has long used plants to combat the effects of arthritis, and new studies concerning fish oil's effect on joints lends added weight to the arthritis-diet connection.

There is ample evidence that oxygen radicals play a major role in the inflammatory response. During an inflammatory reaction, a large number of cells called phagocytes—the "cleanup squad"—can ingest microorganisms or other foreign particles that invade the site of injury or infection. Phagocytes release oxygen radicals that aid in digesting foreign particles.

In some inflammatory diseases, the body seems unable to distinguish foreign particles from its own cells. An example is rheumatoid arthritis.

There is a great deal of excitement in the scientific community involving the development of nutraceuticals to fight the autoimmune diseases in which the body manufactures antibodies against its own tissues and damages itself. The nutraceuticals involve a sort of combination of homeopathic medicine in which a patient is given a substance that has caused the symptoms; voodoo medicine in which animal parts are used; and biotechnology. This technique, referred to us *oral tolerization*, is aimed at inducing tolerance to foreign antigens by feeding the patient small, concentrated amounts of the offending substances. According to the theory, ingesting such concentrated animal proteins will cause suppression of the crippling attacks of autoimmune disorders.

Nutraceuticals are being tested that involve oral doses of such things as chicken-cartilage fibers, egg albumin, concentrate from cows' eyes, and bovine brain extract. Many oral tolerization studies now underway are being sponsored by the National Institutes of Health, pharmaceutical firms such as Eli Lilly, and universities in Israel. Participants in the tests include multiple sclerosis patients, who are ingesting capsules filled with cow brain protein; rheumatoid arthritis patients who are swallowing chicken collagen in orange juice; and patients with the eye disorder, uveitis, who are eating a protein purified from cows' eyes.

Researchers at Harvard Medical School reported in the *Journal of Immunology* in 1993, "Initial clinical trials of oral tolerance in multiple sclerosis, rheumatoid arthritis, and uveitis have demonstrated positive clinical effects with no apparent toxicity and decreases in T cell autoreactivity."

RHEUMATOID ARTHRITIS. An autoimmune disease, that is, a disease where environmental and/or genetic factors trigger an uncontrollable and destructive reaction by the immune system, directed against the body's own tissues. Population studies have indicated that approximately 2.1 million Americans are affected with rheumatoid arthritis. The female to male ratio is about two to one, and the peak age of incidence is thirty-five to fifty-five in males and forty to sixty in females. The disease is characterized by periods of activity and remission. The damage inflicted is not continuous and ongoing, although it does not necessarily heal perfectly. Joint pain and early-morning stiffness are the major symptoms of the disease, and pain is initially felt on movement, but as the disease progresses, pain develops at rest.

GOUT. Arthritis nodosa. Occurs when the body can't properly use its uric acid. Excess uric acid crystallizes in joints, which leads to inflammation. Gout can settle in any part of the body, but in 75 percent of the cases the large joint of the big toe is attacked. An inherited disorder of purine metabolism, occurring mostly in men. Involves a high level of uric acid and sudden and severe onset of arthritis, resulting from deposits of crystals of sodium urate in connective tissue and cartilage.

OSTEOARTHRITIS. A condition that usually results from wear and tear in the mechanical parts of a joint. The cause is unknown, but may be related to age, occupational stress, injuries, obesity, or heredity. There are an estimated 16 million Americans that suffer from osteoarthritis.

Another state of being that affects bone and may or may not be accompanied by arthritis is osteoporosis (see below).

OSTEOPOROSIS. A condition that affects an estimated 24 million Americans, primarily women. In this debilitating disorder, the bones deteriorate due to the excessive loss of bone tissue, and there is an increased susceptibility to bone fractures. People may not know they have osteoporosis until their bones become so weak that a sudden strain, bump, fall, or routine activity like bending to lift groceries causes a bone fracture.

Vitamins and Arthritis

PANTOTHENIC ACID, vitamin B$_5$, may be reduced in arthritis, and there is evidence that supplementation may be beneficial. In two experimental studies done in the 1960s, patients with rheumatoid arthritis who did not respond to medication received from 50 to 500 mg four times daily of pantothenic acid. They all showed improvement of their symptoms after seven days and a relapse after administration of pantothenic acid was stopped.[2]

VITAMIN E may also be helpful in treating arthritis. A controlled study suggests that it may be beneficial in ankylosing spondylitis, also called Marie-Strümpell disease. This is a progressive disease of the joints of the spine, primarily affecting men in their thirties. The typical initial symptom is lower-back pain. After six weeks, patients treated with vitamin E showed a similar significant increase in motility of the spine as patients treated with a drug, diclofenac. Ratings for general well-being showed a similar pattern, but vitamin E had no side effects, while one patient on the drug had GI bleeding.[3]

Vitamin E also helps prevent inflammation of muscle tissue caused by prolonged exercise, probably by protecting cell membranes from oxygen damage. Researchers studied twenty-one sedentary men, half of whom took 800 IU of vitamin E per day for seven weeks prior to running downhill on a treadmill for forty-five minutes. The other half took placebos. Each group consisted of young men in their twenties and older men, fifty-five to seventy-four.[4]

By day twelve after exercise, the vitamin E group—both younger and older men—excreted significantly less byproduct of fat oxidation. They had much lower blood levels of two sub-stances that trigger inflammation. Earlier studies at the USDA Agricultural Research Service suggested the immune system responds to prolonged muscle-damaging exercise much the same as it does to an infection—by launching an attack against damaged muscle tissue to clear it away. But inflammation response may get out of control and damage healthy tissue as well.

Minerals and Arthritis

COPPER. Diet may play a role in general aches and pains not related to an injury, infection, or chronic illness, such as arthritis or migraine headaches. An ARS (Agriculture Research Service) psychologist analyzed patient records from eight separate nutri-tion studies for medications dispensed for such nonspecific pain. The studies involved men, young women, and women past menopause. In five of them, the live-in volunteers requested pain pills two to three times more frequently when their diets were most restrictive. Low copper intakes prompted significantly more requests from men and older women in three of the studies. In another study, young women took more medication when their diets were low in both calcium and manganese (not to be confused with magnesium). And a group of obese young women in a weight-loss study felt more pain when their calories were cut in half. What's more, the young women in the latter two studies made almost as many requests for pain medications dur-ing the nonmenstrual phase of their cycles as they did during menstruation. Women typically take a lot more pain medication when menstruating. This analysis is the first to show a link between diet and nonspecific pain. The findings need to be re-peated in future studies before any recommendations for dietary changes can be made.[5]

COPPER SALICYLATE COMPLEX has been found to be an effective anti-inflammatory agent that may be more potent than aspirin. Doctors and pharmacologists may have laughed at people who wore copper bracelets to combat arthritis. The old wives' tale of copper being helpful against the painful condition seems to have a basis in fact, although perhaps not in the form of a bracelet. Copper's anti-inflammatory effect appears to be related to its ability to form complexes that serve as selective antioxidants, thus reducing the localized tissue inflammation that has resulted from increased oxygen damage.[6] Copper salicylates are believed to be the best copper complexes for the treatment of arthritic pain based on animal studies and uncontrolled human trials. In 140 patients treated with short-term intravenous copper salicylate, 89 percent showed remission of fever, increased joint motility, decreased swelling, and normalization of a blood condition associated with arthritis—ESR (erythrocyte sedimentation rate)—for an average of three years.[7]

BORON. This element is the key to why some populations have a lot of arthritis and others have little. Jamaica, Maritius, Fiji, and Israel were visited by American researchers who tested the boron levels of locally consumed food.[8] They found that excessive use of soluble chemical fertilizers had damaged the soils of the sugar-producing lands. Food grown in these soils were found to have low boron levels. By contrast the foods consumed in Israel had high boron concentrations associated with a low incidence of arthritis. South African researchers have shown that people who eat mostly maize have more arthritis when eating processed maize grown with fertilizer. The American researchers pointed out that in the U.S. boron levels have dropped considerably in fifty years. They say the increased use of fertilizers and genetic selection of plants may be the cause.

In just observational studies, boron supplementation was reportedly effective for about 90 percent of arthritis patients, including those with rheumatoid arthritis, most with complete remission of symptoms. It was especially effective with juvenile patients. Patients normally took 6 to 9 mg of boron daily to achieve symptom relief followed by maintenance doses of 3 mg daily.[9]

How may boron prevent or ease arthritis? Numerous studies suggest that boron interacts with other nutrients and plays a regulatory role in the metabolism of minerals, such as calcium, and subsequently bone metabolism. Although the exact mechanism of action has not been defined, Australian researchers believe it may be mediated by increasing the concentration of steroid hormones such as testosterone and estradiol.[10] Boron is obtained from a diet rich in fruits, vegetables, nuts, and legumes. The daily intake has been estimated to range from 0.3 to 41 mg per day. The wide range is due to the variation in the analytical methods used and differences in the soil content of boron. Large amounts of boron, the Australians say, are well tolerated.

Fats and Arthritis

Fatty fish, walnuts, and flaxseed oil are excellent sources of omega-3 fatty acids, a molecular chain proven to inhibit production of prostaglandins, hormones that, among other things, play a part in inflammation. Since 1985, when a study in *The New England Journal of Medicine* showed that a group of people in the Netherlands who ate about an ounce of fatty fish a day had a reduced risk of heart disease of 50 percent, omega-3 fatty acids have been used to help reduce cholesterol and are now being studied as a possible treatment for other prostaglandin-related disorders such as rheumatoid arthritis and multiple sclerosis.

Researchers believe fish oil works by curtailing production of the body agents called leukotrienes, which promote inflammation. Fish-oil omega-3 fatty acids include eicosapentaenoic acid (EPA) and docosahexaenoic acid (DHA). A number of studies have shown benefits in joint pain and stiffness with fish oil after six to twelve weeks of use.[11] A Danish study, for example, provided added evidence that eating fish oil may ease arthritis. In a test on fifty-one patients with active rheumatoid arthritis, half took fish-oil capsules for three months and half got dummy pills. The fish-oil eaters had significantly less morning stiffness and joint tenderness. The daily amount of fish oil was 3,600 mg, comparable to eating six ounces of fresh mackerel or seven and a half ounces of canned salmon a day. Other research by Swiss investigators shows that eating oily fish like mackerel, sardines, herring, and salmon can work as well as taking fish-oil supplements.

The Danish researchers suggest fish oil could be used along with traditional antiarthritis drugs.[12] But fish oil can be hazardous to some individuals. A study shows it has the potential to depress the immune function, leaving people more vulnerable to infections. Researchers at the Human Nutrition Research Center on Aging at Tufts put twenty-two volunteers on a low-fat diet (30 percent fat calories) for nearly six months.[13] Half got most of their polyunsaturated fats from eating fish—tuna, salmon, or filet of sole—at least once a day, while the other half got them from vegetables. By the end of the study, the fish eaters had a 46 percent weaker response to a skin hypersensitivity test, compared with their responses at the beginning of the study. And their T cells were 24 percent slower to multiply when challenged with a substance that promotes cell division. And some of the chemical signals that orchestrate a coordinated immune response were also significantly depressed. By contrast the vegetable-fat group had a significant increase in these chemical signals, compared to their initial test results, as well as an increase in specific lymphocytes. This runs counter to results of animal studies, in which vegetable-derived polyunsaturated fats tended to suppress immune function. The researchers who conducted the studies said that it should not discourage people from eating fatty fish several times a week as recommended. But those who eat an excess would be wise to get adequate levels of antioxidant nutrients, such as vitamin E and beta-carotene, to counter the effects of fish oil.

The depression in white blood cells, of course, could explain why fish oil apparently helps in arthritis. Arthritis is an autoimmune disease in which white blood cells are overactive.

A six-week dietary supplement of fish-oil triglycerides reduced the function of the white blood cells in normal men. The release of arachidonic acid and its leukotriene metabolites, which play a part in inflammation, was inhibited. This study has positive implications for people prone to rheumatoid arthritis.

Plants and Arthritis

It seems as if "everything old is new again" in the field of nutraceuticals. There is tremendous scientific interest in two ancient folk-medicine substances, turmeric and willow bark, as well as other plants, to treat arthritis.

ADDER'S-TONGUE *(Ophioglossum vulgatum)*, also called dogtooth violet, serpent's-tongue, yellow snowdrop, rattlesnake violet, and yellow snakeleaf. A plant that derives its name from the shape of its leaf, it grows in woods and other shady places throughout the northern and middle United States. It is used by herbalists to treat gout and is related to the compound colchicine, a widely prescribed medicine for gout today. It can be very toxic.

ALFALFA *(Medicago sativa)*, the name of which comes from the Arab word for "father," is a natural flavoring agent for many beverages. The leaves contain beta-carotene, vitamins C, D, and E, and the coagulating vitamin K. It also contains various mineral salts including calcium, potassium, iron, and phosphorous. It is a folk medicine for lower-back pain.

ANGELICA, which is described under cold remedies, is used by herbalists to treat arthritis pain.

BIRCH, SILVER *(Betula pendula)*, is used by herbalists as a diuretic, antiseptic, and tonic. The plant has been used to treat gout and arthritic pain. The young leaves and bark contain tannins, saponins, bitter principles, glycosides, essential oils, and flavonoids *(see* all in glossary).

BLADDER WRACK *(Fucus vesiculosus)* is also called bladder fucus, black tang, cutweed, kelpware, sea oak, and sea wrack. An abundant seaweed with little bladders on its fronds that contain a gel. Found in the Atlantic and Pacific oceans. Herbalists claim it strengthens weak limbs and relieves arthritis, sprains, and strains.

BUTCHER'S-BROOM *(Ruscus aculeatus)* is also called liliaceae, kneeholy, pettier, sweet broom. A member of the lily family, this herb contains saponins similar to those in licorice and sarsaparilla; glycosides; ruscogenins; and neo-ruscogenins *(see* all in glossary). Ruscogenins are similar to the powerful hormones of the adrenal gland. Herbalists use butcher's-broom to treat inflammation, arthritic pain, and hemorrhoidal swelling. In recent scientific experiments, it has been found to constrict arteries and have anti-inflammatory properties. This may explain why Greek physicians reported curing "swelling" with this herb and why the Roman Pliny said it cured varicose veins.

CATECHIN is a naturally occurring flavonoid in acacia and other woody plants. It has been found to inhibit breakdown of collagen caused by either free radicals or enzymes.[14] Collagen is an insoluble protein found in connective tissue, including skin, bone, ligaments, and cartilage. Arthritis destroys cartilage. Catechin is used in medicine today to treat diarrhea, but researchers are finding that it may also be useful in treating arthritis.

CAYENNE *(Capsicum annuum)* is also known as red pepper and green pepper. Derived from the pungent fruit of a plant, it originated in Central and South America where it was used by the natives for many diseases. It contains capsaicin, carotenoids, flavonoids, essential oil, and vitamin C *(see* all in glossary). Cayenne is a stimulant, astringent, laxative, and antispasmodic. It is used to reduce fever. Cayenne is not irritating when uncooked. Cayenne powder or tincture can be rubbed on toothaches, swellings, and inflammations. Herbalists also use it as a rub for inflamed joints and to stop internal or external bleeding.

CELERY SEED *(Apium graveolens)* is also called smallage. One of the first condiments to reach the country of the Gauls and Franks, it was introduced into Northern Europe by military men upon returning home from Roman conquests. Celery seed is used by herbalists as a diuretic and blood cleanser and to treat arthritis. In Europe, celery seed is a common treatment for gout and rheumatism. Some persons are allergic to celery.

CHERVIL *(Anthriscus cerefolium)* is an herb of the carrot family native to Europe. Used as a restorative for the elderly, it was called *cerefolium* because it was said to be a powerful brain stimulant. It is used for gout. As a poultice, it is used for arthritic pains.

CHICORY *(Cichorium intybus)* is also called wild succory. Related to dandelion, in ancient times it was used as a narcotic, sometimes administered before operations. It is used by herbalists to treat arthritis.

CHILI *(Capsicum fastigatum)* is related to cayenne. It is the dried pod of a species of *Capsicum* (*see* glossary) or red pepper. A capsicum poultice has been used with caution for the relief of aches and pains. Modern herbalists use it in pill and powder form, or as a tincture or infusion used in liniments and gargles.

DEVIL'S-CLAW *(Harpagophytum procumbens)* is also called grapple plant and devil's-craw root. A perennial herb introduced into North America relatively recently, it has been used for more than 250 years in South Africa. The natives there use it as a tonic for arthritis.

EPHEDRA *(Ephedra gerardiana, E. trifurca, E. sinica, E. equisetina, E. helvetica)* is also called mahuang and Morman tea. There are about forty species of this herb mentioned in ancient scriptures of India, and it has been used by the Chinese for more than five thousand years. The stems contain alkaloids including ephedrine (*see* both in glossary). Herbalists use the herb to treat arthritis.

EPIMEDIUM (*E pimedium grandiflorum*) is also called lusty goatherb. An herb widely used in Chinese medicine, it contains benzene, sterols, tannin, palmitic acid, linolenic acid, oleic acid, and vitamin E (*see* all in glossary). It is used to treat arthritis.

EVENING PRIMROSE (*Oenothera biennis*) is also called sundrops. The oil has a high content of linolenic acid (GLA), an essential polyunsaturated fatty acid that is converted into prostaglandins (*see* in glossary) and hormones. Evening primrose is used as a tonic for inflammatory conditions and anxiety associated with inflammatory conditions. Herbalists recommend it for arthritics, and it is a popular remedy sold in health-food stores.

HELLEBORE (*Veratrum viride, Helleborus niger*) is also called green hellebore, Indian poke, itchweed, veratrum, false hellebore, and Christmas rose. Herbalists use it to treat gout, rheumatism, and local inflammation. Hellebore is toxic and can cause severe nausea and extreme depression of the nervous system.

HEMP (*Cannabis sativa*) is an herb of the nettle family native to northern India, southern Siberia, and Asia. It was widely cultivated for its narcotic properties. It was used in folk medicine to stem bleeding and to treat arthritis. Use is illegal in the United States.

HOREHOUND (*Ballota nigra*) is also called madweed and black horehound. It was used by the English colonists as a medicine for gout and arthritis. It is soaked in boiling water and applied to the skin to relieve the pain.

HORSERADISH EXTRACT (*Armoracia lapathifolia*) is also called scurvy grass. The grated root from the tall, coarse, white-flowered herb native to Europe. It contains vitamin C and is used for arthritis to relieve pain by stimulating blood flow to inflamed joints. Potential adverse reactions include diarrhea and sweating if taken internally in large amounts.

JUNIPER (*Juniperus communis*) is also called viscum and mistletoe. The berries are used by herbalists to treat urinary problems. It acts directly on the kidneys, according to herbalists, stimulating the flow of urine. The berries have long been used by herbalists to treat gout caused by high uric acid in the blood.

POKEWEED (*Phytolacca americana*) is also called pokeroot and coakum. Native to the southern United States and the Mediterranean area, the dried root reduces inflammation and arthritic pains. It has antibiotic, antiviral, and anti-inflammatory properties. Among its constituents are tannin, formic acid, saponins, and alkaloids (*see* all in glossary). It is prescribed by herbalists for a variety of ailments from swollen glands to weight loss. A member of the bloodberry family, it is an emetic and laxative, with narcotic properties. Both berries and roots contain a dangerous drug. Some people are more sensitive to pokeweed's adverse effects than others, and fatalities have occurred.

PRICKLY ASH BARK (*Zanthoxylum americanum*), known as the toothache tree. A native American herb, the bark and berries have been used for more than two hundred years to treat rheumatism. It has been found to contain coumarins, alkaloids (*see* both in glossary), and lignins.

PRIMROSE (*Primula vulgaris*) is known as the Easter rose. A perennial native to Britain and Europe, it flourishes in meadows, hedges, and ditches. The name comes from the Latin word for first, *primu*, because it was the first rose of spring. Herbalists used it in a tea to treat arthritis and gout.

QUEEN-OF-THE-MEADOW ROOT (*Spiraea ulmaria*) is also called meadowsweet. Indian medicine men used this herb, grown in North America, as a diuretic. It is also used by herbalists to treat gout and arthritis because of its reputed ability to rid the body of uric acid, and to treat inflammation.

QUERCETIN. A bioflavonoid believed to reduce allergies due to its ability to stabilize mast cells and basophils, thereby inhibiting release of histamine, and due to its ability to inhibit certain enzymes and leukotriene involved in the inflammatory response.[15] Rheumatoid arthritis is characterized by substantially increased numbers of mast cells in the fluid and membranes around the joints. These cells release destructive enzymes believed to be a major factor in the tissue destruction in arthritis. Quercetin is a potent inhibitor of mast-cell enzyme release.

RUE *(Ruta graveolens)* is also called garden rue and German rue. An evergreen shrub. The oil is a spice agent obtained from the fresh, aromatic blossoming plants grown in southern Europe and the Orient. Rue is mentioned in the Talmud as a valuable medicine. In the sixth century A.D., it was used to treat gout. It is still used in folk medicine to reduce swelling, to increase local circulation, and to ease arthritis pain. May be toxic and causes sensitivity to light.

TURMERIC *(Curcuma longa)* is a perennial plant native to East India and most of the Pacific islands. It belongs to the ginger family. The active principal of turmeric is curcumin, an anti-inflammatory substance now in clinical trials in India. It has been found to inhibit prostaglandins, hormonelike substances, and arachidonic acid, both involved in inflammation.[16] It is believed to work in a way similar to aspirin.

TURPENTINE TREE *(Pistacia terebinthus, Pinus taeda)* is also known as terebinth and spirits of turpentine. The term *turpentine* is generally used to refer to vegetable juices, liquid or gum, with the essential oil of turpentine. They are generally procured from species of pine, although other trees yield turpentine. *Pistacia terebinthus* is a small tree native to Greece. The common America, or white, turpentine, which is listed as terebinth in the USP (*see* glossary) is from *Pinus taeda*. The oil or "spirit" is a local irritant and somewhat antiseptic. It was used in folk medicine as an expectorant. It was a stimulant to kidney function and was sometimes used in diluted solutions as a diuretic. In large doses, it damages the kidney. Turpentine baths, arranged so that vapors were not inhaled, were given to patients with chronic arthritis. Applied topically as a liniment or ointment, it has been used to treat arthritis and nerve pain. The FDA proposed a ban in 1992 for the use of turpentine oil to treat fever blisters and cold sores.

WILD CARROT (*Daucus carota*) is also called lace flower and Queen Anne's lace. This Eurasian herb contains volatile oil and alkaloids (*see* both in glossary). It is also used in the treatment of gout and arthritis.

WILD THYME EXTRACT (*Thymus vulgaris*) is a plant grown in Eurasia and throughout the United States. The dried leaves are used as a seasoning in foods and in emollients and fragrances. Has also been used as a muscle relaxant.

WILLOW BARK (*Salix alba*) is the original source of salicin, the forerunner of aspirin. There are more than 130 species, most of them in Europe and North America. White willow bark is mentioned in ancient Egyptian, Assyrian, and Greek literature and was used to combat pain and fevers by Galen, Hippocrates, and Dioscorides. Many Native American tribes used it to treat sore muscles and arthritis. In the 1800s, salicylic acid was derived from white willow bark, which then led to a product we call aspirin. Aspirin was shown to be effective against rheumatic fever, general pain, arthritis, gout, and neuralgia. White willow bark is converted through oxidation to salicylic acid within the body.

WINTERGREEN OIL (*Gaultheria procumbens*) is also called spice, teaberry, and deerberry. Obtained naturally from betula, sweet birch, or teaberry oil. Present in certain leaves and bark, but usually prepared by treating salicylic acid with methanol (*see* both in glossary). Wintergreen oil is an old remedy for rheumatism and rheumatic fever and sciatica. Large doses cause vomiting. Ingestion of relatively small amounts may cause severe poisoning and death. Average lethal dose in children is ten milliliters and in adults thirty milliliters. It is very irritating to the mucous membranes and skin and can be absorbed rapidly through the skin. Like other salicylates, it has a wide range of interaction with other drugs, including alcohol, antidiabetic medications, vitamin C, and tranquilizers.

YUCCA *(Yucca liliaceae)* is also called Spanish bayonet. The Southwestern Indians used this herb for hundreds of years to treat pain and inflammation of arthritis and rheumatism. Yucca can occasionally be purgative and cause some intestinal cramping. Long term, it may slow the absorption of fat-soluble vitamins such as A, D, E, and K. An extract of yucca was investigated in a double-blind study, with 149 patients given either yucca saponin extract or a placebo four times daily for one week to fifteen months before reevaluation. Sixty-one percent noted less swelling, pain, and stiffness compared to 22 percent on the placebo.[17]

Allergy

The word *allergy* is a comparatively new one, since it has been used for little more than seventy-five years. It is derived from the Greek word *allos*, meaning "altered," and *ergia*, meaning "reactivity." The conditions that cause an allergic response, however, are as old as mankind. Hieroglyphics describe the death of King Menes of Egypt in 2641 B.C. from the sting of a wasp. There are 35 million allergy sufferers in the United States, according to the National Institutes of Health, and many are not aware that there are new methods of preventing, diagnosing, and treating allergies. They do not know that they no longer need to suffer with an itchy rash or a chronically stuffed nose. They do not have to fight to get air into their lungs. Recent advances in science have revealed new information about how the body musters its defenses against invaders and have led to improvements in diagnosis and therapy of allergies.

One of the major problems with the search for nutraceuticals to prevent and treat illnesses is that many of us are allergic to foods, from tomatoes to peanuts to fish. There is some research that calcium supplementation may reduce allergic reactions, but this is one category of ills for which nutraceuticals may cause more problems than solutions.

In a study—as far back as the 1940s—of patients with acute, severe asthma, injections of the B vitamin niacin reduced the frequency and severity of the attacks. Those who improved frequently relapsed when the vitamin was stopped.[18]

Since plants are so often involved in the allergic response, the search for nutraceuticals that combat allergy is a complicated one. As scientists continue to make strides in understanding the immune system, there is no doubt that nutraceuticals will emerge that will prevent and treat allergies more effectively than the medications we have available today.

Chapter 11

NUTRACEUTICALS TO AID
PERFORMANCE:
BONES AND MUSCLES

While many of us consider our bones—once we have grown to full size—as inanimate as rocks, the truth is that the structures that support and protect all our organs are constantly being broken down and reformed. They are alive and eager recipients of substances we eat and a target of new and very old nutraceuticals.

In order to understand how nutraceuticals may affect our bones, we have to pick them apart. Bone is broken down and removed in a process called *resorption*, while new bone is created in a process called *formation*.

Bone is made mostly of collagen, a protein that provides a soft framework, and calcium phosphate, a mineral that gives strength and hardness. Approximately 99 percent of the body's calcium is contained in the bones and teeth.

There are two types of bone: *trabecular bone*, which makes up the interior of the bone, and *cortical bone*, the dense layer forming the outer portion of the bones. Trabecular bone is also known as spongy bone because it has a porous, spongelike structure. It is this portion of the bone that is most susceptible to osteoporosis, a condition characterized by low bone mass and an increased susceptibility to bone fracture. Trabecular and cortical bones are found throughout the body. Their proportions vary, however. The bones of the spine (vertebrae) and the ends of the long bones of the legs and arms contain a higher percentage of trabecular bone than other areas of the skeleton. This is why osteoporosis typically affects the spine, hips, and wrist.

Nutraceuticals for treating osteoporosis are aimed either at inhibiting bone resorption—the dissolution of bone tissue—or promoting bone formation.

During childhood, new bone is added to the skeleton faster than it is removed, making bones stronger and more dense. This process continues through adolescence and early adulthood until peak bone mass is reached between age twenty-five and thirty-five.

After age thirty-five, in men and women alike, bone removal begins to overtake bone replacement, and bone strength and density begin to diminish.

Eighty percent of bone density is genetically determined. We can only manipulate about 20 percent, but according to Connie Weaver, head of Purdue's Department of Foods and Nutrition, "It's worth working on because a 5 percent increase in bone mass corresponds to a 40 percent decrease in fracture risk."[1]

New research has shown that we can benefit from mineral- and vitamin-based nutraceuticals even in old age. Mineral elements have two basic body functions—building and regulating. Their building functions affect the skeleton and all soft tissues. Their regulating functions include a wide variety of systems, such as heartbeat, blood clotting, maintenance of the internal pressure of body fluids, nerve response, and transport of oxygen from the lungs to the tissues.

Calcium—A Major Bone Nutraceutical

Most of us know by now that the mineral calcium is needed for strong bones and teeth. Almost all of the two or three pounds present in the body are concentrated in bones and teeth. It is present in the body in greater amounts than any other mineral. How much calcium do we need and at what age?

Small amounts of calcium help to regulate certain body processes such as the normal behavior of nerves, muscle tone, irritability, and blood clotting. Although growing children and pregnant and lactating women have the highest calcium needs, all of us need calcium in our diets throughout our lives.

Osteoporosis can be prevented or mitigated if the person can build up enough bone density when young. The bulk of a youngster's bone density—95 percent—is built up by age eighteen. Between the ages of eleven and thirteen, children go through a growth spurt, and their bodies' calcium demand surges.[2] A calcium-sufficient diet, therefore, starting at childhood, is the first step toward optimal bone production. Foods rich in calcium include dairy products, green-leafed vegetables such as broccoli, salmon and some shellfish, and calcium-fortified products such as bread.

Since the majority of bone production occurs by age thirty-five, it is imperative, particularly for those at high risk, to take steps early to promote healthy bone development. But what can you do if you inherited weaker bones and/or you didn't drink your milk when you were a child?

It is important, according to current research, that you obtain an adequate supply of calcium either in your meals or with a calcium nutraceutical. If enough calcium isn't supplied, your blood will leach it from your skeleton. Your bones will then grow thin and weak, with a greater risk of fracture or other injury.

Menopause and Bone

Osteoporosis afflicts 25 million Americans, mostly postmenopausal women. A woman may lose as much as 15 to 20 percent of her bone mass in the first ten to fifteen years following menopause. The loss is particularly acute in the spine. By the age of seventy, women have lost more than 20 percent of the bone they had at age thirty, and men have lost about 10 percent.

Estrogen replacement therapy (ERT) is effective in slowing the bone-thinning effects of estrogen loss and in reducing the risk of osteoporosis and fractures. Studies have shown that ERT is generally most effective in preventing bone loss during the five to ten years following menopause, when bone deterioration is at its peak, but the benefits of ERT administered following menopause can last twenty years or more. Other research has shown effectiveness in hip-fracture prevention with ERT started later in life. Not everyone can or wishes to take estrogen supplements.[3]

Can nutraceuticals prevent or slow bone loss?

New Zealand researchers found calcium supplements significantly slowed bone loss in a study of postmenopausal women and for the first time showed that the effect is lasting. Ian Reid, M.D., of the University of Auckland and his colleagues gave 122 women who were at least three years postmenopausal either a calcium supplement of 1,000 mg a day or a placebo for two years. The rate of bone loss was reduced by one-third to one-half in the women who took the supplements compared to those who took the placebo.[4]

The study has important implications for how much calcium is enough. The recommended daily allowance is 800 mg. Most women, however, ingest only about 500 mg. To boost consumer calcium intake, the New Zealanders suggested food manufacturers fortify bread with calcium.

What about men—do they get enough calcium for their bones?

Men start out with the advantage of having heavier bones, but they may also be at risk for osteoporosis as they age. The prevalence of spinal osteoporosis in men forty-five to seventy-nine years of age is approximately 18 percent. The rate of osteoporosis may increase because of the widespread use of anabolic steroids and protein supplements to build their bodies. Anabolic steroids are related to male sex hormones and stimulate growth, weight gain, strength, and appetite. In addition to adversely affecting bone, they can cause liver cancer and other serious problems. Adding insult to injury, it has been well established that high dietary protein levels result in an increase in urinary calcium excretion. This frequently causes an insufficient amount of calcium in the body.[5]

It was long believed that high calcium intake could lead to kidney stones. A prospective study of 45,619 men, forty to seventy-five years old, who had no history of kidney stones was undertaken by researchers from the Harvard School of Public Health. After adjustment for age, dietary calcium intake was found to decrease, not increase, the risk of symptomatic kidney stones.[6]

In 1993, *The New England Journal of Medicine* reported more than forty studies published since 1988 related to calcium intake and bone mass, bone loss, or bone fragility. Twenty-six reported that calcium intake was associated in some way with bone mass, bone loss, or bone fracture; sixteen did not.[7]

Calcium does not work alone to strengthen bones, however. It needs its partners, calcitonin and vitamin D.

How Much Calcium Is Enough?

A panel of experts convened by the National Institutes of Health recommended in June 1994 that most Americans increase their daily intake of calcium to prevent osteoporosis. The group issued the following recommendations for daily calcium intake: infants, 400 mg to 600 mg (the same as the current RDA); children ages one to ten, 800 mg (the same as the current RDA); people ages eleven to twenty-four, 1,200 mg to 1,500 mg (the current RDA is 1,200 mg); men over age twenty-four, 1,000 mg (the current RDA is 800 mg); pregnant and lactating women, 400 mg more than the current recommendations for their respective age groups; women ages twenty-five to fifty, 1,000 mg (the current RDA is 800 mg); postmenopausal women under age sixty-five, 1,000 mg to 1,500 mg (the current RDA is 800 mg); women over age sixty-five, 1,500 mg (the current RDA is 800 mg). The panel also called for additional research to better define the optimal levels of calcium intake for older men.

Calcitonin—Calcium's Partner

The thyroid, parathyroid, and thymus glands secrete the hormone calcitonin in response to high blood levels of calcium. Calcitonin inhibits the release of calcium from the bone. A commercial preparation of salmon calcitonin is used to treat Paget's disease, which causes the bones to become soft and weak.[8] Salmon calcitonin can slow the rate of bone resorption. The therapy is most useful in patients who are not candidates for estrogen replacement therapy (i.e., women more than fifteen years postmenopausal, men with osteoporosis, women with a family history of breast cancer).

Salmon calcitonin has been available in the United States since 1973 (for Paget's disease) and was approved for postmenopausal osteoporosis in 1984. Calcitonin's use has been limited because of its cost and because it requires self-injections. The first oral form of calcitonin to treat osteoporosis is being tested in patients as of this writing. The researchers have found that the lowest dose (forty units of oral calcitonin) suppressed the normal breakdown of bone more effectively than equivalent doses of intranasal and injected calcitonin.[9]

Calcitonin therapy has been associated with some mild side effects, such as nausea, and while calcitonin's efficacy has been studied for two to three years, longer-term studies have not been completed. Salmon calcitonin can improve mobility and relieve the pain associated with osteoporosis.

Vitamin D—Calcium's Other Partner

A French study found supplementation with vitamin D_3 and calcium reduced the risk of hip fractures and other nonspinal fractures among 3,270 elderly women in 180 nursing homes. A group of 1,634 women received eighteen months of daily supplementation with 1.2 g of elemental calcium and 800 IU of vitamin D_3. The others received placebos. The group with the supplementation had a 43 percent lower incidence of hip fractures and a 32 percent lower incidence of nonspinal fractures. As these results demonstrate, it may never be too late to prevent hip fracture.[10]

Vitamin D, calciferol, speeds production of calcium and is the door opener that allows calcium to pass from our intestines into our bloodstream. Vitamin D is formed in the skin or absorbed through the gastrointestinal tract. Once inside, it is modified in the liver and then transported by the blood to the kidneys, where it turns into an active hormone that processes calcium.

The absence of vitamin D in the food of young animals can lead to rickets, a bone condition. It is soluble in fats and fat solvents and is present in animal fats. Absorbed through the skin, vitamin D_3 is used to treat rickets and other vitamin D deficiency diseases and in the treatment and management of metabolic bone disease associated with chronic renal failure.[11]

Vitamin D also keeps parathyroid hormone (PTH) output in check. If the parathyroid gland in the neck releases too much of its powerful chemical, bone loss is accelerated. Since vitamin D is manufactured in the skin with the aid of sunlight, during the long winter months women may not produce enough of the vitamin to keep the parathyroid gland from spurting too much of its product. In a study of 333 postmenopausal Massachusetts women with a low intake of calcium and vitamin D, it was found that supplementation with vitamin D of 220 IU per day was enough to maintain constant blood levels of parathyroid hormone throughout the year and prevent the seasonal increases.[12]

Aging decreases the capacity of the skin to use vitamin D_3. Recognition of this is important for the elderly, who infrequently avail themselves of sunlight, and when they do, expose just a small area of skin. They depend on this exposure for their vitamin D nutritional needs.[13, 14]

When natural vitamin D production is insufficient, vitamin D supplements, used under strict medical supervision, can aid in calcium absorption. Vitamin D can have serious side effects. Potential adverse reactions include vitamin D intoxication, headache, sleepiness, conjunctivitis, photosensitivity, runny nose, nausea, vomiting, constipation, metallic taste, dry mouth, loss of appetite, diarrhea, frequent urination, weakness, and bone and muscle aches.

There is growing evidence from well-controlled studies that

calcium and vitamin D or both can prevent some portion of age-related bone loss.[15] The Europeans, in particular, suggest that it is never too late to start treatment, and that reductions in fracture rates can occur in as little as eighteen months. Even a 20 percent reduction in the rate of hip fracture would mean forty thousand to fifty thousand fewer hip fractures each year in the United States for an average annual savings of $1.5 billion to $2 billion.[16]

The recommended daily allowance for vitamin D for children up to ten years old is 300 IU; for all adults 200 IU except for pregnant or lactating women, the RDA is 400 IU. (Some women taking vitamin pills and vitamin enriched milk and foods, however, consume as much as 2,000 to 3,000 IUs daily.) The newer reference daily intake issue by the government is 400 IUs of vitamin D for everyone. Intake of 400 IU or higher has been recommended when people have limited exposure to sunlight.

Other minerals are also necessary for bone health and are or will be used as nutraceuticals.

Phosphorus—A Nutraceutical With a Glow

Phosphorus, for example, is present with calcium in almost equal amounts in the bones and teeth. While it is an important part of every tissue in the body, 85 percent of our body's phosphorus—about twenty ounces—is found in bone. It accounts for over 6 percent of bone material. That's enough phosphorus to make two thousand match heads.[17]

Scientists have long believed that since phosphorus and calcium are partners, they should be equal—one to one. They theorized a higher phosphorus ratio in the body caused demineralization of bone, but now they are not so sure. In fact, many believe that phosphorous supplements may help calcium be retained. Indeed, recent studies have shown that high intakes of calcium, phosphorus, and protein result in the best calcium balance of all.[18, 19]

Diphosphonates, nutraceutical phosphorus compounds currently under clinical investigation, bind to bone tissue. They are thought to impede resorption of bone by inhibiting the formation and activity of osteoclasts, the cells involved in bone resorbing. One phosphorus compound, etidronate, is already approved for the treatment of Paget's disease, a bone disorder of unknown cause in which normal bone formation is disrupted and calcium is lost. Etidronate is also approved for high levels of calcium in the blood.[20]

Etidronate was tested over a four-year period in 423 post-menopausal women with osteoporosis. The medication was administered for about two weeks to inhibit bone resorption by bone cells. Then it was discontinued for ten weeks during which time a calcium supplement was given so that osteoblasts could form new bone as a normal part of skeletal remodeling. This etidronate therapy maintained significant increases in spinal and hipbone mineral density and greatly decreased the spinal and hip fracture rate in patients at high risk for breaking bones.[21]

Diphosphonate therapy holds promise as a less expensive option in the treatment of osteoporosis, but further research on its long-term efficacy and safety is in progress. Studies thus far have shown that diphosphonate therapy is associated only with occasional, mild gastrointestinal side effects.

Calcium and vitamin D have long been used to prevent and treat bone disease. Calcitonins and diphosphonates are on the way to becoming the next line of bone-building nutraceuticals.

Magnanimous Manganese

Manganese is an element needed for normal tendon and bone structure and is part of some enzymes. A mineral supplement first isolated in 1774, it occurs in minerals and in minute quantities in animals, plants, and in water. Many forms are used in dyeing. Manganous salts are activators of enzymes and are necessary to the development of strong bones. They are used as nutrients and as dairy substitutes. Manganese is abundant in many foods, especially bran, coffee, tea, nuts, peas, and beans.

A basketball star was plagued by broken bones. When the doctors looked at X rays of his ankle, they saw he had osteoporosis or an osteoporosis-type disease. Examining the star's blood, biologist Paul Saltman of the University of California–San Diego, in La Jolla, found the calcium levels suggested the young man was not synthesizing bone well. Other trace-metal levels in his blood suggested a remarkable imbalance. It turned out the basketball player had been on a macrobiotic diet, a severely restricted, grain-only regimen. When he changed his diet to a regular, well-balanced one and started taking mineral supplements, within six weeks he was back playing basketball.[22]

Manganese may be an important factor not only in preventing osteoporosis but also in regulating the production and release of insulin and in fighting the cell and tissue damage caused by a number of environmental insults.

The first major clue to the basketball player's condition came in a one-year experiment by Saltman and his coworkers in which rats on low-manganese diets developed porous bones. When he and his coworkers at the University of California at San Diego and rheumatologists from the University of Liège in Belgium compared bone samples from fourteen Belgian women with osteoporosis to those of age-matched women without it, they found the only statistically striking difference was in manganese. The blood levels of the trace element in osteoporotic women was a quarter of that in the other group.[23]

Factors such as phytate and fiber in bran, tannins in tea, and oxalic acid in spinach inhibit absorption of many minerals, including manganese. Thus the richest sources of manganese, in wheat bran, tea, and spinach, are unavailable to the body. Though manganese is present in far smaller quantities in meats, milk, and eggs, its higher bioavailability in them can make them an important source.

Studies also show that mineral supplements of iron, magnesium, and calcium can inhibit manganese uptake. The calcium finding is particularly worrisome, according to C. V. Keres of the University of Nebraska's Department of Human Nutrition, because American women, who in general receive far less manganese than even the National Research Council recommends, are being encouraged to offset their risk of developing osteoporosis with calcium pills. In fact, she says, because of their effect on manganese absorption, it is possible that taking these calcium supplements might make the osteoporotic situation worse.[24]

Adverse reactions to manganese include languor, sleepiness, wakefulness, emotional disturbances, and Parkinson-like symptoms. Manganese chloride, citrate, glycerophosphate, and hypophosphite are all *generally recognized as safe* (GRAS) according to the final report of the U.S. Select Committee on GRAS Substances and should continue their GRAS status as nutrients with no limitations other than good manufacturing practices.

Fluoride—Strong Bones and Teeth

Teeth without cavities? Fluoride added to water, toothpaste, or taken by pill or liquid has created a generation of youngsters without or with few areas of decay. It is one of the most successful applications of preventive nutraceuticals. Research has also found that sodium fluoride stimulates bone-mass production in osteoporosis patients from 5 to 30 percent. It increases bone mass by stimulating osteoblasts, or bone-producing cells, particularly in the trabecular or spongelike bone found in the spine.

Some studies have shown that fluoride may lessen the risk of spinal fractures, the most common type of broken bones associated with osteoporosis and the condition that leads to curvature of the spine. Other studies indicate, however, that sodium fluoride may actually increase the risk of hip fractures, and several side effects associated with the use of sodium fluoride require further research, according to Michael Kleerekoper, Henry Ford Hospital, Detroit, Michigan.

A study conducted by Dr. B. Lawrence Riggs and colleagues at the Mayo Clinic in Rochester, Minnesota, however, published in *The New England Journal of Medicine* in 1990, disputed the use of sodium fluoride in increasing bone mass. A four-year clinical study found that the new bone was too weak to prevent the fractures that occur in the vertebrae and cause the back to curve. William A. Peck, president of the National Osteoporosis Foundation, said the results are disappointing, but they do not preclude the possibility that some other fluoride preparation or a lower dose that is more slowly absorbed could be effective. Dr. Peck is vice chancellor and dean at Washington University School of Medicine in St. Louis.[25] Then, in 1994, researchers at the University of Texas Southwestern Medical Center, Dallas, announced the results of a three-year study. Low doses of slow-release fluoride, supplemented with a readily absorbed form of calcium, proved safe and effective in preventing spinal fractures in women with osteoporosis.[26] Charles Y. C. Pak, M.D., and his colleagues found the fluoride rebuilt the already weakened, fragile bone. The cost for the combined fluoride-calcium supplementation is about $1 a day. None of the patients in the fluoride-treated group suffered a hip fracture, gastrointestinal bleeding, pain, or other side effects associated with higher doses of fluoride.

Magnesium—Magnifies Bone Strength

Another mineral, magnesium, is found in all body tissues, but principally in the bones. It is an essential part of many enzyme systems responsible for energy conversions in the body. A deficiency of magnesium in healthy humans eating a variety of foods is uncommon, but it has been observed in some postsurgical patients, in alcoholics, and in certain other disease conditions. Magnesium is widely used as a food-additive buffer, neutralizer, and mineral supplement.

Copper—Policing the Skeleton

Copper aids in the storage and release from storage of iron to form hemoglobin for red blood cells. One of the earliest known metals and an essential nutrient for all mammals. Naturally occurring or experimentally produced copper deficiency in animals leads to a variety of abnormalities, including skeletal defects and muscle degeneration. Copper deficiency is extremely rare in man. The body of an adult contains from 75 to 150 mg of copper. A copper intake of 2 mg per day appears to maintain a balance in adults. An ordinary diet provides 2 to 5 mg daily.

Nutraceuticals for Muscles, Exercise, and Endurance

Without muscles, your bones couldn't move. Your muscles enable you to do everything from clenching your fist to threading a needle. Without muscles you couldn't walk or talk. There are three types of muscles: striped or striated, voluntary muscles that move the bones; the smooth, involuntary muscles that line the blood vessels, stomach, digestive tract, and other internal organs; and the muscles of the heart, which are a kind of cross between smooth and striped muscles.

The striped muscles are capable of strong contractions that you control. The smooth muscles have important but nonemergency functions, so they do not contract as powerfully. Their movements are involuntary, that is, not under conscious control.

The heart muscles have stripes, but the stripes are farther apart than in other striped muscles. The muscles of the heart are involuntary—the heart beats at a certain rate.

The muscles look like a telephone cable. As we age, the resilient fibers of the striped muscles that move our bones are slowly replaced by connective tissue, in a process known as fibrosis. Although this new connective tissue is tough, it is not elastic, so the muscle becomes weak and can no longer contract strongly.

Muscles work by electrochemical signals sent between nerves. The point where the message-bearing nerve fiber links with the muscle fiber is called the motor end plate. When a message reaches the end plate, the plate secretes the powerful chemical acetylcholine, which passes into the muscle fiber and produces jolting electrical charges that get the muscles under way.

Carbohydrates and Muscles

In general it is agreed that the availability of muscle glycogen—a sugar—is the limiting factor in endurance competition. When the muscle glycogen is exhausted, the athlete can no longer perform. Carbohydrate loading or glycogen loading is a dietary procedure whereby high-carbohydrate diets are used to build up muscle glycogen stores. A store of liver glycogen is also necessary to reduce the likelihood of low blood sugar.

When muscles are first depleted of glycogen and then replenished by consumption of a high-carbohydrate diet, the glycogen content of muscle is about twice that achieved with a normal mixed diet. Endurance time correlates with the glycogen content of muscle. Carbohydrate loading entails these steps: depleting the muscle glycogen one week before the event by exercising to exhaustion; consuming a high-protein, high-fat, low-carbohydrate diet for three days; consuming a moderate-protein, low-fat, high-carbohydrate diet for three days immediately preceding the event. The small amount of carbohydrate recommended during the depletion phase is necessary to prevent the effects of ketosis. During the repleting phase, complex carbohydrates are preferred since they are also useful sources of minerals and vitamins and more gradually absorbed.

Initially, carbohydrate furnishes about 90 percent of the energy, and fat about 10 percent. As the competition continues, less energy is derived from carbohydrate and more from free fatty acids. By the end of the competition, most of the energy is derived from fat.

Many of today's athletes are convinced a candy bar, a sports drink, or a bowl of pasta will power them to greater athletic feats. Are such edibles legitimate nutraceuticals?

Candy bars and pasta are made of carbohydrates. In one experiment, eighteen men in their twenties and thirties were tested at the Beltsville Human Nutrition Research Center, Maryland, after eating both high- and low-carbohydrate diets.[27] A third of the men were sedentary. The other two groups either ran (aerobic exercise) or lifted weights (strength training) three to four times a week for an hour or less. After three weeks of getting 62 percent of their calories as carbohydrates, none of the volunteers could pedal a stationary bike significantly longer than when they got 42 percent carbohydrates, nor could their leg muscles overcome any more resistance or their upper bodies bench-press any more weight. Both runners and weight lifters burned significantly more calories per day than the sedentary group. The runners averaged 14 percent more calories daily; the weight lifters who trained the hardest averaged 21 percent more. The findings underscore that people who exercise regularly can eat more calories than sedentary people and still maintain a healthy weight. On the other hand, eating more carbohydrates probably won't improve performance during such exercise. But it can cut down on fat intake, and that may be beneficial.

Protein and Muscle

There is no magic formula for improving performance during exercise and sports. The protein needs of performing athletes include tissue maintenance requirements, allowances for growth by adolescent athletes, and small increments for the development of muscle mass during the conditioning period. No satisfactory evidence exists that additional protein improves work performance or that activity leads to increased cellular destruction of protein. In some cases, protein may not be enough to cover significant losses of nitrogen that occur from the skin during vigorous activity accompanied by profuse sweating in a hot, humid environment. Balance studies have shown that 100 gm of protein per day is adequate to cover all needs of men performing heavy work and perspiring profusely.[28]

Iron and Exercise

Iron is an important part of the compounds necessary for transporting oxygen to the cells and making use of the oxygen when it arrives. It is widely distributed in the body, mostly in the blood, with relatively smaller amounts in the liver, spleen, and bone marrow.

The only way a significant amount of iron can leave the body is through a loss of blood. This is why people who have periodic blood losses or who are forming more blood have the greatest need for dietary iron. Women of childbearing age, pregnant women, and growing children are most likely to suffer from iron-deficiency anemia because of their higher needs. Anemia causes a general lack of energy and a tendency toward fatigue.

It was discovered that women who exercised fifty minutes three times a week experienced a considerable loss of iron in their blood. Roseann M. Lyle, associate professor of health at Purdue and the study's main author, says the research provides further evidence that exercisers need to be knowledgeable about the effects of exercise. During the twelve-week study, previously sedentary women who began exercising but maintained their prestudy eating habits lost five grams of hemoglobin per liter of their blood after the first four weeks of exercise and never regained it during the remaining eight weeks.

All varieties of beans may serve as nutraceuticals because they are rich in iron. Citrus juice taken along with iron supplements or iron-rich food may also serve as a nutraceutical. The vitamin C in the citrus juice helps the body absorb iron. Do not drink tea, however, when eating iron-rich foods. Tannins in tea inhibit iron absorption.[29]

Sports Drinks

Water is of primary concern when profuse sweating accompanies prolonged strenuous exercise. Some individuals may lose as much as two to four liters of sweat (from six to eight pounds of body weight) per hour when competing in endurance events. In addition, with heavy exercise the respiratory loss of water may exceed 130 ml per hour, compared with a normal loss of 15 ml per hour.

The effects of dehydration are:

- fatigue, deterioration in performance
- an increase in body temperature

- reduced volume of extracellular fluid
- reduced urinary volume
- a decline in circulatory function, including lower blood volume, lower blood pressure
- increased pulse rate
- if the dehydration is severe enough, circulatory collapse

A 3 percent weight loss leads to impaired performance; a 5 percent loss can result in some signs of heat exhaustion; a 7 percent loss may produce hallucination and put the individual in the danger zone. A 10 percent loss can lead to heatstroke and circulatory collapse.

Sodium and chloride are also lost during heavy exercise, but most experts believe that they can be replaced during meals after the event.

Supplemental carbohydrates in liquid form may increase endurance, according to studies at the University of Texas at Austin. Researchers in the department of kinesiology tested the effects of carbohydrate supplementation on muscle glycogen utilization and endurance in seven well-trained male cyclists.[30] During each cycling exercise bout, the subjects received either an artificially flavored placebo, a 10 percent liquid carbohydrate supplement, or a solid carbohydrate supplement. Muscle biopsies were taken from their arms during placebo and liquid trials immediately before exercise, after the first 124 minutes, and then after 190 minutes. Subjects then rode to fatigue. After the first 190 minutes, muscle glycogen was greater in the carbohydrate group than in the placebo group. The carbohydrate group was also able to ride more than thirty minutes longer than the placebo riders. The results suggest that carbohydrate supplementation can enhance prolonged, continuous variable-intensity exercise by reducing dependency on muscle glycogen as a fuel source.

Does adding carbonation to carbohydrate drinks have a beneficial effect on exercisers? Researchers at the University of Iowa's Department of Exercise Science wanted to find out. They tested four drinks: a 6 percent carbohydrate, noncarbonated; a 6 percent carbohydrate, carbonated; a 10 percent carbohydrate, noncarbonated; and a 10 percent carbohydrate, carbonated. Subjects were tested on four one-hour treadmill runs in heat. The presence of carbonation in a carbohydrate drink, they found, did not have a significant effect on either gastric emptying or ad libitum drinking. Mean values for sweat rate, percentage of body weight lost, and percentage of fluid replaced by ad libitum drinking were similar for the four trials. Similar changes in heart rate, rectal temperature, and ratings of perceived exertion were also observed during the four one-hour treadmill runs.

Fluids taken before and during an event will not fully replace fluid loss, but partial replacement reduces the risk of overheating, according to American Dietetic Association experts. After the event, they say, athletes should continue to drink water at frequent intervals. The loss of potassium and sodium can be made up at meals later, and they do not have to be included in so-called sports drinks.

Studies of the needs of soldiers in training by researchers at the Western Human Nutrition Research Center, USDA Agricultural Research Service in San Francisco, found that while 100 gm of protein per day and increased carbohydrate diets improve performance, commercial sports drinks do not enhance physical performance compared to water.[31]

Vitamin E and Endurance

Athletes may do well to swallow a vitamin E supplement before exercising. Vitamin E taken before exercise can minimize muscle damage and reduce inflammation and soreness that so often follow a demanding exercise routine. The damage is caused by oxygen radicals, highly reactive oxygen molecules. Among other things, these radicals attack the fats in the muscle cell membranes, which leaves the cells open to injury by other cellular insults.[32]

Drs. Mohsen Meydani and Simin Nikbin Meydani at the Department of Agriculture's Human Nutrition Research Center on Aging at Tufts studied twenty-one sedentary men, half of whom took 800 IU of vitamin E daily for seven weeks prior to running downhill on a treadmill for forty-five minutes. The other half got placebos. Each group consisted of young men in their twenties and older men between fifty-five and seventy-four years of age. By the twelfth day after exercise, the supplemented group —both young and older men—excreted significantly less of a byproduct of fat oxidation. They also had significantly lower blood levels of two substances that trigger inflammation. The benefit was noted in men over fifty-five as well as those in their twenties. Earlier studies at the Agricultural Research Service Center suggested that the immune system responds to prolonged or muscle-damaging exercise much the same way as it does to an infection—by launching an attack against damaged muscle tissue to clear it away for new tissue. But the inflammatory response may get out of control and damage healthy tissue as well.

Vitamin E and Lou Gehrig's Disease (ALS)

Researchers now believe that a deficiency in the antioxidant vitamin E may play an important part in the development of Lou Gehrig's disease, amyotrophic lateral sclerosis (ALS). Cornell University veterinary medical researchers are studying equine motor-neuron disease (EMND) in horses.

Like human ALS patients, EMND horses experience progressive muscle wasting as dying motor neurons fail to transmit signals to muscles. Motor-neuron changes in the spinal cords of human and equine victims of the diseases "are virtually identical—the same cranial nerves are affected and the same ones are spared," according to the Cornell investigators. Weight loss, difficulty standing, and fasciculations (quivering of the leg and shoulder muscles) are others signs of EMND.

There is evidence in EMND horses that an "oxidative insult" may be involved in motor-neuron death, and that a deficiency in protective antioxidants may be at least partially responsible for the disease, according to Dr. Thomas J. Divers, DVM, of Cornell's New York State College of Veterinary Medicine. Blood tests in EMND cases referred to Cornell found "incredibly low, even undetectable levels" of vitamin E, said Divers, an associate professor of medicine. Vitamin E is an antioxidant that counteracts the harmful free radicals that are naturally produced during metabolism in animals and humans.

Coupled with the discovery by researchers at the Massachusetts Institute of Technology and Massachusetts General Hospital of a defective human gene that fails to initiate production of enzymes that protect against oxygen damage in ALS patients, the Cornell finding could indicate an interplay of antioxidant vitamins and enzymes, all working together, to protect humans and horses against neurodegenerative disorders, according to Divers.

He points out horses develop EMND in middle age. They are not pastured where they can eat fresh grass, but rather are fed commercial feeds and cut hay. The commercial horse feeds are low in vitamins, including vitamin E.[33]

Not everyone believes vitamin E may help in the treatment of Lou Gehrig's disease. Dr. Teepu Siddique, a Northwestern University member of an international team that pinpointed the faulty gene in ALS sufferers, says, "I've given antioxidants to ALS patients for years and haven't seen them drop their cane or get better."[34]

The recognition that antioxidant nutrients may have a significant role in the development of ALS may nevertheless lead to prevention or at least more effective treatment.

Antioxidants and Vision

Vision is just as important to the elderly person trying to walk downstairs as it is to a professional basketball player. Approximately 20 percent of Americans aged 65 and older suffer from age-related macular degeneration (AMD), and 45 percent of those aged 75 and older have age-related cataracts (opacity of the lens). The macular is in the center of the retina, the light receptor in the eye. The first symptoms usually are loss of central visual acuity or visual distortion in one eye. No medical therapy has proven effective. The oxidation of the lens proteins in the eye are thought to be a major cause of the lens opacities that impair vision.

In the *Archives of Opthalmology* in January 1993 and in February 1994, groups of researchers reported that antioxidants such as vitamins E and C, selenium, and beta-carotene "suggested a protective effect" against AMD. The higher the levels of antioxidants, the less likely the occurrence of the visually disabling age-related eye problem.

Antioxidants have also been reported to help prevent cataracts. In a two year study performed on 660 subjects enrolled in the Baltimore Longitudinal Study on Aging, it was found that vitamin E appeared to protect against opacities of the lens.

Vitamin A, another antioxidant, of course, has long been known to be vital to vision, particulary night vision.

Plants, Bones, and Muscles

While modern scientists are finding out more about how vitamins and minerals may affect bone and muscle, folk-medicine literature is filled with plants that are reputed to improve athletic prowess and/or deal with bone and muscle problems. The following are just a few of the citations:

ASHWAGANDHA *(Withania somniforal)* is an herb used in India to heal broken bones and as a sedative.

COMFREY *(Symphytum officinale)*, also called knitbone, blackwort, and healing herb, is recommended by herbalists for rapid bone and wound healing. The leaf and root contain allantoin, mucilage, tannins, starch, inulin, steroidal saponins, and pyrrolizidine alkaloids (*see* all in glossary). It has been reported to be toxic when taken internally. Potential adverse reactions include liver dysfunction. Pyrrolizidine alkaloids have been found to cause cancer in laboratory rats, comfrey was banned in Canada in 1989.

REHMANNIA *(Rehmannia glutinosais)* root, also called *sok day–sang day*, is used by Chinese herbalists to purify and nourish the blood, strengthen the kidneys, and heal the bones and tendons. Herbalists say it is useful in building the body during recovery from an illness.

Chapter 12

NUTRACEUTICALS AND THE SKIN

Cleopatra bathed in sour milk, and ladies of the French court rubbed sour wine on their faces. The Queen of the Nile was, in fact, applying lactic acid in her bath, while the mademoiselles were smearing themselves with tartaric acid. All were using nutraceuticals to beautify their skin—the same edible acids that are being touted as "new" ingredients in wrinkle creams today.

In order to understand how ancient and very new nutraceuticals may affect the covering of your body, you have to recognize how the environment, aging, and disease make marks upon skin.

Your skin is your shield of armor, the mirror of your emotions, the largest organ of your body and next to your brain, the most complex. It can also be affected by more than 2,100 diseases.

Your skin performs a number of important jobs. Among these are protecting your body against invasion by bacteria, from injury to the more sensitive tissues within your body, from the rays of the sun, and against the loss of moisture. It is also serves as a sensitive organ of perception. It contains hundreds of pain receptors, plus pressure, heat, and cold receptors.

Your skin is made up of three layers:

- *The epidermis*, the top layer—sometimes called the *horny layer*, is comprised of scales that are actually dead skin cells. They gradually flake away or soak off when wet. The *horny layer* is constantly being replaced by cells pushed toward the surface as new cells are formed in deeper layers.

- *The dermis* sometimes called the *true skin*, lies below the epidermis and atop the subcutaneous layers. It contains blood vessels, nerves, nerve receptors, hair follicles, sweat glands, and oil glands.
- *The subcutaneous* layer contains fat, blood vessels, and nerves. It links the dermis (middle layer) with tissue covering the muscles and bones. It also serves as a smooth and springy base for the skin.

What happens to these three layers as time passes?

The thickness of the skin is reduced by as much as 20 percent. There is a reduction in the network of blood vessels surrounding hair bulbs and sweat and oil glands. Healthy older people perspire more than 70 percent less than younger ones exposed to the same amount of heat. There is a 60 percent decrease in production by the oil glands.

Also, the renewal rate of skin cells is reduced. In young people, the cells renew themselves every three to four weeks and they rise to the skin surface where they are shed. This keeps the skin smooth and fresh in appearance. By the time we reach our thirties or forties, this process takes twice as long. Because of the slowdown in skin-cell turnover as we age, the cells tend to clump together in a process known as *keratinization*, giving the skin a rough, scaly appearance and texture. Sensory perception decreases. Fine lines as well as deep furrows result from changes in elastin and/or collagen fibers, which may become thickened and tangled.

The cells that produce a pigment, melanin, to color skin cells, are reduced. The skin doesn't tan as efficiently when exposed to the sun, and thus a protective barrier against ultraviolet light is weakened.

There is a decline in the healing rate of the skin after injury.

All of the above changes are *intrinsic;* they are caused by changes within the body. Then there are the *extrinsic* changes that are due largely to sun and other environmental factors.

Photoaging, also called *dermatoheliosis, actinic damage,* and *photodamage,* refers to skin damage due to sun exposure. Many of the external signs of aging—wrinkling, mottling, and lesions—can be caused or made worse by photodamage. These are largely preventable.

Formation of growths—benign and malignant—do increase with age. In the United States, basal-cell carcinoma and squamous-cell carcinoma, the most common forms of skin cancer, outnumber all other human malignancies combined.[1] Melanoma is a deadly form of skin cancer diagnosed in about 32,000 Americans per year and killing 6,800 of them.[2] The incidence of melanoma has been growing at the rate of 4 percent per year. As the incidence of skin cancer continues to increase, however, awareness is growing about the dangers of the sun.

Scientists have discovered clues about how chronic exposure to the sun causes sagging, wrinkled, and leathery skin. Researchers at the National Institute of Arthritis and Musculoskeletal and Skin Diseases tested the effects of ultraviolet radiation on skin cells grown in laboratory dishes. The cells produce collagenase, an enzyme that breaks down collagen. Collagen is a connective-tissue protein that supports and provides elasticity for the skin. The researchers found that the sun's rays cause collagenase, the collagen-destroying enzyme, to increase in the dermis, the layer that gives skin its strength and elasticity.[3]

How can your skin be protected from within and without against the sun and other factors that "age" it?

Nutraceuticals—vitamins, derivatives of vitamins, and phytochemicals—are being studied in an effort to prevent skin cancer and to combat the signs of aging as well as other skin problems. Many scientists are investigating the antioxidant nutraceuticals, vitamins A, C, E, selenium, and beta-carotene.

In a large study at Dartmouth College in Hanover, New Hampshire, beta-carotene, the precursor of vitamin A in food, proved ineffective in preventing recurrence of nonmelanoma skin cancers. However, at the University of Arizona, Thomas Moon, M.D., professor of epidemiology, completed a five-year study in which more than 2,200 randomly selected patients with precancerous actinic keratoses received either a placebo or a daily supplement of 25,000 IU of vitamin A. The patients who received vitamin A had higher levels of vitamin A and its precursors, including beta-carotene, in their skins and significantly fewer skin cancers.[4] "The results seem to confirm that vitamin A can help prevent skin cancer, says David Alberts, M.D., director of cancer prevention and control at the university, who worked with Dr. Moon's team.[5] The researchers are now doing further studies using higher megadoses of vitamin A.

Anti-Skin-Cancer Nutraceuticals

A derivative of vitamin A, isotretinoin, is being tested in people abnormally sensitive to the sun. John J. DiGiovanna, M.D., an investigator in the Dermatology Branch of the National Institutes of Health, reported on isotretinoin and patients with xeroderma pigmentosum (XP), a rare hereditary disease. If XP patients are exposed to sunlight, their eyes and their skin can suffer severe damage. XP patients can develop skin cancers before the age of ten and will continue to develop other skin cancers and severe eye problems if not protected from the sun. This condition cannot be cured, and the best treatment is to totally protect the skin and eyes from sun exposure.

Dr. DiGiovanna described the results of a seven-year study in which seven patients with XP were treated with varying doses of systemic isotretinoin.

While a high dose over two years was the most effective in preventing the growth of new skin cancers, he reported, that dosage also proved to have the most serious side effects, such as muscle and bone abnormalities. When the treatment was discontinued, the beneficial effects of isotretinoin were quickly lost.

In the meantime, another vitamin A relative, tretinoin (Retin-A), is a prescription acne drug and wrinkle cream that has been found to have possibilities for preventing skin cancer. In ointment form, the vitamin A product apparently returns precancerous conditions of the skin, dysplastic nevi, to normal, presumably eliminating the risk of developing malignancy. Dysplastic nevi tend to look like moles but are larger and irregularly shaped and unevenly colored. They may be a prelude to melanoma, a deadly skin cancer. Dr. Lynn Schuchter of the University of Pennsylvania conducted the mole studies and reported the nevi faded or disappeared under treatment with Retin-A in six months.[6]

Mace, *Myristica fragrans*, is from the tree that also produces nutmeg and is native to the Banda Islands, the Malay Archipelago, and the Moluccan Islands, India, the West Indies, and Brazil. Both nutmeg and mace are used for flatulence, nausea, and vomiting. They are mildly narcotic. Mace has been found in animals to prevent skin cancer.

Antiwrinkle Nutraceuticals

The possibilities of developing vitamin A derivatives to prevent skin cancer are tremendous, but if such a compound could fight wrinkles, well, the sky's the limit.

Tretinoin (Retin-A) was developed in 1946. The first clinical evaluation in skin lesions that arise from sun exposure was done in 1962. In 1969, Albert Kligman, M.D., of the University of Pennsylvania published the first report of tretinoin's ability to eliminate the signs of acne. Tretinoin was first marketed as Retin-A for acne in 1971. In 1988, a lower-dose Retin-A that was less irritating was put on the market.

Reports began to filter in that tretinoin had possibilities as an antiwrinkle product as well as an acne treatment.

Researchers at the Dermatopharmacology Unit at the University of Michigan Medical Center, Ann Arbor, found that the formation of collagen is significantly decreased in photodamaged human skin, and this process is partly restored by treatment with tretinoin, a factor believed important in preventing wrinkles.[7]

Prompted by reports from the University of Pennsylvania and the University of Michigan that vitamin A preparations have a beneficial effect on photodamaged skin, researchers have been studying tretinoin's benefits for sun-damaged skin.

Gerald Weinstein, M.D., professor and chairman of dermatology at the University of California at Irvine College of Medicine, presented results at an American Academy of Dermatology meeting of the first six months of a 657-patient trial conducted at nine centers. Dr. Weinstein reported that 68 percent of patients using an emollient cream containing .05 percent tretinoin showed improvement. Thirty-eight percent of patients using the same cream without tretinoin also benefited. Patients in the study had only mild or moderate skin damage because the researchers want to test the drug's usefulness for early photoaging.[8]

"This statistically significant difference reflects modest changes for the average patient," said Dr. Weinstein. "Some subgroups may have a better response than others, and that still needs to be sorted out."

Among patients who showed the greatest improvement, 19 percent had used the .05 percent vitamin A cream compared to 11 percent who used the placebo cream.

Dr. Weinstein noted that clinical changes in photodamaged skin such as wrinkling, pigmentation, texture, color, and other characteristics are difficult to measure quantitatively. The researchers were required to develop a scoring method that included the use of photographs to classify the amount of damage in study patients.

The study was double-blind, meaning that neither researchers nor patients knew which tubes contained the active cream. Patients were given the cream alone or active concentrations containing .05, .01, or .001 percent retinoic acid.

Dr. Weinstein speculated that patients' increased attention to their skin, as well as the use of an emollient cream, may have been a factor in improvement.

Some degree of irritation, usually temporary, was reported by approximately 90 percent of patients using the active cream, but was cause to discontinue treatment in only a few cases.

Barbara Gilchrest, M.D., chairwoman, Department of Dermatology, Boston University, presented results to a committee of the U.S. Food and Drug Administration of studies of the use of vitamin A compounds on people with photoaged skin. The committee then unanimously recommended that tretinoin, called Renova, the name of the wrinkle cream, be approved for enhancing the appearance of sun-damaged skin.[9]

Dr. Gilchrest said the most common side effect was skin irritation, which usually declined after the second week. When the treatment was discontinued after 12 months, about half of the participants maintained their improvement for at least six additional months, provided that a sunscreen with a sun protection factor (SPF) of fifteen or higher was used daily.[10]

The use of tretinoin in patients with hyperpigmentation is not new. Acne, eczema, and irritation from shaving may cause postinflammatory hyperpigmentation and freckling. Many physicians, however, have been hesitant to prescribe tretinoin for acne or other disorders in black patients because of side effects such as burning or stinging of the skin, redness, scaling, and pigment changes. Black people sometimes develop irregular disfiguring skin hyperpigmentation due to inflammation. Researchers at the University of Michigan Medical Center, Ann Arbor, investigated the treatment of this hyperpigmentation with topical tretinoin cream. They found that after forty weeks of therapy, facial postinflammatory hyperpigmented lesions were significantly lighter. It also lightens normal skin in black persons.[11]

Vitamin C and the Skin

Vitamin C, in a highly concentrated form, has surprising photoprotective qualities, reported Sheldon R. Pinnell, M.D., chief of dermatology at Duke University.[12] "It can't be washed off, sweated off, or rubbed off, but it's not a sunscreen," he noted.

Dr. Pinnell reported on a study in which ten volunteers applied vitamin C compound to one arm and another compound without vitamin C to the other. Both arms were exposed to ultraviolet B rays, which normally cause sunburn. The vitamin C protected arms did not burn. In another study, live pigs were treated similarly. (Pigs have especially sensitive skin and are prone to sunburns.) Topical vitamin C protected the pigs even though they were exposed to three times the normal dose that would produce sunburn. And the vitamin C protection lasted three days, even though the pigs were scrubbed.

"Vitamin C is different from sunscreens. Sunscreens absorb the ultraviolet rays that are most likely to harm the skin," said Dr. Pinnell. "They can be penetrated by other wavelengths and can easily wear off or be washed away. The vitamin C compound actually destroys the potentially harmful chemicals that form after the ultraviolet rays penetrate the skin."

The Duke researcher and his colleagues point out that vitamin C levels of the skin can be severely depleted after ultraviolet irradiation, which lowers the skin's innate protective mechanism as well as leaving it at risk of impaired healing after sun-induced damage. In addition, vitamin C has been found to show promise as a skin protectant for persons on certain medications that make them sunlight sensitive.

Vitamin C might also be used in the future to help protect the skin against environmental pollutants. Dr. Pinnell reported that it could take several years before a vitamin C compound is approved by the FDA.

Starving Skin Cancer

In another study of vitamin C and the skin, researchers at Washington State University, in an attempt to combat melanoma, the deadly skin cancer, supplemented the drinking water of melanoma-affected mice with vitamin C. They also lowered the dietary levels of two amino acids, tyrosine, and phenylalanine. Starving the body of these two amino acids may eliminate building blocks that melanomas need to sustain growth, according to study head Herbert Pierson, Ph.D., vice president of research and development for Preventive Nutrition Consultants Inc., Woodinville, Washington. Dr. Pierson, who was a guiding force behind the nutraceutical research at the National Cancer Institute, explains that animal proteins abound in these amino acids, while most fruits and vegetables—especially turnips—are low in them. The greatest effect on the melanomas occurred when vitamin C was raised and tyrosine and phenylalanine were lowered, but he cautioned that patients should never limit their tyrosine and phenylalanine without close medical and nutritional supervision.[13]

Vitamin D

Vitamin D is a very odd substance. It needs some sunlight to do its work in the skin to provide the body with healthy bones. Absorbed through the skin, vitamin D_3 is used to treat rickets and other vitamin D deficiency diseases and in the treatment and management of metabolic bone disease associated with chronic renal failure. Vitamin D speeds the body's production of calcium, and is used for its alleged skin-healing properties in lubricating creams and lotions.

How much vitamin D do the elderly need and does the long-term use of sunscreens inhibit the absorption of this necessary vitamin? These questions were addressed by Janet H. Prystowsky, M.D., Ph.D., Herbert Irving assistant professor of dermatology at Columbia University. Providing the body with vitamin D is the only known beneficial effect of sun exposure—it helps prevent rickets and senile osteoporosis.

"Previously, studies on whether sunscreens inhibit the absorption of vitamin D were done in controlled laboratory settings, Dr. Prystowsky said, "and it was found that the long-term use of sunscreens inhibited vitamin D absorption. But as we translate this into 'real life,' we must disagree. We have to wonder how meticulously people apply sunscreen, if it is applied on their entire bodies and in what quality, and how much absorption of sunlight takes place through clothing, which could result in the photosynthesis of vitamin D." "We also know that physical activities and swimming decrease the effectiveness of sunscreens. Given these variables, we find these test conclusions erroneous," Dr. Prystowsky says.

How much vitamin D is necessary? Dr. Prystowsky suggests that the photosynthesis of vitamin D decreases with age and with skin type and is affected by the environment, seasonal changes, and diet.

"We can conclude that the elderly have reduced vitamin D requirements compared to a younger population, and they often have diets that are low in vitamin D due to a lack of fortified dairy products," Dr. Prystowsky said. "However, most adults obtain adequate vitamin D through protected, not deliberate, sun exposure and adequate diets in vitamin D rich foods such as fatty fish, liver, eggs, and fortified foods.

"Dermatologists routinely advise the public to apply sunscreens with an SPF of at least fifteen, wear protective clothing, and limit sun exposure, especially those with fair skin. In the elderly, sun protection is important, since they already have had years of cumulative exposure and are at high risk for many forms of skin cancer." Dr. Prystowsky suggested that the best method to prevent vitamin D deficiency in the elderly is through the intake of oral supplements of 200 IU/d of vitamin D. "This is simple and it is safe. Photoprotection should continue to be advocated for all age groups to minimize actinic damage," Dr. Prystowsky concluded.

The Heartbreak of Psoriasis

A vitamin D nutraceutical, Dovonex, entered the market in March of 1994 to treat psoriasis, a chronic disease of the skin of unknown cause, usually persisting for years with periods of remission and recurrence. Psoriasis is characterized by elevated lesions on various parts of the body covered with dry, silvery scales that drop off. It most often occurs between the ages of ten and thirty and tends to run in families. In most cases, it does not affect general health if it is not neglected. Dovonex is a vitamin D_3 analogue. D_3 is produced in the skin on exposure to sunlight. After entering the bloodstream, it is metabolized in the liver and kidneys to its active form, a hormone called calcitriol. When used as recommended, the synthetic vitamin regulates skin-cell production and development.

Conventional therapies for psoriasis include coal tar, corticosteroids, anthralin, light treatments plus a psoralen (PUVA), methotrexate, and etretinate. The treatments may all have significant side effects. The most frequent side effects with the synthetic vitamin D included burning, itching, and skin irritation, which occurred in approximately 10 to 15 percent of patients.[14]

Vitamin E

Researchers at McGill University, Montreal, Quebec, searched forty-four years of scientific literature to determine if there was any evidence of vitamin E's effectiveness in treating certain skin conditions. They found some "weak or conflicting evidence" that vitamin E is of value in yellow-nail syndrome, epidermolysis bullosa (a chronic skin disease), cancer prevention, insufficient blood flow to the skin, skin ulcers, and collagen manufacture and would healing. They said it was of use in treating atopic dermatitis (a chronic, itching, superficial skin inflammation), chronic herpes disease, psoriasis, subcorneal pustular dermatosis (pus-filled blisters), porphyries (pigmentations), and skin damage induced by ultraviolet light. Still, the researchers said that further research in well-designed controlled trials is needed to clarify vitamin E's role.[15]

The B Vitamins

Vitamin B_2, formerly called vitamin G, is in every plant and animal cell in minute amounts. Riboflavin is a factor in the vitamin B complex and is used in emollients. The B vitamins help to metab- olize protein, carbohydrate, and fat; maintain healthy skin, eyes; and aid formation of red blood cells and antibodies. Symptoms of deficiency include sores or cracking around the mouth, skin prob- lems, and eye disorders. They are necessary for healthy skin and respiration, protect the eyes from sensitivity to light, and are used for building and maintaining human body tissues.

Pantothenic acid, another B vitamin, is reportedly effective for treatment of nerve damage, breathing problems, itching, and other skin problems, and to prevent gray hair, arthritis, allergies, and other ills. There is some controversy in the mainstream med- ical profession over these claims. Deficiencies of this vitamin are reportedly rare. It is found in foods such as peas, whole grain cereals, and lean meat and poultry.

Other Nutraceuticals

Skin and Protein

Protein when eaten is simply burned as fuel for daily activities or stored as fat—not hair. The only people who might see a notice- able improvement in hair quality by consuming protein are those who are severely deficient in that nutrient, such as people with eating disorders or crash dieters who eat tiny portions of food over long periods of time.[16]

Milk and Skin

Hyperimmune milk, mentioned at the beginning of this book, is also being developed to counteract skin disorders such as acne and eczema and even as a deodorant. According to Stolle Milk Biolog- ics, utilization of the unique hyperimmunization process yields antibodies effective against selected human skin bacteria. These bacteria include those associated with acne, body odors, and other skin disorders.[17]

Sharks Are Kind to Skin

Shark liver oil is a rich source of vitamin A, believed to be beneficial to the skin. It is a brown fatty oil that is used in lubricating creams and lotions.

Plant Extracts—Ancient and Modern Beauty Treatments

How about the many plant extracts that have been used through the ages to maintain and beautify the skin? The plant extracts are basically astringents or emollients.

Astringents are substances that cause skin or mucous membranes to pucker and shrink by reducing their ability to absorb water. Often used in skin cleansers and to help stop bleeding. Tannins are used in herbal and conventional medicine for this purpose, and so is witch hazel.

Emollients are preparations that help the skin feel softer and smoother, reduce roughness, cracking, and irritation of the skin. Among the herbs used for this purpose are balm mint and Malva.

Starch is stored by plants and is used in skin products. It is taken from grains of wheat, potatoes, rice, and many other vegetables. In 1992, the FDA proposed a ban on topical starch in astringent drug products and in fever-blister and cold-sore products because it has not been shown to be safe and effective for its stated claims.

Herbs Applied to the Skin

ACACIA GUM *(Acacia vera)* is also called gum arabic, catechu, and Egyptian thorn. Acacia is the odorless, colorless, tasteless dried exudate from the stem of the acacia tree grown in Africa, the Near East, India, and the southern United States. Its most distinguishing quality among the natural gums is its ability to dissolve rapidly in water. The use of acacia dates back four thousand years. It is used today in denture adhesive powder and to give shape to tablets. It is used as a demulcent to soothe irritations, particularly of the mucous membranes, and by herbalists to treat burns. It can cause allergic reactions such as skin rash and asthmatic attacks. Oral toxicity is low.

AMALAKI *(Phyllanthus emblica)* is an herb used for thousands of years in India to treat skin diseases and tumors.

BALM MINT *(Balsamodendron opobalsam)* is also called balm of Gilead. The secretion of any of several small evergreen African or Asian trees with leaves that yield a strong aromatic odor when bruised. Known in ancient Palestine as a soothing medication for the skin. Used in cosmetics as an unguent that is said to soothe and heal the skin.

BAPTISIA *(Baptisia tinctoria)* is also called wild indigo and indigo weed. The roots and leaves are used by herbalists as an anti-inflammatory with antibiotic properties. It has been used to treat all sorts of infections from tuberculosis to sore nipples and swollen glands. It is used either in an ointment or in a tea.

BROOKLIME *(Veronica beccabunga and Veronica americana)* is also called watercress and water pimpernel. An herb that grows abundantly in shallow streams, it is believed to have healing properties. It is used to treat boils, ulcers, abscesses, and pimples. It is said to purge the blood of toxins.

BURDOCK *(Arctium lappa)* is also called bardane and beggar's-buttons. The root, seed, and leaves contain essential oil of this common roadside plant, with nearly 45 percent inulin and many minerals. Herbalists use it for skin diseases, blood purification, urinary problems, and as a tonic. Chinese burdock is used to eliminate excess nervous energy, and the root is considered to have aphrodisiac properties. It is sold in drugstores as an ointment to treat minor burns, cuts, or other skin traumas. Used by Gypsies in a pouch hung around the neck to ward off arthritis. In modern experiments, burdock root extract has been shown to have antitumor effects.

BUTTERBUR *(Petasites hybridus)* is a plant with broad leaves and purplish flowers. The rhizome or leaves of this herb contain essential oil, mucilage, and tannin *(see* all in glossary). The fresh leaves are used for wound dressings.

CAJEPUT *(Melaleuca leucadendron)* is also called cajuput and tea tree. The spicy oil contains, among other ingredients, terpenes, limonene, benzaldehyde, valeraldehyde, and dipentene. Native to Australia and Southeast Asia, it is used to treat fungal infections such as athlete's foot, and as a liniment for a wide variety of ailments. Herbalists use it to relieve itchy scalp and arthritic pains, and it is also used as an antiseptic for cuts.

CALENDULA *(Calendula marigol, Calendula officinalis)* is also called pot marigold. The flower heads contain essential oil containing carotenoids, saponin, resin, and bitter principle *(see* all in glossary). In an oil or ointment, it is used to treat minor skin irritations both by herbalists and traditional pharmacists. An infusion is used by herbalists to treat eruptive skin diseases such as measles.

CAPSICUM, a member of the nightshade family, is native to tropical South America. Herbalists used capsicums as an internal disinfectant and to protect against infectious disease. Plasters are made for arthritic pains. It increases blood flow to the area of application, which results in reduced inflammation of the affected area. The FDA proposed a ban in 1992 for the use of capsicum oleoresin to treat fever blisters and cold sores because it has not been shown to be safe and effective for stated claims in over-the-counter products.

CHICKWEED *(Stelleria media)* is also called starweed and herbal slim. The herb contains saponins, which exert an anti-inflammatory action similar to cortisone, but according to herbalists, it is much milder and without the side effects. Chickweed is also used for weight loss, for skin irritations, itches and rashes, and to soothe sore throat and lungs.

CLEAVERS *(Galium aparine)* is also called catchweed, goose grass, and clivers. A native of Europe, Asia, and North America. The Greeks called it *philantropon* because they considered its clinging habit showed a love of mankind. Used in homeopathic medicine for skin diseases such as psoriasis and scurvy.

CLOVER, RED *(Trifolium pratense)*, is a perennial plant common throughout Europe. It is used in medicine as a tea and sometimes combined with other herbs as a tonic. A salve is made to heal fresh wounds, ulcers, and sores. It is used by some herbalists to help cancer patients.

ELDERFLOWER *(Sambucus nigra, S. canadensis)* is also called sambucus, black elder, bourtree, and Judas tree. An herbal additive to Chinese tea, it contains essential oils, terpenes, glycosides, rutin, quercitrin, mucilage, and tannin. The fruits are high in vitamin C. Elderflower is used to treat burns, rashes, minor skin ailments, and to diminish wrinkles.

EUCALYPTUS *(Eucalyptus globulus)* is also called blue gum tree and dinkum oil. The colorless to pale yellow volatile liquid from the fresh leaves of the tree has a camphorlike odor and is used as a local antiseptic. The chief constituent of eucalyptus, eucalyptol, is used as an antiseptic. Herbalists maintain that as a disinfectant it destroys bacteria, fungi, and viruses. Most commonly, the oil is rubbed directly on the chest or back for all respiratory problems. It is also used in liniments to treat arthritic pains. The FDA proposed a ban in 1992 for the use of eucalyptus oil to treat fever blisters and cold sores, poison ivy, poison sumac, and poison oak and in astringent drugs because it has not been shown to be safe and effective for stated claims in over-the-counter products.

FIGWORT *(Scrophularia nodosa)* is a perennial plant native to Britain and the United States. It used to be hung in houses and barns to ward off witches. Herbalists used it as an ointment to treat eczema, rashes, bruises, scratches, and small wounds and for removing freckles.

FO-TI *(Polygonum multiforum)* is also known as *ho shou wu*. In China, it is one of the most popular herbs and is employed to treat skin ulcers and stomach ulcers as well as abscesses. The Chinese claim this herb has rejuvenating properties and can prevent gray hair and other premature signs of aging.

FUMITORY *(Fumaria officinalis)* is also known as earth-smoke, horned poppy, and wax dolls. An abundant weed in fields, herbalists use it to cure many diseases of the skin. It may also be used as an eyewash to ease conjunctivitis.

GOLDENROD *(Solidago virgauria)* is a perennial that includes 125 species. It was valued for its medicinal properties by herb women in Elizabethan London. The name *Solidago* means "makes whole," and herbalists say it helps to heal wounds, and in fact at one time it was called woundwort. It is used by herbalists as an antiseptic. The pulped leaves, stalks, and flowers are good for staunching blood. The American Indians used it to treat bee stings.

GOTU KOLA *(Centella asiastica)* is also called thickleaved and pennywort. An herb grown in Pakistan, India, Malaysia, and parts of eastern Europe, it is commonly used for diseases of the skin, blood, and nervous system. In homeopathy, it is used for psoriasis, cervicitis, pruritus vaginitis, blisters, and other skin conditions.

HORSERADISH EXTRACT *(Armoracia lapathifolia)* is also known as scurvy grass. The grated root from the tall, coarse, white-flowered herb native to Europe. It contains vitamin C and acts as an antiseptic, particularly in cosmetics. It is applied by herbalists as a poultice to accelerate the healing of stubborn wounds.

HORSETAIL *(Equisetum arvense)* is also called shave grass. The American Indians and the Chinese have long used horsetail to accelerate the healing of bones and wounds. Horsetail is rich in minerals the body uses to rebuild injured tissue. It facilitates the absorption of calcium by the body, which nourishes nails, skin, hair, bones, and the body's connective tissue. The herb helps eliminate excess oil from skin and hair.

HOUSELEEK *(Sempervivum tectorum)* is native to the mountains of Europe and to the Greek islands. Its longevity led to its being named *sempervivum,* which translated means "ever alive." It has been used to treat shingles, gout, and to get rid of bugs. Its pulp was applied to the skin for rashes and inflammation, and to remove warts and calluses. The juice was used to reduce fever and to treat insect stings. Houseleek juice mixed with honey was prescribed for thrush *(see* glossary), and an ointment made from the plant was used to treat ulcers, burns, scalds, and inflammation.

KAVAKAVA *(Piper methysticum)* is also known as kava and 'ava. The Polynesian herb's root is used by herbalists as a remedy for insomnia and nervousness. A compound in kava is marketed in Europe as a mild sedative for the elderly. Other agents in kava have been shown to have antiseptic properties in the laboratory. It is also a reputedly potent analgesic and antiseptic that may be taken internally or applied directly to a painful wound.

LEMON BALM *(Melissa officinalis)* has leaves that contain essential oils, acids, and tannin *(see* glossary). Herbalists use it to cause sweating and lower fevers. Recently, an ointment has been made with lemon balm leaves to relieve symptoms of the herpes simplex virus *(see* glossary).

LETTUCE EXTRACT *(Lactuca elongata)* is an extract of various species of *Lactuca.* Used in commercial toning lotions and by herbalists to make soothing skin decoctions.

LOOSESTRIFE, PURPLE *(Lythrum salicaria)*, also called salicaria extra or spiked loosestrife, is a flowering herb with purple or pink flowers. It is a perennial grown in many parts of the world, in damp, marshy places. Loosestrife has been used since ancient Greek times to calm nerves and soothe skin. The Irish employed it to heal wounds. Herbalists offer it in soothing eye drops and in salves for skin ulcers.

MULLEIN *(Verbascum thapsus)* is a perennial of the figwort family and is native to Europe, Asia, Africa, and the United States. It grows wild. The ashes have been made into soap to restore gray hair to its former color. The crushed flowers reputedly cure warts, and a cloth dipped in hot mullein tea was used for inflammations. It has also been found to have antibiotic properties. During the Civil War, the Confederates relied on mullein for treatment of respiratory problems whenever their medical supplies ran out.

OAK BARK EXTRACT *(Quercus alba)* is also called oak chip extract and stone oak. The extract contains tannic acid (*see* glossary) and is exceedingly astringent. In a wash, the Indians used it for sore eyes and as a tonic. Used in astringents and to treat hemorrhoids.

OAT FLOUR. Flour from the cereal grain that is an important crop grown in the temperate regions. Light yellowish or brown to weak greenish or yellow powder. Slight odor; starchy taste. Makes a bland ointment to soothe skin irritation and is used in powdery form for soothing baths to treat skin irritations, rashes, and hemorrhoids.

PANSY, WILD *(Viola tricolor)*, is also known as johnny-jump-up, heartsease, and violet. A European herb, it is grown for its large, attractive flowers. The herb contains mucilaginous material that is used as a soothing lotion for boils, swellings, and skin diseases. It also contains salicylates, saponins, alkaloids, flavonoids, and tannin (*see* all in glossary). It is also used as a gentle laxative and to treat kidney diseases. The root is both emetic and cathartic.

PILEWORT *(Ranunculus ficaria)* is also called small celandine and buttercup. A little yellow starry blossom, it is widely found under hedges. It has astringent qualities and the herb is considered specific for piles—hence its name. A green pilewort ointment is sold by many herbalists.

POPLAR EXTRACT *(Populus nigra)* is also called balm of Gilead, and extracts of its leaves and twigs were used in ancient times. The buds were mashed to make a soothing salve that was spread on sunburned areas, scalds, scratches, inflamed skin, and wounds. The herb was also simmered in lard for use as an ointment and for antiseptic purposes. The leaves and bark were steeped by American colonists to make a soothing tea. It supposedly helped allergies and soothed reddened eyes.

PRIVET FRUIT *(Ligustrum)* is a common plant used as a hedge in many yards. Its fruits contain mannitol, ursolic acid, and glucose (*see* all in glossary) as well as oleanolic acid and fatty oil. Herbalists also claim that it can prevent premature graying of the hair or loss of vision.

QUEEN'S-DELIGHT *(Stillingia sylvatica)* has a root that contains volatile oil, tannin, and resin. This North American herb is used for the treatment of chronic skin conditions such as eczema and psoriasis. The astringent qualities have led herbalists to use it for hemorrhoid problems.

SAGE. The flowering tops and leaves of the shrubby mints. Spices include Greek sage and Spanish sage. The genus is *Salvia*, so named for the plant's supposed healing powers. Greek sage is used for fruit and spice flavorings. Sage is used by herbalists to treat sore gums, mouth ulcers, as a tonic, and to remove warts. The Arabs believed that it prevents dying. In 1992, the FDA proposed a ban on sage oil in astringent drug products because it has not been shown to be safe and effective for its stated claims.

SAINT-JOHN'S-WORT *(Hypericum perforatum)* is also called amber, blessed, devil's scourge, God's wonder herb, grace of God, goatweed, hypericum, and Klamath weed. A perennial native to Britain, Europe, and Asia, it is now found throughout North America. The plant contains glycosides, volatile oil, tannin, resin, and pectin *(see* all in glossary). It was believed to have infinite healing powers derived from the saint, the red juice representing his blood. A salve made from the flowers is used by herbalists to treat scratches, swellings, and small wounds. The oil is used for burns. The FDA listed Saint-John's-wort as an "unsafe herb" in 1977.

SALICARIA EXTRACT *(Lythrum salicaria)* is also called spiked loosestrife. Extract of a flowering herb that has purple or pink flowers. Used since ancient Greek times as an herb that calms nerves and soothes skin.

SHEPHERD'S PURSE EXTRACT *(Capsella bursa-pastoris)* is also called shepherd's heart. The extract of the herb, a member of the mustard family, is pungent and bitter. It was valued for its astringent properties by early American settlers. Cotton moistened with its juice was used to stop nosebleeds. In an oil-in-water emulsion, it is used as a base for skin preparations. Among its constituents are saponins, choline, acetylcholine, and tyramine *(see* all in glossary). These preparations are used in modern medicine to stimulate neuromuscular function. The herb also reduces urinary tract irritation. It has been shown to contract the uterus and lower blood pressure.

SOLOMON'S SEAL *(Polygonatum officinale)* is a perennial herb. The root was formerly used for its emetic properties, and externally for bruises near the eyes, as well as for treatment of tumors, wounds, poxes, warts, and pimples. In sixteenth-century Italy, it was used in a wash believed to maintain healthy skin. The roots contain allantoin *(see* glossary), used today as an anti-inflammatory and healing agent used in many cosmetics and over-the-counter creams.

SORBIC ACID is a white powder obtained from the berries of the mountain ash. It is also made from chemicals in the factory. Widely used in cosmetics, it produces a velvetlike feel when rubbed in the skin. Practically nontoxic but may cause skin irritation in susceptible people.

SORREL EXTRACT *(Rumex)* is an extract of the various species of the European plant imported to America. The Indians adopted it. It was used for scabs on the skin and as a dentifrice. It was widely used by American medical circles in this century to treat skin diseases.

SPIKENARD *(Aralia racemosa)*, also called nard, is used for acne, rash, and general skin problems.

TOADFLAX *(Linaria vulgaris)* is also called yellow toadflax, snapdragon, butter and eggs, and ranstead. A woody herb native to Europe and introduced in North America and Great Britain. Valued for both external and internal use, it is employed to treat hemorrhoids and skin diseases. The flowers are sometimes mixed with vegetable oils to make a liniment.

TORMENTIL *(Potentilla procumbens, Potentilla tormentilla)* is also called septfoil. Hippocrates used it to treat skin problems. The earliest citation of this plant in England appeared in 1387 recommending it for toothaches. Tormentil is a powerful astringent. Through the years it came to be used for piles, fevers, canker sores, and to relieve pain. It is used by herbalists as a gargle for sore throats and sore mouths. Supposedly a piece of cloth soaked in a decoction of it and covering a wart will cause the growth to turn black and fall off. The same decoction is recommended for sores and ulcers. A fluid extract of the root is used by herbalists to stop the bleeding of the gums and cuts. The root contains more tannin (*see* glossary) than oak bark.

VERVAIN, EUROPEAN *(Verbena officinalis)* is a weed of the verbena family native to Europe and the Far East. It is believed vervain was introduced to Rome by the druids. Hippocrates prescribed vervain for wounds, fevers, and nervous disorders. In England, vervain was used against witches. A decoction made from the whole plant is given for eczema and other skin complaints. It is used as a flavoring in alcoholic beverages.

WALNUT *(Juglans nigra)* is the fruit of a tree that is used by herbalists to promote strength and weight gain, and to treat skin diseases including eczema, herpes, and psoriasis.

WATER LILY *(Nymphaea alba)* is also called water rose, nenuphar, and candock. Cultivated in pools, this beautiful and romantic flower was used in folk medicine to depress sexual function. Externally, white and yellow water lilies were used to treat various skin disorders such as boils, inflammations, tumors, and ulcers.

WILD INDIGO *(Baptisia tinctoria)* is used by herbalists to treat infections of the ear, nose, and throat. The root contains alkaloids, glycosides, and resin *(see* all in glossary). Taken both internally and as a mouthwash, it reputedly heals mouth ulcers and sore gums and helps to control pyorrhea. Externally, in an ointment, it is used to treat infected ulcers and to soothe sore nipples. Used in a douche, it helps vaginal discharges, herbalists say.

WITCH HAZEL *(Hamamelis virginiana)* is a shrub native to eastern states of North America that grows in damp woods. Both leaves and bark are astringent, tonic, and sedative. They naturally contain a high level of tannins *(see* glossary), but products sold in drugstores and supermakets do not contain tannins. Witch hazel is a soothing, mildly astringent agent used to alleviate irritated skin. It can stop minor bleeding.

WOAD *(Isatis tinctoria)* is a biennial widely distributed in Europe, Asia, and North Africa and is a member of the mustard family. The plant is used to treat St. Anthony's fire—any of several inflammatory diseases of the skin—and for plasters and ointments for ulcers and inflammation.

WOUNDWORT *(Stachys palustris)* is also called allheal, clown's wort, donkey's ear, hedge, and dead nettle. There are many varieties of woundwort, but all have the same medical action. The leaves of the downy woundwort have been used instead of lint as surgical dressing. The leaves were believed to have a special power in healing the wounds caused by sword thrusts. Woundwort was used by English herbalists for many years to stop bleeding of the lungs and other internal hemorrhages and to treat severe forms of diarrhea. They claimed that almost any cut or wound would benefit if the newly gathered and washed woundwort leaves were bound to the injury.

Chapter 13

NUTRACEUTICALS FOR BRAIN, MIND, AND EMOTIONS

We all know that why we eat and what we eat has a lot to do with our brain, mind, and emotions. We may overindulge in food when we are sad, happy, or sociable. We can eat something that makes us feel raring to go or uncomfortable or irritable. We may skip a meal and drop our blood sugar so low we can't think clearly. Food, after all, is the fuel for not only our bodies but our brains. The nerve cells in our heads, in fact, communicate with chemicals called *neurotransmitters* made from protein in our diet.

Are there nutraceuticals that benefit our ability to function mentally? As in every other chapter in this book, there are both new and ancient nutraceuticals available. There are also old folk practices to improve thinking or calm emotions that are being studied by modern scientists today.

You probably already use the number one psychoactive nutraceutical in the world—*caffeine*. Do you take a cup of coffee to get you going in the morning? Caffeine can make you more alert and have a better reaction time. It may also make you somewhat anxious and cause a slight tremor in your hands. Microsurgeons who sew minute blood vessels together do not ingest any caffeine hours before operating because they need absolutely steady fingers.

Have you purchased any *Ginkgo biloba* yet? Ginkgo is among

the most popular prescription drugs in Europe. In the United States, it is sold over the counter as a "food."

What is ginkgo? The leaves and nuts of *Ginkgo biloba*—also called maidenhair—are used in ancient Chinese remedies. The ginkgo is supposedly the oldest living tree, having survived some 200 million years. It is said to be the only tree that came through the effects of atomic radiation in Hiroshima, Japan.

Ginkgo has been reported to improve circulation, mental functioning, stop ringing in the ears, and to relieve symptoms of Alzheimer's disease, coldness, emotional depression, Raynaud's disease (a circulatory problem), arthritic disease, hardening of the arteries, dizziness, and anxiety. In recent animal studies at the University of Illinois, ginkgo protected the brains of rats to a significant degree when the animals were given a toxic compound that induces oxygen damage and brain swelling.[1]

Scientists and pharmaceutical firms are excited about another ancient remedy, a tea, *oian ceng ya*, brewed by elderly Chinese from the leaves of *Huperzia serrata* (club moss) to improve memory. In the 1980s, scientists at the Shanghai Institute of Materia Medica and the Zhejiang Academy of Medical Sciences isolated the active components in huperzine (Hup A) and found that it was a remarkably potent inhibitor of acetylcholinesterase (AChE). Acetylcholinesterase breaks down acetylcholine, a chemical in the brain that is vital for memory function. The Chinese have reported that Hup A is effective in treating patients with memory impairment, myasthenia gravis, and multi-infarct dementia (small clots that cause mental deterioration).[2]

Because there is little Hup A in the natural plant, Alan P. Kozikowski, Ph.D., at the Mayo Clinic, Jacksonville, Florida, and chemists at the Shanghai Institute have independently synthesized Hup A. The new nutraceutical has reportedly greater activity and fewer side effects than that of the basic extract.[3]

Alcohol, of course, is one of the oldest nutraceuticals. It has been used since the beginning of time to cheer, calm, relieve emotional and physical pain, and to stimulate. Actually, it is a depressant that, if taken in large amounts, can destroy the brain. The

Chinese have an herb to combat alcohol abuse, kudzu *(Pueraria lobata)*, that pesky vine now spreading unchecked through the southern United States. But in China, an extract from the vine was cited as a medication as early as 200 B.C., and about A.D. 600 a Chinese pharmacopoeia listed the herb as having an antidrunkenness effect. Using Syrian golden hamsters, animals that prefer alcohol to water, two scientists from Harvard Medical School found that extracts of the herb reduced alcohol consumption by about 50 percent.[4]

To document use of the extract, Dr. Wing-Ming Keung, one of the Harvard investigators, went to China and interviewed modern research scientists as well as physicians who offer traditional herbal remedies. Dr. Keung found about 80 percent of three hundred alcoholics treated for two to four weeks lost their desire for alcohol and had no adverse side effects from the herb.

One of Dr. Keung's colleagues at Harvard commented about kudzu research: "It is good to look at nature and folk medicine and realize nature has lots to teach us."

Since practically everything we ingest in one way or another affects our brain, mind, and emotions, volumes would be needed to cover all the scientific research now in progress about nutraceuticals in this category. The information in this chapter concerns just a few interesting research projects and some ancient practices concerning nutrients and phytochemicals that affect mental function.

Vitamins and the Brain

Head trauma, stroke, lung ailments, and other conditions that block the flow of oxygen to the brain cause the release of free radicals—those highly reactive molecules that quickly damage sensitive nerve cells. Neuroscientists have been hard at work trying to determine whether vitamin A, vitamin E, and other antioxidants—which quickly sop up these free radicals—can protect the brain when these conditions occur. Dr. S. Goldstein of the University of Arkansas for Medical Sciences pointed out in the medical journal

Geriatrics that because nerve cells in the adult human do not replicate as colon and bone-marrow cells do, nerve cells must be protected against oxygen damage. "Natural antioxidants such as vitamin C and E and beta-carotene, as well as an optimal caloric and protein intake, should be cornerstones of treatment and prevention in the aging patient."[5]

Vitamin E and Parkinson's Disease

Major medical institutions in the United States and abroad have been investigating whether vitamin E may prove effective in treating such brain conditions as Parkinson's disease and Alzheimer's. Parkinson's disease is a neurological condition that includes rhythmical muscular tremors, rigidity of movement, droopy posture, and a masklike expression. Alzheimer's disease is a deterioration of the brain with severe memory impairment. The exact causes of both maladies are unknown.

A multi-medical-center investigation of vitamin E with and without a medication, selegiline—which inhibits an enzyme, monoamine oxidase, in the brain—started in 1987. Monoamine oxidase works with oxygen to tear apart neurotransmitters, chemical messengers that carry information between nerve cells in the brain. The neurotransmitter most involved in Parkinson's disease is dopamine, which plays an important part in movement. The idea was to determine whether Parkinson's disease progression could be delayed with selegiline and/or vitamin E. The results have been equivocal.

Eight hundred patients with untreated early Parkinson's disease were enrolled in the multicenter program. Patients were assigned to receive either selegiline or vitamin E or both compounds together. The dose of the vitamin was high—2,000 IU per day. In the first report, the University of Rochester Medical Center's Parkinson Study Group noted a 57 percent reduction in the rate of developing symptoms with selegiline therapy, alone or in combination with vitamin E.[6] In a report a year later,

the University of Rochester researchers said the effects of selegiline lasted only nine months and that vitamin E was of no benefit.[7] In another review article of the eight hundred patients
participating in the multicenter trials of vitamin E and selegiline, investigators from Wayne State University School of Medicine, Detroit, Michigan, concluded that selegiline works for
only one year and that vitamin E offered no neuroprotection.[8]

Researchers at Columbia University College of Physicians and
Surgeons, New York, however, reported high dosages of a combination of vitamin E and vitamin C administered to patients with
early Parkinson's disease slowed the progression of symptoms by
an average of 2.5 years compared to a control group who did not
receive these antioxidants.[9]

Does vitamin E have potential as a nutraceutical for parkinsonism? In a meta-analysis of eighty-five parkinsonism studies,
reviewers determined vitamin E may have protectant antioxidant
properties, but not enough research information with patients
was available.[10]

Tardive dyskinesia is another brain condition involving abnormal movements, especially of the tongue, lips, and facial muscles.
One of the causes is high doses of antipsychotic drugs given over
a long period of time. Patients with tardive dyskinesia showed
improvement in the symptoms in four clinical trials—double-
blind and placebo controlled—with vitamin E in dosages of up to
1,600 IU per day.[11]

Vitamin E and A Together May Play a Role in Down's Syndrome and Aging

VITAMIN A is necessary for keen eyesight. Through eyesight, we
gain most of the information we feed our brains. A deficiency of
vitamin A has also been found, at least in laboratory animals, to
affect balance and cause abnormalities in taste and smell, two
senses intimately involved in eating. As with vitamin E, vitamin A
is an antioxidant, and that may be one of its major benefits as far

as the brain is concerned. The two vitamins showed potential in research concerning Down's syndrome. Formerly referred to as mongolism, Down's syndrome is a result of a genetic abnormality that produces mental retardation and usually early death. The blood fats of Down's syndrome patients tend to be easily oxidized. This fat peroxidation causes progressive tissue damage.

A study from the Brain-Behavior Research Center of the University of California, San Francisco, involved twelve Down's patients and twelve normal subjects. Researchers noted that the antioxidant defense system seemed overwhelmed in Down's syndrome, and that blood sample results from Down's patients demonstrated both vitamins A and E were significantly decreased and oxidized blood fats were significantly increased. Vitamins A and E are the major antioxidants in the body that can protect the tissues against this oxidative damage. The California researchers concluded Down's individuals have a greater than normal requirement for both vitamins A and E to help prevent oxidative tissue damage. Could this be why Down's syndrome subjects are at risk for developing Alzheimer's disease and dementia as early as twenty or thirty years of age?

British researchers wanted to find out. They measured the blood levels of vitamin E in twelve Down's syndrome subjects with Alzheimer's. The results showed that these Down's victims did indeed have lower levels of vitamin E than a similar group of twelve Down's subjects without Alzheimer's.[12] One explanation of this finding is that excessive oxidative damage accounts for premature aging. Researchers theorized that since vitamin E protects against oxygen damage to cells, it might protect against the development of Alzheimer's-like dementia in those with Down's syndrome. The researchers concluded that vitamin E may have possible protective action against the inherent risk of Alzheimer's disease in Down's syndrome.

The link between the low levels of the antioxidant vitamins and the rapid aging in the brains of Down's syndrome people has spurred researchers on to determine whether vitamin E and vitamin A may help protect the brains of all of us not only against Alzheimer's but against the ordinary effects of aging of the brain, such as slowed reaction times and benign memory problems. You know the kind—"Where did I put those keys?" or "Why did I open the refrigerator?"

Vitamin C and the Brain Under Stress

Another of the antioxidant vitamins, vitamin C, may also serve as a nutraceutical for the brain, particularly when it is under stress. The level of vitamin C in the brain is second only to that found in the adrenal glands.[13] The adrenal glands produce the hormones needed for "fight or flight" when you feel threatened. They speed the heart rate, increase the blood pressure, and generally rev up the body. These "stress" changes, if they occur too frequently, may cause permanent damage to the brain, heart, and other organs. This has led researchers to believe that vitamin C plays an important role in fighting stress—both emotional and physical. Smoking and drinking alcoholic beverages, for example, physically stress brain tissues because they produce free radicals, those extremely reactive, unstable, damaging molecules. Such bad habits may be made a little less harmful by using vitamin C as a nutraceutical. As do the other antioxidant nutraceuticals, vitamin C helps prevent free-radical damage.

Vitamin C may also have another way of protecting the brain. The interplay between vitamin C and amino acids, the building blocks of protein, suggests that vitamin C may play a vital role in the regulation of messages sent between the brain's nerve cells. Vitamin C has been found to be needed as a helper in the manufacture of *norepinephrine*, a major brain neurotransmitter that acts as a stimulant. It has also been linked to the production of *dopamine*, a neurotransmitter necessary for coordinated movements, and to the production of *tyrosine*, a neurotransmitter that helps produce other neurotransmitters. Vitamin C also participates in the processing of glucose (blood sugar), the brain's primary food.

Brain-Boosting B Vitamins

While new information is being gathered about the use of the antioxidant vitamins as nutraceuticals to protect the brain, the B vitamins have produced more definitive research results in brain and behavior research through the years.

VITAMIN B$_{12}$ (*cyanocobalamin*), as a nutraceutical, may be important in combating Alzheimer's disease as well as depression and panic disorders, according to a number of recent studies. Its utility as a nutraceutical for these conditions apparently lies in its ability to inhibit monoamine oxidase (MAO), an enzyme that works with oxygen to break down brain chemicals involved in movement and mood. MAO activity in the blood has been shown to be increased in patients with senile dementia of the Alzheimer's type.

Swedish researchers, who found B$_{12}$ levels were low and MAO activity high in Alzheimer's patients, gave a group of them B$_{12}$ therapy. The Swedes found the MAO activity in the Alzheimer's patients' brains was significantly reduced to apparently normal levels. Pharmaceutical monoamine oxidase inhibitors (MAOI), such as phenelzine and tranylcypromine, used in treating depression and panic disorders, are more powerful but are used infrequently and with great caution because of their potential serious side effects.

The results of the B$_{12}$ studies have led the Scandinavians to conclude that vitamin B$_{12}$ deficiency plays a significant part in Alzheimer's.[14] The Japanese have added some confirming evidence. Researchers in the department of neuropsychiatry at Yamaguchi University School of Medicine found that giving Alzheimer's patients B$_{12}$ improved intellectual function scores such as memory, emotions, and communication. Improvements in cognitive functions were relatively constant when the vitamin B$_{12}$ was maintained for a prolonged period, the Japanese reported, and there were no side effects.[15] Italian studies have also validated B$_{12}$'s potential usefulness in the treatment of Alzheimer's.[16]

A number of drugs such as antibiotics and those given to treat gout cause malabsorption of vitamin B_{12}. Such a deficiency may affect the behavior of healthy people of any age, but it is particularly significant for older persons. Over the age of sixty, a lack of vitamin B_{12} may be responsible for neurological symptoms ranging from tingling sensations, inability to coordinate muscular movements, weakened limbs, and lack of balance to memory loss, mood changes, disorientation, and psychiatric disorders. Senior citizens may be ingesting enough B_{12} with their food, but more than one in five older Americans has a condition of aging known as *atrophic gastritis*. This means they may no longer produce enough hydrochloric acid for their bodies to utilize the B_{12} taken in. Without the acid, the digestive enzyme that separates B_{12} from the protein swallowed in food does not function properly. The vitamin, therefore, does not travel from the stomach to the rest of the body.

Unfortunately, while the treatment for B_{12} deficiency resulting from atrophic gastritis is simple and inexpensive, the diagnosis is not. One reason is that it is difficult to detect. It doesn't show up on a routine blood workup, yet even a mild deficiency, discernible only with the most sophisticated laboratory tests, can result in neurologic abnormalities.[17] About 30 percent of patients with vitamin B_{12} deficiency symptoms may have apparently normal levels on blood tests, according to researchers at the Department of Neurology, School of Medicine, State University of New York, Buffalo. They maintain vitamin B_{12} replacement should not be withheld from patients with borderline vitamin B_{12} levels, since the consequences of allowing muscle, nerve, and brain damage to worsen clearly outweigh any disadvantage of therapy.[18]

In a review article of seventy-nine studies of subtle B_{12} deficiency, researchers concluded that a long list of psychiatric illnesses or symptoms—especially some cases of mood disorder, dementia, paranoid psychoses, violent behavior, and fatigue—have been documented to be caused by vitamin B_{12} deficiency, among other causes. The conclusion was that these conditions are possibly more commonly caused by B_{12} deficiency than is currently generally accepted, mostly because of a lack of appreciation of the lowest serum B_{12} level that is necessary to protect against the brain manifestations of this deficiency.[19]

Robert Russell, M.D., gastroenterologist, doing research at the USDA Human Nutrition Research Center on Aging at Tufts University, reports the problem is severe enough and widespread enough to say "vitamin B_{12} is probably the single most important nutrient affected by aging."[20]

B_6—A Common Partner

B_6 *(pyridoxine)* is another B vitamin that is a nutraceutical for the brain. It helps metabolize protein; aids in the production of red blood cells; and maintains proper functioning of nervous-system tissue. Vitamin B_6 is believed to act as a partner for more than one hundred different enzymes. A number of the brain chemicals that send messages back and forth between nerves depend upon it for formation. A deficiency in this vitamin is known to cause depression and mental confusion. The occurrence of seizures in experimental animals in response to vitamin B_6 antagonists has been observed by many. Similar seizures were observed in human infants made vitamin B_6 deficient inadvertently when they were fed a commercial infant formula in which the vitamin had not been properly preserved. Certain substances that deplete B_6 also produce deficiency seizures. Patients are likely to have a deficiency of B_6 if they are alcoholics; have burns, diarrhea, heart disease, intestinal problems, liver disease, or overactive thyroid; or are suffering the stress of long-term illness or serious injury. Patients on dialysis or who have had their stomachs removed are also probably deficient in the vitamin.

Numerous studies have suggested that pregnant and lactating women may have dietary intakes of vitamin B_6 that are well below the recommended dietary allowance, which may affect the vitamin B_6 status of their offspring. This nutrient is an essential cofactor in developing the central nervous system and may influence brain growth and cognitive function. Recent work in animals suggests that vitamin B$_6$ deficiency during gestation and lactation alters the function in the brain of certain neurotransmitters thought to play an important role in learning and memory.[21]

Nerve problems in the arms and legs common in diabetics may also be associated with B$_6$ deficiency. Diabetics who experienced nerve symptoms and whose urine contained evidence of B$_6$ deficiency were given 150 mg of the vitamin each day for six weeks. The treatment eliminated symptoms of neuropathy in all subjects. A longer study of six months showed similar results.[22]

Vitamin B$_6$ also reportedly helps rid the body tissues of excess fluid that causes some of the behavioral and physical symptoms of premenstrual tension. Overdosing on B$_6$ is unwise, however. A study reported in the *The New England Journal of Medicine* in 1983 described the loss of balance and numbness suffered by seven young adults who took from two to six grams of pyridoxine daily for several months to a year. Other potential adverse reactions include drowsiness and a feeling of pins and needles in limbs.

Older people, especially older women, may need more vitamin B$_6$ than currently recommended by the government. A three-month study of men and women between sixty-one and seventy-one broadens the age range of data for setting future RDAs for this nutrient.[23] (The current RDAs are based on the needs of younger adults.) The six women in the study required 1.9 mg of B$_6$ compared to the current RDA of 1.6 mg. The men needed 1.96 mg, which is equal to the current 2 mg RDA, leaving no safety margin normally built into an RDA. The findings help to explain why older people repeatedly test more deficient in the vitamin than younger ones. Marginal deficiencies don't produce obvious symptoms and can only be detected through biochemical tests. Since B$_6$ is important for the proper functioning of the nervous system, a persistently low intake could lead to depression, lethargy, confusion, or nervousness. But these symptoms could also result from several other causes.

B_1 Helps to Fuel the Brain

VITAMIN B_1 *(thiamine)*. The link between vitamin B_1 and the brain is strong. Our bodies cannot manufacture the vitamin, yet B_1 is needed to process the only fuel the brain can use—the blood sugar, glucose. Because of this vital need, the nervous system is particularly susceptible to thiamine deficiency. Thiamine treatment as high as 300 mg per day is used in cases of Wernicke's encephalopathy, an acute brain disorder sometimes called "cerebral beriberi." In the early stages, there is mental confusion, inability to think of a word, and making up of "facts." As it progresses, there are delusions, loss of memory, loss of balance, and eye problems. In industrialized countries, when this syndrome is associated with thiamine deficiency, the patients are usually alcoholics.

The Liver and Milk Vitamin

VITAMIN B_2 *(riboflavin)* is also called lactoflavin or hepatoflavin, because milk and liver are its main natural sources. It has a high affinity for your brain and helps explain the long-standing observation that even in severe riboflavin deficiency, its concentration in the brain does not decline appreciably. Ironically, while vitamin B_2 reportedly fights stress and its chemical structure is surprisingly similar to that of chlorpromazine (Thorazine), that powerful tranquilizer depletes vitamin B_2.[24]

The B That Prevents Some Birth Defects

FOLIC ACID, as pointed out in the beginning of this book, has now been proven necessary to the prevention of serious birth defects of the brain and spinal cord (*see* page x).

Folic acid may also have an effect on brain function in the elderly. A review by Dr. E. H. Reynolds of King's College School of Medicine in London concluded that low levels of folic acid are closely tied to psychiatric symptoms in the elderly. One study found that elderly patients with mental disorders, especially dementia, were three times more apt to have low folic acid than others their age.[25]

Even among a group of healthy aged people, those with low folic acid intake scored lower on abstract-thinking ability and memory. Further, even borderline deficiencies "can be harmful to their mental state," says Dr. Reynolds. And low daily doses of folic acid supplements—200 mcg (found in three-fourths of a cup of cooked spinach)—have lifted mood and relieved depression.

In another study were a group of thirty-eight patients with minor neurological signs but with depression, fatigue, lassitude, and burning feet and restless leg syndrome (*see* glossary). Supplementation with folic acid resulted in an easing of the lassitude, fatigue, and depression in about two to three months. The burning feet and restless leg syndrome improved during the first three weeks.[26]

Multivitamins and the Brain

An ordinary multivitamin-mineral supplement was given to thirty Welsh schoolchildren (twelve- and thirteen-year-olds) who had been obtaining micronutrients from their diets at close to recommended dietary allowance (RDA) levels. The study went on for eight months. Thirty of their classmates with similar diets re-ceived placebos, and thirty took no pills. The group taking the supplement had significantly increased scores on a test of nonverbal intelligence compared to both control groups. The supplement provided most vitamins in amounts well above U.S. RDA levels.[27]

Dietary deficiencies in the elderly, especially of vitamins B_6 and B_{12}, niacin, folic acid, thiamine, and vitamin C, have been well documented. Yet clinical signs of deficiency are rare. Much more common are nonspecific symptoms, such as malaise, irritability, or sleepiness, loss of appetite and weight, and impairment of physical performance socially or at work. Therefore, supplemental vitamins may be needed. Most investigators feel that the benefits of multivitamin supplementation greatly outweigh any possible complications from their use.[28]

Minerals for Mood and Mind

There are two classes of minerals: *macronutrients* and *micronutrients*. Your body contains more of the macronutrients—magnesium, sodium, potassium, and chloride—and you require more of them in your diet. The amounts range from hundreds of milligrams to grams. The micronutrients include iron, manganese, copper, iodine, zinc, fluoride, selenium, molybdenum, chromium, aluminum, boron, nickel, silicon, and vanadium. Micronutrients, also called *trace elements*, are found in tiny amounts—so small they are often measured in micrograms. Your body contains some trace elements even though there is no known need for them. These include aluminum, antimony, barium, boron, bromine, gallium, germanium, gold, lithium, mercury, silver, strontium, and titanium.

There is one trace element, however, that has been used as a nutraceutical through the ages: lithium, a light metal that exists in the earth's crust.

LITHIUM has been used as a medicine since ancient Greece, when it was prescribed for gout, rheumatism, and kidney stone. Small amounts of the salts are used today as a nutraceutical to treat manic-depressive illness, also called bipolar disorder, with its episodes of both mania and severe, disabling depression. Psychiatric researchers believe it is caused by a chemical imbalance in the brain. Lithium was introduced as a medication to treat manic-depressive disorders in 1949. Its exact mechanism of action is unknown, but it does work for some patients for whom nothing else helps. Lithium has a narrow margin of safety and may have severe side effects.

CALCIUM, a fairly soft, silvery white, alkaline earth metal, is the fifth most abundant element. Calcium is most often thought of as a nutraceutical for bones, teeth, and stomach acid, but its ingestion may also have an effect on mood.[29] A Texas A&M professor,

Kaymar Arasteh, told a meeting of the American Psychological Association that depressed patients given 1,000 mg of calcium gluconate plus 600 IU of vitamin D twice a day for four weeks showed significant elevation in mood compared to a control group of depressed patients who received placebos. Dr. Arasteh noted that calcium's effect on nerves in the brain and on mood is biphasic . . . that is, a little stimulates the nerves and elevates mood, but a lot can depress nerve activity and mood.

Amino Acids—Messengers of the Mind

While there is scientific interest in minerals for the mind, there is a greater emphasis on nutraceuticals based on the very stuff that controls thinking, emotions, and behavior—*amino acids*. They provide the building blocks from which proteins are constructed. Protein not only creates body tissue—muscles, bone, hair, and nails—it also transports oxygen and carries the genetic code of life to all your cells. As if that weren't enough, protein is used by your body to manufacture antibodies (disease fighters), hormones (gland messengers), and neurotransmitters (nerve-cell messengers).

Your brain is almost completely regulated by amino acids made from protein, and their journey from your plate to your head depends on the content of your meals, your physical condition, your activity, and your environment. Amino acids are extremely powerful in small doses and are versatile in changing roles, depending on where they are used in the body. It is not surprising, therefore, that one of the hottest areas in pharmaceutical research today involves amino acids.

Of the twenty amino acids that go into building the millions of proteins, nine cannot be manufactured by your body in sufficient quantities to sustain growth and health and must be obtained from your diet. These nine are called *essential* amino acids because they are essential for maintaining good health. They are *isoleucine, threonine, leucine, tryptophan, lysine, valine, methionine, histidine* (thought to be essential only in children), and *phenylalanine*.

"Nonessential" amino acids that can be obtained from your diet or manufactured in your intestines and liver are *alanine, arginine, asparagine, aspartic acid, cysteine, glycine, glutamic acid, glutamine, serine, taurine,* and *tyrosine.*

That they are essential to your brain and body and are derived from food, however, does not mean amino acids are harmless and should be taken lightly. The amino acid levels in your body are exquisitely balanced. By overloading your system with one, you can affect the others, which may produce serious adverse effects on your body and brain.

The following are amino acids used as nutraceuticals. They are either on the market or in testing in the laboratory.

TRYPTOPHAN. A tremendous amount of research is now in progress with this amino acid. First isolated in milk in 1901, tryptophan is being studied as a means to calm hyperactive children, induce sleep, and fight depression and pain. Serotonin, which is derived from dietary tryptophan, is one of the many neurotransmitters involved in modulating pain perception. Clinical application for tryptophan may be as a mild analgesic that can be used in combination with other pharmaceuticals. In a number of studies, tryptophan from two to three grams daily raised the pain thresholds in patients suffering from chronic facial pain and dental pain.[30] It has also been used as an aid to smokers who wish to quit the habit since it reportedly prevents nicotine withdrawal symptoms.

Tryptophan is a precursor of an important neurotransmitter, serotonin, low levels of which are believed to play a part in depression. Tryptophan is also a precursor of an important neurohormone, melatonin. Disorders of melatonin levels and rhythms are suggested to be a cause of depression, abnormal sleep, Alzheimer's disease, and some age-related disorders. Tryptophan is also a precursor of niacin, which is a critical helper in many biochemical processes, notably energy metabolism. Lack of it can cause neurological disorders. There is evidence that stress and/or dietary lack of tryptophan may make deficiencies of serotonin and melatonin common.[31]

Over-the-counter tryptophan was withdrawn from the market. In 1989 and 1990, more than 1,200 cases of eosinophilia-myalgia syndrome (EMS) were reported to the CDC Department of Health Services; three patients died. All patients reported use of L-tryptophan supplements before the onset of illness. The most commonly reported symptoms were muscle and joint pains followed by shortness of breath or cough and rash. Fluid retention occurred in half, and fever was common. The cause was found to be a contaminant in the tryptophan, not the amino acid itself.[32]

TYROSINE, high in poultry and fish, is another amino acid that is being studied as a nutraceutical. Tyrosine serves as a building block for epinephrine and norepinephrine, neurotransmitters involved in strong emotions and alertness. Tyrosine is carried across the protective filter—the blood-brain barrier. Tyrosine also helps produce thyroid hormone and is used in antistress medications and antidepressant medications.

METHIONINE, an essential amino acid, has been found to have antidepressant effects when metabolized with vitamin B_{12} into a compound called S-adenosyl methionine (SAM). In several studies this compound was found to be as effective as some antidepressant drugs now widely used, ameliorating symptoms such as guilt, suicidal ideation, slowness of movement, work problems, and lack of interest. It was also reported to be more rapid in taking effect than conventional antidepressant drugs, with many patients showing improvement after four to seven days as compared to the ten days to two weeks it usually takes with other medications. It also apparently has fewer side effects. It is still in testing in Europe and the United States.[33]

Other amino acids and their uses by the body—and therefore their potential as nutraceuticals—are as follows:

HISTIDINE is used by the body for growth, nerve function, and blood-vessel dilation.

PHENYLALANINE with **TYROSINE** acts as a building block of nor-epinephrine, the neurotransmitter that stimulates the nerves and promotes appetite.

ASPARTIC ACID, a nonessential amino acid, is a major neuro-transmitter substance. The sweetener aspartame is also derived from it.

GLUTAMIC ACID is a major stimulating neurotransmitter sub-stance. It acts as a catalyst and its salts are used as tranquilizers. It is in monosodium glutamate.

SERINE helps produce the neurotransmitter acetylcholine, in-volved in memory.

GLYCINE inhibits signals between nerve cells.

TAURINE is involved in nerve stimulation and is now believed to be essential for fetal and infant brain and nervous-system develop-ment. It also aids digestion.

Choline—The Elusive Memory Nutraceutical

Choline is found in fish, meats, egg yolks, soy products, oatmeal, rice, peanuts, and pecans. It is taken from the digestive tract by the blood and carried to the brain, where it becomes acetyl-choline, the neurotransmitter that plays a vital part in memory. Possibly because nature recognized its importance, it is the only neurotransmitter that can be made from another dietary compo-nent besides protein. It can be derived from lecithin, which is found in large amounts in eggs.

While the exact role and requirement of choline in the diet remains unknown, the brain is unable to make it, and choline must be derived from the diet or manufactured in the liver. Researchers are pursuing the idea that the impairment in certain diseases and in old age of the brain's system for using choline may be prevented or minimized with choline-based materials added to the diet.

An effort has been made to increase the building blocks of acetylcholine by increasing lecithin, the normal source of choline in the diet. Lecithin, from the Greek meaning "egg yolk," is found in large amounts in egg yolks and is commercially isolated from eggs, soybeans, and corn. It is a widely used antioxidant in food and cosmetic products. Purified lecithin, which is more con-centrated than that sold in health-food stores, raises blood levels of choline, but as yet there are no definitive studies on the bene-fits of lecithin. One large food company, Lipton, attempted to develop a lecithin-laced chicken soup in the late 1980s, but it was not marketed.

Scientists know that as we age, the capability of transferring information from one cell to another or to a large target organ is markedly reduced. In part, this is due to the amount of acetyl-choline and in part to the ability to use what is there. N-acetyl-transferase is an enzyme that helps produce acetylcholine. One of the most consistent neurochemical findings is the reduced activity of acetyltransferase in the normal aged human, and its marked weakness in the brains of Alzheimer's victims, causing reduced manufacture of acetylcholine.[34] Three pharmacologic approaches are being attempted by researchers to enhance the use and pro-duction of acetylcholine:

- To increase the availability of the building blocks of acetyl-choline—lecithin and choline.
- To inhibit acetylcholine degradation by inhibiting acetyl cholinesterase.
- To directly stimulate the receptors for choline in the brain by sending in a compound that imitates it.

The search for a nutraceutical that will increase the amount or availability of acetylcholine in the brain has, as yet, not been very successful, but the quest continues full speed because of the burgeoning aging population.[35]

Pain and the Brain

Pain is sensed by nerve endings around the body but it is evaluated by the brain. Capsaicin, the active dried principle of the dried ripe fruits of *Capsicum spp*, also known as *chili peppers*, was first cited in the medical literature by Christopher Columbus's physician on the explorer's second visit to the New World in 1994.[36] The doctor, Diego Alvarez Chanca, wrote that the chili pepper seemed to have medicinal value. Capsaicin is the most potent of a group of compounds that give chilies their fiery bite. Chili peppers contain anywhere from 0.1 percent to 1.0 percent capsaicin, depending on the variety, soil, and climate. The firey chemicals are the peppers' defense against predators, but humans have eaten them and used them in herbal remedies for thousands of years. Capsaicin is used to test pain sensitivity in animals and humans. The same sensation in food delights many diners. Capsaicin as capsicum BPC has been available for more than fifty years to treat arthritis and other pains. In the past few years, it has been reintroduced as an analgesic treatment with wide applications.

Capsaicin injected into the skin or painted on the skin induces an intense burning with a surrounding area of reduced sensation. This is due to the release of *substance P* from nerve endings. *Substance P* is an important transmitter of sensory input, the initial release results in pain. Continued application eventually depletes the nerve endings, leading to loss of that particular pain sensation. If frequent applications are continued for a long time, researchers believe it may be possible to prevent the nerve from storing enough substance P, and thus prevent the pain signal from being sent again to the brain.[37]

Capsaicin solution is used to treat painful conditions characterized by the same symptoms that capsaicin itself produces such as burning, numbness, and pain. Thus it is used for herpes pain and various other nerve pains such as those due to diabetes, stump pain, and trigeminal neuralgia, an excruciating face pain. More recently it has been used to treat cluster headache, psoriasis, arthritis, postmastectomy pain, and itching associated with kidney dialysis. In a nasal spray, it is used to relieve nonallergic stuffy nose. It is also used to help stimulate the bladder. The most familiar capsaicin medicines of the topical ones now on the market is Zostrix, which is used to alleviate pain from conditions that affect millions of people—arthritis, diabetic nerve damage, and shingles, a viral condition.

D-phenylalanine is a form of an amino acid being used to combat pain. In an experimental double-blind crossover study, after two weeks of DPA at 250 mg three times a day, seven out of twenty-one chronic-pain patients taken off all other medications noted over 50 percent pain relief, which was not seen or maintained while on a placebo. One patient improved while on the placebo, while thirteen patients noted no significant pain relief from either DPA or the placebo.[38]

When the Head Aches

CHAMOMILE, ROMAN *(Anthemis nobilis)* is a native of Europe and grows wild in all the temperate parts of the continent. In moderate doses, the flowers are used to soothe indigestion, gas, colic, gout, and headaches. A strong infusion acts as an efficient emetic. The oil has stimulant and antispasmodic properties; it is useful in treating gas and is added to purgatives to prevent cramps. If you are allergic to ragweed, chrysanthemums, or asters, you may be allergic to chamomile because it is a member of the same plant family. The FDA issued a notice in 1992 that chamomile has not been shown to be safe and effective as claimed in OTC digestive-aid products.

FEVERFEW *(Chrysanthemum parthenium* OR *Pyrethrum parthenium* OR *Tanacetum parthenium)* is also called flirtwort, bachelor's button, maydes' weed, or wild quinine. A small, hardy perennial herb, a member of the chamomile family *(see* above), it was introduced into Britain from Southeast Asia. Since ancient times it has been used by physicians for its action on the uterus. The name *feverfew* is derived from the word *febrifuge*, which means "to lower fever," the most common use for the herb by ancient Greek physicians. It is now being investigated as a preventative for migraines.

GARLIC. Mentioned in other chapters for its usefulness as a nutraceutical, garlic also has painkilling capabilities. Three Rutgers University researchers reported in 1992 at the American Chemical Society meeting in Washington, D.C., that chemicals in garlic may protect the liver from damage caused by large doses of the widely used over-the-counter painkiller acetaminophen and may prevent growth of lung tumors associated with tobacco smoke. Such research reports have been criticized by scientists, who say that it is difficult to do double-blind studies in which neither the subjects nor the scientists know which compound contains the placebo and which the garlic.

Nine patents have been issued in Japan for painkilling compounds that use garlic as a primary ingredient.

GROUND IVY *(Glechoma hederacea)* is also called alehoof, benth, cat's-foot, devil's candlesticks, hale house, hay house, May house, hay-maids, hedge maids, thunder vine, and tun-hoof. A common plant on wastelands, it is used by herbalists for headaches, and backaches caused by sluggishness of the liver or obstruction of the kidneys. It contains tannin, volatile oil, bitter principle, and saponin (*see* all in glossary).

GUARANA *(Paullinia cupana)* is a native of tropical America. The seeds of this wood vine are used by Brazilian Indians in a traditional beverage. The caffeine content of the plant is two and a half times that of coffee. It also contains tannins. The plant was introduced into France by a physician who had been working in Brazil. It came to be used to treat migraine and nervous headaches, neuralgia, paralysis, urinary-tract irritation, and other ailments, as well as for chronic diarrhea. The caffeine (*see* glossary) is assumed to be effective for migraine relief and the tannins (*see* glossary) for the beneficial effects on diarrhea.

JAMAICA DOGWOOD *(Piscidia erythrina).* The bark is collected from trees grown in Texas, Mexico, and the Caribbean. It contains glycosides, flavonoids, and resin (*see* all in glossary). It is used in the West Indies to treat pain, including that of migraine.

KOLA NUT *(Cola acuminata),* also called cola and guru nut, is collected from a tree that grows in tropical Africa and is cultivated in South America. The seeds contain caffeine, theobromine, tannin, and volatile oil (*see* all in glossary). It is used for stimulation to counteract fatigue and as a diuretic. Herbalists use it to treat some types of migraine headache and diarrhea caused by anxiety. It is also used to treat depression.

LAVENDER *(Lavandula vera)* is an evergreen of the mint family native to the Mediterranean coast and cultivated in France, Italy, and England. The name is derived from the Latin word *lavare,* which means "to wash." Lavender flowers contain large amounts of essential oils that have antispasmodic, antiseptic, and carminative activity. Herbalists used lavender oil to promote relaxation and to treat headaches. Lavender tea is used in folk medicine for stomach gas and to relieve anxiety. The FDA issued a notice in 1992 that lavender compound tincture has not been shown to be safe and effective as claimed in OTC digestive-aid products.

PRIMROSE *(Primula vulgaris),* also called Easter rose, is a perennial native to Britain and Europe and flourishes in meadows, hedges, and ditches. The name comes from the Latin word for first, *primu,* because it was the first rose of spring. Herbalists used it in a tea to treat arthritis, gout, and migraines and as a general blood cleanser. A decoction of the root is given for catarrh, coughs, and bronchitis. It is also used to cure insomnia.

QUININE, also called bichinine, biquinate, chinine, and many other names, is a drug derived from cinchona bark (*see* glossary), from a tree that grows wild in South America. A white, crystalline powder, almost insoluble in water, it was introduced as a Western medication in 1888 to treat malaria. It is used as a local anesthetic. Cinchonism (quinine poisoning), which may consist of nausea, vomiting, disturbances of vision, ringing in the ears, and nerve deafness, may occur from an overdose of quinine. If there is a sensitivity to quinine, such symptoms can result after ingesting tonic water. Quinine more commonly causes a rash, blurred vision, a headache, limb and back pain, loss of appetite, and unusual bleeding or bruising. In 1992, the FDA proposed a ban on quinine in internal analgesic products because it has not been shown to be safe and effective for its stated claims.

ROSEMARY (*Rosmarinus officinalis*) contains rosmaricine, the derivatives of which possess smooth-muscle stimulant activity and some analgesic properties. The herb possesses essential oils that reputedly calm and soothe irritated nerves and upset stomach. Rosemary is also high in minerals such as calcium, magnesium, phosphorus, sodium, and potassium. Used in an herbal tea for headaches.

WOOD BETONY (*Stachys officinalis*), also called wort, is a common herb of North America. It has been used for centuries to treat diarrhea, and as an astringent and sedative. An ingredient in it has been found to be active against tuberculosis. Wood betony has been used by herbalists to treat heartburn, gout, nervousness, cough, bladder and kidney stones, asthma, and fatigue. It is reputedly good for chronic headaches. The root is both emetic and purgative. The leaves contain mild laxative and astringent agents. A tea brewed from the plant is used in the treatment of stomach disorders.

WHITE WILLOW BARK (*Salix alba*) is the original source of salicin, the forerunner of aspirin. There are more than 130 species, most of them in Europe and North America. White willow bark is mentioned in ancient Egyptian, Assyrian, and Greek literature and was used to combat pain and fevers by Galen, Hippocrates, and Dioscorides. Many Native American tribes used it for headache relief. White willow bark is converted through oxidation to salicylic acid within the body.

WOODRUFF *(Asperula odorata)* is a perennial native to Europe, Asia, and North Africa and cultivated in the United States. It was used in the Middle Ages as a drink for jaundice and liver complaints. Its leaves were laid on open wounds. It was combined with other herbs as a cure for migraine and bladder problems and as a tonic for nervous conditions. Used in an herbal tea for migraine headache. The FDA issued a notice in 1992 that woodruff has not been shown to be safe and effective as claimed in OTC digestive-aid products. It may cause bleeding.

Other Plants and the Brain

ANEMONE *(Anemone ranunculaceae)*, also called windflower, pulsatilla, and lily of the field. Common throughout Europe. References to the small herb can be found in Greek and Chinese ancient medicinal literature. Anemone is still used today as a homeopathic remedy for various emotional ills.

BALM *(Melissa officinalis)*, also called lemon balm and sweet balm. A sweet-tasting herb introduced into Britain by the Romans, it has been used from early times in England for nervousness.

BLUE FLAG *(Iris versicolor)*, also called flag lily, fleur-de-lis, liver lily, poison flag, and wild iris. The rhizome contains salicylic and isophthalic acids, volatile oil, iridin, a glycoside gum, resin, and sterols *(see* all in glossary). Herbalists use it in herbal medicines as both a relaxant and stimulant.

BRAHMI *(Hydrocotyle asiatica)* is an herb used in India to relieve anxiety and to treat epilepsy and leprosy and named for the ancient Indian alphabet.

BURDOCK (*Arctium lappa*), also called lapp, bardane, and beggar's-buttons. The root, seed, and leaves contain essential oil of this common roadside plant. It contains nearly 45 percent inulin (*see* glossary) and many minerals. Herbalists use it as a tonic. Chinese burdock is used to eliminate excess nervous energy, and the root is considered to have aphrodisiac properties.

CHAMOMILE (*Matricaria chamomilla*), also called camomile. There are English, Roman, German, and Hungarian varieties of the plant. The daisylike white and yellow heads of these flowers contain sesquiterpene lactones, essential oil, calcium, coumarin, and tannic acid (*see* all in glossary). Chamomile is widely used as a tea for digestive ills and for tranquilization and insomnia. The oil is used with crushed poppy heads as a poultice for toothaches and neuralgia. Herbalists claim that chamomile tea prevents nightmares.

CLOVER, RED (*Trifolium pratense*) is a perennial common throughout Europe and is used in medicine as a tea and sometimes combined with other herbs as a tonic. It is reputedly good for the nerves because of its sedative properties.

DAMIANA (*Turnera diffusa, Turnera aphrodisiaca*), also called pastorata. The leaves contain volatile oil, hydrocyanic glycoside, bitter principle, tannin, and resin (*see* all in glossary). The drug is used by herbalists as a mild aphrodisiac for both sexes. It is reputed to be the safest of plant aphrodisiacs. It is also believed to counteract depression.

DILL (*Anethum graveolens*) is a hardy herb native to southern Europe and western Asia as well as the Americas. It was said by the ancient Greek physician Galen that it "procureth sleep." The name *dill* is derived from a Saxon word meaning "to lull." It is used by herbalists to treat symptoms of colic in children and insomnia in adults caused by indigestion. Dill in hot milk is recommended by herbalists as a drink that calms the nerves.

HELLEBORE *(Veratrum viride, Helleborus niger)*, also called green hellebore, Indian poke, itchweed, veratrum, false hellebore, and Christmas rose. Employed by ancient physicians to treat insanity. The doctors believed that patients brought to near death by the medication would be shocked into sanity. Hellebore is used by homeopathic physicians as a means to slow heartbeats. Hellebore is toxic and can cause severe nausea and extreme depression of the nervous system.

HEMLOCK *(Conium maculatum)*, also called poison parsley, is found in many parts of Europe and the Americas. The hemlock is related to parsnip, carrot, celery, fennel, and parsley. It is famed as the poison used to execute ancient Greeks. It was mixed with opium and used as a suicide drink for old, frail Roman philosophers. The narcotic drug conium comes from the dried, unripe fruit of the hemlock. Herbalists once used it as a sedative and antispasmodic and an antidote to other poisons.

HOPS *(Humulus lupulus)*, also called silent night, is widely cultivated. This plant has been used in folk medicine for its calming effect on the body. Contains an estrogenlike ingredient as well as volatile oil, lupulin, bitter principle, and tannin *(see* all in glossary). It is used to relieve gas and cramps and to stimulate appetite. It is used in a poultice to relieve sciatica and arthritis, toothaches, and other nerve pain. It has been used to induce sleep and as a tonic in wine. Both Abraham Lincoln and England's King George III reportedly relied on hops to promote a restful calm at bedtime. Hops flowers were listed in the USP *(see* glossary) for ninety years. The lupulin content of hops has antifungal and antibiotic activity.

HYSSOP *(Hyssopus officinalis)* is a perennial herb native to southern Europe. It was used to calm the nerves.

JAPANESE TURF LILY *(Ophiopogon japonicus)*, also called creeping lily root and dwarf lilyturf. The bulbs are used by herbalists to give clients a sense of inner well-being and to relieve insomnia and fearfulness.

JASMINE *(Jasminum officinale, Gelsemium sempervirens)*, also called Carolina jessamine, gelsemium root, and yellow jessamine. The jasmine flower has been brewed in tea for centuries to aid relaxation. The rhizomes and roots contain the alkaloid gelsemine, a potent analgesic that is used to treat the severe pain in the face known as tic douloureux or trigeminal neuralgia. Herbalists also claim that jasmine oil rubbed on the body increases sexual interest. It can be highly toxic and can cause death by respiratory arrest.

JUJUBE DATE *(Ziziphus jujuba)*, also called *da t'sao*. The Chinese jujube date is commonly used in a wide variety of herbal formulas. It is found dried in most oriental markets. It is used to enhance the taste and benefits of soups and stews and to energize the body. Chinese herbalists believe it relieves nervous exhaustion, insomnia, apprehension, forgetfulness, dizziness, and clamminess.

LADY'S SLIPPER *(Cypripedium calceoulus)* is used to treat anxiety, stress, insomnia, neurosis, restlessness, tremors, epilepsy, and palpitations. Herbalists claim it is also useful for depression. It contains volatile oils, resins, glucosides, and tannin *(see* all in glossary).

LEMON BALM *(Melissa officinalis)*. The leaves of this herb contain essential oils, acids, and tannin *(see* glossary). Herbalists use it to calm nervous tension and elevate mood.

LETTUCE EXTRACT *(Lactuca)*. Various species of lettuce are used by herbalists to make soothing skin decoctions. During the Middle Ages, lettuce was used as a valuable narcotic, and its milky juice, lactuca, was used with opium to induce sleep.

WILD LETTUCE *(Lactuca virosa)* is known as lettuce opium. The dried leaves contain latex, alkaloids, and terpenes *(see* all in glossary). It is used by herbalists to treat insomnia, restlessness, and anxiety, especially in children. It is also used to treat coughs, colic pains, and painful menstruation. It also reputedly eases arthritic pain.

LIME BLOSSOM *(Tilia europaea)*, also called linden, has flowers that contain essential oils, mucilage, flavonoids, coumarin, and vanillin (*see* all in glossary). Herbalists used it for relaxation from nervous tension and to lower blood pressure.

LOVAGE *(Ligustrum scoticum)*, also known as shunis, is an ingredient in perfumery from an aromatic herb native to southern Europe and grown in monastery gardens centuries ago for medicine and food flavoring. It has a hot, sharp, biting taste. The yellow-brown oil is extracted from the root or other parts of the herb. It has a reputation for improving health and inciting love; Czechoslovakian girls reportedly wear it in a bag around their necks when dating boys. It supposedly has deodorant properties when added to bathwater.

PASSIONFLOWER *(Passiflora incarnata)* is used in over-the-counter homeopathic medicines for temporary relief of simple nervous tension and insomnia. An extremely popular herb in Europe, where it is often used to induce relaxation and sleep. It has been shown that an extract of the plant depresses the motor nerves of the spinal cord. One of the ingredients in passionflower is serotonin (*see* glossary), a neurotransmitter that is low in persons who are depressed.

POPPY *(Papaver somniferum)*, also known as opium poppy, red poppy, California poppy, and papaver. Early monasteries grew poppies for use in hospitals for pain relief, and the sap was used throughout the Middle Ages during crude surgical operations and after serious battlefield injuries. The exudate from the poppies contains alkaloids (*see* glossary) with sedative and hypnotic properties. They are generally used as sedatives, narcotics, and analgesics. They are used to treat diarrhea, pain, coughs, sweating, and insomnia.

SCHISANDRA *(Schisandra chinesis)* is an herb used by Chinese women as an aphrodisiac and a youth tonic. It is a mild sedative. It is also believed to increase stamina. Schisandra has been shown in modern scientific laboratories to protect against the narcotic and sedative effects of alcohol and barbiturates. It is used as a tea. Contraindicated in persons with high blood pressure, epilepsy, and increased pressure on the brain.

SHANKA PUSPI *(Confolvulus mycrophyllus)* is an herb used in India to treat anxiety and mild pain.

SWEET FERN *(Polypodium vulgare)*, also called wood licorice, common polypody, female fern, and rock brake. The root of this fern that is distributed throughout Europe, South Africa, Siberia, Asia, and North America was used in folk medicine to treat melancholy and intestinal obstructions. The resin is considered to be useful against worms and as a purgative. It also possesses demulcent properties. Sweet fern is also reportedly useful as an appetite stimulant.

VACHA *(Acorus calamus)* is an herb used in India as a tranquilizer and aphrodisiac.

VALERIAN *(Valeriana officinalis)* is a perennial native to Europe and the United States that was reputed to be a love potion. Its vapor was found to kill the bacillus of typhoid fever after forty-five minutes. The herb has been widely studied in Europe and Russia, and the major constituents, the valepotriates, have been reported to have marked sedative, anticonvulsive, blood-pressure lowering, and tranquilizing effects. It has been used for centuries to treat panic attacks. In Germany, valerian preparations have been in use for more than a decade to treat childhood behavioral disorders, supposedly without the side effects experienced with pharmaceuticals for that purpose. It has been reported that it also helps concentration and energy. Prolonged use of valerian may result in side effects such as irregular heartbeat, headaches, uneasiness, nervousness, and insomnia. Large doses may cause paralysis.

VERVAIN, EUROPEAN (*Verbena officinalis*) is a weed native to Europe and the Far East. It is believed vervain was introduced to Rome by the Druids. Hippocrates prescribed vervain for wounds, fevers, and nervous disorders. In England, vervain was used against witches. Homeopathic medicine has used it to treat nervous disorders and epilepsy. In the United States it is used as a flavoring in alcoholic beverages.

As with any chemicals, you have to use your head if you want to protect your brain. Vitamins should be taken in moderation. Common sense should prevail before you swallow any substance that may affect your mind, including those aimed at pain relief or as an insomnia cure.

Chapter 14

NUTRACEUTICALS FOR WOMEN ONLY

Women *are* different from men. Adult females, unlike adult males, have to deal with menstruation, pregnancy, and menopause, and they are generally smaller in stature. Their need for and the effects from nutraceuticals may be gender specific.

Before, During, and After Menstruation

Each month during a woman's fertile years, her hormones rise and fall in her bloodstream. One of her ovaries releases an egg, which travels down her fallopian tube to her uterus. This takes about five days. During the few days preceding ovulation, the lining of the uterus becomes thickened and engorged with blood. This prepares her womb for fertilization of the egg by a visiting sperm. If the egg and the sperm do not meet, the thickened lining sloughs off and blood passes out of her vagina. The phenomena is repeated approximately every twenty-eight days. The two major sex hormones, estrogen and progesterone, control various physical swings. Associated with those changes may be water retention, breast tenderness, and mood swings. These emotional alterations are called premenstrual syndrome (PMS). They usually occur in the week before menstruation begins.

Premenstrual Syndrome (PMS)

The syndrome, despite much publicity in the lay press, is not well understood. No symptom is unique to PMS, and cardinal PMS symptoms such as irritability, depression, and appetite changes are prominent in other conditions, such as depression, personality disorders, and marital discord.[1] Studies with nutraceuticals have produced interesting but not definitive results.

Because premenstrual food cravings, especially for carbohydrates and sweets, and an increase in appetite are prominent PMS symptoms, various aspects of nutrition have long been implicated in the causes of PMS. In a review of twelve controlled trials of vitamin B_6 administration, the most commonly proposed therapy, only weak evidence of any positive effect of the vitamin was reported.[2]

Multiple nutritional factors were studied in ten PMS patients and ten control women. Each woman gave blood at two-to-three-day intervals throughout three menstrual cycles. No difference between PMS patients and controls was noted in levels of vitamin A, vitamin E, or magnesium. However, an excess of copper and a deficiency of zinc were observed in the luteal (after the egg enters the uterus) phases of PMS patients. The significance of these changes is as yet uncertain, but it is known that the trace metals are important cofactors in many liver enzyme pathways involving vitamins and hormone metabolism.[3]

In another study, magnesium was given during the luteal phase to thirty-two PMS patients for two to four months in a controlled study in which neither the subjects nor the physicians knew which were the real pills and which were the placebos. Magnesium turned out to be significantly more effective than the placebo in relieving symptoms.[4]

Can calcium ease the stress of women around menstruation time? In a study at USDA Grand Forks Human Nutrition Center, North Dakota, ten women received 1,300 mg of calcium daily. United States women average little more than 600 mg in their daily diets. Women in the study experienced fewer PMS-type mood changes, such as irritability, anxiety, crying, and depression, while on the higher calcium intake. They also reported fewer negative changes in behavior and concentration, such as poorer work performance and overall efficiency, avoiding social contacts, forgetfulness, confusion, and accidents. And the extra calcium significantly reduced complaints of physical distress, such as headache, backache, and cramps during menstruation.

Menstrual Cramps, Bloating, and Nutraceuticals

Menstrual pain varies. Some women have dull pain in the abdomen or back, others have severe cramping abdominal pain. Typically, pain is most acute at the beginning of a period. Painful periods are common.

Since time began, women have been trying to relieve these uncomfortable symptoms. While hormonal medications, psychopharmaceuticals, and diuretics are available by prescription, and "water pills" and a variety of mild painkillers are sold over the counter for the symptoms of premenstrual tension, nutraceuticals are used worldwide for this purpose. Not all are harmless, and many are ineffective, but some may be useful. The following describes some of the substances.

BUTTERBUR *(Petasites hybridus)* is a plant with broad leaves and purplish flowers. The rhizome or leaves of this herb contain essential oil, mucilage, and tannin *(see* all in glossary). It is used for painful menstrual periods, to induce sweating, and to reduce fluid retention.

CHASTE *(Vitex agnus-castus)* is also known as vitex, hemp tree, and monk's pepper. The fruit contains volatile oil, glycosides, and flavonoids *(see* all in glossary). In ancient times, the berries were used to suppress libido in temple priestesses. The herb is used to regulate the menstrual cycle of women, premenstrual syndrome (PMS), and menopause.

COLLINSONIA *(Collinsonia canadensis)* is also known as stoneroot.

The root contains saponin, alkaloid, tannin, and resin (*see* all in glossary). It is used by herbalists to treat hemorrhoids, varicose veins, and diarrhea. It is also used to treat the discomfort of menstruation, but in 1992, the FDA proposed a ban on collinsonia in oral menstrual drug products because it has not been shown to be safe and effective for its stated claims.

COUCH GRASS *(Agropyroni repens)*, also called dog grass or twitch grass. A weed that dogs and cats will seek out when they have upset stomachs. Herbalists use it to cool fevers and soothe internal irritation or inflammation. The roots possess both diuretic and demulcent properties and have been used by herbalists for centuries to treat bladder problems in humans. Couch grass contains high concentrations of mucilage, which gives the plant its soothing effect on mucous membranes. The plant is also reported to have antibiotic activity. Herbalists use it to treat menstrual problems, but in 1992, the FDA proposed a ban on couch grass in oral menstrual drug products because it has not been shown to be safe and effective for its stated claims.

CRAMP BARK *(Viburnum opulus)*, also called viburnum extract. It is the extract of the fruit of a hawthorn shrub or tree used by herbalists to relax the uterus during painful periods. It is also used to prevent threatened miscarriage and in the treatment of excessive blood loss during periods, especially those associated with menopause.

CYPERUS *(Cyperus rotundus)*, also called sedge root, is a common wayside weed closely related to ancient Egyptian papyrus. The root contains essential oils including pinene and sesquiterpenes (*see* glossary). It is used by herbalists to treat stomach cramps, menstrual irregularities, and depression.

DONG QUAI *(Angelica sinensis)*, also known as *tang kwei*, has a root used for the treatment of female gynecological ailments, particularly menstrual cramps, irregularity, and malaise during the menstrual period. It is also used to relieve the symptoms of menopause.

EVENING PRIMROSE *(Oenothera biennis)*, also called sundrops, has leaves and seed oil used by herbalists to treat painful breasts, premenstrual tension, and as a tonic for inflammatory conditions. The oil has a high content of linoleic acid, an essential polyunsaturated fatty acid that is converted into prostaglandins *(see* glossary) and hormones.

PASQUEFLOWER *(Anemone pulsatilla)* is a low, perennial herb with white or purple flowers. It is used by herbalists to treat painful periods. It is also used to treat asthma, insomnia, and other tension-induced conditions. (It also reputedly alleviates painful conditions of the testes.) The antibacterial effects are used by herbalists to treat skin infections.

PERIWINKLE *(Catharanthus roseus, Vinca rosea)* is an everblooming perennial herb or small shrub popular in gardens. The tropical periwinkle is an example of a folk medicine that has made its way into modern medicine. In 1953, Dr. Faustino Garcia reported at the Pacific Science Congress that the plant, taken orally, is a folk medicine in the Philippines for the treatment of diabetes. Researchers at the Eli Lilly Company screened the plant and found that it showed good anticancer activity in test animals. The result was the discovery of two alkaloids that are useful in treating cancer. The plant has also been found useful in treating diabetes. Periwinkle has been found to stop external hemorrhages, probably because it contains tannins *(see* glossary). The effect of controlling menstrual hemorrhaging may be due to vincamine, which dilates blood vessels.

VIBURNUM EXTRACT *(Carrifoliacea)*, also called haw bark, is the extract of the fruit of a hawthorn shrub or tree used by herbalists as a uterine antispasmodic. It is also used commercially in fragrances and in flavorings.

Inducing Menstruation

An *emmenagogue* is an agent that induces or increases menstrual flow. Among the herbs used for this purpose are

BLACK HAW *(Viburnum prunifolium)*, also called American sloe or stagbush. The stem and root bark contain coumarins, arbutin, salicin, and tannin (*see* all in glossary). It was used by herbalists to treat spasms of the uterus and to treat all forms of menstrual disorders.

CRAMP BARK *(Viburnum opulus)*, also called guelder rose or snowball tree. The bark contains hydroquinones, arbutin, coumarins, tannins, and catechins (*see* all in glossary). It is used to induce menstruation and to treat cramps and the discomfort of menstruation. It has also been used to prevent miscarriage and to treat the symptoms of menopause.

FENUGREEK *(Trigonella graecum)* is one of the oldest known medicinal plants. Use of fenugreek dates back to ancient Egyptians and Hippocrates. A folk remedy reputed to be an aphrodisiac, it is used to induce menstruation.

LIFE-ROOT *(Senecio aureus)*, also called golden ragwort, is an herb that contains alkaloids and resins (*see* both in glossary) and is used as a uterine tonic by herbalists. It is reportedly useful in treating the symptoms of menopause and for delayed or suppressed menstruation. It is also used as a general tonic for debilitated states.

MOTHERWORT *(Leonurus cardiaca)* is known by many names, such as heart wort, mother weed, mother herb, heart gold, heart heal, and lion's-tail. It is used worldwide in folk medicine as a tonic for the uterus due to its alkaloid content. The plant reputedly induces menstruation. Motherwort has also been used to treat high blood pressure, as a sedative and antispasmodic, and as a douche for the treatment of vaginitis.

Contraception

There are many choices of effective contraceptive techniques today ranging from the rhythm method to sterilization. The "pill," which uses female hormones, has literally changed society with its ease of administration and nearly certain prevention of pregnancy. It is interesting that the most popular birth control pill today is based on ancient practices.

CARROTS *(Daucus carota)*. There is epidemiological evidence that, when brewed in tea, the roots can block conception.

NEEM TREE *(Azadirachta indica)*, a native of India and Burma, is related to mahogany that now thrives throughout arid tropical regions of the world. There is evidence that materials from the seeds may work like contraceptives. Exploratory trials in male mammals, including monkeys, show that some compounds in neem reduce fertility without inhibiting sperm production. Furthermore, the reduced fertility effects seem to be temporary. Some twenty thousand wives of Indian army personnel recently partook in a test using neem oil as a spermicide, and the results were encouraging.

SOUTHERNWOOD *(Artemisia abrotanum)* is native to southern Europe and widely grown in English gardens. It belongs to the Compositae family. Pliny thought it had aphrodisiac qualities when placed under a mattress. It reputedly made hair grow on bald heads. Used in herbal teas as a sedative. It is also used by herbalists to bring on delayed menstruation, which gave it a nickname, "lad's love."

WILD YAM ROOT *(Dioscorea paniculata)*, also called colicroot, rheumatism root, and Chinese yam. The most widely prescribed birth control pill in the world, Desogen, is made from the wild yam, confirming what the ancient Mexican women knew all along. They used wild yam as a contraceptive. Japanese researchers in

1936 discovered glycoside saponins of several Mexican yam species from which steroid saponin (*see* glossary), primarily diosgenin, could be derived. These derivatives were then converted to progesterone, an intermediate in cortisone production. Steroid drugs derived from diosgenin include corticosteroids, oral contraceptives, androgens, and estrogens. For more than two centuries American herbalists used wild yam roots to treat painful menstruation, ovarian pain, cramps, and problems of childbirth. Wild yam root has also been used to treat gallbladder pain and ease the passage of gallstones.

Fertility and Nutraceuticals

As couples wait longer to have children, they are increasingly exposed to pollutants in the air, water, and food that may cause them to have trouble conceiving. New diagnostic techniques and drugs as well as microsurgical procedures are making it possible to have children despite most problems. Infertility is not a new problem, however, and the ancients used many plants to try to produce a successful pregnancy. The following are a sampling of traditional remedies.

LONGANBERRY (*Euphoria longana*), also called *long yen rou*, or dragon's eye is a red-fruited herb. The berries are used by herbalists to make a strong tonic that reputedly strengthens the reproductive organs of women and counteracts anemia, forgetfulness, and hyperactivity. It is also an herbal remedy for low blood sugar.

MUIRA-PUAMA (*Liriosma ovata*) is a Brazilian herb used primarily to treat impotence, frigidity, and diarrhea.

SQUAW VINE (*Mitchella repens*), also called partridgeberry or checkerberry, is an American trailing plant used for painful or absent menstruation. Also used to prepare the womb for childbirth. It acquired its name because it was popular among American Indian tribes during pregnancy.

Pregnancy and Childbirth

Whatever the mother takes in her body may affect her unborn child. The following information about vitamins to prevent birth defects describes some of the latest research.

Vitamins Preventing Birth Defects

The link between vitamins in the diet and birth defects has been suspected for many years. Recent evidence, as pointed out earlier in this book, suggests that folic acid taken prior to conception and early in pregnancy can reduce the fetus's risk of neural-tube birth defects, a condition where the protective channel around the nerves in the spinal cord does not properly close. Neural-tube defects, including spina bifida (incomplete fusion of some of the vertebrae), can cause early death or paralysis. Neural-tube defects occur in about 1.2 per 1,000 births in the U.S.A. and with Down's syndrome constitutes one of the two most common major birth defects.

Vitamin A, retinoic acid, may also help prevent birth defects. Vitamin A plays a pivotal role in normal development. Retinoic acid helps determine the shape and pattern of a broad array of the body's organs, including parts of the brain and spinal column, the face, the limbs, the heart, the skeleton, and the skin. In a number of papers published in 1990s, the vitamin A results come primarily from animals, but researchers believe that they are likely to apply to human development.

A study of 22,776 pregnancies was done to evaluate whether multivitamins that contained folic acid, taken early in pregnancy, would protect against neural-tube defects. The group of women who *did not* use folic-acid-containing vitamins gave birth to almost four times more infants with neural-tube defects than those who had taken the vitamins.[5]

Other studies have pointed out that women who take multivitamins prior to and during pregnancy are also less likely to have a child born with birth defects of the brain and spine, according to medical epidemiologist Dr. Joseph Mulinare, who led the study at the National Centers for Disease Control in Atlanta.[6]

The federal researchers found that women who took multivitamins—at least three times a week—regularly in the three months prior to and after becoming pregnant were 50 percent less likely to produce children with brain and spinal-cord malformations. It could be the multivitamins are having an effect on the fetus, said Dr. Mulinare, or it could be something special about women who are multivitamin users versus women who are not.

Phytochemicals and Birth

Through the centuries, women have handed down from generation to generation advice about foods and herbs that may help with discomfort that may occur during pregnancy and during delivery and to aid the flow of milk in breast-feeding mothers.

Morning sickness—the nausea that often accompanies the first weeks of pregnancy—may be relieved, herbalists believe, by the following:

FALSE UNICORN (*Chamaelirium luteum*), also known as helonias. The North American Indians used this herb as a tonic and to strengthen the reproductive system. It is used by herbalists today to treat painful and irregular menstruation, threatened miscarriage, and nausea during pregnancy. It is also used a general tonic for the genitourinary tract and for heartburn and loss of appetite. Large doses will cause nausea and vomiting.

GOLDENROD (*Solidago virgauria*) is a perennial in a genus that includes 125 species. It was valued for its medicinal properties by herb women in Elizabethan London. The name *Solidago* means "makes whole," and herbalists say it helps to heal wounds, and in fact at one time it was called woundwort. It is used by herbalists as an antiseptic. Used in an herbal tea as a tonic and for morning sickness.

GROUNDSEL *(Senecio vulgaris)* is part of an enormous worldwide genus of between two thousand and three thousand species. Groundsel was used in European and American folk medicine to ease painful menstruation. American Indians used it to speed childbirth. In general, the plant has been used to induce sweating, to rid the body of excess fluid, and as a tonic. Cases of liver toxicity from its use have been reported by the National Centers for Disease Control in Atlanta.

SWEET CICELY *(Myrrhis odorata)* is a perennial herb native to Britain and many parts of the world. It was used as a preventative against the plague. In Alaska and other areas throughout North America, the root was used for a tonic for invalids and new mothers. Used in an herbal tea as a tonic.

The Pain of Childbirth

Did primitive women really have their babies in the field and go back to work, as legend has told us, or did they down a few herbs while they were out there to ease the pain of childbirth? There is no doubt that having a baby hurts, and following are some of the ancient remedies for the pain.

BLACK COHOSH *(Cimicifuga racemosa)* is also called black snakeroot, bugbane, and rattleroot. The root contains various substances including glycosides, estrogens, and tannins (*see* all in glossary). Herbalists used it to relieve nerve pains, menstrual pains, and the pain of childbirth. It is also used to speed delivery and to reduce blood pressure. Black cohosh is also believed to have sedative properties. In 1992, the FDA proposed a ban on black cohosh in oral menstrual drug products because it has not been shown to be safe and effective for its stated claims.

BLUE COHOSH *(Caulophyllum thalictroides)*, also known as papooseroot or squawroot, has a rhizome that contains active ingredients including saponin, glycosides, and phosphoric acid (*see* all in glossary). Herbalists use it for menstrual irregularities and pain and to ease the pain of childbirth.

After Birth

Sometimes, bleeding becomes a problem after the birth of a baby. The folk medicine practioners had remedies. The following are examples.

REHMANNIA (*Rehmannia glutinosa*), also called *sok day–sang day*, is a root used by Chinese herbalists to purify and nourish the blood, strengthen the kidneys, and heal the bones and tendons. Herbalists say it is useful in building the body during recovery from an illness. It is given to women to treat menstrual irregularities and infertility, as a tonic during pregnancy, and to stop postpartum hemorrhage.

TRILLIUM (*Trillium liliaceae*), also called bethroot, Indian balm, and ground lily. The dried rhizome contains tannin (*see* glossary). Used by herbalists to treat painful menstrual symptoms, various types of hemorrhage, and diarrhea.

Breast Feeding—Best but Not Necessarily Easy

Almost everyone agrees that if possible, breast feeding is best for a baby. It not only reduces the baby's risk of infection, it strengthens the bond between mother and child. However, problems can arise to make breast feeding difficult. In most women, the milk arrives a few days after delivery and the breasts become swollen and sore. For any unusual problems, of course, a physician should always be consulted. A *galactogogue* is a compound that aids the flow of milk in breast-feeding mothers, and women have used the following herbs for that purpose through the centuries, but no one should use them today without consulting a physician first.

BLESSED THISTLE *(Cnicus benedictus)* is also called holy thistle. The plant contains tannin, lactone, mucilage, and essential oil *(see all in glossary)*. It is used by herbalists to increase the flow of milk in breast feeding. It also reputedly breaks up blood clots, relieves jaundice, stops bleeding, increases appetite, and lowers fevers. The FDA issued a notice in 1992 that blessed thistle has not been shown to be safe and effective as claimed in OTC digestive-aid products or in oral menstrual drugs.

CARAWAY *(Carum carvi)* is a native of southeastern Europe and western Asia. The use of this herb dates back to ancient Egypt. The seeds are used to ease intestinal gas and colic and to stimulate the appetite. It is also used by herbalists to treat bronchitis, laryngitis, and to relieve menstrual pains. It has been used to increase the flow of mother's milk.

VERVAIN, EUROPEAN *(Verbena officinalis)* is a weed used to increase the flow of milk in new mothers.

Menopause—Stopping the Flow

There is a season in life when the menstrual cycle—including ovulation and menstrual periods—ends. The term *menopause* is used in the popular sense to mean the months or even years before and after this change in life. About 25 percent of women do not notice any changes at menopause, except the cessation of periods. Another 50 percent notice slight physical and/or mental changes. The remaining 25 percent have inconvenient or even distressing symptoms—physical discomforts such as hot flashes, sweating, dryness of the vagina, palpitations, joint pains, and headaches. They may also suffer depression, anxiety, irritability, decreased ability to concentrate, lack of confidence, and sleeping difficulties. These symptoms can last from a few weeks to more than five years.

Since menopause is a natural event in life, many times the

uncomfortable symptoms are downplayed by doctors and families, and many women are reluctant to take medication for them. Since ancient times, women have been using herbs to deal with the discomfort. Whether or not the folk therapies work is still a matter of trial and error. But new research is showing that some nutritional deficiencies may play a part in exacerbating the symptoms. Here are some of the remedies being tried.

Vitamin E has been recommended for the hot flashes that often annoyingly make their appearance during menopause. Bioflavonoids, especially hesperidin, with vitamin C are also reputedly effective in helping ameliorate the hot flashes. The following herbs have a long history of being used by women to ease the discomfort of menopause:

BLESSED THISTLE (*Cnicus benedictus*), which is also used to ease menstruation, has been employed for centuries by herbalists to treat the symptoms of menopause.

DONG QUAI, mentioned above under menstruation, is also used to relieve the symptoms of menopause.

GINSENG (*Panax ginseng*, Asia; *Panax quinquefolius*, North America; *Eleutherococcus senticosus*, Siberian ginseng). Chinese esteem ginseng as an herb of many uses. They have been using it in medicine for more than five thousand years. The Chinese and Koreans also use it in combination with chicken soup. The word *Panax* comes from the Greek *panakos*, a panacea. Among its active ingredients are amino acids, essential oils, carbohydrates, peptides, vitamins, minerals, enzymes, and sterols (*see* all in glossary). In the Orient, it is esteemed for its abilities to preserve health, invigorate the system, and prolong life. It is taken in an herbal tea as a daily tonic. North American Indians used ginseng as a love potion. It has been found to normalize high or low blood sugar. Russian scientists are studying ginseng for the treatment of insomnia and general debility. Japanese scientists recently reported isolating a number of compounds rare in nature from ginseng, some of which have anticancer properties, tranquilizing effects, or aphrodisiac properties. No wonder it has been used through the centuries for the symptoms of menopause.

LADY'S MANTLE (*Alchemilla xanthochlora*) is a common European herb covered with spreading hairs. The dried leaves and flowering shoots have been used for centuries by herbalists to concoct love potions and to treat menstrual problems, diarrhea, and wounds. It contains tannin, glycosides, and salicylic acid (*see* all in glossary). Widely used by herbalists throughout Europe, it is prescribed for easing the changes of menopause.

Vaginal Discharges

GOLDENSEAL (*Hydrastis canadensis*) is also called puccoon root and yellowroot. The American Indians were the first to use it for sore eyes. Early pioneers, along with many Indian tribes, used it as a general tonic. The rhizome and root are used by herbalists to treat heavy menstrual periods, and as a general tonic for the female reproductive tract. It is also used for penile discharge, eczema, and skin disorders. Herbalists claim it dries and cleanses the mucous membranes and is good for liver dysfunction and for all inflammations. It reputedly has potent antibiotic and antiseptic properties. It contains berberine (*see* glossary). It is contraindicated during pregnancy and for persons suffering from high blood pressure and ischemia (insufficient blood flow). The FDA issued a notice in 1992 that *Hydrastis canadensis,* and hydrastis fluid extract have not been shown to be safe and effective as claimed in OTC digestive-aid products and in oral menstrual products.

ROSE (*Rosa gallica*) is a popular flower, and the use of its petals dates from very ancient times. Ancient pharmacists used them as purgatives, astringents, and tonics, and for chronic lung diseases, diarrhea, and vaginal discharges. The medicinal properties of the petals are generally considered mild. The buds and petals are astringent. Rosebuds are high in vitamin C, astringent tannins, and phenolic compounds (*see* all in glossary).

VINEGAR, which is used in popular over-the-counter douches today, has been used for hundreds of years. Vinegar is about 4 to 6 percent acetic acid. Acetic acid occurs naturally in apples, cheese, grapes, milk, and other foods. No known toxicity but may cause an allergic reaction.

Bladder Problems

CAPSAICIN. Women, because of their anatomy, are prone to bladder problems. Scientists have sought to control the "uninhibited bladder," which can lead to incontinence and damage to the upper urinary tract. One treatment reported in 1994 was the instillation of capsaicin, the pungent extract from red pepper. There are reported capsaicin-sensitive nerves in the bladder that help to control its function. In experiments at the State University of New York Health Science Center at Brooklyn, five out of twelve patients with poor bladder control showed "highly satisfactory improvement."[7]

Vitamins for the Mature Woman

Older women can increase spine bone density by getting extra vitamin D during the dark days of winter in addition to getting adequate calcium. The lack of sunlight in the temperate zone from midfall to midspring leads to a deficiency in the vitamin, which helps the body absorb calcium and phosphorus from foods and deposit these minerals in bones. Researchers measured bone density in 247 women past menopause during a year-long study. In addition to getting 800 mg of calcium per day, half the women got an extra 400 IU of vitamin D, while the other half got a placebo. Both groups gained about the same amount of density of their spines during the summer and fall months when exposure to the sun prompts the skin to manufacture enough of the vitamin, and both lost density during the winter and spring months, but the group getting extra vitamin D lost only half as much, giving them an overall increase in spinal bone of 0.85 percent for the year compared with no net gain for the placebo group. Unfortunately, 400 IU of the vitamin is difficult to get from the diet, so vitamin supplements would be necessary.[8]

Extra vitamin C at each meal can help women get more iron from the less available sources—vegetables, grains, and legumes. In a ten-week study, women of childbearing age ate a diet low in meat and high in plant foods, from which iron is harder to absorb. During half the experiment, they got a 500-mg vitamin C supplement with each meal, and during the other half, a placebo. The supplement didn't increase either blood hemoglobin or iron reserves, but it significantly boosted the active thyroid hormone T3.[9] Studies with rats have shown that iron deficiency reduces levels of T3, which regulates the body's metabolism. The results support findings from earlier studies showing that vitamin C can enhance iron absorption from plant foods. Getting enough iron has long been a problem for younger women and is becoming more important among those who cut back on consumption of red meat. Adding a glass of orange or grapefruit juice or a serving of fresh strawberries or broccoli to meals can help overcome the problem.[10]

Women who consume low levels of beta-carotene and vitamin C are up to six times more likely to develop cervical cancer than are women who eat proper amounts of these nutrients.[11]

A growing body of research is showing that several nutrients, including the antioxidants vitamin C and beta-carotene, and the B vitamins folic acid and vitamin B_{12}, can help prevent the development of cancers of the uterine, cervix, and endometrium. These nutrients may also play a role in suppressing cancer growth once it has started. The best evidence thus far has come from studies on large groups of women. Those groups of women whose diets contained the highest amounts of beta-carotene, vitamin C, and/or folic acid had a lower risk of developing cervical or endometrial cancer.[12]

Surveys show that not only older women but those in the age group nineteen to fifty years may not be getting enough of a number of nutrients in their diets. Fully 70 percent of women (eighteen to fifty) are consuming less than the RDA for vitamin E, vitamin B$_6$, folic acid, and calcium.[13] It may well be that improving the nutrition in their diets by fortifying food with nutraceuticals or taking the compounds in pill form may do much to prevent many of the ills that plague women only.

Chapter 15

NUTRACEUTICALS, THE LAW, THE COMPETITION, AND THE FUTURE

When a five-thousand-year-old man was discovered frozen in the Italian Alps, scientists were puzzled about the two mushrooms he had carried tied together in a leather pouch. They tested the mushrooms and found a type of fungus from which penicillin is derived. Was this ancient Alpine hiker carrying the first prehistoric first-aid kit?

"If this theory proves true," says Abbey S. Meyers, executive director of the National Organization for Rare Disorders, "we can only lament that it took another five thousand years to rediscover what mankind should have known all along. And this is why scientists should reexamine this important area of investigations—the therapeutic use of nutritional supplements—in the context of our free-market system where the government protects healthy consumers and compassionately helps the ill."[1]

As you have read in this book, a tremendous amount of information is being gathered about the use of food, nutrients, and phytochemicals in the prevention and treatment of diseases. But a big legal question remains as a roadblock in the United States—when is a food a pharmaceutical or a pharmaceutical a food?

The U.S. Food and Drug Administration (FDA) maintains a *medical food is a specially formulated and processed food for patients who are seriously ill or who require the product as a major factor in their treatment.*[2]

According to the FDA, medical foods *are:*

- For oral or tube feeding.
- Ones that claim a preventive and/or therapeutic purpose.
- Labeled for the dietary management of a specific medical disorder, disease, or condition, for which there are distinct nutritional requirements.
- Intended for use under medical supervision.[3]

The FDA says medical foods are *not:*

- Foods that make health claims but are marketed to us.
- Foods just recommended by physician or health-care professionals as part of our diet to reduce the risk of a disease or a medical condition or to promote weight loss.
- Dietary supplements that we can purchase from retail outlets or by mail order.

Before 1972, medical foods were considered drugs and were regulated to ensure use under medical supervision. In 1972, the FDA reclassified these products from drugs to *foods for special dietary use* to promote their development and availability. Today, millions of patients receive medical foods in hospitals, private homes, and nursing homes. Medical foods are marketed for the dietary management of malnutrition, lung, liver, kidney, and heart diseases. One of the newest is a prescription drink specially formulated for people with Parkinson's disease that adjusts protein and carbohydrate intake.

A *drug*, on the other hand, according to FDA regulations, *diagnoses, relieves, or cures a disease.*

But what about nutraceuticals that may be used by the general population to prevent and to treat ailments?

Problems

If the National Cancer Institute's multimillion-dollar search for elements in diet that can prevent or aid in the treatment of cancer is successful, will those elements become foods, drugs, or something in-between—nutraceuticals? The NCI researchers had better consult the regulations from their sister agencies—the FDA and the Federal Trade Commission—before any claims are made.

Under the current system in the United States, advertising for foods and nonprescription drugs is regulated by the Federal Trade Commission. Marketing approval, composition, and product labeling for prescription and nonprescription drugs, as well as most foods, are regulated by the FDA. The labeling and production of meat and poultry products are regulated by the United States Department of Agriculture.

The FDA's broad new limitations on marketing claims for vitamins, minerals, and herbs took effect July 1, 1994. The agency says the new regulations are to prevent false or unproven health claims and to help the public make "informed choices."

The FDA maintains that more than five hundred products have no scientific or medical support for their health claims. The federal courts have repeatedly rebuked the FDA for some of its actions against dietary supplements. For example, the FDA seized gel caps containing black-currant-seed oil and evening-primrose oil, alleging that the caps were "food" and the oil inside an "unapproved food additive." A federal court called the FDA "nonsensical" and added that black-currant-seed oil is not only healthy, but a leading treatment for chronic fatigue syndrome.[4]

The FDA has the authority to pursue unsubstantiated health claims on a case-by-case basis. For example, FDA officials seized products from Thorne Research Inc., a Sandpoint, Idaho, manufacturer of dietary supplements, including a calcium product marketed as Osteocap. The product name, said the FDA, implied a treatment for osteoporosis. What happened? Thorne continued to sell the product but marketed under a new name, Oscap.[5]

While frustrated, the FDA officals sometimes go overboard. In 1992, FDA personnel and sheriff's officers raided the offices of a Kent, Washington, physician and nutritionist. Though an associate of the doctor's was ultimately charged with selling "adulterated" drugs, the raid prompted a public outcry because the raiders barged into the doctor's office with their guns drawn and scared the vitamins out of the patients, who were seeking nutrients for their health.[6]

So where do such FDA actions leave nutraceuticals, which fall outside the traditional concept of either a food or a drug?

Dr. Stephen L. DeFelice, who has been spearheading the drive for recognition of nutraceuticals, says a new regulatory process must be created for their review and approval. At the same time, in the interest of efficiency, care should be taken to incorporate rather than duplicate the roles of established regulatory agencies.

"We have a law that has two concepts—one of food and the other of drug," he says. "Under the present law, if a food is used for the cure, mitigation, or prevention of a disease, it's considered a drug and is subject to regulation as a drug. All of the expensive testing involved with a new-drug application would apply."

The FDA, of course, is there to protect us from fraud and from potentially harmful products. Under 1974 FDA regulations, food is misbranded and illegal to sell if claims are made about the prevention or treatment of any diseases or symptoms.

The provisions of the Nutrition Labeling and Education Act (NLEA) and the Dietary Supplement Act of 1992 were the first major changes in food labeling regulations since 1974. Under the new NLEA final regulations, health-related claims must go through an administrative procedure to receive FDA approval. Approval is based on the totality of publicly available scientific evidence, including well-designed studies and significant agreement among experts.

The process may take a long time. The folic-acid recommendations to prevent birth defects took more than ten years.

Since May 8, 1994, food producers have had to comply with most of the FDA's new labeling requirements. Advertising is not covered by NLEA. The Federal Trade Commission, however, has indicated it may apply the same criteria to advertising that the FDA does to labels.

Dr. DeFelice and his colleagues are trying to get new legislation passed similar to the Orphan Drug Act.

Dr. DeFelice, the former chief of clinical pharmacology at the Walter Reed Army Institute of Research, was a principal proponent of the 1983 Orphan Drug Act, which encourages pharmaceutical companies to develop medications for small groups of patients suffering from relatively rare diseases. He himself studied carnitine—a naturally occurring substance in muscle, liver, and meat extracts. A small number of people are born with an inability to make carnitine, and they suffer from weak muscles. To them, carnitine supplementation is vital.

The Orphan Drug Act regulations give drug companies exclusive rights to rare-disease pharmaceuticals they develop, such as carnitine, for seven years. Until the act was passed, few pharmaceutical companies developed such medications because there was little profit to be made.

Nutraceutical research is likely to be less expensive than pharmaceutical research because many of the products occur naturally in plants or are easily obtained vitamins and minerals, according to Dr. DeFelice.

However, if the companies cannot patent a product or have exclusive rights to it, then they are not going to spend the money for research and development. It is almost impossible to patent a food or a nutrient or a phytochemical, since they are common and available. If a company does the research and development to isolate and prove the health benefits of a certain nutraceutical, the producer must then have some sort of protection for the resulting claim to earn back the money spent on research and development and to make a profit. Such a regulation would be similar to the Orphan Drug Act.

"I think there's a vast world out there of natural-substance deficiencies that create disease states that, once treated, can be reversed," Dr. DeFelice says. Specific disease states and medications create nutritional deficiencies that should be treated with supplements, he believes.[7]

Dr. DeFelice maintains an interdepartmental commission—known as the Nutraceutical Commission (NUCOM)—should be created to administer the review and approval requirements of nutraceuticals as well as to work across government lines with the FDA, FTC, and USDA and their respective functions.

Under the new regulatory process, Dr. DeFelice says, companies would be able to decide whether to pursue a potential new product development as a food, a drug, or a nutraceutical. If a company chooses to develop a product as a nutraceutical, an option prior to conducting studies would be to submit to NUCOM a summary of the company's proposed product development, following guidelines developed by NUCOM.

Study requirements for a potential new nutraceutical product would be open and flexible. Given the broad role of nutrients, for example, epidemiological data may frequently provide significant evidence in addition to clinical studies.

Companies Need Economic Incentives

Hercules A. Segalas, managing director of Paine Webber, Inc., New York, compares American, European, and Japanese nutraceutical efforts:

"While it appears we will have to wait for many years for nutraceuticals to become truly plentiful on our supermarket or specialty-retailing shelves, especially if the Food and Drug Administration does not act to incentivize food companies to spend research dollars in this area, there is no stopping the trend toward healthful foods—or perhaps equally important, what are perceived as healthful. Unlike the health-food consumers of the past, who were often viewed as 'far-out' eaters of wheat germ and seaweed, healthful eating is now mainstream. More and more consumers are taking an interest in their health, exercising more, and watching their diet. Indeed, nearly 35 percent of all new food products launched in 1992 were in a no or low category concerning calories, fat, salt, sugar, or cholesterol. There are some six thousand reduced-fat foods on grocery shelves today."[8]

Most nutraceuticals, however, will be to fortify foods or to supplement them. Herbert Pierson, Ph.D., former head of the National Cancer Institute's Designer Foods Research Program and now affiliated with the Seattle-based Preventive Nutrition Consultants, Inc., says, "The technology is there, but FDA approval is needed."[9]

Indeed, new nutraceuticals are already on the market but cannot be claimed as such. The Dow Chemical Company, for example, has a food additive, HPMC (hydroxypropylmethylcellulose), that can, researchers at the University of Michigan have shown, lower blood cholesterol.

Both the potential nutraceutical and the food additive are derivatives of cellulose extracted from wood. The food additive is now being used in small amounts to thicken cheese, cakes, and puddings.

In the University of Michigan study—which was funded by Dow—HPMC was tested in three different groups of people. Blood cholesterol levels dropped an average of 32 percent in a one-week trial in ten healthy young men. In a second experiment on twelve people with mildly elevated blood cholesterol levels, HPMC reduced cholesterol levels by an average of 22 percent over two weeks. Side effects were minimal, according to the researchers, consisting mostly of a feeling of bloating. The University of Michigan's Jennifer Bressman, Ph.D., associate professor of pharmaceutics, and her colleagues said the drug appears to work by thickening the food and slowing its movement through the intestines. The speculation is that this either lowers the efficiency with which the digestive system processes cholesterol and dietary fats or else slows the absorption of cholesterol by the intestines.[10]

HPMC could fortify a cookie and the cookie would then be a nutraceutical available in the supermarket to lower cholesterol.

Researchers at the Agricultural Research Service of the United States Department of Agriculture have developed two other food additives that are potential nutraceuticals.

Oatrim consists of amylodextrin—shortened fragments of starch—and beta-glucans, the principal fiber in oats and barley. Twenty-four volunteers, who were selected because of their mildly elevated cholesterol, ingested the Oatrim. About one-half cup of Oatrim a day added to a variety of foods significantly reduced artery-clogging LDL cholesterol, but it did not lower the beneficial HDL cholesterol. The volunteers not only had a drop in cholesterol, they also lost weight, averaging 4.5 to 5 pounds. That happened even though their calorie intake increased during the study in an effort to stem weight loss. Also, their glucose tolerance—the ability to process sugar from a meal—improved, reducing the risk of diabetes.

Barley is rich in tocotrienols, which along with tocopherols are in vitamin E. Several studies have found that tocotrienols are better antioxidants than tocopherols. Other studies have shown that the consumption of barley helps in lowering the plasma cholesterol levels, since tocotrienols inhibit the enzyme that controls cholesterol manufacture in the liver.[11]

ARS has licensed Oatrim to a joint venture between ConAgra and A. E. Staley and a partnership between Quaker Oats and Rhone Poulenc. ConAgra puts Oatrim in several of its Healthy Choice products now commercially available to food companies for modifying meats, baked goods, and other foods. The Healthy Choice hamburger with Oatrim is 96 percent fat free and is still juicy.[12] The Oatrim may also help lower cholesterol, but the company cannot by law make any claims about Oatrim as a nutraceutical.[13]

Another version of the oats and barley derivative, B-Trim, was also developed by ARS scientists. New beverages ranging from fruit or vegetable juices to diet colas could contain this nutraceutical. The drinks would have the soluble fiber for health reasons and yet have a consistency perceived as no thicker than ordinary beverages. B-Trim is similar to Oatrim but is mixed into a beverage, cooled, and then resheared by a blender to give the beverage less viscosity. Orange juice with O.1 percent added B-Trim from barley was slightly more viscous than plain orange juice, but the difference could only be sensed by a viscometer. B-Trim is rich in beta-glucan, a component of some grains that has been found to help lower blood cholesterol and thus reduce the threat of heart disease. George Inglett, a chemist with USDA ARS, developed

B-Trim. He envisions "nutraceutical" sports and soft drinks, wines, cappuccino, and iced teas enriched with B-Trim, vitamins, and other nutrients and flavored to suit individual preferences.[14]

The FDA prohibits assertions that dietary fiber and antioxidant vitamins such as beta-carotene or vitamin C can prevent cancer or cardiovascular disease, and that fish oils can prevent heart disease. Thus, you won't hear of the cholesterol-lowering benefits of the oat-barley nutraceuticals, at least not for a while.

Other Nations Accept Nutraceuticals

Other nations are not being hamstrung by the bureaucratic "Is it a food or drug?" debate.

In France, fish oil capsules have received drug approval. In Germany, the United Kingdom, and other European Economic Community nations, herbal remedies represent a significant share of the pharmaceutical market.[15]

Japan is way out in front as far as nutraceuticals are concerned. They now hold 57 percent of the patents awarded for plant-derived foods in the world. In 1984, the Education, Science, and Culture Ministry of Japan provided $7 million to joint research teams among universities to study the potential and actual benefits of food components in the prevention and treatment of disease. The concept of *food for specified health use (FOSHU)* came from these government-sponsored studies.[16] The FOSHU system was approved in July 1991. The category is expected to reach $8 billion within a couple of years. The Agricultural, Forest, and Fisheries Ministry and the Health and Welfare Ministry encouraged industry to develop technologies and information about the health benefits of food components. FOSHU are incorporated under the established regulatory umbrella without requiring extremely high costs. A key nonprofit organization—the Japan Health Food and Nutrition Food Association—was set up to guide companies through the approval process. First the nutritional components are examined, then an application is made for the food product itself. Among the criteria for FOSHU are that the product must have a clear medical and health benefit and that the amount for consumption should be based on medical and nutritional knowledge. The product should be one that is normally consumed in ordinary dietary plans and that is not nutritionally deficient compared with similar types of food.[17]

FOSHU products that are approved are licensed and clearly labeled with both the medical benefit and the precautions for cooking, use, and storage. A brochure must explain possible risks. To help consumers, the government is considering allowing only certified stores staffed by FOSHU nutritionists to sell their products.

The Japanese have a product, Relax Time gum, on the market that contains herbs that can be claimed to ease stress. They have Ginseng Rush soda and Yen Sum beer, which contain ginseng, which can be advertised to help stimulate the body. The French also have a beer that supposedly increases sexual desire. It contains ginger, cardamon, ginseng, licorice, and about six other herbs.[18]

Immune milk that lowers cholesterol and blood pressure is on the market in Taiwan.[19]

Dr. DeFelice believes both the U.S. food and pharmaceutical companies will take a big hit from European and Japanese companies by the end of the twentieth century: "The present situation is analogous to the recent history of the U.S. auto industry. The United States is standing still while Europe and Japan are moving forward."[20]

Nutraceuticals Today and Tomorrow

The Japanese and French nutraceuticals may not be vital to health, but America's farmland has the potential to become America's pharmacy. Purdue University researchers in Indiana are exploring the possibility of developing soybeans to produce proteins used in cancer therapy or human and animal vaccines. Lab cultures now used to make those proteins are expensive, but producing the proteins in soybean fields could lower the cost of these drugs to consumers, Purdue researchers say.[21]

No matter what the products are called—nutraceuticals, pharm-foods, or designer foods—the category exists and will be growing.

First of all, the public wants more control over their health care, and nutraceuticals are one way to get it. People are already using nutraceuticals on their own without scientific research or regulations to protect them. One in three persons, according to a report in the *The New England Journal of Medicine*, report using at least one unconventional therapy in the past year, and a third of these saw providers for unconventional therapy. David Eisenberg, M.D., and his colleagues at Harvard Medical School and the Institute for Social Research at the University of Michigan surveyed 1,539 adults about their use of conventional services and unconventional therapy. The frequency of use of unconventional therapy in the United States is far higher than previously reported.[22]

In some cases, ancient usage, modern science, and commercial promotion have met on a product and changed the marketplace. Yogurt, for example, was never seen on grocery shelves thirty years ago, but it is now in almost every supermarket. It is both a food and a drug, since it contains lactobacilli that have been found to prevent and to treat diarrhea. Fiber, particularly oat fiber, is another example of popular, scientific, and commerical interests meeting. Everyone seems to agree that it can lower cholesterol and fight colon cancer. Wheat germ is another example of an old practice making its way into the scientific arena because of its high vitamin E content.

In 1988, the National Cancer Institute guidelines pointed out that the potential for dietary changes to reduce the risk of cancer is considerable, and that the existing scientific data provide evidence that is sufficiently consistent to warrant prudent interim dietary guidelines that will promote good health and reduce the risk of some types of cancer. The NCI estimated that 35 percent of cancers may be related to dietary components. The NCI hopes to reduce cancer mortality by 50 percent by the year 2000.[23]

The National Cancer Institute, the National Heart Institute, the American Heart Association, and the American Cancer Society all have programs to research and improve health through diet.

University researchers are hard at work trying to find out what elements in foods are beneficial and how they can be increased in diets and medicines. In 1992, Johns Hopkins Medical Institution in Baltimore trumpeted the discovery of an anticancer substance in broccoli. In 1993, the prestigious institution opened one of the world's first laboratories dedicated to finding and testing a variety of edible plants with cancer-protective properties. The scientists have already found, for example, that not all types of broccoli have the same concentration of sulphoraphane, the protective chemical in this vegetable. In addition, they have discovered that different plants produce different kinds of chemoprotective molecules. Paul Talalay, M.D., who head the lab, is conducting studies with his colleagues to develop plants with high amounts of protective compounds that are safe to eat.[24] Texas A&M's Vegetable Improvement Center researchers, for example, have created a carrot with higher levels of beta-carotene. They have also developed vaccines in bananas and a super onion that may help prevent colon cancer. Rutgers University and Harvard University are also hard at work on nutraceuticals.

A survey by Nancy Childs, Ph.D., a marketing professional at St. Joseph's University, Philadelphia, found that 55 percent of the major food companies surveyed were either doing research and development in the field or watching it carefully.

There is now evidence that antioxidant vitamin supplementation can prevent or delay the onset of certain cancers, heart disease, and some types of brain dysfunction, as described in this book. Supplemental B vitamins are also capable of preventing certain brain disorders and specific birth defects.

Fueling the great strides now being made in all fields of medical research is a new understanding of the human body's immune system and the ability to manipulate it to prevent and treat disease.

Developments in genetics are making it possible to create animal nutraceutical factories. A glass of milk or a tomato-and-lettuce sandwich may replace the vaccination needle.

New investigations of old folk-medicine practices are turning up effective nutraceuticals.

Nutraceuticals are also being used to prevent deterioration after a disease has struck.

Certainly not all the research projects described in this book will have successful and long-lasting results. But many will, and you do have more choices about what you eat and the medicines you take.

E. J. Guardia of Kraft's General Foods had the following to say about the future at a meeting of the Food Science Department of Rutgers University:

"It used to be that a salable food product was one that just looked, smelled, and tasted good, but there is a health and wellness trend."

He says it began as a collection of single food fads, like eating mounds of oat bran, but it is developing and expanding. He says consumers look for taste first, but once they've determined that the product tastes good, a great many will also check to see what's included . . . and what's left out.

"In essence, the consumers will be saying to us food manufacturers: 'Give me a broad spectrum of foods with outstanding taste, convenience, value, and variety—and that make me healthy."

He said the food manufacturers will respond, if there are significant changes in government regulations, with a sort of combination food and drug.[25]

Judy McBride from the Agricultural Research Service points out that scientists are still discovering trace elements and vitamins. There may be a lot more carotenoids yet to be discovered. She said Japanese eat thirty foods a day. Apples, pears, and grapes have boron, which is good for you, but if you only eat oranges, you may not get the boron you need.

She says in the future it may be possible to test babies to see if they are salt sensitive and likely to get high blood pressure. Then you could adjust their diets accordingly.[26]

Nutraceuticals, because they prevent and treat disease, will compete with both drugs and foods by the year 2000. The quest for nutraceuticals is exciting and has really just begun, even though it often involves studying ancient uses of foods and medicines.

The food industry, the pharmaceutical industry, and government agencies including the FDA and the FTC as well as the National Institutes will have to work together to develop nutraceuticals that will treat and prevent diseases. It will be well worth it to individual companies and agencies as well as to the population at large.

Nearly 72 percent of deaths in the U.S.A. can be attributed to eight causes with a dietary association, namely heart disease, cancers, strokes, alcohol, related accidents and suicides, diabetes, chronic liver disease, and atherosclerosis. The major risk factors for these diseases are obesity, high blood pressure, and pollutants, especially cigarette smoking. The most prevalent morbidity conditions are osteoporosis and diverticular disease. Both the latter have dietary associations, namely calcium metabolism and intestinal physiology affected by dietary fiber respectively.

Paul LaChance, Ph.D., chairman of Rutgers University's Department of Food Science and a member of the team that developed food for the astronauts, says, "It is far wiser to advocate dietary recommendations that provide for thwarting as many dietary-associated diseases as possible."[27]

Up to 40 percent of the scores of very sick, elderly patients admitted to Mount Sinai Medical Center are malnourished even though they are apparently well cared for. They suffer from hidden malnutrition.[28]

Stephen L. DeFelice, M.D., chair of the Foundation for Innovation in Medicine and the person who coined the term "nutraceuticals," maintains that by the year 2000 companies will be marketing "smart drinks" that have been clinically proven to make people smarter and functional energy foods that truly deliver energy to those who need it.[29]

In fact, there are companies already marketing functional drinks. They are being sold, at this writing, under names such as Mo'Beta, SunBolt, Fib Pep, and Vita-J. Whether they are true nutraceutical drinks, offering more than juices and vitamins, remains to be proven. SunBolt, for example, is made by the same people who make the sports drink Gatorade. A mixture of carbohydrates, vitamin C, and caffeine, SunBolt is marketed as an alternative to orange juice or soda. Its very name, however, conjures up its placement in the market as an energy drink. And then there is Femme Vitale that was introduced in 1994 by Odwall. A mixture of vitamins, herbs, and fruit juices, it is aimed at "women's health needs," including combating osteoporosis and premenstrual syndrome.

Commenting in general and not about any specific product, Dr. DeFelice at the American Chemical Society meeting in Washington, D.C., in 1994, said that "current near-sighted marketing efforts based on the advertising of unproven benefits will quickly become relic techniques of the past."

Who will lead the way to the nutraceutical revolution?

Dr. DeFelice claims that, as has already happened in the biotechnology area, small entrepreneurial companies will formulate proprietary products, sponsor clinical trials, and storm the marketplace with profit margins that far exceed those of the present food and future pharmaceutical industries. Like the American car industry, the giant food and drug companies, taken aback by this new threatening competition will adjust and enter the nutraceutical market.

As researchers understand how chemicals in food affect the bodies of various age groups and persons with certain physicial conditions or diseases, the possibilities of marketing nutraceuticals are great.

Hippocrates said in 400 B.C., "Let food be your medicine and medicine be your food."

Nutraceuticals—which may be both a food and a medicine—may soon supplement our diets, bolster our immunity, and when needed, enhance our medical therapy.

A

Acetylcholine. A neurotransmitter that is released by nerve cells and acts either on other nerve cells or on muscles and organs throughout the body.

ACTH. Adrenocorticotropin hormone, a hormone controller.

Action potential. An electric burst that travels the length of the nerve cell and causes the release of a neurotransmitter.

Active immunity. Immunity produced by the body in response to stimulation by a disease-causing organism or a vaccine.

Adrenal gland. Your two adrenal glands, one on top of each of your kidneys are about the size of a grape. Each adrenal gland has two parts. The first part is the medulla, which produces epinephrines and norepinephrine, two hormones that play a part in controlling your heart rate and blood pressure. Signals from your brain stimulate the production of these hormones. The second part is the adrenal cortex, which produces three groups of steroid hormones. The hormones in group one control the levels of various chemicals in your body. For example, they prevent the loss of too much sodium and water into the urine. Aldosterone is the most important hormone in this group. The hormones in the second group have a number of functions. One is to help convert carbohydrates, or starches, into energy-providing glycogen in your liver. Hydrocortisone is the major hormone in this group. The third group consists of the male hormone androgen and the female hormones estrogen and progesterone. Sex hormones are also produced by the testes and ovaries.

Agonist. A drug, hormone, or neurotransmitter that binds to a receptor site and triggers a response.

AIDS (acquired immunodeficiency syndrome). A life-threatening disease caused by a virus and characterized by a breakdown of the body's immune system.

Albumin. A group of simple proteins composed of nitrogen, carbon, hydrogen, oxygen, and sulfur that are soluble in water. Albumin is usually derived from egg white and employed as an emulsifier in foods and cosmetics.

Alkaloids. Compounds of vegetable origin, some of which have great dietary importance. Usually derived from a nitrogen compound such as pyridine, quinoline, isoquinoline, or pyrrole, designated by the ending -*ine*. Examples are atropine, morphine, nicotine, quinine, codeine, caffeine, cocaine, and strychnine. The alkaloids are potent and include the hallucinogen mescaline and the deadly poison brucine. There are alkaloids that act on the liver, nerves, lungs, and digestive systems.

Allantoin. A uric-acid derivative. Applied topically, it is used in skin preparations because of its ability to help heal wounds and skin ulcers and to stimulate the growth of healthy tissue.

Allergen. Any substance that causes an allergy.

Allergy. An inappropriate response of the immune system to normally harmless substances.

Allylic sulfides. Found in garlic and onions, these compounds may protect against cancer-causing agents by stimulating production of a detoxification enzyme, glutathione-S-transferase.

Alzheimer's disease. A deterioration of the brain with severe memory impairment.

Amino acids. Building blocks of proteins and neurotransmitters. There are about twenty amino acids, eight of which are called essential because the body cannot synthesize them and they must be obtained from food. Combinations with B₆ are used to treat splitting, peeling nails. Arginine, lysine, and phenylalanine were banned by the FDA from over-the-counter diet pills, February 10, 1992.

Aminophylline. An antiasthmatic drug belonging to the xanthine family of medications that widen the airways and stimulate the respiratory center in the brain.

Amygdalin. A glycoside (organic compound) found in bitter almonds, peaches, and apricots. It has been a controversial substance because claims have been made that it can fight cancer in a compound called laetrile. Such claims have not been accepted by conventional U.S. scientists, but the compound is widely available in Mexico.

Angiotensin. A powerful elevator of blood pressure. It is produced by the action of renin, an enzyme made in the kidney. All the components of the renin-angiotensin system have been found in the brain, and there are indications they are part of the brain's mechanism for regulating blood pressure as well as for telling you whether you should drink fluid.

Antagonist. A drug, hormone, or neurotransmitter that blocks a response from a receptor site.

Antibody. A protein in the blood formed to neutralize or destroy foreign substances or organisms (antigens). Each antibody is tailor-made for an antigen.

Antigen. A foreign protein that can cause an immune response by stimulating the production of antibodies in the body.

Arbutin. A diuretic and anti-infective derived from the dried leaves of the berry family, including blueberries, cranberries, and bear berries (*see* Uva-ursi), and from most pear plants. This may explain why cranberry juice is reputed to ward off and to treat urinary-tract infections.

Aspartic acid. A nonessential amino acid.

Astringent. Substance that causes skin or mucous membranes to pucker and shrink by reducing their ability to absorb water. Often used in skin cleansers and to help stop bleeding. Tannins are used in herbal and conventional medicine for this purpose and so is witch hazel.

Astringent resins. *See* Astringent and Resin.

Astringent tannins. *See* Astringent and Tannins.

Atherosclerosis. Fatty deposits on the inner walls of the arteries.

Autoantibody. An antibody that reacts against a person's own tissue.

Autoimmune. A condition in which the body manufactures antibodies against its own tissues and damages itself. Arthritis and lupus are examples of autoimmune diseases.

Autonomic nervous system. The division of the nervous system that regulates the involuntary vital functions, such as the activity of the heart and breathing. Governs the excitation and relaxation of muscles. One part of the system, the sympathetic, widens airways to the lungs and increases the flow of blood to the arms and legs and prepares the body for fight or flight. The other part, the parasympathetic, slows the heart rate and stimulates the flow of digestive juices. Although the sympathetic and parasympathetic cooperate in the functional rhythm of most organs, the muscles surrounding the blood vessels are affected only by the signals from the sympathetic system. The trigger for constriction or relaxation of the blood vessels involves two sets of receptors, the alpha and the beta. Among the compounds that act on the sympathetic nervous system are epinephrine and norepinephrine (*see* both). Among the compounds that act on the parasympathetic system is acetylcholine (*see*).

B

B cells (B lymphocytes). Small white blood cells crucial to the immune defenses. They are derived from bone marrow and are the source of antibodies.

Bacterium. A microscopic organism composed of a single cell. Many but not all bacteria cause disease.

Balm mint. *Balsamodendron opobalsam*, Balm of Gilead. The secretion of any of several small evergreen African or Asian trees with leaves that yield a strong aromatic odor when bruised. Known in ancient Palestine as a soothing medication for the skin. Used in cosmetics as an unguent that is said to soothe and heal the skin.

Basophil. A white blood cell that contributes to inflammatory reactions. Along with mast cells, basophils are responsible for the symptoms of allergy.

Benzene. A solvent obtained from coal and used in nail-polish remover. Also used in varnishes, airplane dopes, lacquers, and as a solvent for waxes, resins, and oils. Highly flammable. Poisonous when ingested and irritating to the mucous membranes. Harmful amounts may be absorbed through the skin. Can also cause sensitivity to light in which the skin may break out in a rash or swell. Inhalation of the fumes may be toxic. The Consumer Product Safety Commission voted unanimously in February 1978 to ban the use of benzene in the manufacture of many household products.

Benzopyrene. A hydrocarbon found in coal tar, cigarette smoke, and in the atmosphere as a product of incomplete combustion. Highly toxic and a cancer-causing agent.

Berberine. Mild antiseptic and decongestant used in eye lotions. Derived as yellow crystals from various plants. Used as a dressing for skin ulcers.

Beta-blockers. Drugs that slow heart activity and thus lower blood pressure. They are used to treat angina (chest pain), high blood pressure, and irregular heart rhythms. They are given after a heart attack to reduce the likelihood of fatal irregular heartbeats or further damage to the heart muscle. These drugs are also prescribed to improve heart function in damaged hearts. Beta-blockers may also be used to prevent migraine headaches, to reduce anxiety, to control fluid pressure in the eye, and for an overactive thyroid. There are two types of beta receptors: Beta 1 receptors are located mainly in the heart muscle and beta 2 are in the airways and blood vessels. They work by occupying the beta receptors in these areas. By blocking these receptors, they block the stimulating action of the nerve-stimulating chemical, norepinephrine. Thus they reduce the force and speed of the heartbeat, prevent the dilation of the airways to the lungs, and prevent the dilation of the blood vessels surrounding the brain and leading to the extremities. Drugs for the heart act mainly on beta 1 receptors. Beta-blockers are usually not prescribed for people who have poor circulation, partularly in the legs and arms. Beta-blockers should not be stopped suddenly after prolonged use because it may worsen the symptoms of the disorders for which they were prescribed. They should not be taken with foods, beverages, or over-the-counter medications that contain caffeine or alcohol or are high in sodium content. The combination may increase heartrate or elevate blood pressure.

Beta-carotene. Provitamin A. Found in all plants and in many animal tissues. It is the chief yellow-coloring matter of carrots. Oral doses of beta-carotene (180 mg/day) given for two weeks to normal volunteers significantly increased the T cells in their blood that are involved in immunity. Low levels of beta-carotene in serum or plasma have been associated with subsequent development of lung cancer. No official recommended daily allowance for adults, but 6 mg daily have been recommended. Current research seems to indicate that it may lower risk of cancer of the lung, stomach, and mouth; may lower risk of cardiovascular disease. Too much carotene in the blood can lead to carotenemia, a pale yellow-red pigmentation of the skin that may be mistaken for jaundice. It is a benign condition, and withdrawal of carotene cures it. Beta-carotene has less serious side effects than vitamin A.

Beta-glucans. Polysaccharides that yield sugars (glucose) on hydrolysis when exposed to water treatment. Beta-glucan is in cellulose and is found in edibles such as oat fiber and barley.

Biochemical. A substance that is produced by a chemical reaction in a living organism. Some can also be made in the laboratory.

Bioflavonoids. Sometimes called vitamin P. Coloring compounds such as rutin, esculin, and tangeretin in plants. Bioflavonoids have various biological activities in mammals, and are being studied to determine if they have anticancer and blood vessel protection properties.

Biotechnology. The use of living cells or parts of cells to perform procedures and to make products.

Bitter principles. A group of chemicals in plants that are bitter tasting. They differ chemically, but most derive from the iris or pine families. Bitter principles reputedly stimulate the secretion of digestive juices and stimulate the liver. They are being scientifically investigated today as antifungals and antibiotics as well as anticancer agents. The bitter principle in mallow plants is being investigated as a male contraceptive. Other bitter principles in herbs are used to combat coughs and as sedatives.

C

Caffeine. A stimulant drug that occurs in coffee, tea, and cola, it is considered the most commonly consumed drug in the United States. Caffeine is used to treat breathing problems in newborns. It is sometimes added to many analgesic medications. Potential adverse reactions include insomnia, restlessness, nervousness, mild delirium, headache, excitement, agitation, muscle tremors, fast heartbeat, nausea, vomiting, loss of water, and skin sensitivity. Interacts with theophylline and beta-blockers (*see*) to create excessive central nervous stimulation. Contraindicated in gastric or duodenal ulcer, irregular heartbeat, or those who have had heart attacks. Caffeine-containing beverages should be restricted in patients who have palpitations. Tolerance or psychological dependence may develop. Americans reportedly consume 2 billion pounds of coffee and 500 million pounds of tea each year. The FDA review panel determined caffeine safe and effective as a stimulant in doses of 100 mg to 200 mg no more often than every three to four hours.

Calcium. The adult body contains about three pounds of calcium, 99 percent of which provides hardness for bones and teeth. Approximately 1 percent of calcium is distributed in body fluids, where it is essential for normal cell activity. If the body does not get enough calcium from food, it steals the mineral from bones. Abnormal loss of calcium from bones weakens them and makes them porous or brittle and susceptible to fractures. Calcium deficiencies can result in osteopenia (less bone than normal, a condition preceding osteoporosis) and osteoporosis (a severe decrease in bone mass with diagnosable fractures), which affects 25 percent of women after menopause. The percentage of calcium absorption declines progressively with age. The RDA for calcium is 1,000 mg for adults. There is also some evidence that an intake of about 1,000 mg of calcium may protect against hypertension or high blood pressure. Adverse reactions from intravenous use include tingling sensations, a sense of oppression or heat, and with rapid IV injection, faintness. There may be a mild fall in blood pressure, but with rapid IV injection there is possible dilation of the blood vessels, slowed heartbeat, irregular heartbeat, or cardiac arrest. With oral ingestion, irritation, hemorrhage, and constipation. With IV administration, a chalky taste; with oral calcium chloride, GI hemorrhage, nausea, vomiting, thirst, abdominal pain. Other reactions to calcium include too much calcium in the blood, frequent urination, and kidney stones. Interaction with cardiac glycosides may increase digitalis toxicity. Calcium is contraindicated in irregular heartbeat, high blood calcium, or kidney stones. It should be used cautiously in patients with sarcoidosis and kidney or heart disease. Oxalic acid found in rhubarb and spinach, phytic acid in bran and whole cereals, and phosphorus in milk and dairy products may interfere with absorption of calcium. Caffeine and alcoholic beverages may also make calcium channel blockers less effective. Rhubarb, bran, whole-grain cereals, milk, and other dairy products taken with calcium supplements may make the supplements ineffective.

Capsaicin. The principal pungent constituent of hot peppers. It is being studied for use as an analgesic and as an anti-inflammatory medication.

Capsicum. A member of the nightshade family, it is native to tropical South America. Herbalists used capsicums as an internal disinfectant and to protect against infectious disease. Plasters are made for arthritic pains. It increases blood flow to the area of application, and the increased blood flow results in reduced inflammation of the affected area. The FDA issued a notice in 1992 that capsicum and capsicum fluid extract have not been shown to be safe and effective as claimed in OTC digestive-aid or in oral menstrual drug products. The FDA also proposed a ban in 1992 for the use of capsicum oleoresin to treat fever blisters and cold sores because it has not been shown to be safe and effective for stated claims in OTC products. *See also* Cayenne and Capsaicin.

Carbohydrate. Starches and sugars contain a high proportion of carbohydrates. These are chemicals that contain carbon, hydrogen, and oxygen. Gums and mucilages are complex carbohydrates and are ingredients in soothing herbs and medications.

Carcinogen. A substance that causes cancer.

Carcinogenesis. The development of cancer.

Carcinoma. A malignant tumor that grows from epithelial tissue (*see*).

Carcinoma in situ. A cancer of the outer layer of cells only; one that has not invaded underlying tissues.

Carnitine. Vitamin B_T, found in muscle, liver, and meat extracts. It is a thryoid inhibitor and stimulates fatty-acid oxidation.

Carnosine. A peptide found in the muscle of humans and numerous animals. L-carnosine is being tested for use as an aid in wound healing.

Carotene. A yellow pigment occurring in yellow vegetables, egg yolk, and other foods. The body converts it into vitamin A.

Carotenoids. Found in parsley, carrots, sweet potatoes, and most green, red, and yellow vegetables and fruits. These are vitamin A precursors that are antioxidants and cell-differentiation agents (cancer cells are nondifferentiated). There are hundreds of carotenoids in nature, both in foods and other plants. Many of them are not yet identified.

Catechin. Found primarily in wood such as mahogany, it is used as an astringent (*see*), particularly to treat diarrhea.

Catecholamines. A group of self-made chemicals such as neuro-transmitters and hormones, which can be made synthetically. Among the major catecholamines are dopamine, norepinephrine, and epinephrine (*see* all). The catecholamines help regulate blood pressure, heart rate, breathing, muscle tone, metabolism, and central-nervous-system function.

Cayenne. *Capsicum annum.* Red pepper. Green pepper. Derived from the pungent fruit of a plant, it originated in Central and South America where it was used by the natives for many diseases, including diarrhea and cramps. It contains capsaicin (*see*), carotenoids, flavonoids, essential oil, and vitamin C. Cayenne is a stimulant, astringent, laxative, and antispasmodic. Cayenne is not irritating when uncooked. Cayenne powder or tincture can be rubbed on toothaches, swellings, and inflammations. It is reported by herbalists to lower blood pressure and serum cholesterol. Modern scientists report that cayenne prevents the absorption of cholesterol. Herbalists use it as a rub for inflamed joints and to stop internal or external bleeding. *See also* Capsicum.

Cell. The smallest living unit that is able to grow and reproduce. A single cell may be a complete organism such as bacteria or may represent a specialized cell that is part of a large plant or animal.

Cervix. The narrow outer end of the uterus.

Chili. *Capsicum fastigatum.* Chili is the dried pod of a species of capsicum (*see*) or red pepper. The small pods have been used for dyspepsia (*see*) and dilated blood vessels arising from drunkenness. A capsicum poultice has been used with caution for the relief of aches and pains. Modern herbalists use it in liniments and gargles.

Cholecystokinin. A hormone produced by the small intestine during the movement of food from the stomach into the intestine. It causes the contraction of the gallbladder, thus releasing bile into the small intestine, where the enzymes and other components of bile aid digestion. It has also been found in the brain and may help to stop eating.

Choline. Found in most animal tissues, either free or in combinations such as lecithin or acetylcholine. Choline is being studied for its effects on brain neurotransmission and memory.

Chromosome. One or more small rod-shaped elements in a cell that contains genetic information.

Cinchona bark. *Cinchona ledgeriana.* Jesuits' powder. Peruvian bark. The extract of the bark of various species of cinchona cultivated in Java, India, and South America. The source for quinine (*see*) until the drug was made synthetically, it possesses antiviral, antimalarial, and fever-reducing properties. Large amounts of cinchona slow the heart rate. In addition to its use to treat malaria, cinchona is used to stimulate the appetite and as a tonic. It stimulates digestion. It is a common ingredient in over-the-counter medications. Potential adverse reactions include nausea, dizziness, deafness, and buzzing in the ears.

Citric acid. One of the most widely used acids in cosmetics and foods, it is derived from citrus fruit by fermentation of crude sugars. Employed as a preservative, sequestering agent, and to adjust acid-alkali balance. The clear, crystalline, water-absorbing chemical is used to prevent scurvy, a deficiency disease, and as a refreshing drink with water and sugar added.

Complement. A complex series of blood proteins whose action "complements" the work of antibodies. Complement destroys bacteria, produces inflammation, and regulates immune reactions.

Coumarin. Tonka bean. Cumarin. A fragrant ingredient of tonka beans, sweet woodruff, cramp bark, and many other plants. It is made synthetically as well. It has anti-blood-clotting effects and anticlotting agents are derived from it. Coumarin is prohibited in foods because it is toxic by ingestion and carcinogenic. It causes bleeding in cattle. Cinnamic acid or its derivatives are the precursors of coumarin.

Cruciferous vegetables. A family of plants characterized by flowers and fruits that bear a cross. The genus being studied intensively for nutraceuticals at this writing are the *Brassica*, which include brussels sprouts, cauliflower, and broccoli. These vegetables contain large quantites of some substances that have been shown to inhibit chemically induced cancers in animals.

Cyanide. Widely found in trace amounts in the plant kingdom—root crops, grains, and fruit kernels contain high levels. It has been reported to reduce oxygen availability in the blood even in low doses.

Cytokines. Powerful chemical substances secreted by cells and part of the immune defense system. Cytokines include lymphokines produced by lymphocytes and monokines produced by monocytes and macrophages.

D

Dendrites. Spiderlike projections from the cell body, which receive and send messages between nerve cells.

Digitalis. The name is from *digitalis*, a Greek word relating to the fingers, a reference to the flowers of this plant, which look like fingers. Foxglove and fairy glove are included in this genus of perennial flowering plants of the family *Schrophulariacea*. D. *Lanata* and D. *purpurea*, purple foxglove, are the main sources of the medications used to treat congestive heart failure and other heart diseases.

Diuretic. Drug used to remove excess fluids from the body by increasing the flow of urine.

DNA (deoxyribonucleic acid). The complex substance that makes up genes; it contains the genetic information for all organisms.

Dopamine. 3-hydroxytyramine. An intermediate in tyrosine metabolism and the precursor of norepinephrine and epinephrine. It is a brain chemical that initiates movement.

Double-blind clinical trial. A placebo (*see*) is designed to look, feel, and taste exactly like the substance being tested, so that neither the investigator nor the subjects know who is taking the active ingredient.

Dysplasia. Abnormality in size, shape, and organization of adult cells, often a premalignant condition.

E

E. coli. A type of bacteria normally found in the gut of most animals, including humans. Much of the work scientists have done using recombinant DNA (*see*) techniques has used *E. coli* as a carrier because it is well understood.

Endorphins. Self-made tranquilizers and painkillers. Each is composed of a chain of amino acids and acts on the nervous system to reduce pain.

Enzymes. Substances in the body necessary for accomplishing chemical changes such as processing sugar to create energy or breaking down food in the intestines for digestion.

Ephedra. *Ephedra gerardiana. E. trifurca. E. sinica. E. equisetina. E. helvetica.* Ma huang. Morman tea. About forty species of this herb are mentioned in ancient scriptures of India. Used by the Chinese for more than five thousand years. The stems contain alkaloids (*see*) including ephedrine (*see*). Herbalists use the herb to treat arthritis, asthma, emphysema, bronchitis, hay fever, and hives.

Ephedrine. This alkaloid is derived from the plant *Ephedra equisetina* and others of the forty species of *Ephedra*, or produced synthetically. Ephedra has been used for more than five thousand years in Chinese medicine and has become more and more popular in Western medicine. It acts like epinephrine (*see*) and is used as a bronchodilator, nasal decongestant, to raise blood pressure, and topically to constrict blood vessels. *See also* Ephedra.

Epidemiological study. A study that measures the incidence of disease in large population groups and looks for associations with various genetic or environmental factors.

Epidermis. The outer portion of the skin.

Epidermoid cancer. Malignancy of the outermost layer of tissue, either the epidermis or resembling the epidermis (*see*).

Epinephrine. Adrenaline. The major hormone of the adrenal gland, which increases heart rate and contractions, vasoconstriction or vasodilation, relaxation of the muscles in the lungs and intestinal smooth muscles, the processing of sugar and fat.

Epithelial tissues. *See* Epithelium.

Epithelium. The cellular covering of internal and external body surfaces, including the lining of vessels and small cavities. The epithelium consists of cells joined by small amounts of cementing substances and is classified according to the number of layers and the shape of the cells.

Essential oil. The oily liquid obtained from plants through a variety of processes. The essential oils are called volatile because most of them are easily vaporized. The only theories behind calling such oils essential are (1) the oils were believed essential to life and (2) they were the "essence" of the plant. The use of essential oils as preservatives is ancient. A large number of oils have antiseptic, germicidal, and preservative action. A teaspoonful may cause illness in an adult, and less than an ounce may kill.

Estrogen. A hormone produced by the ovaries that is mainly responsible for female sexual characteristics. Estrogen influences bone mass by slowing or halting bone loss, improving retention of calcium by the kidneys, and improving the absorption of dietary calcium by the intestine. Estrogen is given to relieve menopausal symptoms, prevent or relieve aging changes in the vagina and urethra, and to help prevent osteoporosis.

F

Fatty acids. Compounds of carbon, hydrogen, and oxygen that combine with glycerol to make fats.

Fiber. Found in whole grains and many vegetables, fiber helps speed cancer-causing compounds through the digestive system; discourages growth of harmful bacteria while bolstering healthful ones; may encourage production of a healthier form of estrogen.

Fibrin. An insoluble protein formed in blood as it clots. Derived from fibrinogen.

Fibrinogen. A clotting factor; an inactive plasma protein that is activated by thrombin to form fibrin (*see*).

Flavonoids. A compound in a plant such as a pigment. Most plants and vegetables contain flavonoids. Bioflavonoids have biological effects. Rutin, for example, has chelating properties and influences the functioning of minute blood vessels. It is believed flavonoids block receptor sites for certain hormones that promote cancers.

Formic acid. Colorless, pungent, highly corrosive, it occurs naturally in apples and other fruits. It is used as a flavoring. Chronic absorption is known to cause protein in the urine, and it caused cancer when administered orally in rats, mice, and hamsters. In 1992, the FDA proposed a ban on formic acid in lice-killing products because it has not been shown to be safe and effective for its stated claims.

Free radicals. Highly reactive molecules generated when a cell "burns" its foods with oxygen to fuel life processes. Free radicals act like "loose cannons" rolling around and damaging cells. This damage is thought to be a first step in cancer development. Antioxidants such as vitamin C, vitamin E, and a number of phytochemicals found in food can suppress free radical cell damage.

Fungi. A group of simple plantlike organisms that don't have the green coloring known as chlorophyll. Fungi include mushrooms, yeasts, rusts, molds, and smuts.

G

Gallic acids. *See* Phenolic acids.

Gamma-aminobutyric acid (GABA). A compound found in high concentrations in the brain that functions as an inhibitory neurotransmitter.

Gene. The smallest genetic unit of a chromosome. It is a piece of DNA that contains the hereditary information for the production of a protein.

Gene mapping. Scientists can find the location of genes on a chromosome so they know which genes control which traits. When they do this, they are mapping genes.

Genetic engineering. The technique of removing, modifying, or adding genetic material in living cells to produce a new substance or new function. This includes adding or deleting genes, as well as preventing, or turning off, the expression of particular genes.

Genistein. A plant estrogen found in the urine of people with diets rich in soybeans and to a lesser extent in the cabbage-family vegetables. This compound seems to block the growth of new blood vessels, essential for some tumors to grow and spread. Sheep grazing on some clovers are prone to reproductive failure because of genistein in the plants.

Genome. The genetic information contained in one complete set of chromosomes.

Genotype. The hereditary makeup or genetic constitution of an individual organism, distinguished from its physical appearance or visible traits (phenotype).

Germanium. In the earth's crust, it is a naturally occurring isotope that is recovered from residues from the refining of zinc and other sources. It is also present in some coals. It is used in infrared transmitting glass and electronic devices.

Germ plasm. The total genetic variability available in particular populations of an organism, usually represented by the seeds or reproductive cells, such as eggs and sperm—also called germ cells.

Ginseng. *Panax ginseng* (Asia). *Panax quinquefolius* (North America). *Eleutherococcus senticosus* (Siberian ginseng). Chinese esteem ginseng as an herb of many uses. They have been using it in medicine for more than five thousand years. The Chinese and Koreans also used it in combination with chicken soup. *Panax* comes from the Greek *panakos*, a panacea. Among its active ingredients are amino acids, essential oils, carbohydrates, peptides, vitamins, minerals, enzymes, and sterols. In the Orient, it is esteemed for its abilities to preserve health, invigorate the system, and prolong life. It is taken in an herbal tea as a daily tonic. North American Indians used ginseng as a love potion. It has been found to normalize high or low blood sugar. Russian scientists are studying ginseng for the treatment of insomnia and general debility. Japanese scientists recently reported isolating a number of compounds rare in nature from ginseng, some of which have anticancer properties, tranquilizing effects, or aphrodisiac properties.

Glucagon. A neurotransmitter involved in glucose metabolism and hunger.

Glucoalkaloid. An organic compound of vegetable origin that has a sugar component.

Glucose. Sugar that occurs naturally in blood, grape, and corn sugars. A source of energy for animals and plants. Sweeter than sucrose. It is used medicinally for nutritional purposes and in the treatment of diabetic coma. Used to soothe the skin.

Glucosides. Compounds with sugar with an alcohol.

Glutamic acid. A nonessential amino acid.

Glutathione S-transferase. Cloves, caraway, dill weed, parsley, lemongrass oil, and celery have been found to have significant amounts of substances that stimulate the production of glutathione S-transferase (GST) in the body, a detoxifying enzyme that can combat cancer-causing agents.

Glycine. A nonessential amino acid, usually derived from gelatin.

Glycosides. A class of drugs used in heart failure. Many flowering plants contain cardiac glycosides. The most well-known are foxglove, lily of the valley, and squill. The cardiac glycosides have the ability to increase the force and power of the heartbeat without increasing the amount of oxygen needed by the heart muscle. Among the glycosides are cyanogens, goitrogens, estrogens, and saponins. They are found in lima beans, cassava, flax, legumes, broccoli and other brassicas, most legumes, and grasses.

Granulocytes. Phagocytes filled with granules containing potent chemicals that allow the cells to digest microorganisms. Neutrophils, eosinophils, basophils, and mast cells are examples of granulocytes.

Gum. True plant gums are the dried exudates from various plants obtained when the bark is cut or other injury is suffered. Gums are soluble in hot or cold water, and sticky. Gums are also used as emulsifiers, stabilizers, and suspending agents. Today, the term resin is usually used instead of *gum*, both for natural and synthetic sources.

H

Helper T cells. A subset of T cells that are essential for turning on antibody production, activating killer T cells, and initiating many other immune responses.

Herpes simplex virus I (HSV I). Virus that causes cold sores or fever blisters on the mouth or around the eyes. It can be transmitted to the genital region. The latent virus can be reactivated by stress, trauma, other infections, or suppression of the immune system.

Herpes simplex virus II (HSV II). Virus that causes painful sores of the anus or genitals, which may lie dormant in nerve tissue and can be reactivated to produce the sores.

Hesperidin. A compound in orange juice that has been found to be an anticancer agent in laboratory experiments.

HIV (human immunodeficiency virus). The virus that causes AIDS.

Humoral immunity. Immune protection provided by soluble factors such as antibodies, which circulate in the body's fluids or "humors," primarily serum and lymph.

Hybrid. Plant or animal offspring from parents that have distinctly different genetic makeups. Using traditional breeding, crossing two different varieties of plants or two purebred lines of animals produces hybrids. Crossbreeding can take place on the molecular level in genetic engineering.

Hydrocyanic glycoside. A combination of hydrocyanic acid and a sugar.

Hydroquinones. Used in strong solution to bleach dark spots on the skin. In weaker solutions, it is used in bleach and freckle creams and in suntan lotions. A white, crystalline phenol that occurs naturally but is usually manufactured in the laboratory. Application to the skin may cause allergic reactions. It can cause depigmentation in a 2 percent solution. Ingestion of as little as one gram (one-thirtieth of an ounce) has caused nausea, vomiting, ringing in the ears, delirium, a sense of suffocation, and collapse. Industrial workers exposed to the chemical have suffered clouding of the eye lens.

Hypoglycemia. Low blood sugar—the opposite of diabetes.

Hypothalamus. Brain control area involved in emotions, movement, and eating. Less than the size of a peanut and weighing a quarter of an ounce, this small area deep within the brain also oversees appetite, blood pressure, sexual behavior, and sleep and sends orders to the pituitary gland.

I

Immunoglobulins. Family of large protein molecules, also known as antibodies.

Indoles. A compound found in cabbage, brussels sprouts, and kale, they seem to induce protective enzymes.

Initiation. An event that alters the genetic code of a cell or causes some other basic, permanent damage, predisposing that cell to later become a cancer cell. Chemical carcinogens, viruses, radiation, and other factors are thought to be capable of causing initiation.

Interleukins. A major group of lymphokines and monokines.

Inulin. A sugar from plants. It is injected intravenously to determine kidney function and is also used in bread for diabetics.

Iodine. Discovered in 1811 and classed among the rarer earth elements, it is found in the earth's crust as bluish black scales. Nearly two hundred products contain this chemical, including both prescription and over-the-counter medications. Iodine is an integral part of the thyroid hormones, which have important metabolic roles, and is an essential nutrient for humans. Iodine deficiency leads to thyroid enlargement or goiter.

Iridin. Extract from *Iris versicolor* (blue flag) by extraction with ale.

Iridine. A protamine from the sperm of rainbow trout.

Irigenin. From the rhizome of *Iris florentia*. The rhizome contains salicylic acid (*see*), isophthalic acids, volatile oil, iridin, a glycoside (*see*), gum, resin, and sterols. Herbalists use it as a cathartic and emetic and to treat liver complaints, swollen glands, hepatitis and jaundice, skin diseases, and loss of appetite. It is promoted in herbal medicines as both relaxing and stimulating.

Isophthalic acid. Derived from xylene, a hydrocarbon, and used to make polyester and plasticizers.

Isothiocyanates. Found in mustard, horseradish, and radishes, they seem to induce protective enzymes.

L

Lactone. Occurs in nature as odor-bearing components of various plants. Also made synthetically.

Latex. Synthetic rubber. Component of chewing-gum base. The milky, usually white juice or exudate of plants obtained by tapping.

Legumes. Plants that include seeds in a pod, such as beans and peas. The Leguminosae family includes over 18,000 species and is one of the most economically important plant families in the world. They include the phytochemicals being studied as nutraceuticals. Phytochemicals from legumes are already utilized as food additives, fungicides, and anticancer agents.

Leukocytes. All white blood cells.

Leukoplakia. Small, whitish patches on the oral mucosae, believed to be premalignant lesions of oral cancer.

Lignin. Binding agent in animal feed from plant fibers. There is no reported use of the chemical and no toxicology information is available.

Liminoids. Found in citrus fruits, they seem to induce protective enzymes.

Linoleic acid. An essential fatty acid (*see*) prepared from edible fats and oils. Component of vitamin E and a major constituent of many vegetable oils, for example, cottonseed and soybean. Used in emulsifiers and vitamins. Large doses can cause nausea and vomiting.

Linolenic acid. Polyunsaturated acid produced in the body as a metabolite of linoleic acid. A nutrient used in the treatment of eczema. Alpha-linolenic acid in the diet of Mediterranean people is believed to be important in the prevention of heart disease.

Lupulin. From the hop plant *Humulus lupulus*, it contains lupulone, which is active against fungus and bacteria and humulone, which is an antibiotic.

Lycopene. An antioxidant found in tomatoes and red grapefruit. Seems to be a good antioxidant.

Lymph. A liquid found within the lymphatic vessels, containing white blood and some red blood cells. These cells, collected from tissues throughout the body, flow in the lymphatic vessels through the lymph nodes, and eventually into the blood. Lymph is an important part of the body's ability to fight infection and disease.

Lymph nodes. Small bean-shaped organs of the immune system, distributed widely throughout the body and linked by lymphatic vessels. Lymph nodes are closets for B, T, and other immune cells.

Lymphatic vessels. A bodywide network of channels, similar to the blood vessels, that transport lymph to the immune organs and into the bloodstream.

Lymphocytes. Small white blood cells produced in the lymphoid organs and paramount in the immune system.

Lymphokines. Powerful chemicals secreted by the lymphocytes. These soluble molecules help direct and regulate immune re-sponses.

M

Macrophage. A large and versatile immune cell that acts as a microbe-devouring phagocyte, an antigen-presenting cell, and an important source of immune secretions.

Mannitol. A diuretic that increases pressure on the machinery of the kidney and thus increases flow. Also elevates blood plasma passage through tissue, resulting in enhanced flow of water into fluids outside the cells. Used in the treatment of scanty urination, to reduce pressure inside the eye, and to prevent acute kidney failure.

MAO inhibitors. *See* Monoamine Oxidase Inhibitors.

Mast cell. A granulocyte found in tissue. The contents of mast cells, along with those of basophils, are responsible for the symptoms of allergy.

Metastasis. Transfer of disease from one organ or part of the body to another not directly connected with it.

Methanol. Methyl alcohol. Wood alcohol. Wood spirit. A solvent and denaturant obtained by the destructive distillation of wood. Methanol is highly toxic and readily absorbed from all routes of exposure.

Microorganisms. Tiny organisms that can only be seen under a microscope—such as bacteria and viruses.

Minerals. Inorganic materials found in the earth's crust.

Molecule. The smallest amount of a specific chemical substance that can exist alone.

Monoamine. Containing one amine group.

Monoamine oxidase. An enzyme that acts in the nervous system to break down certain types of neurotransmitters (chemical messengers sent between nerve cells) such as dopamine, norepinephrine, and serotonin (*see* all).

Monoamine oxidase inhibitors (MAOIs). A class of antidepressant medications usually prescribed for people who have not responded to tricyclics (*see*) or who have certain forms of depression with symptoms including an increase in weight, appetite, or sleep. MAOIs may also be used for cases of mixed anxiety and depression, depression accompanied by pain, panic disorder, post–traumatic stress disorder, and bipolar depression. The drug works by raising the level of neurotransmitters by preventing their destruction by enzymes. People taking MAOIs must adhere to a special diet because of the interaction of the medications with certain foods. Foods that contain tyramine, such as cheeses, yogurt, sour cream, beef or chicken livers, and red wines, should be avoided. The combination of MAOIs and tyramine can shoot up blood pressure to dangerous levels. Symptoms include headache, increased or decreased heart rate, nausea and vomiting, sweating, fever or cold clammy skin, and chest pain.

Monokines. Powerful chemical substances secreted by monocytes and macrophages. These soluble molecules help direct and regulate the immune responses.

Monoterpenes. Found in parsley, carrots, broccoli, cabbage, cucumbers, squash, yams, tomatoes, eggplant, peppers, mint, basil, and citrus fruits, they have some antioxidant properties. Have been found to inhibit cholesterol production and aid protective enzyme activity.

Mucilage. A solution in water of the sticky principles of vegetable substances. Used as a soothing application to the mucous membranes.

Mucin. A secretion containing carbohydrate-rich proteins. It is found in saliva and the lining of the stomach.

Mucosa. Mucous membrane lining the digestive tract.

Mutation. A permanent change in the genetic material that will be passed on to new generations of cells.

N

Natural killer cells (NKs). Large granule-filled lymphocytes that take on tumor cells and infected body cells. They are known as "natural" killers because they attack without first having to recognize specific antigens.

Neoplasm. Tumor. Any new and abnormal growth.

Neo-ruscogenin. *See* Ruscogenin.

Neuron. The basic nerve cell of the central nervous system containing a nucleus within the cell body, an axon (a trunklike projection containing neurotransmitters), and dendrites (spiderlike projections that send and receive messages).

Neurotensin. A peptide of thirteen amino acid derivatives that helps to regulate blood sugar by its effects on a number of hormones, including insulin and glucagon. It is also thought to play a part in pain suppression.

Neurotransmitters. Molecules that carry chemical messages between nerve cells. Neurotransmitters are released from a nerve cell, diffuse across the minute distance between two nerve cells (synaptic cleft), and bind to a receptor at another nerve site.

Neutrophil. A large white blood cell that is an abundant and important phagocyte.

Nitrate, potassium, and **sodium.** Potassium nitrate is used as a color fixative in the still. Sodium nitrite has the peculiar ability to react chemically with muscle protein to impart red-bloodiness to processed meats. The nitrites also convey tanginess to the palate but most importantly, they resist the growth of *Clostridium botulinum* spores. Nitrites, however, combine with natural stomach and food chemicals (secondary amines) to create nitrosamines, among the most powerful cancer-causing agents.

Nitrate, Potassium, and **Sodium.** Potassium nitrate, also known as saltpeter and niter, is used as a color fixative in cured meats. Sodium nitrate, also called Chile saltpeter, is used as a color fixative in cured meats. Nitrates are also used as drugs to treat heart attacks. They dilate blood vessels and increase blood flow.

Nitro-. A prefix denoting one atom of nitrogen and two of oxygen. *Nitro* also denotes a class of dyes derived from coal tars. Nitro dyes can be absorbed through the skin. When absorbed or ingested, they can cause a lack of oxygen in the blood. Chronic exposure may cause liver damage.

Nitrosamines. Cancer-causing agents formed in the gastrointestinal tract from reactions in which nitrites and nitrates combine with amines, organic compounds present naturally in the body.

Nobelitin. A substance in citrus fruit that has been found in laboratory studies to have anticancer properties.

Norepinephrine. Noradrenaline. A hormone released by the adrenal gland, it possesses the ability to stimulate that epinephrine does but has minimal inhibitory effects. It has little effect on the lungs, smooth muscles, and metabolic processes and differs from epinephrine in its effect on the heart and blood vessels.

NSAID. The abbreviation for nonsteroidal anti-inflammatory drug. This category includes aspirin, ibuprofen, and naproxen, among others.

Nucleic acids. Large, naturally occurring molecules composed of chemical building blocks known as nucleotides. There are two kinds of nucleic acids, DNA and RNA.

O

Oleic acid. Obtained from various animal and vegetable fats and oils, it is used in synthetic butter, cheese, and spice flavorings and as a lubricant and binder in various foods. The FDA has determined it is generally recognized as safe (GRAS).

Oxalic acid. Occurs naturally in many plants and vegetables, particularly in the Oxalis family; also in many molds. Some plants such as rhubarb, spinach, and amaranthus are high in it. Oxalic acid has the ability to bind some metals such as calcium and magnesium and has therefore been suspected of interfering with the metabolism of these minerals.

P

Palmitic acid. A mixture of solid organic acids obtained from fats. Palmitic acid occurs naturally in allspice, anise, calamus oil, cascarilla bark, celery seed, butter acids, coffee, tea, and many animal fats and plant oils. It forms 40 percent of cow's milk.

Papilloma. A benign tumor derived from epithelial tissue.

Parathyroid gland. One of four corners of the thyroid gland (*see*), these pearl-sized glands produce parathyroid hormones, which work with calcitonin from the thyroid gland to control calcium in the blood. Calcium not only has a role in developing bones and teeth but is also involved in blood clotting and nerve and muscle function.

Parkinson's disease. Chronic neurologic disease characterized by tremors, rigidity, and an abnormal gait. The most common variety is Parkinson's disease of unknown cause, or paralysis agitans. Postencephalitic parkinsonism is the diseaselike state occurring after brain inflammation.

Pectin. Found in roots, stems, and fruits, this soluble fiber forms an integral part of such plant structures. The richest sources of pectin are lemon and orange rind, which contain about 30 percent of this polysaccharide. It is used in antidiarrheal medications. Pectins have also been reported to lower cholesterol and blood sugar.

Peptidases. Enzymes that cleave peptides.

Peptide. Two or more amino acids chained together in head-to-tail links. Generally larger than simple amino acids or the monoamines, the largest peptides discovered thus far have forty-four amino acids. Neuropeptides signal the body's endocrine glands to balance salt and water. Opiate peptides can help control pain and anxiety. The peptides work with amino acids. A peptide is present at two tenthousandths of its partner amino acid or a hundredth the amount of a monoamine.

Phagocytes. Large white blood cells that contribute to the immune defenses by ingesting microbes or other cells and foreign particles.

Phenol. Carbolic acid. Obtained from coal tar. Occurs in urine and has the characteristic odor present in coal tar and wood. Phenol compounds are found in many plants, such as willow bark and wintergreen. It is a general disinfectant and anesthetic for the skin. Ingestion of even small amounts may cause nausea, vomiting, and circulatory collapse, paralysis, convulsions, coma, and greenish urine, as well as necrosis of the mouth and gastrointestinal tract. Fatal poisoning can occur through skin absorption. Although there have been many poisonings from phenolic solutions, it continues to be used in commercial products. Swelling, pimples, hives, and other skin rashes following application to the skin have been widely reported. A concentration of 2 percent causes burning and numbness. The Food and Drug Administration issued a notice in 1992 that phenol has not been shown to be safe and effective for stated claims in OTC products including astringent (*see*) drugs and insect bites and stings.

Phenolic acids (tannins). Found in parsley, carrots, broccoli, cabbage, tomatoes, eggplant, peppers, citrus fruits, whole grains, and berries, they have antioxidant properties, inhibit formation of nitrosamine, a cancer-causing agent, and affect enzyme activity.

Phenotype. The physical characteristics or visible traits of an organism.

Phosphoric acid. A colorless, odorless solution made from phosphate rock. Mixes with water and alcohol.

Pinene. A synthetic flavoring agent that occurs naturally in angelica root oil, anise, star anise, asafetida oil, coriander, cumin, fennel, grapefruit, juniper berries, oils of lavender and lime, mandarin orange leaf, black pepper, peppermint, pimenta, and yarrow. It is the principal ingredient of turpentine (*see*).

Pituitary gland. The pea-sized gland situated at the base of the brain, once thought to be the master gland that gave "orders" to other glands. It is now known that the pituitary gland takes its orders from the hypothalamus (*see*). The pituitary then sends out orders to the other glands in your body. The frontal lobe of the gland produces six hormones: growth hormone, which regulates growth; prolactin, which stimulates the breasts and has other functions as yet not clearly understood; and four other hormones that stimulate the thyroid, adrenals, ovaries in women, and testes in men. The back lobe of the pituitary produces two hormones: antidiuretic hormone, which acts on the kidneys and regulates urine output; and oxytocin, which stimulates the contraction of the womb during childbirth.

Placebo. An inert or innocuous substance given in place of medication.

Plant estrogens. A host of estrogens have been identified in plants. Although they are considerably less active than those in animals, chronic exposure may lead to the accumulation of levels that are active in humans. *See also* Genistein.

Plant sterols. Vitamin D precursors found in broccoli, cabbage, cucumbers, squash, yams, tomatoes, eggplant, peppers, soy products, and whole grains. They cause cells to differentiate.

Plasma. The fluid portion of the blood or lymph that carries in solution a wide range of ions, minerals, vitamins, antibodies, proteins, enzymes, and/or other essential substances.

Plasmid. A small, circular piece of DNA that carries selected genes as well as directions to reproduce itself when put into a host cell. Plasmids cannot survive outside a host cell.

Platelet. A component of blood that plays an important role in blood coagulation.

Polyphenolic. Having a number of phenol (*see*) molecules.

Precursor. A substance turned into another active or more mature substance by a biologic process. Beta-carotene is a precursor of vitamin A because the body can use it to make Vitamin A.

Promotion. An intermediate stage of cancer development during which initiated (*see*) cells, in the presence of promoters, move further along the pathway to cancer. The promotion stage may take several decades in humans.

Prostaglandins. PGA. PGB. PGC. PGD. A group of extremely potent hormonelike substances present in many tissues. More than sixteen are known with effects such as dilating or constricting blood vessels, stimulation of intestinal or bronchial smooth muscle, uterine stimulation, antagonism to hormones, and influencing fat metabolism. Various prostaglandins in the body can cause fever, inflammation, and headaches. Prostaglandins or drugs that affect prostaglandins are used medically to induce labor, prevent and treat peptic ulcers, control high blood pressure, treat bronchial asthma, and to induce delayed menstruation. Aspirin and other NSAIDs (*see*) tend to inhibit prostaglandin production.

Proteins. Organic compounds made up of amino acids. Proteins are among the major constituents of plant and animal cells.

Q

Quercetin. A bioflavonoid found in many plants but usually obtained from the inner bark of a species of oak tree common in North America. The active ingredient, isoquercitin, has been found to block allergic and inflammatory reactions by inhibiting an antibody, IgE, responsible for the majority of allergic reactions and by inhibiting leukotrienes and prostaglandins involved in producing inflammation.

Quercitrin. A pale, yellow glycoside obtained from barks. Some glycosides have the ability to increase the force and power of the heartbeat without increasing the amount of oxygen needed by the heart muscle.

Quinine. A drug derived from the bark of the cinchona tree, which grows wild in South America. White crystalline powder, almost insoluble in water, it was introduced in the West in 1888 as a medication to treat malaria. It is used as a local anesthetic in hair tonics and sunscreen preparations and to relieve muscle cramps. When taken internally, it reduces fever. It is in over-the-counter cold and headache remedies as well as bitter lemon and tonic water, which may contain as much as 5 mg per 100 ml.

Quinones. Derived from aniline and other coal tar products. Toxic by inhalation, a strong irritant to the skin and mucous membranes. Used to manufacture dyes, hydroquinone, fungicides, and oxidizing agents.

R

Receptor. A protein molecule that may also be composed of fat and carbohydrate that resides on the surface or in the nucleus of a cell and recognizes and binds a specific molecule of appropriate size, shape, and charge. Receptors are activated by specific nerve chemicals, hormones, or drugs and can be regarded as "biological locks" that can be "opened" only with specific keys.

Receptor binding assay. A technique to determine the presence and amount of a drug, neurotransmitter, or receptor in a biological system.

Recombinant DNA. The DNA formed by combining segments of DNA from different types of organisms. Recombinant DNA technology is one technique of genetic engineering.

Recombinant DNA technology. A broad range of techniques involving the manipulation of genetic material of organisms, including technologies by which scientists isolate genes from one organism and insert them into another. The term is often used synonymously with *genetic engineering* and to describe DNA sequences isolated from and transferred between organisms by genetic-engineering techniques.

Releasing factors. Produced by the hypothalamus and then sent to the pituitary, where they cause the release of appropriate hormones. Among those that have been found are luteinizing hormone–releasing hormone (LHRH), which affects the release of the sex hormones, and thyroid hormone-releasing factor (TRF), which affects the release of the thyroid hormone. Both LHRH and TRF have behavioral effects. LHRH, for example, enhances mating behavior. TRF can cause stimulation of the thyroid and thus body metabolism.

Resin. The brittle substance, usually translucent or transparent, formed from the hardened secretions of plants. Among the natural resins are damar, elemi, and sandarac. Synthetic resins include polyvinyl acetate, various polyester resins, and sulfonamide resins. Resins have many uses in cosmetics. They contribute depth, gloss, flow, adhesion, and water resistance. Toxicity depends upon ingredients used.

Restless leg syndrome (RLS). Occurs at bedtime and is described as "running in bed." Relief occurs with movement, and symptoms occur when stationary. Symptoms are vague, with twitching and muscular discomfort.

Retinoid. A derivative of vitamin A, created in the laboratory by altering certain aspects of the retinol molecule. Among the retinoids in use are etretinate, 13-cRA, and transretinoic acid.

Retinol. Vitamin A as found in fish oils, liver, butter, egg yolks, and whole milk.

RNA (Ribonucleic acid). A nucleic acid that is found in the cytoplasm and also in the nucleus of some cells. One function of RNA is to direct the manufacture of proteins.

Ruscogenin. A sugar from *Ruscus aculeatus*. It is used in the treatment of hemorrhoids.

Rutin. Pale yellow crystals found in many plants, particularly buckwheat. Used as a dietary supplement for capillary fragility. No known toxicity.

S

Salicin. A chemical derived from the bark of several species of willows and poplar trees. Aspirin and other salicylates are derived from salicin or made synthetically.

Salicylates. Aspirin. Amyl-. Phenyl-. Benzyl-. Menthyl-. Glyceryl-. Salts of salicylic acid. A number of foods naturally contain salicylate, such as almonds, apples, apricots, blackberries, boysenberries, cherries, cloves, cucumbers, currants, gooseberries, grapes, nectarines, oil of wintergreen, oranges, peaches, pickles, plums, prunes, raisins, raspberries, strawberries, and tomatoes. The salts are used as sunburn preventatives and antiseptics. Aspirin is acetylsalicylic acid. Nonacetylated salicylates, such as sodium salicylate, salsalate (Disalcid and others), and choline magnesium trisalicylate (Trilisate and others), do not interfere with platelet function as aspirin does and may be safer than acetylated salicylates for aspirin-intolerant patients. Salicylates interact with many medications.

Salicylic acid. Occurs naturally in wintergreen leaves, sweet birch, and other plants. Synthetically prepared by heating phenol with carbon dioxide. It has a sweetish taste and is used as a preservative and antimicrobial. Used externally as an antiseptic agent, fungicide, and skin-sloughing agent, it is antipuretic (anti-itch). It is used as an antimicrobial at 2 to 20 percent concentration in lotions, ointments, powders, and plasters. It is also used in making aspirin. It is used as a keratolytic drug applied topically to slough the skin in the treatment of acne. It can be absorbed through the skin. The Food and Drug Administration issued a notice in 1992 that salicylic acid, while useful for removing warts, is not effective as an external pain or itch reliever in insect bite or sting, poison ivy, poison sumac, and poison oak over-the-counter drug products.

Saponin. Any of numerous glycosides—natural or synthetic compounds derived from sugars—that occur in many plants such as soap-bark, soapwort, or sarsaparilla. Characterized by their ability to foam in water. Saponins are believed to reduce blood cholesterol. They can be beneficial or deleterious. They may be either steroidal or triterpenoid in structure.

Scavenger cells. Any of a diverse group of cells that have the capacity to engulf and destroy foreign material, dead tissue, or other cells.

Serotonin. A neurotransmitter thought to play a role in temperature regulation, mood, and sleep. It is believed that its level can be raised by eating carbohydrates. Inhibits secretions in the digestive tract, stimulates smooth muscles, and affects appetite. It may be useful for victims of seasonal depression and people who want to stop smoking.

Serum. The clear portion of the blood, separated from its solid elements.

Sesquiterpenes. In recent years, more than six hundred plants have been identified as containing these substances, and more than fifty are known to cause allergic contact dermatitis. Among them are arnica, chamomile, and yarrow.

Silicic acid. Silica gel. White, gelatinous substance obtained by the action of acids on sodium silicate. Odorless, tasteless, inert, white, fluffy powder when dried. Insoluble in water and acids. Absorbs water readily. Used in face powders, dentifrices, creams, and talcum powders as an opacifier. Soothing to skin.

Sinesetin. A substance in citrus fruit that has been shown in laboratory studies to have anticancer activity.

Spleen. A lymphoid organ in the abdominal cavity that is an important center for immune-system activities.

Squamous cell cancer. Malignancy arising from the squamous cells, a layer of the epithelium consisting of flattened, plate-shaped cells.

Starch. Starch is stored by plants and is taken from grains of wheat, potatoes, rice, corn, beans, and many other vegetable foods. Insoluble in cold water or alcohol but soluble in boiling water. Comparatively resistant to naturally occurring enzymes, and this is why processors "modify" starch to make it more digestible.

Steroidal saponins. *See* Steroids and Saponin.

Steroids. Class of compounds, some of hormonal origin such as cortisone, used to treat the inflammations caused by allergies. Cholesterol, precursors of certain vitamins, bile acids, alcohols, and many plant derivatives such as digitalis are steroids. Steroids can reduce white-blood-cell production, prostaglandins, and leukotrienes. Natural and synthetic steroids have four rings of carbon atoms but have different actions according to what is attached to the rings. Oral contraceptives are steroids.

Sterol. Any class of solid, complex alcohols from animals and plants. Cholesterol is a sterol and is used in hand creams. Sterols are lubricants in baby preparations, emollient creams and lotions, emulsified fragrances, hair conditioners, and hand creams and lotions. No known toxicity.

Substance P. Self-made chemical that alerts the body to pain.

Succinic acid. Occurs in fossils, fungi, lichens, etc. Prepared from acetic acid. The acid is used as a plant-growth retardant. A buffer and neutralizing agent in food processing. A germicide and mouthwash and used in perfumes and lacquers. Has been employed medicinally as a laxative.

Suppressor T cells. A subset of T cells that can turn off antibody production and other immune responses.

Sympathetic nervous system. One of the major divisions of the autonomic nervous system; it regulates involuntary muscle actions such as the beating of the heart and breathing. The sympathetic nerves that leave the brain and spinal cord, pass through the nerve-cell clusters (ganglia), and are distributed to the heart, lungs, intestines, blood vessels, and sweat glands. In general, sympathetic nerves dilate the pupils, constrict small blood vessels, and increase heart rate. They are the nerves that prepare us for fight or flight. The other part of the autonomic system, parasympathetic nerves, slow things down after you stop exercising or the danger has passed. The system also involves circulating substances produced by the adrenal glands.

Synapse. The minute space between two neurons or between a neuron and an organ across which nerve impulses are chemically transmitted.

T

T cells. Small white blood cells that orchestrate and/or directly participate in the immune defenses. Also known as T lymphocytes, they are processed in the thymus and secrete lymphokines.

Tangeretin. A substance from tangerines found to be anticarcinogenic in experiments.

Tannic acid. It occurs in the bark and fruit of many plants, notably in the bark of the oak and sumac, and in cherry, coffee, and tea. Used medicinally as a mild astringent, and in sunscreen preparations, eye lotions, and antiperspirants. Tea contains tannic acid, and this explains its folk use as an eye lotion.

Tannins. A broad group of plant-derived phenolic compounds characterized by their ability to precipitate proteins. Some are more toxic than others, depending upon their source. Those found in tea are being studied as nutraceuticals. Tannins, however, can be antinutritional and may make some proteins and digestive enzymes not readily digestible. Iron absorption, for example, is inhibited by tea.

Terpenes. A class of unsaturated hydrocarbons. Their removal from products improves the products' flavor and gives them a more stable, stronger odor. However, some perfumers feel that the removal of terpenes destroys some of the original odor. Used as an antiseptic.

Theobromine. The alkaloid found in cocoa, cola nuts, tea, and chocolate products, closely related to caffeine. It is used as a diuretic, smooth-muscle relaxant, heart stimulant, and blood-vessel dilator. In 1992, the FDA proposed a ban on theobromine sodium salicylate in oral menstrual drug products because it has not been shown to be safe and effective for its stated claims.

Theophylline. An alkaloid found with caffeine in tea leaves, it is prepared synthetically for pharmaceutical use. A smooth-muscle relaxant, diuretic, heart stimulant, and vasodilator introduced in 1929, it is used to treat bronchial asthma, angina, and peripheral vascular disease.

Thrombus. A blood clot that forms within the heart or a blood vessel and remains attached to its point of origin.

Thrush. A fungal infection of the mouth.

Thymus. A primary lymphoid organ, high in the chest, where T lymphocytes proliferate and mature.

Thyroid. The thyroid is a butterfly-shaped gland located in the neck with a "wing" on either side of the windpipe. The gland produces thyroxine, which controls the rates of chemical reactions in the body. Generally, the more thyroxine, the faster the body works. Thyroxine needs iodine to function.

Tissue culture. A technique in which portions of a plant or animal are grown on an artificial culture medium. In many instances, entire plants can be grown from one tissue-culture sample. Organs and entire animals cannot be grown from tissue-culture cells, even in the case of lower forms of animals such as a starfish, which can naturally regrow parts of itself.

Tolerance. A state of nonresponsiveness to a particular antigen or group of antigens.

Trachea. Windpipe. The main trunk of the tubes by which air passes to and from the lungs.

Transgenic animal, plant, or **crop.** An animal, plant, or crop in which the hereditary DNA has been altered through genetic engineering by adding DNA from a source other than its parent.

Tricyclic. An organic compound comprised of only three-ring molecular structures, which may be identical or different. *See* tricyclic antidepressants.

Tricyclic antidepressants. The most widely used class of antidepressant medications. Tricyclics are usually the first to be prescribed for patients with what is known as major depression.

Turpentine. *Pistacia terebinthus.* Pinus taeda. Terebinth. Spirits of turpentine. The term *turpentine* is generally used to refer to vegetable juices, liquid, or gum with the essential oil of turpentine. They are generally procured from species of pine, although other trees yield turpentine. *Pistacia terebinthus* is a small tree native to Greece. The common American, or white, turpentine, which is listed as terebinth in the *United States Pharmacopeia*, the official publication for drug product standards, is from *Pinus taeda*. The oil or "spirit" is a local irritant and somewhat antiseptic. It was used in folk medicine as an expectorant. It was a stimulant to kidney function and was sometimes used in diluted solutions as a diuretic. In large doses, it damages the kidney. It was also used to treat intestinal gas and colic, chronic diarrhea and dysentery, typhoid fever, internal hemorrhages, bleeding, worms, vaginal discharge, and absence of menses. Turpentine baths, arranged so that vapors were not inhaled, were given to patients with chronic arthritis. Terebinth was also used in enema form to treat constipation. Applied topically as a liniment or ointment, it has been used to treat arthritis and nerve pain. It was also used topically to treat and promote the healing of burns and to heal parasitic skin diseases. Terebene, which is derived from oil of turpentine, is used orally or by inhalation as an antiseptic and expectorant. The FDA proposed a ban in 1992 on the use of turpentine oil to treat fever blisters and cold sores, in insect bite and sting drug products, and in those to treat poison ivy, poison sumac, and poison oak because it has not been shown to be safe and effective for stated claims in these over-the-counter products. The FDA also put sulfurated oils of turpentine on the ban list for oral menstural drugs.

Tyramine. A derivative of tyrosine it is a chemical present in mistletoe and many common foods and beverages. It raises blood pressure but usually causes no problem because enzymes in the body hold it in check. When drugs are used that inhibit the major enzyme that restrains its actions, monoamine oxidase (MAO), the blood pressure can shoot to dangerous levels when foods and beverages containing significant levels of tyramine are ingested. Among the foods that are high in tyramine are cheese, beer, wines, pickled herring, chicken livers, yeast extract, canned figs, raisins, bananas, avocados, chocolate, soy sauce, fava beans, meat tenderizers, eggplant, tea, cola, beef liver, and yogurt. Among the drugs that inhibit the enzyme and may lead to a serious rise in blood pressure are the MAO-inhibitors (*see*), anti-TB drugs, such as isoniazid, and anticancer drugs, such as procarbazine.

U

Ursolic acid. Bearberry. Privet fruit. Found in leaves and berries of *Arctostaphylos uva-ursi (see)*. Used as an emulsifying agent in pharmaceuticals and foods.

Usnic acid. Antibacterial compound found in lichens. Pale yellow, slightly soluble in water.

USP. Abbreviation for *United States Pharmacopeia*, the official publication for drug product standards.

Uterine tumors. Cancers of the uterus, the womb. They include cancer of the cervix, the opening of the womb, and of the corpus, body of the womb, and of the endometrium, lining of the womb.

Uva-ursi. *Arctostaphylos uva*, also called bearberry. An astringent used to treat bladder problems, it is believed its action is due to the high concentration of the antiseptic, arbutin. Arbutin, in passing through the system, yields hydroquinone, a urinary disinfectant. Uva-ursi leaves also contain anesthetic principles that numb pain in the urinary system and the herb has been shown to have antibiotic activity. Crude extracts of uva-ursi reportedly possess some anticancer property. In 1992, the FDA proposed a ban on uva-ursi extract in oral menstrual drug products because it has not been shown to be safe and effective for its stated claims.

V

Vanilla. Extracted from the full-grown, unripe fruit of the vanilla plant of Mexico and the West Indies.

Vanillin. Occurs naturally in vanilla (*see*) and potato parings but is an artificial flavoring. Odor and taste of vanilla. Made synthetically from eugenol; also from the waste of the wood-pulp industry. One part vanillin equals four hundred parts vanilla pods. Used in flavorings.

Vasoactive intestinal peptide (VIP). Present in both the gut and brain, its peripheral effects include lowering blood pressure by causing vasodilation, suppressing secretion of stomach acid, and stimulating secretion in the small intestine and colon. VIP is a neurotransmitter that may play a part in arousal. It also stimulates the release of a number of pituitary hormones including growth hormone and prolactin and may thus help to regulate the hormone glands.

Virus. An extremely small structure that has genes and a protein coat, but cannot reproduce by itself. Viruses cannot be seen by standard optical microscopes; they are only visible by using electron microscopes. To reproduce, a virus must enter a cell and use parts of that cell to grow. Viruses can be used to carry genes from one cell to another.

Vitamin A. Exists in two main forms in nature: as retinol, found only in animal sources, and as certain carotenoids, found mainly in yellow fruits and vegetables. Carotenoids are only one-third as potent as retinol. High levels of vitamin E can block the conversion of beta-carotene into vitamin A.

Vitamin C. Helps to form the connective tissue collagen; promotes wound healing; keeps blood vessels strong; enhances iron absorption. Deficiencies may cause bleeding gums, easy bruising, slow-healing wounds, painfully swollen joints, and impaired digestion. The recommended daily allowance for newborns to six months is 30 mg. Infants six months to one year, 35 mg. Children one to three years, 40 mg. Children four to ten years, 45 mg. Children eleven to fourteen years, 50 mg. Children fifteen years and over and adults, 60 mg. Used to prevent scurvy, in extensive burns, postoperative wound healing, severe fever, or chronic disease states. Also used to prevent vitamin C deficiency in those with poor diet or increased requirement. Current research indicates that vitamin C may reduce the risk of cancer of mouth, esophagus, and stomach; may reduce risk of cataracts; may protect lungs against pollutants; may ease common colds. Higher intakes associated with higher beneficial high-density cholesterol levels and lower blood pressure.

Vitamin E. Tocopherol. Antioxidant vitamin prevents cell-membrane damage; protects red blood cells; helps in tissue-growth repair. Protects fat in the body's tissues from abnormal breakdown. Experimental evidence shows vitamin E may protect the heart and blood vessels and retard aging. Used as a dietary supplement and as an antioxidant for essential oils, rendered animal fats, or a combination of such fats with vegetable oils. Helps form normal red blood cells, muscle, and other tissues. The recommended daily allowance for newborns to six months is 4 IU. Infants from six months to one year, 6 IU. Children over one year to three years, 9 IU. Children four to ten years, 10 IU. Males eleven years and over, 12 IU. Females eleven years and over, 12 IU. Pregnant women, 15 IU. Lactating women, 16 to 18 IU. Used to treat vitamin E deficiency in premature infants and in patients with impaired fat absorption. Current research indicates that vitamin E may lower the risk of cardiovascular diseases (hardening of the arteries, angina, heart attack, and stroke) by reducing oxidation of harmful LDL cholesterol, inhibiting platelet (*see*) activity, and preventing blood clots; may enhance immune response in the elderly; may prevent toxicity of some drugs; may cut risk of cancers and cataracts. Mineral oil and cholestyramine resin inhibit GI absorption of oral vitamin E. Harmful effects are rare, but prolonged use of more than 250 mg daily may lead to nausea, abdominal pain, vomiting, and diarrhea. Large doses may also reduce the amounts of vitamins A, D, and K absorbed from the intestines.

Vitamins. Chemical compounds that are vital for growth, health, metabolism, and physical and mental well-being. Some vitamins aid enzymes—the workhorses of the body that perform chemical reactions. Other vitamins form parts of hormones—the directors sent out from glands to turn on other organs. There are two basic types of vitamins—fat soluble and water soluble. The fat soluble such as vitamin A can accumulate in the body and cause problems if taken in excessive amounts. The water-soluble vitamins such as vitamin C cannot be stored to any great degree and must be obtained through foods.

Volatile oil. The volatile oils give off vapors, usually at room temperature. The volatile oils in plants such as peppermint or rose produce the aroma. The volatile oils in plants stimulate the tissue with which they come in contact whether they are inhaled, ingested, or placed on the skin. They can relax or stimulate, irritate or soothe, depending upon their source and concentration.

GOVERNMENT RECOMMENDATIONS FOR NUTRIENTS; BENEFITS;

NUTRACEUTICAL POTENTIAL; RISKS; AND FOOD SOURCES

The United States government has changed the standards for the intake of vitamins, minerals, and other nutrients. Since May 1994, the labeling on foods changed to *daily values.*

Daily values (DV) comprise two sets of references for nutrients, daily reference values (DRVs) and reference daily intakes (RDIs).

DAILY REFERENCE VALUES (DRVS)

These are for nutrients for which no set of standards previously existed, such as fat, cholesterol, carbohydrates, proteins, and fibers. DRVs for these energy-producing nutrients are based on the number of calories consumed per day. For labeling purposes, two thousand calories has been established as the reference for calculating percent daily values. This level was chosen, in part, because many health experts say it approximates the maintenance calorie requirements of the group most often targeted for weight reduction: postmenopausal women.

DRVs for the energy-producing nutrients are calculated as follows:

- Fat based on 30 percent of calories.
- Saturated fat based on 10 percent of calories.
- Carbohydrates based on 60 percent of calories.

- Protein based on 10 percent of calories.
- Fiber based on 11.5 grams of fiber per 1,000 calories.

The DRVs for cholesterol, sodium, and potassium, which do not contribute calories, remain the same no matter what the calorie level.

REFERENCE DAILY INTAKES (RDIS)

A set of dietary references based on and replacing the recommended dietary allowances (RDAs) for essential vitamins and minerals and, in selected groups, protein. You will continue to see vitamins and minerals expressed as percentages on the label, but these figures now refer to the Daily Reference Values.

The following are the reference daily intakes (RDIs) and the older recommended dietary allowances (RDAs) so that you can compare the "recommendations." Also included are the known benefits, potential nutraceutical supplementation, risks, and good food sources, and when possible, what destroys the vitamins and minerals in foods.

VITAMIN A

RDI: 5,000 international units (IU)
RDA: Women, 4,000 IU
       Men, 5,000 IU

Known benefits: A fat-soluble vitamin, it is involved in the formation and maintenance of healthy skin, hair, and mucous membranes. Vitamin A helps us to see in dim light and is necessary for proper bone growth, tooth development, and reproduction.

Potential as a nutraceutical: An antioxidant vitamin, it may help prevent certain cancers and be useful against problems of aging skin. Beta-carotene, its precursor, is under study as a nutraceutical to ward off cancer and heart disease and to delay cataracts.

Risks: High doses can cause pressure on the brain, birth defects, blurred vision, joint pains, and appetite loss.

Good food sources: Liver, kidney, egg yolk, spinach, carrots, apricots, and broccoli.

Destroyers: Frying vitamin A foods at high temperatures; exposing vitamin A foods to air for extended periods.

VITAMIN C
RDI: 60 milligrams (mg)
RDA: 60 mg

Known benefits: Teeth and bone formation, bone fracture, and wound healing. Resistance to infections and other diseases.

Potential as a nutraceutical: An antioxidant vitamin, it may help prevent heart disease and cancer and build immunity against infections, including the common cold.

Risks: High doses can cause kidney stones, diarrhea, and nausea.

Good food sources: Green peppers, citrus fruits, cantaloupe, broccoli, brussels sprouts, honeydew melon, and strawberries.

Destroyer: Cooking, smoking.

THIAMINE (B₁)
RDI: 1.5 mg
RDA: 1.0–1.1 mg

Known benefits: A water-soluble vitamin, it helps the body release energy from carbohydrates during metabolism. It also plays a vital role in the normal functioning of the nervous system.

Potential as a nutraceutical: May combat depression, fight fatigue, increase mental alertness, and decrease pain. Also being studied to prevent heart disease and bladder cancer.

Risks: May cause allergylike symptoms in high doses and drowsiness.

Good food sources: Fortified ready-to-eat cereals, sunflower seeds, meats, cooked oatmeal, and split peas.

RIBOFLAVIN (B$_2$)
    RDI: 1.7 mg
    RDA: 1.2–1.3 mg

Known benefits: Aids enzymes in the metabolism of proteins, sugars, and fats. Essential for growth.

Potential as a nutraceutical: May be useful against AIDS and to treat skin disorders and infertility. Is also being studied as a cancer preventative.

Risks: Decreases effects of antidepressants.

Good food sources: Beef liver, milk, brewer's yeast, sunflower seeds, broccoli, and beef.

Destroyer: Sunlight, water, estrogen, and alcohol.

NIACIN (B$_3$)
    RDI: 20 mg
    RDA: 13–14 mg

Known benefits: Reduces blood levels of cholesterol; vital to mental and emotional health; aids metabolism of carbohydrates, fats, and amino acids.

Potential as a nutraceutical: To lower cholesterol, to prevent cancer, and to help in the treatment of AIDS.

Risks: High doses can cause nausea, irregular heart rhythm, liver problems, asthma, and peptic ulcers.

Good food sources: Chicken, salmon, beef, peas, peanut butter, fortified pasta and breads, swordfish, veal, fortified ready-to-eat cereals.

Destroyers: Cooking, so cook vegetables in a minimal amount of water and roast or broil beef, veal, lamb, and poultry. Pork keeps about the same amount of niacin regardless of cooking method.

CALCIUM
    RDI: 1 gram (g)
    RDA: 800 mg

Known benefits: A mineral used for building bones and teeth and in maintaining bone strength. Calcium is also used in muscle contraction, blood clotting, and maintenance of cell membranes.

Potential as a nutraceutical: Already widely used in medications for the heart and bones. May help prevent colon cancer.

Risks: High doses may cause kidney stones, nausea, constipation, abdominal pain, and deposits in soft tissue.

Good food sources: Yogurt, milk, cheese, tofu, sardines, oysters, dried apricots, whole-wheat bread, broccoli, dry beans, and fortified cereals.

Destroyer: Cooking.

IRON
    RDI: 18 mg
    RDA: Women, 15 mg
             Men, 10 mg

Known benefits: Strengthens chemical links in the brain; it carries oxygen in the body as part of hemoglobin in the blood and myoglobin in the muscles.

Potential as a nutraceutical: Help for the immune system; may aid learning.

Risks: Nausea and liver disease. High levels may cause heart disease in adults; overdose can be lethal to children.

Good food sources: Liver, oysters, beef, apricots, blackstrap molasses, raisins, fortified pasta, white rice, and most breads.

Destroyer: Cooking, so cook for the minimum amount of time and use the minimum amount of water in recipes that call for water.

VITAMIN D
    RDI: 400 IU
    RDA: 200–400 IU

Known benefits: Helps build and maintain teeth and bones; needed for body to absorb calcium.

Potential as a nutraceutical: May help prevent cancer. Is already being used to treat psoriasis. May help immunity. Being used to prevent broken bones.

Risks: Large doses may cause heart problems.

Good food sources: Cod-liver oil, halibut, eggs, salmon, tuna, milk (enriched with vitamin D), and sardines.

Destroyer: Smog, mineral oil, cortisone.

VITAMIN E
    RDI: 30 IU
    RDA: 8 IU

Known benefits: Needed for healthy heart and skeletal muscles. Helps form red blood cells.

Potential as a nutraceutical: An antioxidant vitamin that may protect against heart disease and cancer. It may also be beneficial in the treatment of arthritis and certain skin problems.

Risks: Large doses may cause diarrhea, but it is one of the safest vitamins.

Good food sources: Oils, almonds, sunflower seeds, whole wheat, wheat germ, peanuts, peaches, and prunes.

Destroyer: Heat, freezing.

VITAMIN B$_{12}$
RDI: 6 micrograms (mcg)
RDA: 3 mg

Known benefits: Needed for normal growth, a healthy nervous system, and normal red-blood-cell formation.

Potentail as a nutraceutical: May be useful in the treatment of brain and nerve disorders of aging.

Risks: Great margin of safety but may cause allergic reactions in some people and can worsen gout.

Good food sources: Clams, beef liver, oysters, mackerel, sardines, crab, and herring.

Destroyer: Alcohol, estrogen, sleeping pills.

FOLIC ACID
RDI: 0.4 mg
RDA: 400 mcg

Known benefits: Regulates cell division and new red-blood-cell division.

Potential as a nutraceutical: Prevention of brain and nerve birth defects; may prevent cancer of the cervix and throat as well as other forms of malignancy.

Risks: High doses can mask B_{12} deficiency, a potential source of nerve damage.

Good food sources: Liver, brewer's yeast, green leafy vegetables, black-eyed peas, and lentils.

Destroyers: Birth control pills, sunlight, aspirin, cooking, and storage.

VITAMIN B₆
    RDI: 2 mg
    RDA: 2 mg

Known benefits: Helps use protein to build body tissues and aids in the metabolism of fat. The need for this vitamin is directly related to protein intake. As the intake of protein increases, the need for vitamin B_6 increases.

Potential as a nutraceutical: May help the immune system and be useful as a pain medication.

Risks: May be toxic to nerves if taken in large amounts.

Good food sources: Bananas, plantains, chicken, potatoes, green peas, spinach, walnuts, liver, oatmeal, and wheat germ.

Destroyer: Long storage, alcohol, estrogen, cortisone.

PHOSPHORUS
    RDI: 1 g
    RDA: 800–1,200 mg

Known benefits: Needed for strong bones and teeth.

Potential as a nutraceutical: May reduce the pain of arthritis and reduce the effects of stress.

Risks: May cause fatigue, swelling, headaches, muscle cramps, numbness, unusual thirst, abdominal pain, bone or joint pain, confusion, and decreased output of urine.

Good food sources: Eggs, fish, grains, glandular meats, meat, poultry, yellow cheese, nuts, legumes, and milk.

IODINE
    RDI: 150 mcg
    RDA: 150 mcg

Known benefits: Aids metabolism, particularly of fat; important to thyroid gland function.

Potential as a nutraceutical: May aid in the treatment of anemia, chest pain, hardening of the arteries, arthritis, and certain infections of the skin.

Risks: May adversely affect the thyroid gland, cause irregular heartbeat, skin rash, and bloody stools.

Good food sources: Seafood, kelp, iodized salt, dairy products.

MAGNESIUM
    RDI: 400 mg
    RDA: 300–400 mg

Known benefits: Needed for healthy arteries, bones, heart, muscles, nerves, and teeth. Activates enzymes needed to release energy.

Potential as a nutraceutical: Medication to counteract heart-attack damage.

Risks: May cause abdominal pain, appetite loss, diarrhea, irregular heartbeat, mood changes, nausea, fatigue, urinary problems, and vomiting.

Good food sources: Fresh green vegetables, oysters, scallops, unmilled wheat germ, soybeans, corn, oil-rich seeds and nuts, and milk.

ZINC
    RDI: 15mg
    RDA: 15 mg

Known benefits: Boosts the immune system and helps fight disease; element in more than one hundred enzymes—proteins that are essential to digestion and other functions.

Potential as a nutraceutical: May prevent the growth of abnormal cells associated with cancer and other diseases. May have antiviral capabilities.

Risk: May reduce immunity when taken in large doses.

Good food sources: Meat, grains, breads, eggs, oysters, and lima beans.

Destroyer: Fat-soluble vitamins may decrease absorption of the mineral.

COPPER
    RDI: 2mg
    Estimated safe and adequate daily dietary intake: 2–3 mg
    (was no official RDA because of lack of information, so estimate was given instead)

Known benefits: Needed for healthy blood, bones, circulatory system, and skin.

Potential as a nutraceutical: May ease arthritis pain, protect against cancer and heart disease, and reduce inflammation.

Risks: May cause anemia, nausea, vomiting, muscle aches, and abdominal pain.

Good food sources: Liver, whole grains, almonds, dried legumes, nuts, and seafood.

Destroyer: Cereals, zinc, and vegetables may interfere with copper absorption and utilization.

BIOTIN
RDI: 0.3 mg
Estimated safe and adequate daily dietary intake: 100–200 mcg

Known benefits: Helps make fatty acids and aids in oxidizing fatty acids and carbohydrates; helps use of protein, folic acid, pantothenic acid, and niacin.

Potential as a nutraceutical: May aid the metabolism of fats in persons with high cholesterol and sugars in diabetics.

Risks: None known.

Good food sources: Egg yolk, liver, unpolished rice, nuts, chicken, whole grains, and brewer's yeast.

PANTOTHENIC ACID
RDI: 10 mg
Estimated safe and adequate daily dietary intake: 4–7 mg

Known benefits: Stimulates adrenal glands, aids cellular metabolism, helps metabolize cholesterol and fatty acids, maintains healthy digestive tract.

Potential as a nutraceutical: May help prevent birth defects, mental fatigue, sleep disturbances, headaches, muscle spasms, and breathing problems.

Risks: Diarrhea and water retention.

Good food sources: Brewer's yeast, beef liver, bran, peanuts, sesame seeds, eggs, soybeans.

Destroyer: Food processing, sleeping pills, alcohol, tobacco, caffeine, and estrogen.

NATURAL NUTRACEUTICAL DIET

EAT AT LEAST 2–4 SERVINGS OF FRUITS A DAY
Eat at least one vitamin A rich selection every day. Fruits rich in vitamin A include apricots, cantaloupe, mango, and papaya. Eat at least one vitamin C rich selection every day. Fruits rich in vitamin C include oranges, grapefruit, kiwi, cantaloupe, honydew, papaya, mango, raspberries, strawberries, and watermelon.

A Serving of Fruit

- A whole fruit such as a medium apple, banana, or orange
- A half a grapefruit
- A melon wedge
- ¾ cup of juice
- ½ cup of berries
- ½ cup of cooked or canned fruit
- ¼ cup of dried fruit

EAT 3–5 SERVINGS OF VEGETABLES A DAY
Vegetables high in vitamin A include broccoli, bok choy, carrots, kale, turnips, Swiss chard, beet and mustard greens, spinach, romaine lettuce, winter squash, sweet potatoes, and tomatoes. Vegetables rich in vitamin C include asparagus, bok choy, broccoli, brussels sprouts, cabbage, cauliflower, green bell peppers,

and tomatoes. Eat cabbage family (cruciferous) vegetables several times a week. Research indicates that cruciferous vegetables may have natural anticancer properties. These types of vegetables include broccoli, brussels sprouts, bok choy, cabbage, cauliflower, and various greens such as mustard, turnip, and beet greens, kale, and Swiss chard.

A Serving of Vegetables

- ½ cup of cooked vegetables
- ½ cup of chopped raw vegetables
- 1 cup leafy raw vegetables such as lettuce or spinach

EAT AT LEAST ONE HIGH-FIBER SELECTION EVERY DAY

Breads, cereals, and other grain products are high in fiber. Almost all fruits and vegetables are good sources of fiber. Cooked dried peas and beans and dried fruits are especially high in fiber.

A Serving of Fiber (whole-grain, enriched)

- 1 slice of bread
- ½ hamburger bun or English muffin
- A small roll, biscuit, or muffin
- 3 to 4 small or 2 large crackers
- ½ cup cooked cereal, rice, or pasta
- 1 ounce of ready-to-eat breakfast cereal

EAT 2–3 SERVINGS OF PROTEIN A DAY

Meat, poultry, fish, eggs, dry beans and peas, nuts, and seeds.

A Serving of Protein

- Amounts should total 5 to 7 ounces of cooked lean meat, poultry, or fish a day.
- Count 1 egg, ½ cup cooked beans, or 2 tablespoons peanut butter as equal to one ounce of meat.

EAT 2–3 SERVINGS A DAY OF MILK, CHEESE, OR YOGURT

Three servings are needed by women who are pregnant or breast-feeding and for teens; four servings for teens who are pregnant or breast feeding.

A Serving of Calcium-Rich Foods

- 1 cup of milk
- 8 ounces of yogurt
- 1½ ounces of natural cheese
- 2 ounces of processed cheese

Try to keep fats, sweets, and alcoholic beverages to a moderate level.

EXAMPLES OF RECIPES WITH NATURAL NUTRACEUTICALS

You can make choices that will provide you with healthy, good-tasting foods that will supply the natural nutraceuticals described in this book. The more you learn about the natural protectants in food, the better your choices will be.

SUPER STEAK

Round steak is one of the leanest cuts of beef. Making this recipe with tomatoes canned without salt and ¼ teaspoon of salt provides 50 mg less sodium per serving than making the same recipe with tomatoes canned with salt. Choose a whole-grain roll and noodles or rice to go with this main dish for two servings from the bread group. Serve with a fresh fruit cup for desert; include some kiwi for added color and flavor. Add a serving of milk and you have something from each of the food groups.

¾ pound beef round steak, boneless

½ cup celery, sliced

1 tablespoon onion, chopped

1 tablespoon flour

16 oz. can tomatoes, no salt added

2 tablespoons water

1 tablespoon parsley, chopped

1 tablespoon soy sauce, low sodium

½ teaspoon ginger root, minced

¼ teaspoon salt

⅛ teaspoon ground cloves

⅛ teaspoon red-pepper flakes

1 bay leaf

To prepare:

1. Trim all fat from steak. Slice across the grain diagonally into thin strips.
2. Heat nonstick frypan. Cook steak, celery, and onion until steak is browned.
3. Stir flour into beef mixture. Add remaining ingredients. Bring to a boil; reduce heat, cover, and cook over low heat for 40 minutes or until meat is tender.
4. Serve over noodles or rice.

4 servings, about ¹/₂ cup each
Each serving provides about 2 ounces cooked meat; 1 serving
(¹/₂ cup) cooked vegetables.
See text for benefits of nutraceuticals in soy sauce, tomatoes, red
pepper, onions, celery, etc.

Per serving (not including noodles or rice):

Calories	 140	Cholesterol	. . . . 43 mg
Total fat	. . . . 3 gm	Sodium	. . . . 245 mg
Saturated fatty acid	. . . 1 gm		

SPINACH ORANGE SALAD

Fruits and vegetables served together give you a double benefit. The light orange-juice dressing adds a sweet-tart flavor. Serve this salad with a baked chicken breast, seasoned lima beans, and a hot crispy roll. If you wish, an angel food cake with a lightly sweetened fruit topping will cap off this good meal.

4 cups spinach, torn into pieces

2 medium oranges, sectioned

½ cup red onion, sliced

⅔ cup mushrooms, sliced

¼ cup orange juice

2 tablespoons vinegar

½ teaspoon vegetable oil

½ teaspoon ground ginger

¼ teaspoon pepper

To prepare:

1. Place spinach in bowl. Add orange sections, onion, and mushrooms. Toss lightly to mix.
2. Mix orange juice, vinegar, oil, ginger, and pepper well. Pour over spinach mixture. Toss.
3. Chill.

4 servings, about 1 cup each
Each serving provides 1½ cup (1 cup leafy raw and ¼ cup raw) vegetables; ½ serving fruit.
Check text for benefits of nutraceuticals in mushrooms, oranges, onions, etc.

Per serving:

Calories *110*
Total fat . . . . *8 gm*
Saturated fatty acid . . . *trace*

Cholesterol *0*
Sodium . . . . *25 mg*

WONDERFUL WHOLE-WHEAT CORNMEAL MUFFINS

This is a tasty, high-fiber, low-fat muffin that will be a treat at any meal and provide the basic fiber you need for the day.

⅔ cup yellow cornmeal, degerminate

⅔ cup whole-wheat flour

1 tablespoon sugar

2 teaspoons baking powder

⅛ teaspoon salt

⅔ cup skim milk

2 egg whites

2 tablespoons oil

To prepare:

1. Preheat oven to 400° F.
2. Grease 8 muffin tins or use paper liners.
3. Mix dry ingredients thoroughly.
4. Mix milk, egg whites, and oil. Add to dry ingredients. Stir until dry ingredients are barely moistened. Batter will be lumpy.
5. Fill muffin tins two-thirds full.
6. Bake until lightly browned—about 20 minutes.

   8 muffins

Per serving:

Calories 130	Cholesterol .... 35 mg
Total fat .... 4 gm	Sodium .... 146 mg
Saturated fatty acids ... 1 gm	

BRAVO BROCCOLI SOUP

Broccoli is a super food filled with nutraceuticals that can help prevent a number of diseases (*see* text). Here is a soup with onion that also contains beneficial nutraceuticals, including a lot of calcium and polyphenols.

1½ cups broccoli, chopped (10-ounce package of frozen chopped broccoli can be used instead of fresh broccoli that will slightly increase calories and sodium)

¼ cup celery, diced

¼ cup onion, chopped

1 cup chicken broth, unsalted

2 tablespoons skim milk

¼ teaspoon salt (optional)

Dash, pepper

Dash, ground thyme

¼ cup Swiss cheese, shredded, (may use low-sodium, low-fat cheese to reduce fat and sodium content)

2 tablespoons cornstarch

To prepare:

1. Place vegetables and broth in saucepan. Bring to boil, reduce heat, cover, and cook until vegetables are tender—about 8 minutes.
2. Mix milk, cornstarch, salt, pepper, and thyme; add to cooked vegetables. Cook, stirring constantly, until soup is slightly thickened and mixture just begins to boil.
3. Remove from heat. Add cheese and stir until melted.

4 servings, about 1 cup each

Per serving:

Calories 110
Total fat . . . . 3 gm
Saturated fatty acids . . . 2 gm

Cholesterol . . . . 9 mg
Sodium . . . . 252 mg

BROILED SENSATIONAL SESAME FISH

Fish, sesame seeds, and parsley, as well as lemon juice, contain beneficial nutraceuticals, as you can read in the text, including protease in sesame seeds.

1 pound cod fillets, fresh or
    frozen

1 teaspoon margarine,
    melted

1 tablespoon lemon juice

1 teaspoon dried tarragon
    leaves

$1/8$ teaspoon salt (optional)

Dash, pepper

1 tablespoon sesame seeds

1 tablespoon parsley,
    chopped

To prepare:

1. Thaw frozen fish in refrigerator overnight or defrost briefly in microwave oven. Cut fish into 4 portions.
2. Place fish on a broiler pan lined with aluminum foil. Brush margarine over fish.
3. Mix lemon juice, tarragon leaves, salt, and pepper. Pour over fish.
4. Sprinkle sesame seeds evenly over fish.
5. Broil until fish flakes easily with a fork—about 12 minutes.
6. Garnish each serving with parsley.

4 servings, about $2^1/_2$ ounces each

Per serving:

Calories *110*		*Cholesterol* . . . . *46 mg*
Total fat . . . . *3 gm*		*Sodium* . . . . *155 mg*
Saturated fatty acids . . . *trace*		

ROYAL RICE-PASTA PILAF

A low-fat recipe with high carbohydrates and the benefits of green onions, peppers, mushrooms, and of course garlic. See benefits in text.

⅓ cup uncooked brown rice	2 tablespoons green pepper, chopped
1½ cups chicken broth, unsalted	2 tablespoons fresh mushrooms, chopped
⅓ cup thin spaghetti, broken into ½- to 1-inch pieces	1 clove garlic, minced
	½ teaspoon savory
2 teaspoons margarine	¼ teaspoon salt (optional)
2 tablespoons green onions, chopped	⅛ teaspoon pepper
	1 tablespoon slivered almonds, toasted*

To prepare:

1. Cook rice in 1 cup of broth in a covered saucepan until almost tender—about 35 minutes.
2. Cook spaghetti in margarine over low heat until golden brown— about 2 minutes. Stir frequently; watch carefully.
3. Add browned spaghetti, vegetables, remaining ½ cup of chicken broth, and seasonings to rice.
4. Bring to boil, reduce heat, cover, and cook over medium heat until liquid is absorbed—about 10 minutes.
5. Remove from heat; let stand 2 minutes.
6. Garnish with almonds.

4 servings, about ½ cup each

Per serving:

Calories *135*	*Cholesterol* *0*
Total fat . . . . *4 gm*	*Sodium* . . . . *177 mg*
Saturated fatty acids . . . *1 gm*	

*Toast almonds in 350°F (moderate) oven until lightly browned, 5–12 minutes. Or, toast in heavy pan over medium heat for 10–15 minutes, stirring frequently. If served without almonds, the pilaf has 125 calories and 3 gm of total fat per serving.

FAST CHILI

Chili, onions, and kidney beans have a lot of nutraceuticals, as the text describes. It is quick and easy and has less fat, sodium, and calories than the traditional dish. It also contains capsaicin, a natural painkiller. See page 323.

½ pound lean ground beef

15½-ounce can kidney beans, drained (save liquid)

⅓ cup bean liquid

1 cup no-salt-added canned tomato puree

¼ cup onion, minced

1½ tablespoons chili powder

To prepare:

1. Cook beef in hot frying pan until lightly browned. Drain off fat.
2. Stir in remaining ingredients.
3. Bring to a boil. Reduce heat, cover, and simmer 10 minutes.

Serve with mixed salad greens, with reduced-calorie dressing, whole-wheat rolls, and juice-pack canned pineapple chunks, and you have a healthy, well-balanced meal with nutraceuticals, as you will have read about the specific ones in the text.

4 servings, about ¾ cup each

Per serving:

Calories 230
Total fat . . . . 9 gm
Saturated fatty acids . . . 3 gm

Cholesterol . . . . 34 mg
Sodium . . . . 390 mg

OATMEAL APPLESAUCE COOKIES

Applesauce adds pectin and moistness to this low-calorie, low-fat, and low-sodium version of oatmeal cookies. The oats, as you read in the text, help to lower cholesterol.

1 cup unbleached flour
1 teaspoon baking powder
1 teaspoon ground allspice
¼ teaspoon salt
½ cup margarine
½ cup sugar

2 egg whites
2 cups rolled oats, quick cooking
1 cup unsweetened applesauce
½ cup raisins, chopped

To prepare:

1. Preheat oven to 375° F (moderate).
2. Grease baking sheet.
3. Mix flour, baking powder, allspice, and salt.
4. Beat margarine and sugar until creamy. Add egg whites; beat well.
5. Add dry ingredients.
6. Stir in oats, applesauce, and raisins. Mix well.
7. Drop by level tablespoonfuls onto baking sheet.
8. Bake 11 minutes or until edges are lightly browned.
9. Cool on rack.

About 5 dozen cookies

Per cookie:

Calories *45*
Total fat .... *2 gm*
Saturated fatty acids ... *trace*

Cholesterol *0*
Sodium .... *36 mg*

PEPPY PUMPKIN CUPCAKES

These cupcakes provide a nutrient-plus desert. The pumpkin is high in vitamin A and the raisins add iron.

1 1/2 cups whole-wheat flour

1 cup unbleached flour

3/4 cup sugar

2 tablespoons baking powder

2 teaspoons ground cinnamon

1/2 teaspoon ground nutmeg

1/4 teaspoon salt

6 egg whites, slightly beaten

1 cup skim milk

1/2 cup oil

1 cup canned pumpkin

3/4 cup raisins, chopped

1 tablespoon vanilla

To prepare:

1. Preheat oven to 350° F (moderate).
2. Place 24 paper baking cups in muffin tins.
3. Mix dry ingredients thoroughly.
4. Mix remaining ingredients; add to dry ingredients. Stir until dry ingredients are barely moistened.
5. Fill paper cups two-thirds full.
6. Bake about 20 minutes or until toothpick inserted in center of a cupcake comes out clean.
7. Remove cupcakes from tins and cool on rack.
8. Freeze cupcakes that will not be eaten in the next few days.

24 cupcakes

Per cupcake:

Calories 140
Total fat . . . . 5 gm
Saturated fatty acids . . . 1 gm

Cholesterol . . . . 34 mg
Sodium . . . . 132 mg

MEXICAN SNACK PIZZA

A low-fat, low-calorie pizza with a Mexican flavor. The beans and whole-wheat muffins provide a delicious fiber treat.

2 whole-wheat English muffins

¼ cup tomato puree (no-salt-added can reduce sodium)

¼ cup kidney beans, canned, drained, chopped

1 tablespoon green pepper, chopped

½ teaspoon oregano leaves

¼ cup mozzarella cheese, part skim milk, shredded (low-sodium, low-fat cheeses can be substituted)

¼ cup lettuce, shredded

To prepare:
1. Split muffins; toast lightly.
2. Mix puree, beans, onions, green pepper, and oregano. Spread on muffin halves. Sprinkle with cheese.
3. Broil until cheese is bubbly, about 2 minutes.
4. Garnish with shredded lettuce.

4 servings

Per pizza (½ English muffin):

Calories 95	*Cholesterol* . . . . 4 mg
Total fat . . . . 2 gm	*Sodium* . . . . 300 mg
Saturated fatty acid . . . 1 gm	

FRUITY FINGER SNACK

A healthy snack that is cool, refreshing, and fun for both children and adults. It is a good replacement for a sweet, sugary drink that supplies almost no vitamins and minerals.

1½ tablespoons (1½ envelopes) unflavored gelatin

¾ cup water

6-ounce can frozen grape- or apple-juice concentrate

To prepare:

1. Lightly grease a 9-by-5-inch loaf pan or plastic ice-cube trays.
2. Soften gelatin in water in a small saucepan for 5 minutes.
3. Heat over low heat, stirring constantly, until gelatin dissolves. Remove from heat.
4. Add fruit-juice concentrate; mix well. Pour into pan.
5. Cover and refrigerate. Chill until set.
6. Cut into 1-inch cubes. Keep covered during refrigerator storage.

45 cubes

Per cube:

Calories *10*
Total fat . . . . *trace*
Saturated fatty acids . . . *trace*

Cholesterol *0*
Sodium . . . . *1 mg*

HIGH-PERFORMANCE SHAKE

An easy and delicious way to help get the calcium you need for your bones and the neurotransmitters you need for your brain.

1 cup nonfat yogurt	½ teaspoon vanilla
2 tablespoons nonfat powdered milk	1 tablespoon honey
1 ripe banana, sliced	Dash of nutmeg or cinnamon

1 serving

Whirr all ingredients in a blender until smooth and serve.

Per glass:

Calories	339	Potassium	352 mg
Fat	1 gm	Serotonin	15 mcg
Calcium	602 mg	Tryptophan	1.62 mg

Introduction—What Is a Nutraceutical and Why Should You Care?

1. Stephen DeFelice, M.D., *Regulatory Affairs* 5 (Summer 1993):169.

2. Tadayasu Furukawa, Ph.D., "The Nutraceutical Rules: Health and Medical Claims: 'Food for Specified Health Use' in Japan." *Regulatory Affairs* 5 (1993):189–206.

3. Herucles Segalas, managing director, PaineWebber, Inc., New York, "The Next Generation of Food Products: Healthy Foods," *Regulatory Affairs* 5 (1993):265–80.

4. R. W. Smithells et al., "Further Experience of Vitamin Supplementation for Prevention of Neural Tube Defect Recurrences," *The Lancet* (May 7, 1983):1027–31.

5. James Mills, M.D., et al., "The Absence of a Relation Between the Periconceptional Use of Vitamins and Neural-Tube Defects," *The New England Journal of Medicine* (1989):321, 430–35.

6. Aubrey Milunsky, MBBCh, DSc, et al., "Multivitamin/Folic Acid Supplementation in Early Pregnancy *Reduces* the Prevalence of Neural Tube Defects," *Journal of the American Medical Association* 262, no. 20 (November 24, 1989):2847–52.

7. Martha Werler, ScD, et al., "Periconceptional Folic Acid Exposure and Risk of Occurent Neural-Tube Defects," *Journal of the American Medical Association* 269, no. 10 (March 10, 1993):1257–61.

8. Centers for Disease Control and Prevention. "Recommendations for the use of folic acid to reduce the number of cases of spina bifida and other neural tube defects," *MMWR* 41, no. RR-14 (1992):1233–38.

9. Tufts University, *Diet & Nutrition Letter* 8, no. 9 (November 1990):1.

10. R. Wood et al., "Effect of butter, mono- and polyunsaturated fatty

acid–enriched butter, trans fatty acid margarine, and zero trans fatty acid margarine on serum lipids and lipoproteins in healthy men," *Journal of Lipid Research* 34, no. 1 (January 1993):1–11; Marian Burros, "Now What? U.S. Study Says Margarine May Be Harmful," *New York Times*, October 7, 1992, p. 1.

11. "Health Doubts Cut Into Margarine Sales," *Wall Street Journal*, April 26, 1993, p. B1.

12. "Study that links margarine to possible heart disease draws criticism," Associated Press report, *Newark Star-Ledger*, October 8, 1992.

13. "The Effect of Vitamin E and Beta-Carotene on the Incidence of Lung Cancer and Other Cancer in Male Smokers," *The New England Journal of Medicine* 330 (1994):1029–35.

14. Rebecca Voelker, "Recommendations for Antioxidants: How Much Evidence is Enough?" *Journal of the American Medical Association* 27, no. 15 (April 20, 1994):1148–49.

15. Ibid.

16. National Heart, Lung and Blood Institute publications; Human Nutrition Information Service, U.S. Department of Agriculture; and American Heart Association publications.

17. Molly O'Neill, "Eating to Heal: Mapping Out New Frontiers," *New York Times*, February 7, 1990, p. C1.

18. "Think of It: An Anticancer Breakfast Bar," *Health & Human Development Research* (Penn State) (Spring 1993):26.

Chapter 1: What Now Purple Cow?

1. Lee R. Beck, Ph.D., personal communication with author, May 3, 1993.

2. United States Department of Agriculture, Agricultural Research Service, *Quarterly Report of Selected Research Projects* (July 1 to September 30, 1992):7.

3. William Velander et al., "Purification Challenges for Recombinant Protein C From the Milk of Transgenic Pigs," paper presented April 6, 1992, before the Division of Analytical Chemistry at the American Chemical Society national meeting, San Francisco.

4. Iris Taylor, "Enzon Seeks FDA Green-Light to Test Blood Substitute," *Newark Star-Ledger*, June 30, 1994, p. 1.

5. "Foods of the Future: The New Biotechnology and FDA Regulations," *Journal of the American Medical Association* 269, no. 7 (February 17, 1993):1223.

6. Wayne M. Barnes, "Variable Patterns of Expression of Luciferase in Transfenic Tobacco Leaves," *Proceedings of the National Academy of Sciences* 87 (December 1990):9183–87.

7. Hugh Mason, Ph.D., personal communication with author, June 2, 1993.

8. David Russell, paper presented at the 208th American Chemical Society Meeting, Washington, D.C., August 22, 1994.

9. Ibid.

10. Bob Ortega, "Vaccine Designing Scientists Go Bananas," *Wall Street Journal*, March 9, 1994, p. B6.

11. Eben Shapiro, "The Long, Hard Quest for Foods that Fool the Palate," *New York Times*, September 29, 1991, p. F5.

12. "Position of the American Dietetic Association: Biotechnology and the Future of Food," *Journal of the American Dietetic Association* 3, no. 2 (February 1993):189–92.

13. National Research Council, "Statement of Policy: Foods Derived from New Plant Varieties," *Federal Register* 57 (May 29, 1992):22984–23005.

14. H. I. Miller, "Foods of the Future: The New Biotechnology and FDA Regulation," *Journal of the American Medical Association* 269, no. 7 (February 17, 1993):910–12.

15. Stuart Gannes, "Nutrition Alert! Genetically Altered Foods. They're Coming to Grocery Shelves," *Self*, March 1993, 152.

16. Ron Cowen, "Medicine on the Wild Side," *Science News* 138 (November 3, 1990):221.

17. Roger Miller, "Can Herbs Really Heal?" *FDA Consumer*, June 1987, 30–35.

Chapter 2: Diet and Clues to Cancer Prevention

1. Vincent DeVita Jr., M.D., director of the National Cancer Institute, statement made during U.S. Senate Appropriation Hearings, March 5, 1986, and

U.S. House of Representatives Appropriation Hearings, March 11, 1986.

2. Ibid.

3. American Cancer Society special report, January 31, 1984.

4. Walter Troll, Department of Environmental Medicine, New York University Medical Center, "Prevention of cancer by agents that suppress production of oxidants," paper presented at the 204th American Chemical Society National Meeting, Washington, D.C., August 23, 1992.

5. Roland Phillips, "Role of Lifestyle and Dietary Habits in Risk of Cancer Among Seventh-Day Adventists," *Cancer Research* 35 (November 1975): 3513–22.

6. Ibid.

7. Peter Greenwald, M.D., "Cancer Prevention Trials to Clarify Relationships Between Diet and Cancer," presented at "Nutrition in the 90s: Setting the Table for the Future," sponsored by the American Medical Association, New York, New York, January 14, 1993.

8. Ibid.

9. Ibid.

10. Ibid.

11. Maxwell D. Parkin, "Cancers of the Breast, Endometrium and Ovary: Geographic Correlations," *European Journal of Cancer and Clinical Oncology* 25, no. 12 (1989):1917–25.

12. A. Tannenbaum, "Genesis and growth of tumors: Ill effects of a high-fat diet," *Cancer Research* 2 (1942):468–75.

13. K. K. Carroll and H. T. Khor, "Dietary fat in relation to tumorigenesis," *Progress Biochem Pharmcol* 10 (1975):308–53.

14. Geoffrey Howe, "Nutritional Epidemiology of Postmenopausal Breast Cancer in Western New York," *American Journal of Epidemiology* 137, no. 2 (1993).

15. P. J. Goodwin, M.D., and N. F. Boyd, M.D., "Critical Appraisal of the Evidence that Dietary Fat Intake is Related to Breast Cancer Risk in Humans," *Journal of the National Cancer Institute* 79, no. 3 (September 1987).

16. Parkin, "Geographic Correlations."

17. "Study Shows Link Between Diet and Breast Cancer," *Tel Aviv University Report* (October 12, 1986).

18. "Breast Cancer Recurrence Linked to Fat," *University of Texas Lifetime Health Letter* (March 1993):8.

19. Geoffrey Howe et al., "Review: Dietary Factors and Risk of Breast Cancer, Combined Analysis of 12 Case-Control Studies," *Journal of the National Cancer Institute* 82, no. 7 (April 4, 1990):56–63.

20. Paul Knekt, "Serum Vitamin E Level and Risk of Female Cancers," *International Journal of Epidemiology* 17 (1988):281–88.

21. Ibid.

22. Charles Butterworth et al., "Folate Deficiency and Cervical Dysplasia," *Journal of the American Medical Association* 267, no. 4 (January 22, 1992):528–33.

23. Charles E. Butterworth, Jr., M.D., "Folic Acid and Cancer," a paper presented at "Beyond Deficiency: New Views on the Function and Health Effects of Vitamins," sponsored by the New York Academy of Sciences, New York, New York, February 1992.

24. C. E. Butterworth et al., "Folate Deficiency."

25. C. E. Butterworth et al., "Improvement in Cervical Dysplasia Associated With Folic Acid Therapy in Users of Oral Contraceptives," *American Journal of Clinical Nutrition* 35 (January 1982):73–82.

26. P. R. Palan et al., "Plasma levels of antioxidant beta-carotene and alpha tocopherol in uterine cervix dysplasias and cancer," *Journal of Nutrition and Cancer* 15, no. 1 (1991):13–20

27. La Vecchia et al., "Dietary Vitamin A and the Risk of Intraepithelial and Invasive Cervical Neoplasia," *Gynecologic Oncology* 30, no. 2 (June 1988):187–95.

28. Wassertheil-Smoller et al., "Dietary Vitamin C and Uterine Cervical Dysplasia," *American Journal of Epidemiology* 114, no. 5 (November 1981):714–24.

29. K. E. Brock et al., "Nutrients in diet and plasma and risk of in situ cervical cancer," *Journal of the National Cancer Institute* 80, no. 8 (June 15, 1988):580–85.

30. Laara E. Parkin, D.M. and C. S. Muir, "Estimates of Worldwide Frequency of 16 Major Cancers in 1980," *International Journal of Cancer* 41 (1988):184–97.

31. Fabio Barbone, Austin Harland, and Edward Partridge, "Diet and Endometrial Cancer: A Case-Control Study," *American Journal of Epidemiology* 137, no. 4 (1993):393–403.

32. Greenwald, "Cancer Prevention Trials."

33. Nancy Potischman et al., "Breast Cancer and Dietary and Plasma Concentrations of Carotenoids and Vitamin A," *American Journal of Clinical Nutrition* 52 (1990):909–15.

34. David Hunter et al., "A Prospective Study of the Intake of Vitamins C, E, and A and the Risk of Breast Cancer," *The New England Journal of Medicine* 329 (July 22, 1993):234–40.

35. *Journal of the National Cancer Institute*, October 7, 1992.

36. "Study Finds New Evidence That Diet High in Vegetables and Grains May Protect Against Colon Cancer," American Cancer Society release, Atlanta, Georgia, October 6, 1992.

37. Michael Thun, "Aspirin Use and Reduced Risk of Fatal Colon Cancer," *The New England Journal of Medicine* 325, no. 23 (December 5, 1991):1644–46.

38. Geoffrey Howe et al., "Dietary Intake of Fiber and Decreased Risk of Cancers of the Colon and Rectum: Evidence from combined analysis of 13 case-control studies." *Journal of the National Cancer Institute* 84, no. 24 (December 16, 1992):1887–96.

39. Gladys Block, "Vitamin C and Cancer Prevention: The Epidemiologic Evidence," *American Journal of Clinical Nutrition* 53 (1991):275.

40. Ibid., 270–82.

41. E. R. Greenberg et al., "A Clinical Trial of Antioxidant Vitamins to Prevent Colorectal Adenoma," *The New England Journal of Medicine* 3 (July 21, 1994):189–90.

42. John Vena, Ph.D., "Bladder Cancer and Vitamin A," *Nutrition and Cancer* (December 1992).

43. L. N. Kolonel et al., "Relationship of dietary vitamin A and ascorbic acid intake to the risk for cancers of the lung, bladder, and prostate in Hawaii," *National Cancer Institute Monograph* 69 (1985):137.

44. Curtis Mettlin et al., "Vitamin A and Lung Cancer," *Journal of the National Cancer Institute* 62, no. 6 (June 1979):1435–38.

45. Ibid.

46. M. Ward Hinds et al., "Dietary Vitamin A, Carotene, Vitamin C and Risk of Lung Cancer in Hawaii," *American Journal of Epidemiology* 119, no. 2 (1984):227–37.

47. John E. Connett, Ph.D., et al., "Relationship Between Carotenoids and Cancer: The Multiple Risk Factor Intervention Trial (MRFIT) Study," *Cancer* 64 (1989):126–34.

48. Steinmetz et al., "Vegetables, Fruit, and Lung Cancer in the Iowa Women's Health Study," *Cancer Research* 53 (1993):536–43.

49. G. Gridley et al., "Vitamin Supplement Use and Reduced Risk of Oral and Pharyngeal Cancer," *American Journal of Epidemiology* 135, no. 10 (May 15, 1992):1083–92.

50. Ibid.

51. Block, "Vitamin C and Cancer Prevention," 270–82s.

52. Ibid.

53. Harvey Risch et al., "Dietary Factors and the Incidence of Cancer of the Stomach," *American Journal of Epidemiology* 122, no. 6 (1985):947–57.

54. Ibid.

55. Ibid.

56. Ibid.

57. Block, "Vitamin C and Cancer Prevention."

58. Ibid., 273s.

59. "Supplements Reduce Deaths in a High-Risk Population in China," National Cancer Institute Report, Bethesda, Maryland, September 14, 1993.

Chapter 3: Nutraceuticals That Fight Cancer

1. A. B. Caragay, "Cancer Preventive Foods," *Food Techonology* 46, no. 4 (1992):65–68.

2. L. O. Dragsted, M. Strube, and J. C. Larsen, "Cancer-protective factors in fruits and vegetables; biochemical and biological background," *Pharmacology and Toxicology* 72, suppl. 1 (1993):116–35.

3. "Foods Can Be Potent Cancer-Fighting Weapons," *Lifetime Healthletter* (University of Texas Health Science Center) 5, no. 1 (January 1993):4–5.

4. W. Troll, and A. R. Kennedy, "Protease Inhibitors as Cancer Chemopreventive Agents," *Cancer Research* 49 (1989):499–502.

5. A. R. Kennedy et al., "Effects of various preparations of dietary protease

inhibitors on oral carcinogenesis in hamsters induced by DMBA," *Nutritional Cancer* 19, no. 2 (1993):191–200; and L. N. Su, W. A. Toscano., Jr, and A. R. Kennedy, "Suppression of phorbol ester–enhanced radiation-induced malignancy in vitro by protease inhibitors is independent of protein kinase C," *Biochemistry Biophysical Communication* 176, no. 1 (April 15, 1991):18–24.

6. "Diet and Cancer. Where Do Matters Stand?" *Archives of Internal Medicine* 153 (January 11, 1992); Committee on Diet and Health: Food and Nutrition Board, National Research Council, *Diet and Health: Implications for Reducing Chronic Disease Risk* (Washington D.C.: National Academy Press, 1989); "Nutrition and Cancer: Cause and Prevention," American Cancer Society special report, January 31, 1984.

7. "Diet and Cancer. Where Do Matters Stand?" Review of recommendations made by the National Research Council in its 1982 report, "Diet, Nutrition, and Cancer."

8. *Science News* 135 (June 7 and 24, 1988):390.

9. L. O. Dragsted et al., "Cancer-protective factors."

10. Ibid.

11. A. Mandal and G. D. Stoner, "Inhibition of N-nitrosobenzyl-methyamine–induced esophageal tumorigenesis in rats by ellagic acid," *Carcinogenesis* 11, no. 1 (January 1990):55–61.

12. Y. H. Heur et al., "Synthesis of Ellagic Acid O-alkyl Derivatives and Isolation of Ellagic Acid as a Tetrahexanoyl Derivative from *Fragaria ananassa*," *J Natural Products* 55, no. 10 (October 1992):1402–7.

13. Bandaru S. Reddy and Chinthalapally V. Rao, Division of Nutritional Carcinogenesis, American Health Foundation, "Chemoprevention of Colon Cancer by Thiol and Sulfur-Containing Compounds," paper presented at the 204th American Chemical Society Meeting, Washington, D.C., August 24, 1992.

14. Dragsted et al., "Cancer-protective factors."

15. Reddy and Rao, "Chemoprevention of Colon Cancer."

16. J. A. Albrecht, H. W. Schafer, and E. A. Zottola, *Journal of Food Science and Nutrition* 55, no. 1 (1990):181–83.

17. Dragsted et al., "Cancer-protective factors."

18. G. D. Stoner et al., "Inhibitory Effects of Phenethyl Isothiocyanate on N-nitrosobenzylmethylamine Carcinogenesis in the Rat Esophagus," *Cancer Research* 51, no. 8 (April 15, 1991):2063–68.

19. K. Doerr-O'Rourke et al., "Effect of phenethyl isothiocyanate on the metabolism of the tobacco-specific nitrosamine 4-(methylnitrosamino)-1-(3-pyridyl)-1-butanone by cultured rat lung tissue," *Carcinogenesis* 12, no. 6 (June 1991):1029–34.

20. R. M. Speights and P. J. Perna, "Fructo-O Gliosaccharides: Multifunctional and Healthful Carbohydrates from Sucrose," paper presented at the Fourth Chemical Congress of North America, New York, New York, August 26, 1991.

21. Stephen Barnes, "The Isoflavone Genistein: A Good Reason for Eating Soy," paper presented at the 208th American Cancer Society National Meeting, Washington, D.C., August 21, 1994.

22. Reddy and Rao, "Chemoprevention of Colon Cancer."

23. Rodolfo Saracci, "The Diet and Cancer Hypothesis: Current Trends," *Medical Oncology and Tumor Pharmacotherapy* 7, no. 2/3 (1990):99-107.

24. Natalie Angier, "Chemists Learn Why Vegetables Are Good for You," *New York Times*, April 13, 1993, p. C1.

25. G. Howe et al., "Dietary Intake of Fiber and Decreased Risk of Cancer of the Colon and Rectum," *Journal of the National Cancer Institute* 16:84, no. 24 (December 1992):1887–96.

26. "Use Natural Food to Increase the Fiber Content of Your Diet," *Mayo Clinic Health Letter* 4, no. 3 (March 1986):1.

27. H. Benjamin et al., "Inhibition of benzo(a)pyrene-induced mouse forestomach neoplasia by dietary soy sauce," *Cancer Research* 51, no. 11 (June 1, 1991):2940–42.

28. P. C. Billing, P. M. Newberne, and A. R. Kennedy, "Protease Inhibitor Suppression of Colon and Anal Gland Carcinogenesis Induced by Dimethylhydrazine," *Carcinogenesis* 11, no. 7 (July 1990):1083–86; M. Messina and S. Barnes, "The role of soy products in reducing risk of cancer," *Journal of the National Cancer Institute* 83, no. 8 (April 17, 1991):541–46.

29. Michael W. Pariza, paper on soybeans presented at the American Chemical Society Meeting, Washington, D.C., August 24, 1992.

30. *Proceedings of the National Academy of Sciences* (April 1992).

31. L. Schweigerer and T. Fotsis, "Angiogenesis and angiogenesis inhibitors in pediatric diseases," *European Journal of Pediatrics* 151, no. 7 (July 1992):472–76.

32. Stephen Barnes et al., "Soybeans Inhibit Mammary Tumors in Models of Breast Cancer," *Mutagens and Carcinogens in the Diet* (New York: Wiley-Liss, 1990), 239–53.

33. G. Peterson and S. Barnes, "Genistein and biochanin A inhibit the growth of human prostate cancer cells but not epidermal growth factor receptor tyrosine autophosphorylation," *Prostate* 22, no. 4 (1992):335–45; F. Traganos et al., "Effects of genistein on the growth and cell cycle progression of normal human lymphocytes and human leukemia MOLT-4 and hl-60 cells," *Cancer Research* 52, no. 22 (November 15, 1992):6200–08; K. Kiguchi et al., "Genistein-induced cell differentiation and protein-linked DNA strand breakage in human melanoma cells," *Cancer Communication* 2, no. 8 (1990):271–77.

34. Stephen Barnes, "The Isoflavone Genistein: A Good Reason for Eating Soy," paper presented at the 208th American Cancer Society National Meeting, Washington, D.C., August 21, 1994.

35. Johanna Dwyer, *Journal of the American Dietetic Association* (1994):739–43.

36. Kim Mujo, managing director, Central Research Laboratories, Japan, "Preventive Effect of Green Tea Polyphenols on Rat Colon Carcinogenesis," paper presented at the 204th American Chemical Society National Meeting, Washington, D.C., August 23, 1992.

37. C. S. Yang and Z. Y. Wang, "Tea and Cancer Prevention," paper presented at the 208th American Chemical Society Meeting, Washington D.C., August 21, 1994.

38. Yukihiko Hara, Ph.D., general manager, Food Research Laboratories, Mitsui Norin Co., Japan, "Prophylactic Functions of Tea Polyphenols," paper presented at the 204th American Chemical Society Meeting, Washington, D.C., August 23, 1992.

39. Mujo, managing director, Central Research Laboratories, Japan, "Preventive Effect of Green Tea."

40. American Medical Association Council on Scientific Affairs, "Diet and Cancer: Where Do Matters Stand?" *Archives of Internal Medicine* 153 (January 11, 1993):50–58.

41. Y. Zhang et al., "A Major Inducer of Anticarcinogenic Protective Enzymes From Broccoli: Isolation and Elucidation of Structure," *Proceedings of the National Academy of Sciences* 89, no. 6 (March 15, 1992):2399–403.

42. J. J. Michnovicz and H. L. Bradlow, "Induction of Estradiol Metabolism by Dietary Indole-3-carbinol," *Journal of the National Cancer Institute* 82, no. 11 (June 6, 1990):947–49.

43. H. L. Bradlow et al., "Effects of dietary indole-3-carbinol on estradiol metabolism and spontaneous mammary tumors in mice," *Carcinogenesis* 12, no. 9 (September 1991):1571–74.

44. Ibid.

45. Christopher Beecher, Ph.D., University of Illinois College of Pharmacy, paper presented at Rutgers University's "Symposium on Phytochemicals," Piscataway, New Jersey, March 16–17, 1993.

46. *RD: Research and Development* 24 (March 1992):34.

47. Ellen Miseo, Ph.D., "Phytochemicals in Citrus Juice Could Contain Natural Anticancer Compounds," presented at the 204th American Chemical Society National Meeting, Washington, D.C., August 23, 1992.

48. John Attaway, director of scientific research, State of Florida Department of Citrus, "Citrus Juice Flavonoids With Anticancer Properties," presented at the 204th American Chemical Society National Meeting, Washington, D.C., August 28, 1992.

49. Ibid.

50. Marc Bracke, "The Citrus Flavonoid Tangeretin Enha ces Cell-Cell Adhesion and Inhibits Invarions of Human MCF-7/6 Breast Carcinoma Cells," paper presented at 208th American Chemical Society National Meeting, August 21, 1994, Washington, D.C.; Widmer W. W. et al., "The Potential for Citrus Phytochemicals in Hypernutritious Foods," paper presented at the 208th American Chemical Society National Meeting, Washington, D.C., August 21, 1994.

51. Ibid.

52. M. A. Helser, J. H. Hotchkiss, D. A. Roe, "Influence of fruit and vegetable juices on the endogenous formation of nitrosoproline and N-nitrosothiazolidine-4-carboxylic acid in humans on controlled diets," *Carcinogenesis* 13, no. 12 (December 1992):2277–80.

53. Y. H. Heur et al., "Synthesis of Ellagic Acid."

54. Alan Conney, Ph.D., paper on antioxidants presented at Rutgers Continuing Professional Education in Food Science Course "Designer Foods II," Piscataway, New Jersey, March 16–17, 1993.

55. S. Belman et al., "Papilloma and carcinoma production in DMBA-initiated, onion-oil-promoted mouse skin," *Nutrition and Cancer* 14, no. 2 (1990):141–48.

56. Michael Weiner, Ph.D., *Weiner's Herbal* (Mill Valley, Calif: Quantam Books, 1990), 243.

57. *RD: Research and Development* 24 (March 1992):34.

58. K. W. Singletary and J. M. Nelshoppen, "Inhibition of 7,12-dimethyl-benz(a)anthracene (DMBA)–induced mammary tumorigenesis and of in vivo formation of mammary DMBA-DNA adducts by rosemary extract," *Cancer Letter* 60, no. 2 (November 1991):169–75.

59. O. I. Aruoma et al., "Antioxidant and pro-oxidant properties of active rosemary constituents: carnosol and carnosic acid," *Xenobiotica* 22, no. 2 (February 1992):257–68.

60. H. T. Huang, "Rosemary," paper presented at Rutgers University's "Symposium on Phytochemicals," Piscataway, New Jersey, March 16–17, 1993.

61. Karen Schaich, Ph.D., "Curcuminoids," paper presented at Rutgers University's "Symposium on Phytochemicals," Piscataway, New Jersey, March 16–17, 1993.

62. H. H. Tnesen et al., "Studies on curcumin and curcuminoids," *Journal of Pharmaceutical Science* 76, no. 5, (May 1987):371–73.

63. Regina Zeigler, Ph.D., MPH, "Studies of Cancer-Fighting Foods Show Promise but Aren't Yet Conclusive," paper presented at "Nutrition in the 90s: Setting the Table for the Future," sponsored by the American Medical Association, New York, New York, January 14, 1993.

64. Dragsted et al., "Cancer-Protective Factors."

65. Martin Lipkin, M.D. and Harold Newmark, M.S., "Effect of Added Dietary Calcium on Colonic Epithelial-Cell Proliferation In Subjects At High Risk for Familial Colonic Cancer," *The New England Journal of Medicine* 313, no. 22 (November 28, 1985):1381–88.

66. Ibid.

67. Paul Newberne et al., "Experimental Evidence on the Nutritional Preven-

tion of Cancer," *Nutrition and Cancer Prevention,* eds. Thomas Moon and Marc Micozzi (New York: Marcel Dekker, 1989), 65.

68. B. S. Reddy et al., "Chemoprevention of Colon Carcinogenesis by the Synthetic Organoselenium Compound 1,4-phenylenebis (methylene) selenocyanate," Division of Nutritional Carcinogenesis, American Health Foundation, Valhalla, New York.

69. Ibid.

70. Steven Zeisel, M.D., Ph.D., "Choline: An Important Nutrient in Brain Development, Liver Function and Carcinogenesis," *Journal of the American College of Nutrition* 11, no. 5 (1992):473–81.

Chapter 4: Diet and the Heart at Risk

1. C. A. Barger, professor of physiology, Harvard Medical School, paper presented at the American Heart Association's Twelfth Science Writers Forum, Monterey, California, January 13–16, 1985.

2. *1992 Heart and Stroke Facts* (Dallas, Texas: American Heart Association).

3. "Lowering Blood Cholesterol to Prevent Heart Disease," *Journal of the American Medical Association* 253, no. 14 (April 12, 1985):2080–86.

4. *1992 Heart and Stroke Facts.*

5. *1992 Heart and Stroke Facts,* 13.

6. "Triglyceride, High Density Lipoprotein and Coronary Heart Disease," *National Institutes of Health Consensus Statement* 10, no. 9 (February 26–28, 1992).

7. J. Fruebis, S. Parthasarathy, and D. Steinberg, "Evidence for a concerted reaction between lipid hydroperoxides and polypeptides," *Proceedings of the National Academy of Sciences* 89, no. 22 (November 15, 1992):10588–92.

8. G. M. Rubanyi, "Vascular Effects of Oxygen-Derived Free Radicals," *Free Radical Biological Medicine* 4 (1988):107–120.

9. *1992 Heart and Stroke Facts,* 13.

10. D. Atkins et al., "Cholesterol Reduction and the Risk for Stroke in Men—A Meta-analysis of Randomized, Controlled Trials," *Annals of Internal Medicine* 119, no. 2 (July 15, 1993):136–45.

11. *1992 Heart and Stroke Facts*, 11.

12. Gerald Reaven, M.D., professor of medicine and diabetes, Stanford University, Stanford University news release, September 24, 1986.

13. *1992 Heart and Stroke Facts*, 4.

14. Ibid.

15. Ibid.

Chapter 5: Nutraceuticals That Combat Cardiovascular Disease

1. M. J. Stampler et al., "Vitamin E Consumption and the Risk of Coronary Disease in Women," and E. B. Rimm et al., "Vitamin E Consumption and the Risk of Coronary Heart Disease in Men," *The New England Journal of Medicine* 328 (1993):1444.

2. M. Steiner, "Effects of vitamin E on platelet function and thrombosis," *Agents Actions* 22 (1987):357–58.

3. *1992 Heart and Stroke Facts*, 4.

4. M. J. Stampler et al., "Vitamin E Coronary Heart Disease in Women," and E. B. Rimm et al., "Vitamin E Coronary Heart Disease in Men."

5. S. K. Gaby and L. J. Machlin, "Vitamin E," *Vitamin Intake and Health: A Scientific Review* (New York: Marcel Dekker, 1991), 71–101.

6. Ibid.

7. Terrence Yau, "Vitamin E May Safeguard Bypass Hearts" (paper presented at the American Heart Association Meeting, Dallas, 1990) *Science News*, November 24, 1990, p. 333.

8. K. F. Gey et al., "Plasma Levels of Antioxidant Vitamins in Relation to Ischemic Heart Disease and Cancer," *American Journal of Clinical Nutrition* 45 (1987):1368–77.

9. David Stipp, "Studies Showing Benefits of Antioxidants Prove Potent Tonic for Sales of Vitamin E," *Wall Street Journal*, April 13, 1991, p. B1.

10. M. J. Pinsky, "Treatment of Intermittent Claudication with Alpha-tocopherol," *Journal of the American Podiatry Association* 70 (1980):454–58.

11. C. V. Soong et al., "Lipid peroxidation as a cause of lower-limb swelling following femoro-popliteal bypass grafting," *European Journal of Vascular Surgery* 7, no. 5 (September 1993):540–45.

12. "Vitamin-Rich Blood May Prevent Angina," *Science News*, January 12, 1991, p. 23.

13. Orvile Lavander, "People Can't Substantially Raise Vitamin E Levels in Their Blood by Diet Alone," *Quarterly Report of Selected Research Projects* (United States Department of Agriculture, Agricultural Research Service) (April 1–June 30, 1993):9.

14. Joseph Palca, "Vitamin C Gets a Little Respect," *Science* 254 (October 18, 1991):373–76.

15. Gaby and Machlin, "Vitamin E."

16. Paul Jacques, ScD, "Relationship of Vitamin C Status to Cholesterol and Blood Pressure," paper presented at the New York Academy of Sciences seminar "Beyond Deficiency: New Views on the Function and Health Effects of Vitamins," New York City, February 9–12, 1992.

17. Ibid.

18. S. K. Gaby and V. N. Singh, "Vitamin C," *Vitamin Intake and Health: A Scientific Review*, eds. Suzanne Gaby, Adrianne Bendich, Vishwa Singh, and Lawrence Machlin (New York: Marcell Dekker, 1991), 123–25.

19. R. M. Acheson and Dr. Willaims, "Does Consumption of Fruit and Vegetables Protect Against Stroke?" *The Lancet* 1 (1993):1191–93.

20. *Science News* 137 (May 12, 1990):292.

21. E. Ginter and V. Chovathova, "Vitamin C and Diabetes Mellitus," *Nutrition and Health: A Scientific Review* (New York: Marcel Dekker, 1991); S. K. Gaby and V. N. Singh, "Vitamin C," in *Vitamin Intake and Health: A Scientific Review* (New York: Marcel Dekker, 1991).

22. B. D. Cox, W. J. Butterfield, "Vitamin C Supplements and Diabetic Cutaneous Capillary Fragility," *British Medical Journal* 3 (1975):205.

23. Robert E. Pecoraro, M.D. and Mei Chen, M.D., "Ascorbic Acid Metabolism in Diabetes Mellitus," *Annals New York Academy of Science* 498 (1987):248–58.

24. D. A. McCarron et al., "Blood Pressure and Nutrient Intake in the U.S.," *Science* 224 (1984):1392–98.

25. *Science News* 137 (June 9, 1990):367.

26. *Science News* 137 (June 9, 1990):367.

27. J. M. Graziano et al., "Beta-carotene Therapy for Chronic Stable Angina," *Circulation* 82, suppl. 2–5 (1990).

28. "Long-term study finds carotenoids can reduce heart attack," *University of North Carolina News Reports* (February 25, 1994).

29. S. K. Gaby, "Vitamin B_6," paper presented at "Vitamin Intake and Health: A Scientific Review," sponsored by the New York Academy of Sciences, New York, New York, February 1992.

30. S. K. Gaby and A. Bendich, "Vitamin B_{12}," in *Vitamin Intake and Health: A Scientific Review* (New York: Marcel Dekker, 1991), 193–97.

31. S. K. Gaby and A. Bendich, "Vitamin B_6," in *Vitamin Intake and Health: A Scientific Review* (New York: Marcel Dekker, 1991), 163–74.

32. S. K. Gaby and A. Bendich, "Folic Acid," in *Vitamin Intake and Health: A Scientific Review* (New York: Marcel Dekker, 1991), 175–83.

33. P. L. Canner et al., "Fifteen-year mortality in coronary drug-project patients: long-term benefit with niacin," *American College of Cardiology* 8 (1986):1245–55.

34. S. K. Gaby, "Niacin," in *Vitamin Intake and Health: A Scientific Review* (New York: Marcel Dekker, 1991), 189–91.

35. Dawn Jones, "The Secrets of Vitamin K," *Touchstone* (University of Wisconsin) (January 1990):17–21.

36. M. de Lorgeril et al., "Mediterranean Alpha-Linolenic Acid-Rich Diet in Secondary Prevention of Coronary Heart Disease," *The Lancet* 343 (1994):1454–54.

37. K. Folkers et al., "Biochemical rationale and myocardial tissue data on the effective therapy of cardiomyopathy with coenzyme Q_{10}," *Proceedings of the National Academy of Sciences* 82, no. 3 (1985):901–4.

38. T. Fujioka et al., "Clinical study of cardiac arrhythmias using a 24-hour continuous electrocardiography recorder: Antiarrhythmic action of coenzyme Q_{10} in diabetics," *Tohoku Journal of Experimental Medicine* 141 (suppl) (1983):453–63; S. Imanishi et al., "CoQ_{10} and Supraventricular Tachyarrhythmias," *Japanese Journal of Experimental Medicine* 58 (1981):216–19.

39. J. B. Lombardini and M. W. Cooper, "Elevated blood taurine levels in acute and evolving myocardial infarction," *Journal of Laboratory Clinical Medicine* 98, no. 6 (1981):849–59.

40. T. Fujita et al., "Effects of increased adrenomedullary activity and taurine in young patients with borderline hypertension," *Circulation* 75 (1987):525.

41. J. M. Belizan et al., "Reduction of blood pressure with calcium supplemen-

tation in young adults," *Journal of the American Medical Association* 249 (1983):1161–65.

42. "Calcium Supplement May Lower Cholesterol," *University of Texas Lifetime Health Letter* (March 1993):8.

43. "Yet Another Reason to Drink Your Milk," *Tufts University Diet and Nutrition Letter* 9, no. 11 (January 1992):1.

44. R. B. Singh et al., "Nutritional Modulators of Lipoprotein Metabolism in Patients with Risk Factors for Coronary Heart Disease: Diet and Moderate Exercise Trial," *Journal of the American College of Nutrition* 11, no. 3 (1992):391–98.

45. D. M. Roden, "Magnesium treatment of ventricular arrhythmias," *American Journal of Cardiology* 63, no. 14 (1989):43g–46g; C. DeCarli et al., "Serum magnesium levels in symptomatic atrial fibrillation and their relation to rhythm control by intravenous digoxin," *American Journal of Cardiology* 57 (1986):956–59.

46. B. M. Altura and B. T. Altura, "Cardiovascular risk factors and magnesium: relationships to atherosclerosis, ischemic heart disease and hypertension," *Magnesium Trace Element: A Review* 10, nos. 2–4 (1992–92):182–92.

47. S.S. Gottlieb et al., "Effects of Intravenous Magnesium Sulfate on Arrhythmias in Patients With Congestive Heart Failure," *American Heart Journal* 125, no. 6 (June 1993):1645–50.

48. Pat Phillips, "Magnesium May Extend Survival After Myocardial Infarctions," *Medical Tribune* (September 23, 1993):2.

49. B. M. Altura and B. T. Altura, "Cardiovascular risk factors and magnesium: relationships to atherosclerosis, ischemic heart disease, and hypertension," *Magnesium Trace Element: A Review* 88, (1993):451–73.

50. "Magnesium: Potential Benefits for the Heart, Bones and More," *University of Texas Lifetime Health Letter* 65, no. 5 (May 1993):1.

51. Kent Woods and Susan Fletcher, "Long-term outcome after intravenous magnesium sulphate in suspected acute myocardial infarction: the second Leicester Intravenous Magnesium Intervention Trial (Limit-2)," *The Lancet* 343 (April 2, 1994):816–19.

52. Mildred Seelig, M.D., MPH, "Cardiovascular Consequences of Magnesium Deficiency and Loss: Pathogenesis, Prevalence and Manifestations— Magnesium and Chloride Loss in Refractory Potassium Repletion," *American Journal of Cardiology* 63 (1989):4g–21g.

53. Robert Lewis et al., "Effect of Manganese on High-Density and Low-Density Lipoprotein in Sprague Dawley Rats" (Departments of Chemistry and Nutrition, University of Maine, Orono, Maine 04469).

54. Louis Tobian, M.D., "Cavemen's Diet," paper presented at the American Heart Association's Twelfth Science Writers Forum, Monterey, California, January 13–16, 1985.

55. M. F. McCarty, "Insulin Resistance in Mexican Americans—A Precursor to Obesity and Diabetes?" *Nutrition 21 Medical Hypotheses* 41, no. 4 (October 1993):308–15.

56. Richard Anderson, *Agricultural Research Service Research Briefs* (April–June 1991):8.

57. Forrest Nielsen and David Milne, "Diets high in sugar fructose significantly increased cholesterol levels," *Quarterly Report of Selected Research Projects* (USDA, Agricultural Research Service) (January 1–March 31, 1993):11.

58. Jack Sari, *Agricultural Research Service Research Briefs* (April–June 1991):4.

59. *Quarterly Report* (USDA, Agricultural Research Service) (July–September 1992):3.

60. L. M. Klevay and J. L. Sullivan, "The iron paradigm of ischemic heart disease," *American Heart Journal* 117 (1989):1188.

61. "But Maybe You Should Watch the Tea," *Science News* 133 (March 12, 1988):174.

62. *Research and Science*, report from North Shore University Hospital—Cornell University Medical College (June 1994):1.

Chapter 6: Plants That Help the Heart

1. James Duke, "Some Folk Remedies for Diabetes," *Quarterly Report of Selected Research Projects* (United States Department of Agriculture) (April 1–June 30, 1993):9.

2. Robert Baker, "Potential Dietary Benefits of Citrus Pectin and Fiber," paper presented at "Nutrition and Health Benefits of Citrus Products," Institute of Food Technologists Meeting, Chicago, Illinois, July 10–14, 1993.

3. James Cerda, "The Role of Pectin in Cholesterol Regulation," paper presented at the 208th American Chemical Society Meeting, Washington, D.C., August 23, 1994.

4. L. F. Tinker et al., "Consumption of Prunes as a Source of Dietary Fiber in Men With Mild Hypercholesterolemia," *American Journal of Clinical Nutrition* 53, no. 5 (May 1991):1259–65.

5. "Prune fiber or pectin compared with cellulose lowers plasma and liver lipids in rats with diet-induced hyerlipidemia," *Journal of Nutrition* 124, no. 1 (January 1994):31–40.

6. Joan Sabate, M.D., et al., "Effects of Walnuts on Serum Lipid Levels and Blood Pressure in Normal Men," *The New England Journal of Medicine* 328 (1993):603–7.

7. Norman Salem, Jr. et al., "Purslane" (letter), *The New England Journal of Medicine* (November 16, 1989).

8. Yukihiko Hara, Ph.D., general manager, Food Research Laboratories, Mitsui Norin Co., Japan, "Prophylactic Functions of Tea Polyphenols," and Kim Mujo, managing director, Central Research Laboratories, Japan, "Preventive Effect of Green Tea Polyphenols on Rat Colon Carcinogenesis," papers presented at the 204th American Chemical Society National Meeting, Washington, D.C., August 23, 1992.

9. Andrew Waterhouse, Edwin Frankel, and J. Bruce German, et al., "The Phenolic Antitoxidants in Wine: Levels and Effects," paper presented at the 208th American Chemical Society Meeting, Washington, D.C., August 22, 1994.

10. C. Baum-Baicker, "The Health Benefits of Moderate Alcohol Consumption: A Review of the Literature," *Drug Alcohol Dependence* 3 (June 15, 1985):207–27.

11. "Garlic Medicine: Cures in Cloves?" *Science News*, September 8, 1990, p. 157.

12. John O'Brien, "The First World Congress on the Health Significance of Garlic and Garlic Constituents," *Trends in Food Science and Technology* (Elsevier Science Publishers) (December 1990):155–57.

13. Ibid.

14. Nilofer, Qureshi, "Hypocholesterolaemic Effect of Dietary Commerical Garlic Powder, Aged Garlic Extract, Garlic Oil or Allyl Cysteine," paper presented at First World Congress on the Health Significance of Garlic and Garlic Constituents, Washington, D.C., August 28–30, 1990.

15. "Garlic Effective in Hypercholesterolaemia," *Journal of the Royal College of Physicians* (January/February 1994).

Chapter 7: Fish, Fat, and the Healthy Heart

1. D. Kromhout et al., "The Inverse Relation Between Fish Consumption and 20-Year Mortality from Coronary Heart Disease," *The New England Journal of Medicine* 312 (1985):1205.

2. Jim Matthews, "Pharmaceutical Perspectives on Omega-3," paper presented at "Designer Foods II: Phytochemicals in Disease Prevention," sponsored by Rutgers University Department of Food Science, Piscataway, New Jersey, March 16–17, 1993.

3. Charles Marwick, "International Conference Gives Boost to Including Omega Fatty Acids in Diet," *Journal of the American Medical Association* 263, no. 16 (April 25, 1990):2152–53.

4. J. A. Glomset, "Fish, Fatty Acids and Human Health," *The New England Journal of Medicine* 312 (1985):1253.

5. Ibid.

6. B. E. Phillipson et al., "Reduction of Plasma Lipids, Lipoproteins and Apoproteins by Dietary Fish Oils in Patients with Hypertriglyceridemia," *The New England Journal of Medicine* 312 (1985):1210.

7. "Fish Oil Helps Keep Newly Opened Coronary Arteries Clear," *University of Texas Lifetime Health Letter* (September 1993):6.

8. *The New England Journal of Medicine* 319 (1988):733; *Journal of the American College of Cardiology* 9 (1987):64A; *Circulation* 78, suppl. 20: II (1988):634.

9. "International Conference Gives Boost to Including Omega Fatty Acids in Diet," *Journal of the American Medical Association* 263, no. 16 (April 25, 1990):2153–54.

10. *Gallagher Report* (January 28, 1985).

11. Kromhout et al., "The Inverse Relation."

12. J. Matthews, "Pharmaceutical Perspectives on Omega-3," paper presented at Designer Foods II: Phytochemicals in Disease Prevention, Rutgers University Department of Food Science, Piscataway, New Jersey, March 16–17.

13. Ibid.

14. "A Prudent Diet Enhanced With Fruits, Vegetables and Complex Carbohydrates Cuts Heart Disease Risk," *University of Texas Lifetime Health Letter* (September 1993):6.

15. M. Wheeler et al., "Metabolic Response to Oral Challenge of Hydrogenated Starch Hydrolysate Versus Glucose in Diabetes," *Diabetes Care* 13, no. 7 (July 1990):773–840.

Chapter 8: Nutraceuticals That Boost Immunity

1. W. R. Beisel, "History of nutritional immunology: introduction and overview," *Journal of Nutrition* 122, suppl. 3 (March 1992):591–96.

2. "The Language of the Cells," *UCSF Magazine* 3, no. 2–3 (June–September 1980):4–6; "Taming Rogue Immune Reactions," *Science*, July 20, 1990, p. 249.

3. Ronald R. Watson, Ph.D., "Nutrition and Immunity," *Contemporary Nutrition* 6, no. 5 (May 1981).

4. J. B. Blumberg, "Considerations of the RDA for Older Adults," *Clinics in Applied Nutrition* 1 (1991):9–18.

5. Bruce Ames, Ph.D., Introductory remarks, 1992 VNIS Health Communicators Conference, Captiva Island, Florida, March 27–29, 1992.

6. J. S. Prasad, "Effect of vitamin E supplementation on leukocyte function," *American Journal of Clinical Nutrition* 33 (1980):606–8.

7. M. Kamimura, "Anti-inflammatory activity of vitamin E," *Journal of Vitaminology* 18, no. 4 (1972):204–9.

8. W. R. Beisel, "Single Nutrients and Immunity," *American Journal of Clinical Nutrition* 35 (suppl.) (1982):417–68.

9. R. L. Baehner et al., "Autooxidation as a Basis for Altered Function By Polymorphonuclear Leukocytes," *Blood* 50, no. 2 (August, 1977): 321–35.

10. Simin N. Meydani, M. Meydani, et al., "Effects of Vitamin E Supplementation on Immune Responsiveness in the Aged," *Annals of the New York Academy of Sciences* 570 (1989):283–90.

11. R. K. Chandra, "Effect of vitamin and trace-element supplementation on immune responses and infection in elderly subjects," *The Lancet* 341 (January 30, 1993):306–7.

12. M. Chavance et al., "Immunologic and nutritional status among the elderly," in *Lyphoid Cell Functions in Aging*, ed. A. L. deWeek (Rijswijk, Netherlands: Evrage, 1984).

13. R. E. Hodges et al., "Factors affecting human antibody response: pyridoxine deficiencies," *American Journal of Clinical Nutrition* 11 (1962):180–86.

14. Research program description, United States Department of Agriculture Human Nutrition Research Center on Aging at Tufts University, Boston, 1992.

15. "Vitamins May Boost Immunity in Elderly," *University of Texas Lifetime Health Letter* 5, no. 1 (January 1993):7.

16. A. E. Axelrod, "Immune processes in vitamin-deficiency states," *American Journal of Clinical Nutrition* 24, (1971):265–71.

17. R. Anderson, "The immunostimulatory, anti-inflammatory and anti-allergic properties of ascorbate," in *Advances in Nutritional Research*, vol. 6, ed. H. H. Draper (New York: Plenum Press, 1984), 19–45.

18. A. Bendich, "Vitamin C and immune responses," *Food Technology* 41, (1987):112–14.

19. Robert Jacobs, "Skimping on Vitamin C," *Agricultural Research Service Briefs* (July–September 1992):1.

20. "Supplements of glutathione may boost older people's flagging immune response," *Quarterly Report of Selected Research Projects* (USDA, Agricultural Research Service) (July–September 1993):6.

21. A. Sommer et al., "Increased Risk of Respiratory Disease and Diarrhea in Children with Preexisting Mild Vitamin A Deficiency," *American Journal of Clinical Nutrition* 40 (1984):1090–95.

22. W. R. Beisel et al., "Single-Nutrient Effects on Immunologic Functions," *Journal of the American Medical Association* 245, no.1 (January 2, 1981):53–58.

23. Beisel, "Single Nutrients and Immunity."

24. Sommer et al., *American Journal of Clinical Nutrition* 40 (1984):1090–95.

25. "Vitamin A Treatment Recommended for Children Hospitalized With Measles," *Pediatrics*, June 1993, p. 26.

26. "Vitamin A Supplementation and Childhood Morbidity," *The Lancet* 342 (December 4, 1993):1420–21.

27. M. L. Barreto et al., "Effect of Vitamin A Supplementation on Diarrhea and Acute Lower-Respiratory-Tract Infections in Young Children in Brazil," *The Lancet* 344 (1994):228–31.

28. William Gottlieb, "Encyclopedia of Minerals," in *Sourcebook on Food and Nutrition*, 3d ed. (Chicago: Marquis Academic Media, 1982):102–8.

29. R. K. Chandra et al., "Iron status, immune response and susceptibility to infection," in *Iron Metabolism* (Ciba Foundation Symposium 51), ed. H. Kies, (Amsterdam: Elsevier/Excerpta Medica/North-Holland, 1977):249–68.

30. John Britton et al., "Dietary Magnesium, Lung Function, Wheezing, and Airway Hyper-reactivity in a Random Adult Population Sample," *The Lancet* 334 (August 6, 1994):357–62.

31. J. D. Bogen et al., "Zinc and immunocompetence in elderly people: effects of zinc supplementation for three months," *American Journal of Clinical Nutrtion* 48 (1988):655–63.

32. I. Lombeck et al., "Hair zinc of young children from rural and urban areas in North Rhine–Westphalia," *European Journal of Pediatrics* 147, no. 2 (1988):179–83; J. P. van Wouwe et al., "Subacute zinc deficiency in children with recurrent upper respiratory tract infections," *European Journal of Pediatrics* 146, no. 3 (1987):293–95.

33. W. Al-Nakib et al., "Prophylaxis and treatment of rhinovirus colds with zinc gluconate lozenges," *Journal of Antimicrobial Chemotherapy* 20, no. 6 (1987):893–97.

34. G. A. Eby, D. R. Davis, and W. W. Halcomb, "Reduction in duration of common colds by zinc gluconate lozenges in a double-blind study," *Antimicrobial Agents Chemotherapy* 25, no. 1 (1984):20–24.

35. R. K. Chandra, "Excessive Intake of Zinc Impairs Immune Responses," *Journal of the American Medical Association* 252, no. 11 (1984):1443–46.

36. Dayong Wu and Simin Meydani, "Antioxidant Glutathione and Immunity," paper presented at Experimental Biology 94, Anaheim, California, April 24–28, 1994.

Chapter 9: Plants, Minerals, and Vitamins That Fight Infections From Colds to AIDS

1. Kitta MacPherson, "Pill-packing plants: infection-fighting role discovered for aspirin's relative," *Newark Star-Ledger*, December 17, 1993, p. 41.

2. Yukihiko Hara, Ph.D., general manager, Food Research Laboratories, Mitsui Norin Co., Japan, "Prophylactic Functions of Tea Polyphenols," paper presented at the 204th American Chemical Society Meeting, Washington, D.C., August 23, 1992.

3. *University of Texas Lifetime Health Letter* (March 1993):2.

4. Kevin Tracy, M.D., "Cost of Common Cold," *Medical News Alert* (Univer-

sity of California, Davis Medical Center) (February 1993).

5. R. L. Korets, "My Grandmother's Intravenous Chicken Soup," *Gastroenterology* 105, no. 1 (July 1993):299–300; S. G. Cohen, "The chicken in history and in the soup," *Allergy Proceedings* 13, no. 2 (March–April 1992):105–12; "Excerpts from classics on chicken soup, *Allergy Proceedings* 12, no. 1 (January–February 1991):57–59, (discussion) 47–56.

6. "Chicken Soup Passes a Scientific Examination," press release from the American Lung Association, San Francisco, California, May 17, 1993.

7. Sandra Blakeslee, *New York Times*, November, 22 1994, p. c3.

8. Linus Pauling, Ph.D., "Why you need vitamin C to fight your cold," *Medical Tribune*, Educational Service, "The Good Drugs Do Better Your Health," 1970.

9. Margaret Morrison, "What About Vitamin C?" *FDA Consumer* (October 1974) (publication no. [FDA] 75-2015).

10. "Does Vitamin C Clear the Smoke?," *Science* 265 (August 12, 1994):871.

11. S. K. Gaby and V. N. Singh, "Vitamin C," in *Vitamin Intake and Health: A Scientific Review* (New York: Marcel Dekker, Inc., 1991).

12. K. A. Mink et al., "Amelioration of rhinovirus colds by vitamin C supplementation," *Medical Virology*, eds. L. M. DeLaMaza and E. M. Peterson (New York: Elsevier, 1988), 356.

13. C. A. Clemetson, "Histamine and ascorbic acid in human blood," *Journal of Nutrition* 110, no. 4 (1980):662–68; J. C. Bucca, et al., "Effect of vitamin C on histamine bronchial responsiveness of patients with allergic rhinitis," *Annals of Allergy* 65 (1990):311–14; S. Pavlovic and R. Fraser, "Effects of different levels of vitamin C intake on anaphylaxis," *Medical Intern* 26, no. 3:235–44.

14. "Vitamins may stave off full-blown AIDS," *Medical Tribune*, March 24, 1994, p. 5.

15. Gregg Coodley, M.D., "Beta-carotene and Immune Response in HIV-Infected Patients," paper presented at "Carotenoids in Human Health," symposium sponsored by the New Academy of Sciences, San Diego, California, September 5, 1992.

16. Robert Service, "An Anti-HIV Vitamin?," *Science* 265 (July 15, 1994).

17. Hideo Nakane, research assistant at the Aichi Cancer Center Research Institute in Nagoya, Japan, "Tea polyphenols as a novel class of inhibitors for HIV reverse transcriptase," paper at the 204th American Chemical Society

Meeting, Washington, D.C., August 25, 1992.

18. X. J. Yao, "Mechanism of Inhibition of HIV-1 infection in vitro by purified extract of *Prunella vulgaris,*" *Virology* 187, no. 1 (March 1992):56–62.

Chapter 10: Nutraceuticals to Ease Arthritis and Allergies

1. *Food Allergy: Adverse Reactions to Foods and Food Additives,* eds. by Dean Metcalf, M.D., Hugh Sampsen, M.D., and Ronald Simpson, M.D. (Boston: Blackwell Scientific Publications, 1991).

2. E. C. Barton-Wright and W. A. Elliott, "The pantothenic acid metabolism of rheumatoid arthritis," *The Lancet* 2 (1963):862–63.

3. G. Blankenhorn, "Vitamin E: Clinical research from Europe," *Nutrition Dietary Consult* (June 1988).

4. *Human Nutrition, Quarterly Report of Selected Research Projects* (USDA Agricultural Research Service) (July 1–September 30, 1992), 2.

5. Grand Forks Human Nutrition Research Center, Grand Forks, North Dakota, *Human Nutrition, Quarterly Report of Selected Research Projects* (July 1–September 30, 1992), 4.

6. J. R. Sorenson and W. Hangareter, "Treatment of rheumatoid and degenerative diseases with copper complexes: A review with emphasis on copper salicylate," *Inflammation* 2, no. 3 (1977):217–38.

7. Ibid.

8. R. E. Newham, "Agricultural Practices Affect Arthritis," *Nutrition Health* 7, no. 2 (1991):89–100.

9. "Arthritis or skeletal fluorosis and boron," letter to *International Clinical Nutrition Review* 11, no. 2 (1991):68–70; R. E. Newham, "Boron beats arthritis," *Proc ANZAAS* (Canberra, Australia: Australian Academy of Science, 1979).

10. Samman S. Naghii, M.R., "The Role of Boron in Nutrition and Metabolism," *Progress Food Nutrition Science* 17, no. 4 (1993):331–49.

11. Melvyn Werbach, "Arthritis," in *Nutritional Influences on Illness: A Sourcebook of Clinical Research* (Tarzana, California: Third Line Press, 1993), 578–79.

12. R. I. Sperling, reported in *Medical World News,* July 1986.

13. Simin Meydani, "Eating Fish Every Day of the Week Can Be Too Much," *Quarterly Report of Selected Research Projects* (USDA Agricultural Research

Service) (July 1–September 30, 1993).

14. N. Blumenkrantz and J. G. Asboe-Hansen, "Effect of (+)-catechin on con-
    nective tissue," *Scand J Rheumatol* 7 (1978):55–60.

15. H. Ogasawara, J. E. Middleton Jr., "Effect of selected flavonoids on hista-
    mine release (HR) and hydrogen peroxide (H²O₂) generation by human
    leukocytes," *Journal Allergy Clinical Immunology* 75 (1985):184; H. Neshino,
    "Quercitin interacts with calmodulin, a calcium regulatory protein," *Experi-
    mentia* 40, no. 2 (1984):184–85; J. T. Yoshimoto, et al., "Flavonoids: Potent
    Inhibitors of arachidonate 5-lipoxygenase," *Biochem Biophys REs Commun*
    116 (1983):612–18.

16. D. L. Flynn, M. F. Rafferty, and A. M. Boctor, "Inhibition of 5-hydroxy-
    eicosatetraenoic acid," *Prostaglandins, Leukotrienes and Medicine* 22, no. 3
    (June 1986):357–60.

17. R. Bingham et al., "Yucca plant saponin in the management of arthritis," *J
    App Nutr* 27 (1975):45–50.

18. F. E. Maisel and E. Somkin, "Treatment of asthmatic paroxysms with nico-
    tinic acid," *Journal of Allergy* 13 (1942):397–403.

Chapter 11: Nutraceuticals to Aid Performance: Bones and Muscles

1. Chris Sigurdson, "Eat Your Dinner," *Forefront: Advancing the Forefront of
   Knowledge for Food, Agriculture and Natural Resources* (Purdue University) 4,
   no. 4 (fall 1993).

2. Laurence Demers, Ph.D., "Test to Measure Bone Breakdown," paper presented at the Association of Clinical Scientists, Newport, Rhode Island,
   August 10, 1993.

3. "It's Important, but Don't Bank on Exercise Alone to Prevent Osteoporosis,
   Experts Say," *Journal of the American Medical Association* 263, no. 13 (April 4,
   1990):1751–53.

4. Ian Reid, M.D., et al., "Effect of Calcium Supplementation on Bone Loss in
   Postmenopausal Women," *The New England Journal of Medicine* 328, no. 7
   (February 18, 1993):503-5.

5. Nweze Nnakwe, "The Comparison of Mineral Intake and Excretion of Anabolic Steroid Users and Nonusers," American Chemical Society Meeting,
   Denver, Colorado, April 4, 1993.

6. Gary Curhan, M.D., et al., "A Prospective Study of Dietary Calcium and Other Nutrients and the Risk of Symptomatic Kidney Stones," *The New England Journal of Medicine* 328 (1993):833–38.

7. Reid et al., "Effect of Calcium Supplementation."

8. M. S. Caalvo et al., "Elevated secretion and action of serum parathyroid hormone in young adults consuming high-phosphorus, low-calcium diets assembled from common foods," *Journal of Clinical Endocrinology Metabolism* 66, no. 4 (1988):823–29.

9. Naomi Pfeiffer, "Oral calcitonin tested in UK," *Medical Tribune*, February 16, 1994, p. 9.

10. Marie Chapuy, Ph.D., et al., "Vitamin D_3 and Calcium to Prevent Hip Fractures in Elderly Women," *The New England Journal of Medicine* 327 (1992):1637–42.

11. M. Meydani and S. Meydani, *U.S. Department of Agriculture Research Reports* (April–June 1991):4, 7.

12. Elizabeth Krall, Ph.D., et al., "Effect of vitamin D intake on seasonal variations in parathyroid hormone secretion in postmenopausal women," *The New England Journal of Medicine* 321 (1989):1777–83.

13. Ibid.

14. Julia Maclaughlin and Michael Holick, "Aging Decreases the Capacity of the Human Skin to Produce Vitamin D," *Journal of Clinical Investigation* 7 (October 1985):1536–38.

15. "Osteoporosis," *Merck Manual* (Rahway, New Jersey: Merck & Co., 1987), 1297.

16. News release, Penn State, Hershey, Pennsylvania, August 17, 1993.

17. Neil McAleer, *The Body Almanac* (New York: Doubleday, 1985), 112.

18. M. Hegsted et al., "Urinary calcium and calcium balance in young men as affected by level of protein and phosphorus intake," *Journal of Nutrition* 111 (1981):553–62.

19. Sally Schuette and Helen Linkswiler, "Calcium," in *Present Knowledge in Nutrition* Washington, D.C.: Nutrition Foundation, 1984), 400–409.

20. "New Osteoporosis Therapies Appear Closer," *Journal of the American Medical Association* 263, no. 13 (April 4, 1990):1753.

21. S. T. Harris et al., "Four-year study of intermittent cyclic etidronate treatment of postmenopausal osteoporosis: three years of blinded therapy fol-

lowed by one year of open therapy," *American Journal of Medicine* 95, no. 6 (December 1993):555–56.

22. P. D. Saltman and L. G. Strauss, "Role of trace minerals in osteoporosis," *Journal of the American College of Nutrition* 12, no. 4 (August 1993):384–89.

23. J. Ratoff, "Reasons for boning up on manganese," *Science Digest*, September 27, 1986, p. 199.

24. S. M. Potter, C. V. Kies, and A. Rojhani, "Protein and fat utilization by humans as affected by calcium phosphate, calcium carbonate, and manganese gluconate supplements," *Nutrition* 6, no. 4 (July–August 1990):309–12; C. Kies, "Mineral utilization of vegetarians: impact of variation in fat intake," *American Journal of Clinical Nutrition* 48, suppl. 3 (September 1988):884–87; S. E. Scjeideler, "Interaction of dietary calcium, manganese, and manganese source on chick performance and manganese utilization," *Biological Trace Elements* 29, no. 3 (June 1991):217–28.

25. "Doubt Raised on Bone Disease Treatment," *New York Times*, March 22, 1990, p. 23.

26. "Slow-Release Fluoride Plus Calcium Citrate Checks Osteoporosis" (Southwestern news release, April 18, 1994, from report in *Annals of Internal Medicine*, April 18, 1994).

27. "Eating More Carbohydrates," *Agricultural Research Service Quarterly Research Reports* (May 5, 1993):12.

28. American Dietetic Association, "Nutrition and Physical Fitness," in *Sourcebook on Food and Nutrition* 3 ed. (New Providence, New Jersey: Marquis Academic Media, 1982).

29. "Purdue Study: If You Work Out, Work In More Iron" (special report), February 23, 1993.

30. B. B. Yaspelkis III et al., "Carbohydrate supplementation spares muscle glycogen during variable-intensity exercise," *Journal of Applied Physiology* 75, no. 4 (October 1993):1477–85.

31. Herman Johnson, Ph.D., nutritional physiologist, Agricultural Research Service, "The Requirements for Fluid Replacement During Heavy Sweating and Benefits of Carbohydrates and Minerals," paper presented at the American Chemical Society National Meeting, Colorado, April 1, 1993.

32. M. Meydani and S. Meydani, *U.S. Department of Agriculture Research Reports* (April–June 1991):4, 7.

33. "Vitamin Deficiency Considered in Equine Form of Lou Gehrig's Disease," *Veterinary Viewpoints*, (Cornell University) (Spring 1993):1.

34. David Stipp, "Scientists Pinpoint Gene That Causes Inherited Cases of Lou Gehrig's Disease," *Wall Street Journal*, March 4, 1993, p. 40.

Chapter 12: Nutraceuticals and the Skin

1. Barbara A. Gilchrest, M.D., *Skin and Aging Processes* (Boca Raton, Florida: CRC Press, 1982).

2. American Cancer Society (Atlanta, Georgia), "Cancer Facts and Figures—1993."

3. M. J. Peterson, C. Hansen, and S. Craig, "Clues Provided on How Sunlight Causes Aging of Skin," *Journal of Investigative Dermatology* 99 (1992):440–44.

4. Y. M. Peng et al., "Micronutrient concentrations in paired skin and plasma of patients with actinic keratoses: effect of prolonged retinol supplementation," *Cancer Epidemiology Biomarkers* 2, no. 2 (March–April 1993):145–50.

5. "Your Diet May Defend Against Skin Cancer," *Sun & Skin News* (Skin Cancer Foundation) 10, no. 2 (1993):3.

6. "Cream for wrinkles may fight cancer," *Newark Star-Ledger*, May 18, 1993, p. 2.

7. E. M. Christopher et al., *The New England Journal of Medicine* 329 (1993): 530–35.

8. Gerald Weinstein, M.D., "Retinoic Acid in the Treatment of Photoaged Skin," paper presented at the annual meeting of the American Academy of Dermatology, December 4, 1989.

9. "Can Retin-A Repair Skin Aged by the Sun?" news release from the Skin Cancer Foundation, New York, New York, March 19, 1993.

10. Ibid.

11. Stella Bulengo-Ransby et al., "Topical Tretinoin (Retinoic Acid) Therapy for Hyperpigmented Lesions Caused by Inflammation of the Skin in Black Patients," *The New England Journal of Medicine* 328 (1993):1438–43.

12. D. Darr et al., "Topical vitamin C protects porcine skin from ultraviolet radiation–induced damage," *British Journal of Dermatology* 127, no. 3 (September 1992):247–53.

13. G. G. Meadow, H. F. Pierson, and R. M. Abdallah, "Ascorbate in the treatment of experimental transplanted melanoma" *American Journal of Clinical Nutrition* 54, suppl. 6 (December 1991):1284–91S.

14. Press conference for introduction of Dovonex, Westwood-Squibb, New York City, March 10, 1994.

15. K. Pehr and R. R. Forsey, "Why don't we use vitamin E in dermatology?" *Canadian Medical Association Journal* 149, no. 9 (November 1, 1993):1247–53.

16. "The Beautiful Skin Yogurt Diet and Other Fables," *Tufts University News-Letter* 8, no. 8 (October 1990):3.

17. Stolle Milk Biologics International Skin Care Products informational brochure, May 1988.

Chapter 13: Nutraceuticals for Brain, Mind, and Emotions

1. D. C. Dorman et al., "Effects of an extract of Ginkgo biloba on bromethalin-induced cerebral lipid peroxidation and Edema in Rats," *American Journal of Veterinary Research* 53, no. 1 (January 1992):138–42.

2. X. U. Chang, Ph.D., Chinese Academy of Sciences, "Synthesis of Huperzine A Analogues and Their Inhibitory Activities of Acetylcholinesterase," paper presented at the 206th American Chemical Society Meeting, Chicago, Illinois, August 25, 1993.

3. Alan Kozikowski, "An Improved Synthetic Route to Huperzine A; New Analogues and Their Inhibition of Acetylcholinesterase," paper presented at the 206th American Chemical Society Meeting, Chicago, Illinois, August 25, 1993.

4. William Dicke, "Chinese Herb Remedy Curbs Alcohol Desire," *New York Times*, November 2, 1993, p. 14.

5. S. Goldstein, "The biology of aging: looking to defuse the genetic time bomb," *Geriatrics* 48, no. 9 (September 1993):76–82.

6. I. Shoulson, "An interim report of the effect of selegiline on the progression of disability in early Parkinson's disease," *European Neurology* 32, suppl. 1 (1992):46–53.

7. "Effects of tocopherol and deprenyl on the progression of disability in early Parkinson's disease. The Parkinson Study Group," *The New England Journal of Medicine* 328, no. 23 (June 10, 1993):1715.

8. P. A. Lewitt, "Neuroprotection by anti-oxidant strategies in Parkinson's disease," *European Neurology* 33, suppl. 1 (1993):24–30.

9. S. Fahn, "A pilot trial of high-dose alpha-tocopherol and ascorbate in early Parkinson's disease," *Annals of Neurology* 32, suppl. (1992):128–32S.

10. D. S. Collier et al., "Parkinsonism treatment: Part III—Update," *Annals of Pharmacotherapy* 26, no. 2 (February 1992):227–33.

11. L. Bischot et al., "Vitamin E in extrapyramidal disorders," *Pharmacology World Science* 15, no. 4 (August 20, 1993):146–50.

12. Shantilal N. Shah, Ph.D., and Ronald C. Johnson, Ph.D., "Antioxidant Vitamin A and E Status of Down's Syndrome Subjects," *Nutrition Research* 9 (1989):705–15.

13. G. Milner, "Ascorbic Acid in Chronic Psychiatric Patients—A Controlled Trial," *British Journal of Psychiatry* 109 (1963):294–99; and N. Subramanian, "On the Brain Ascorbic Acid and Its Importance in the Metabolism of Biogenic Amines," *Life Sciences* 20, no. 9 (1991):1479–84.

14. B. Regland et al., "Vitamin B_{12}–induced reduction of platelet monoamine oxidase activity in patients with dementia and pernicious anemia," *European Archives of Psychiatry Clinical Neuroscience* 240, no. 4–5 (1991):288–91.

15. T. Ikeda et al., "Treatment of Alzheimer-type dementia with intravenous mecobalamin," *Clinical Therapeutics* 14, no. 3 (May–June 1992):426–37.

16. L. Parnetti et al., "Platelet MAO-B activity and vitamin B_{12} in old-age dementias," *Molecular Chemistry and Neuropathology* 16, no. 1–2 (February–April 1992):23–32.

17. "Even Mild Lack of B_{12} could hurt seniors," *Diet and Nutrition Letter*, (Tufts University) 9, no. 11 (January 1992):1.

18. E. J. Fine and E. D. Soria, "Myths about Vitamin B_{12} deficiency," *Southern Medical Journal* 84, no. 12 (December 1991):1475–81.

19. J. Dommisse, "Subtle vitamin B_{12} deficiency and psychiatry: a largely unnoticed but devastating relationship," *Medical Hypotheses* 34, no. 2 (February 1991):131–40.

20. Robert Russell, *Agricultural Research Services Research Briefs* (April–June 1991):5.

21. T. R. Guilarte, "Vitamin B_6 and Cognitive Development: Recent Research Findings from Human and Animal Studies," *Nutrition Review* 51, no. 7 (July 1993):193–98.

22. S. K. Gaby, "Vitamin B_6" in *Vitamin Intake and Health: A Scientific Review* (New York: Marcel Dekker, 1991), 163–74.

23. J. R. Saltzman et al., "Bacterial Overgrowth without Clinical Malabsorption in Elderly Hypochlorhydric Subjects," *Gastroenterology* 106, no. 3 (March 1994):615–23.

24. Richard Rivlin, "Riboflavin," in *Present Knowledge in Nutrition*, 5th ed., 318–31. The Nutrition Foundation, Washington, D.C., 1984.

25. E. H. Reynolds, "Interictal Psychiatric Disorders: Neurochemical Aspects," *Advances in Neurology* 55 (1991):47–58.

26. M. I. Boetz, "Neurological Correlates of Folic Acid Deficiency: Facts and Hypotheses," in *Neurology, Psychiatry, and Internal Medicine* (New York: Raven Press, 1979), 435–61.

27. D. Benton and G. Roberts, "Effect of vitamin and mineral supplementation on intelligence of a sample of schoolchildren," *The Lancet* 1 (1988):140–43.

28. Robert Young and John Blass, "Nutrition and the Aged," in *Sourcebook on Food and Nutrition*, 3d ed. (New Providence, New Jersey: Marquis, 1982), 368–72.

29. Arasteh Kaymar, "Elevation of Mood with Calcium and Vitamin D," paper presented at the 95th annual meeting of the American Psychological Association, New York City, August 31, 1987.

30. S. Seltzer et al., "The effects of dietary tryptophan on chronic maxillofacial pain and experimental pain tolerance," *Journal of Psychiatric Research* 17 (1982–83):181–86; T. B. King, "Pain and Tryptophan," *Journal of Neurosurgery* 53, no. 1 (1980):44–55.

31. B. P. Maurizi, "The Therapeutic Potential for Tryptophan and Melatonin: Possible Roles in Depression, Sleep, Alzheimer's Disease and Abnormal Aging," *Medical Hypotheses* 32 (1990):233–42.

32. "Clinical Spectrum of Eosinophilia-Myalgia Syndrome," *Morbidity and Mortality Weekly Report* (Centers for Disease Control) 39, no. 6 (February 16, 1990):1–3.

33. E. H. Reynolds, "Folic Acid, S-adenosyl Methionine and Affective Disorders," *Psychological Medicine* 13, no. 4 (1991):705–10.

34. Arthur Winter, M.D., and Ruth Winter, M.S., *Eat Right Be Bright* (New York: St. Martin's Press, 1988), 193.

35. B. W. Volger, "Alternative in the treatment of memory loss in patients with Alzheimer's disease," *Clinical Pharmacology* 10, no. 6 (June 1991):447–56.

36. "Hot Stuff: Peppers May Stop Pain," *What's Happening in Chemistry?* American Chemical Society's Annual Compendium of Selected Research Highlights (1994):42–43.

37. I. M. C. Clarke, "Peppering Pain," *The Lancet* 342 (November 6, 1993):1130.

38. K. Budd, "Use of D-phenylalanine, an enkephalinase inhibitor, in the treatment of intractable pain," *Advancements in Pain Research Therapy* 5 (1983):305–8.

Chapter 14: Nutraceuticals for Women Only

1. Ken Muse, M.D., "The Premenstrual Syndrome," *Current Science* 3, no. 6 (December 1991):865–69.

2. J. Kleijenen et al., "Vitamin B_6 in the treatment of premenstrual syndrome: a review," *British Journal of Obstetrics and Gynecology* 97 (1990):847–52.

3. C. J. Chuong et al., "Vitamin A levels in premenstrual syndrome," *Fertility and Sterility* 54 (1990):643–47.

4. F. Facchinetti et al., "Oral magnesium successfully relieves premenstrual mood changes," *Obstetrics and Gynecology* 78 (1991):177–81.

5. C. H. Park et al., "Is there etiologic heterogeneity between upper and lower neural-tube defects?" *American Journal of Epidemiology* 136, no. 12 (December 15, 1992):1493–501.

6. J. Mulinare, "Epidemiologic Associations of Multivitamin Supplementation and Occurrence of Neural-Tube Defects," *Annals of New York Academy of Sciences* 678 (1989):130–36.

7. Nitti, Victor "Intravesical capsaician for treatment of neurogenic bladder," *The Lancet* 343 (June 11, 1994):1448.

8. *Agricultural Research Services Research Briefs* (U.S. Department of Agriculture) (April–June 1991):1.

9. Janet Hunt, Grand Forks Human Nutrition Research Center, Grand Forks, North Dakota, *Agricultural Research Services Research Briefs* (January–March 1992):1.

10. Paul Lachance, "Diet-Health Relationship," in *Food Safety Assessment* (Washington, D.C.: American Chemical Society, 1992), 279–95.

11. Frank L. Meyskens, M.D., "Beta-carotene effects in precancer," paper presented at "Beyond Deficiency: New Views on the Function and Health Effects of Vitamins," New York Academy of Sciences, New York City, February 9–12, 1992.

12. Ibid.

13. LaChance, "Diet-Health Relationship."

Chapter 15: Nutraceuticals, the Law, the Competition, and the Future

1. Abbey Meyers, "Nutraceuticals and the Orphan Drug Act," *Regulatory Affairs* 5 (1993):241–58.

2. "Nutraceuticals: Using Food to Treat Disease," *Biopharm* (July–August 1993):18–19.

3. The Orphan Drug Act, 1983.

4 . "FDA Pans Dietary Supplement Bill," *Newark Star-Ledger*, October 19, 1993, p. 2.

5. Paulette Thomas, "FDA Moves to Limit Marketing Claims About Vitamins, Minerals and Herbs," *Wall Street Journal*, December 15, 1993, p. B3.

6. Ibid.

7. Stephen Felice, M.D., personal communication with author, December 12, 1993.

8. Hercules Segalas, "A Comparison of the U.S., European & Japanese Nutraceutical Health and Medical Claim Rules," paper presented at the Foundation for Innovation in Medicine's seminar, New York City, January 13–14, 1993.

9. Pierson, Herbert, Ph.D., "Food Phytochemical Pharmacology—The Basis for Designer Food Development," *Regulatory Affairs* 5 (1993):219–22.

10. Jerry Bishop, "Dow Food Additive Lowers Cholesterol in Blood, Data Say," *Wall Street Journal*, June 15, 1993, p. B8.

11. Eugenios Katsanidis, "Evolution of Barley Flour/Wild Rice Antioxidant Properties in Ground Beef," paper presented at the 208th American Chemical Society Meeting, Washington, D.C., August 21, 1994.

12. George Inglett, developer of Oatrim at ARS, personal communication with author, April 28, 1994.

13. Volunteers in the first human study of ARS-developed Oatrim," *Quarterly Report of Selected Research Projects* (October 1–December 31, 1993):2.

14. Inglett, George, National Center Agricultural Utilization, USDA, "Low-viscosity beverage process using soluble beta-glucan enrichment," paper

presented at the 204th American Chemical Society National Meeting, Washington, D.C., August 22, 1992.

15. Fran LaBell, "Europe, Japan open doors to medicinal food products," *Food Processing* April 1993, 60–63.

16. Tadayasu Furukawa, Ph.D., "The Nutraceutical Rules: Health and Medical Claims: Food for Specific Health Use in Japan," *Regulatory Affairs* 5 (1993):189–202.

17. Ibid.

18. Linda Gilbert, "From Soothing Noodles to Smart Cookies," paper presented at "Designer Foods II," Rutgers University, Piscataway, New Jersey, March 16–17, 1993.

19. Lee Beck, Ph.D., personal communication with author, April 28, 1994.

20. Stephen DeFelice, "Nutraceutical Revolution: Global Implications," *Regulatory Affairs* 5 (1993):169–72.

21. Purdue University release, "Pharmaceutical pharming may be in our future," October 1993.

22. David Eisenberg, M.D., et al., "Unconventional Medicine in the United States: Prevalence, Costs, and Patterns of Use," *The New England Journal of Medicine* 328 (1993):246–52.

23. Riva Butrum, Ph.D, et al., "NCI dietary guidelines: rationale," *American Journal of Clinical Nutrition* 48 (1988):888–95.

24. *Johns Hopkins Medical Institution News Tips*, November 11, 1993.

25. E. J. Guardia, paper presented at "Designer Foods II" seminar, Rutgers University Department of Food Science, Piscataway, New Jersey, March 17, 1993.

26. Judy McBride, personal communication with author, January 1994.

27. Paul LaChance, Ph.D., "Food Safety Assessment," paper presented at the 204th American Chemical Society Meeting, Washington, D.C., 1992.

28. James Bennet, "Hidden Malnutrition Worsens Health of Elderly," *New York Times*, October 10, 1992, p. 1.

29. Stephen DeFelice, M.D., "Nutraceuticals in the Year 2000," paper presented at the 208th American Chemical Society Meeting, Washington, D.C., August 21, 1994.